DEVELOPING HIGH PERFORMANCE LEADERS

Every leader has human resource management and development responsibilities. Using a behavioral science perspective, *Developing High Performance Leaders* will enable leaders throughout the various business sectors to increase the yield on their organization's human capital and help their team members achieve their goals.

In this instructive book, Philip Harris centers his teaching around five key aspects of the leadership process:

- human behavior and performance;
- communications;
- cultural influences;
- organizational relations;
- change management.

A selection of strategies to take forward into practice is offered to the reader and the text is organized with a view to the leader sharing the knowledge obtained from this volume. For personal or group growth, each chapter is framed in terms of four "I's": Introduction, Input, Interaction, and Instrumentation, to provide an ideal framework for any adult education endeavor.

Developing High Performance Leaders is for all human resource development professionals, supervisors, managers, and executives concerned with the career development of themselves and their team.

Philip Robert Harris is President of Harris International, Ltd. and author of fifty-four professional books. He was previously Vice President of Copley International Corporation and St. Francis College (NYC, USA). He has been a visiting professor and lecturer in many universities worldwide, including The Pennsylvania State University, Temple University, the East–West Center in Hawaii, and Sophia University–Tokyo.

DEVELOPING HIGH PERFORMANCE LEADERS

A behavioral science guide for the knowledge of work culture

Philip Robert Harris

Routledge
Taylor & Francis Group

LONDON AND NEW YORK

First published 2013
by Routledge
4 Park Square, Milton Park, Abingdon, Oxon OX14 4RN
605 Third Avenue, New York, NY 10017

Routledge is an imprint of the Taylor & Francis Group, an informa business

© 2013 Philip Robert Harris

British Library Cataloguing in Publication Data
A catalogue record for this book is available from the British Library

Library of Congress Cataloging-in-Publication Data
Harris, Philip R. (Philip Robert), 1926-
    Developing high performance leaders/Philip R. Harris.
        p. cm.
    1. Leadership. 2. Personnel management.
    3. Employee motivation. 4. Performance.
    I. Title.
HD57.7.H3697 2012
658.4'092–dc23   2011049401

ISBN: 978-0-415-50069-2 (hbk)
ISBN: 978-0-415-50068-5 (pbk)
ISBN: 978-0-203-11880-1 (ebk)

Typeset in Bembo by Sunrise Setting Ltd.

Dedication

To my first leadership models, my parents, Gordon Roger and Esther Delahanty Harris, and to all high performers who strive to improve their skills and contributions as both local and global leaders. This volume is also a special memorial to my late life partner, Dr Dorothy Lipp Harris.

CONTENTS

List of exhibits   ix

Foreword by Leonard Nadler   xii

Preface   xiv

Acknowledgments   xvii

About the author   xviii

  Prologue: the organization as an energy exchange   1

1 High performance leaders for a knowledge culture   4

2 Leading in a high performance work environment   18

3 Increasing performance at work   40

4 Improving leadership communication skills   73

5 Influencing work culture at home and abroad   100

6 Enhancing organizational and team relations   134

7 Leading in the management of change   162

8 Developing people through learning   202

9 Energizing personnel through meetings   253

10 Future of leadership in the twenty-first century   286
    contributed by Dr William Howe

    Epilogue: the learning leader   301

    Afterword by Michael McManus   310

    Glossary of abbreviations   311

    Further reading   313

    Notes   318

    Index   322

EXHIBITS

1.1	Astronauts on the Moon	5
1.2	The Indomitable Dean Lipp	7
1.3	Middle Eastern transnational houses of wisdom	11
1.4	The GEO leadership system	15
2.1	Profile of a high performing business leader	19
2.2	The leadership continuum	23
2.3	The high performance management inventory	31
3.1	Anne Millians-Roche is President/Broker of Owens Realty Network	41
3.2	Maslow's hierarchy of needs	43
3.3	Analyzing human behavior at work	46
3.4	Motivation and behavior responses: achievement or adjustment	47
3.5	Four competencies in HRD	52
3.6	The high performance organization	53
3.7	"She beat the SEC team over sex harassment"	55
3.8	Critical pay-off functions exercise	58
3.9	Leadership motivation inventory	61
3.10	Human resources inventory	65
4.1	Profile of an electronic HPL	74
4.2	Communication and perception	75
4.3	A model of interactive communication	77
4.4	The how of communication	81
4.5	Hindrances to effective communications	82
4.6	How to further leadership communications	84
4.7	Internet effects	86
4.8	Meeting functional analysis: task behavior	90
4.9	Meeting functional analysis: maintenance behaviors	91
4.10	Management communications inventory	92
4.11	Organizational communications analysis	96

5.1	Profile of an international HPL	101
5.2	BAFA BAFA – a cross-cultural training simulation	115
5.3	What is a quality circle?	120
5.4	Cross-cultural relations inventory (CRI)	121
5.5	Organizational culture survey instrument (OCS)	125
6.1	Profile of a HP scuba dive master and manager	135
6.2	Conflicting forces affecting work relationships	137
6.3	Team problem solving strategies	145
6.4	Dimensions of conflict	147
6.5	Criteria for a helping relationship	150
6.6	Individual behavior analysis (team member)	152
6.7	Team performance survey	159
7.1	Profile of a HP thinker	163
7.2	Leadership in the management of change	165
7.3	Human development – changes in activities	168
7.4	Historical perspective on human progress	169
7.5	Altering the equilibrium of forces	172
7.6	Case for change in leadership development	175
7.7	Trends in organizational change	181
7.8	Stages of organizational growth	184
7.9	Systems analysis	189
7.10	Creative risk taking	189
7.11	Change inventory for leaders	191
7.12	Force field analysis inventory	195
8.1	Profile of a HP inventor	203
8.2	Action learning planning model	207
8.3	Planning model sequence	208
8.4	Planning interview strategy	211
8.5	Ten steps in training needs analysis for a job role	211
8.6	Program planning agreement	212
8.7	Selecting alternative learning activities	214
8.8	Schedule for a high performance leadership institute	217
8.9	Checklist for training materials and supplies	219
8.10	Guidelines for training adults	221
8.11	Strategy for concluding the training program	223
8.12	Personal information form	247
8.13	Pre-training self-evaluation inventory	248
8.14	High performance leadership institute	250
9.1	Profile of a high performing CEO	254
9.2	A world of connections	258
9.3	Discussion group guidelines by Robert Letwin	264

9.4	Hollow Square game	267
9.5	Hollow Square exercise: briefing sheet	268
9.6	Creative thinking techniques	272
9.7	Meetings management planning inventory	280
9.8	Managing people skills inventory (MPSI)	283
10.1	Profile of a HP futurist	288
10.2	Preparing for the future questionnaire	300
E.1	ExxonMobil's policy with peak performers	303
E.2	Diverse high performers	304

FOREWORD

There has always been a need for leadership in society, particularly in the business and professional worlds. What is new is the increased emphasis on the need for high performance leaders. For some people high performance leadership means that leaders are more active, get more done, and generally function like hurricanes each time they arrive at the office or participate in a meeting. Such people are *heavy* performance leaders, not *high* performance leaders. Today's challenges call for leaders whose level of performance is not hectic, but highly directed toward helping organizations reach goals and accomplish missions.

There have been many books, in recent years, addressing this topic. Very few, however, have focused on the responsibility of high performance leaders in the area of human resources. This recognition is what makes this volume distinctive and so important for those who seek to become or remain high performance leaders. Given the constant accumulation of new knowledge and the rapidity of change, it is essential that high performance leaders become directly involved in continuous learning, as Dr Harris points out in this text. It is essential for those leaders to provide learning (HRD) for all those in their organizations, including themselves. In a knowledge culture, lifetime learning is the norm.

Currently, it is satisfying to find an increasing recognition of the impact of culture on organizations. Those of us who have worked in the international arena and with multinational companies have come to understand the importance of recognizing cultural differences, while promoting cultural synergies. Until recently, one only talked of culture when discussing other countries; for most people, the terms *international* and *cross-cultural* meant the same thing. The realization is slowly emerging, within the global marketplace, that culture influences every group, organization, and country. And it is an important factor in understanding relationships, in communicating, and in providing leadership.

As a case in point, many in the United States perceive themselves as part of a melting-pot society. That is, new people arriving in the country were expected to slowly lose their "cultural baggage" and become "Americans." This was symbolized by a big pot, with a spigot at the bottom. Various kinds of people entered the pot at the top, but when the spigot was turned on at the bottom, what came out were people that all looked exactly the same. They were "Americans." As years have passed, and immigration increased again, it is possible to recognize a new reality – that the US is, instead, a pluralistic society. Even more important is the realization that a pluralistic community can endure and become successful just because of the diversities that stimulate that society. Diversity can revitalize a nation, as well as institutions and individuals.

The same trend is now apparent in our organizations. At one time, it was important for new employees to be indoctrinated (beyond merely receiving orientation) and to change to fit the company image. Of course, this attitude still exists today, but it is not nearly as pervasive as in the past. Organizations have recognized that diversity is not to be equated with disaster. Even an occasional organizational deviant can be helpful, and they are often among the most creative people in the organization. The global, multicultural organization calls for a different kind of leadership than we have had in the past. It requires leaders prepared to accept cultural behavior that is constantly changing, partially because of technological innovations. In fact, key executives may themselves even be catalysts in fostering planned changes.

The insights and input that Dr Harris provides in this work are an important contribution to the literature of HRD and leadership. In addition, the author provides interactive exercises and instrumentation that can take abstract theories and put them into an organizational perspective.

This is certainly not a volume to be read once and then placed on a leader's shelf or in the corporate library. It is a timely book to be read, and then selectively re-read from time to time as needed. The full value of the data gathering instruments may not be apparent at first reading, but they are significant tools for the person who seeks to be a high performance leader. This is a text to be utilized as a continuing resource by managers, trainers, and consultants seeking to become leaders who capitalize on human assets.

Leonard Nadler, PhD, Professor Emeritus,
George Washington University, Washington, DC

PREFACE

Not all managers, executives, and professionals are necessarily leaders, but, if they are high performers, they exercise some leadership. With the world of work in transition, such leadership is needed to transform the work environment through people, beginning with one's own self-development. The meaning and scope of the leadership to be acquired will be explored in this book, but our rationale can be simply stated: increasing productivity, service, and profitability depend primarily upon improved human performance. High performing leaders are needed to guide and stimulate twenty-first century organizations. Corporations, agencies, associations, and other institutions have limited material, technological, and capital resources. As Peter Drucker reminded us, the fourth factor – human resources – is virtually unlimited in its potential. The leadership challenge in organizations today is to learn how to capitalize on human assets to enhance a system's effectiveness. Managers confront this task during times of unprecedented change when the use of technology increases and its cost seemingly, along with the number of human workers required, decreases. However, with new knowledge workers, costs and quality seemingly go up.

To energize information and knowledge workers, managers, administrators, and their leaders have to exercise greater behavioral science skills with people. At a Business Week executive conference on "Gaining the Competitive Edge," Hank Koehn, when chairman of the Trimtab Consulting Group, forecasted that we are moving away from a capital-intensive, physical-resource-based economy toward a human resource and knowledge-based economy. Literally, today's globalization requires a *knowledge culture*. The repositioning will result in a need for fewer managers, especially at the middle level, but for more leaders capable of inspiring knowledge workers, especially in varied, advanced technologies.

Developing High Performance Leaders is written for those who aim to be top performers themselves, while enabling their associates to join in this career development process. The author's premise is that all supervisors, managers, and executives, whether in the private or public sectors, have such a HRD responsibility. This volume takes cognizance of the role change which requires them to spend more time in their own and others' professional development. The post-industrial work environment necessitates that leaders be lifelong learning facilitators. This book is composed to help readers meet these challenges. Because the subject matter deals with the "human" aspects of work learning and performance, it may also appeal to any practitioner in the people service business, from health service and criminal justice to real estate and sales. It is especially relevant to engineers, technicians, computer experts, and information technologists, as well as those in the expanding service occupations. The materials provided are most applicable to those whose previous education and training may not have emphasized human relations or people skills.

Furthermore, many work specialists are assigned to a training function on a lateral transfer, often on a temporary basis. Too often, they have no background in the behavioral sciences, group dynamics, or adult education, but are expected to pick up such knowledge on the job. For them, as well as for beginning HRD specialists and meeting planners, this text may be of value. *Developing High Performance Leaders* is intended for those with leadership responsibilities within any industry or profession. Its message is meaningful in high- or low-tech industries, as well as within the helping professions. In the disappearing industrial work culture, many employees were designated as "subordinates" or "laborers." In the "meta-industrial" or knowledge work situation, human assets are perceived by leaders as co-workers, colleagues, and associates. The new paradigm of managerial thought envisions this work force as the capital investment of an enterprise. In this Information Age, talent is more important than tenure. A worker's values and competencies are to be treasured. Thus, this book is written for those in management and the professions who wish to make the most of a more diverse, complex, multicultural, and educated personnel.

In the Prologue that follows, I propose that readers view their own organization as an energy exchange system. With that model as a rationale, the opening chapter examines contemporary strategies for a high performance leadership within a knowledge-based global environment. The closing chapter is an exercise in "mind stretching" about leadership in the future, whether on this planet or off-world.

These ten chapters consider the essence of leadership and effectiveness with people from a behavioral science perspective. The five aspects of the leadership process center around understanding:

1 human behavior and performance;
2 communications;
3 cultural influences;
4 organizational relations;
5 change management.

Within that context, two strategies are offered – action learning and research – particularly relative to one's leadership role regarding meetings. For personal or group growth, each of these chapters is framed in terms of four "I's":

1 *Introduction*, for the objectives or overview of that information segment or learning module. A profile of an actual high performance leader is provided to motivate readers.

2 *Input*, which summarizes behavioral science management thinking on each subject for a manager's consideration.
3 *Interaction*, which illustrates the possibilities for sharing the information and insights by the leader with his or her team through group process.
4 *Instrumentation*, which can be used for human factor data gathering and personal development relative to the chapter theme.

In effect, we have provided readers with a design for a High Performance Leadership Development Institute. That is a 3–6 day course or workshop which can be incorporated into any adult education endeavor. These sessions can be grouped together or spread out, such as on a weekly or monthly basis. Each day has a different theme, as explained in these chapters. Each day is divided into two learning modules of 3–4 hours. This approach can be adapted to a university or college course with students, as well as to continuing management training with workers.

An Epilogue summarizes my thinking relative to the role of the learning leader. Finally, Further Reading offers the thinking manager further resources to advance leadership capability. Included is a directory of select leadership books and publications useful in HRD efforts, as well as a directory of internet websites and other media. The total text is organized with a view to the leader sharing learning obtained from this volume's content.

My assumption is that every leader has human resource management and development responsibilities. Human resource management centers on those personnel activities that range from recruitment and selection to health and safety, benefits and incentives, performance evaluation, and so on. In the knowledge culture, these activities are no longer left to personnel specialists; rather, line management plays an active role in such matters, especially in smaller, fast-growth companies. Akin to that effort is HRD, a series of organized learning activities conducted within a specified time and designed to produce behavioral change, such as through education and training sessions, whether within or without the organization.

To increase the yield on the organization's human capital, this book shares some specific ways to exercise leadership in development of people. The arrangements and details for this learning program can be handled by a task force established to coordinate this learning systematically. Such a planning group could be composed of high performing members of the organization. Later, they should be involved in the project as instructors, facilitators, or discussion leaders. The pay-off should be enhanced learning and improved performance by all who participate in both the planning and the intensive learning experience. Certainly, it should promote more shared leadership relative to the human side of enterprise. Such an undertaking is an organizational commitment to help personnel make the transition to a new work culture. In this changing workplace environment, those with leadership skills play an increasingly important role in workforce transformation. They are not only high performers themselves, but mentor others to follow their example.

Philip Robert Harris, PhD,
La Jolla, California, USA

ACKNOWLEDGMENTS

I am grateful to Dr Leonard Nadler, considered the "father" of HRD (human resource development), for his inspiring Foreword, and to Dr Michael McManus, founder of the California International Business University, for his insightful After-word about the significance of this book . Also, I thank Dr William S. Howe who provided input in the last chapter on the future of leadership. I am especially beholden to those at Leadership Resources, Inc., who first provided me with information and opportunities related to the behavioral science approach to management and leadership. In addition to Dr Nadler, I am particularly indebted to these helpful colleagues at LRI: Drs Gordon Lippitt, Drex Sprecher, Ken Sowers, Woody Sears, and Ken Haygood. Among my professional colleagues, I particularly value the support received from the late Drs James Grier Miller and James Cribbin, as well as Dr Eileen Sheridan Wibbeke. Finally, I am most obliged to the US Marine Corps and other international clients who enabled me to test the leadership theories and learning materials that are the basis of this book.

ABOUT THE AUTHOR

Philip Robert Harris is President of Harris International Ltd. in La Jolla, California. He received his PhD and MS in psychology from Fordham University, and his BBA degree from St. John's University. Dr Harris was first licensed as a psychologist in 1959 by the University of the State of New York. He also attained the rank of GS15 as a Federal Government consultant.

For the past sixty years, Dr Harris has been engaged in leadership development as a management and organizational psychologist. His behavioral science research focus has been on change, culture, communication, and management, but more recently as a space psychologist on human factors related to living and working off-world. Dr Harris has now authored or edited fifty-four professional books, and two science-based space novels. In addition, he has published some 275 professional articles in international publications or as chapters in others' volumes. He has been editor of three professional journals, in addition to being co-editor of the *Managing Cultural Differences* series for Elsevier Publishing. For ten years, he served on the editorial advisory board of the *European Business Review* in the UK, as well as being Book Review Editor for *Behavioral Science*. Dr Harris has been a consultant on six major media projects to produce learning systems for such producers as NBC's *Sunday Today Show*, Westinghouse Learning Corporation, and the US Marine Corps. In addition to numerous research grants, such as the US Office of Naval Research, Dr Harris has received many awards – e.g. a Fulbright professorship to India from the US State Department; a NASA Faculty Fellowship; the Torch Award from the American Society of Training and Development for outstanding HRD contributions; and New York City's Young Man of the Year for 1959 from the Junior Chamber of Commerce.

In his global management practice, Dr Harris has successfully served more than 200 human systems – multinational corporations, government agencies, military services, consulting organizations, and trade/professional associations. A former Senior Scientist at Netrologic Inc., he was also vice president of Copley International Corporation, as well as of St. Francis College (NYC). Dr Harris has been a visiting professor and lecturer in many universities worldwide, including The Pennsylvania State University, Temple University, the East–West Center in Hawaii, and Sophia University–Tokyo.

During his multifaceted career, Dr Harris has also been a Senior Associate for Leadership Resources, Inc.; a fellow of the National Training Laboratory (NTL); an Associate Fellow of the American Institute of Aeronautics and Astronautics; project research consultant for the State of California's POST Command College for law enforcement executives. This scholar has been an educator for sixty-five years, and, at eighty-five, he is still teaching graduate courses on his books at the California International Business University. Readers are invited to visit his internet website, http://www.wix.com/philharris/drphiliprharris, or see his Amazon Books author profile.

PROLOGUE

The organization as an energy exchange

Have you ever thought of organizations as energy exchange systems? Behavioral scientists suggest this as a new way to look at the institutions with which we are affiliated. This dynamic view helps us to envision our corporation, agency, or association as a system for the exchange of natural and human energy, both physical and psychic. Our image of the organization not only affects our behavior and performance, but also that of our co-workers and clients. If we are to encourage high performance by people, perhaps we should begin by revising obsolete notions we have about the enterprises in which we are involved. In any event, this is the conceptual model we offer as the backdrop for the messages in this book.

A concept is like an intellectual hook around which we may string many ideas; it is a construct that can be formulated into numerous applications. "Concept" is similar to the Greek word *paradigm*, which refers to a framework of thought that helps us to organize human experience. Too often, people think only in terms of words or sentences; leaders think in terms of concepts. That is why this book will share many concepts with readers, starting with the model of the organization as an energy exchange system (organization energy exchange, OEE). Our concern in this text is to foster top performance, so perhaps we should begin by examining how our organization channels or uses the energies of its human assets.

Each organization receives input from its environment and a pattern of internal activity transforms that energy into output, thus provoking new materials, information, and effort. Sound familiar? It is the cybernetic model of how our own human system – the body – operates, and is replicated in communication and computer exchanges. Jonas Salk maintained that humankind replicates biological models in the social systems we create, so it is understandable that the operation of our body may provide us with prototypes for organizational activities.

As managers adapt or abandon archaic organizational models from the Industrial Age, innovative leaders adopt more creative concepts such as OEE. In this way of thinking, our enterprise is seen as an open system engaged in constant transactions with its environment. This system includes many subsystems, called subsidiaries, branches, divisions, departments, or offices. All are continuously engaged in energy exchanges within the organization and outside with other systems. These energy transactions affect the behavior and performance of personnel in a corporation, an industry, a region, a country, and even internationally, because our company or agency is but a micro system, part of one or more macro systems. The definitive book on the subject, *Living Systems* (Miller 1978), examines the concept in terms of cell, organ, organism, group, organization, society, and global systems.

Now this may sound like heady stuff straight from the world of biology and physics, but it has practical implications for executives, managers, and those in any profession. Let us look at some of the applications for those who aspire to be leaders in high performance:

1 *Quality of the work environment.* There is much concern today about the quality of life and our environment. Therefore, we rightly organize to combat energy waste and pollution, as well as to preserve or conserve natural resources. Real leaders are equally concerned about the quality of work life and the organizational environment. They analyze their systems to counteract human energy waste and pollution, such as underused employees or workers whose energies are misdirected. Such leaders study how machines and technology can enhance human performance, for instance through the introduction of office automation or factory robotics. Leaders in the new work culture give priority to the conservation and development of human resources.

Physicists tell us that energy transactions take place in a field of force, such as a magnetic field, operating in space and time. Behavioral scientists, such as the late Kurt Lewin, conceive of the organization as also having a unique space at a point in time. It, too, is a field of driving and resisting forces that alter the status quo (the equilibrium between the forces that affect growth and development). For example, if a reader tries to introduce some of the insights obtained from this book into his or her office or plant, one may anticipate that some people or forces will support this effort to improve performance, while others will oppose the concepts for a variety of reasons.

Inside every organization's space, a variety of energy exchanges or transactions take place among the personnel. The pattern of these interchanges represents the individual desires and aspirations, prejudices and biases, information and misinformation of the people who make up that human system. The same may be said for external systems that impact the organization, such as customers, suppliers, contractors, unions, and government agencies. Thus, a high performance leader is not only concerned about the performance of one's workers or management, but also about the clients, competitors, regulators, and all those outside the enterprise who impact employee productivity.

2 *The management process.* Every *aspect of the management* or leadership process can be re-examined in the context of the OEE paradigm. If we take the core concepts which make up the themes of this book, each can be redefined in terms of the energy exchange conceptual model. For example, in Chapter 1, we view leadership as guiding the generation of worker and group energy toward achieving

personal and organizational goals through excellent performance. Such leadership involves control of the management and record keeping of energy efforts by personnel. It also may include reward, which is the reinforcement or support of proper energy.

In Chapter 2, we consider human behavior and performance in terms of an individual effort toward personal and organizational goals. In Chapter 3, we look at communication as an exchange of energy between people and groups. In Chapter 4, we regard culture as establishing the values and customs to which a particular group of people devotes its energies. In Chapter 5, we examine organizational relations as a mechanism for maximizing cooperative energy. In this context, conflict between people or groups represents a disagreement on energy use. If it is not properly channeled, conflict energy may undermine performance. In Chapter 6, we analyze change as the altering of energy priorities, while planning becomes the setting of such priorities for energy use.

Every dimension of management, then, can be perceived in this framework of energy and its exchange. With reference to work performance, leaders seek effective use of human energy to improve morale and teamwork. As a result, productivity and service increase. Leaders also discover ways to minimize the waste of organizational energy. People can learn better ways to direct their energies, as shown in Chapter 7. Since so much time of managers and their colleagues is spent at meetings, Chapter 8 suggests learning as a means for making them more productive by properly using the energies of all involved. Chapter 9 proposes ways to make better use of energy at meetings. Finally, Chapter 10 looks at how leadership energy may be used in the future.

In the high technology, fast growth environment requiring top performance, leaders learn to capitalize on the organization's human resources. Play with the OEE concept, analyze it from different angles, then share it with co-workers. Devote a staff meeting to getting input from colleagues on how it could be applied to improve performance in one's own organization. Our associates may have many valuable ideas for conserving employee energy, including their own. Given the opportunity to contribute, we may be surprised by their proposals for more creative employment of their own energies. For example, when this is done with a sales team, members may come up with imaginative approaches for focusing group energies in the achievement of targets and objectives.

Researchers estimate that the average person only realizes about forty percent of his or her potential. The leader's goal should be to foster a creative environment that stretches people's capacities, energizing them to perform beyond their present level. The pages that follow provide some strategies for tapping into that sixty percent of unused ability or promise within all of us.

1

HIGH PERFORMANCE LEADERS FOR A KNOWLEDGE CULTURE

Introduction

High performing knowledge workers

Leadership is not exercised within a vacuum. It is manifest within a context of a society or organization. In this century, high performing leadership is essential because we function within a more complex environment, a knowledge culture. Leaders today need competence to operate effectively within a national culture, a global business culture, and an organizational culture. These various cultures influence a leader's behavior and decisions.

Within these cultures, leaders also work within multiple worlds or psychological spaces. There is a private world or perceptual field that influences our behavior, making us unique individuals. There is also the public world outside ourselves – the external reality. Within that larger arena are the human systems of which we are a part, representing our organizational world or culture. The continuing theme now in all such systems is rapid, constant change, often spurred on by new technological advances and expansion of knowledge. As a result, individuals and institutions, as well as their larger societies, must adjust more quickly. Similarly, those who would be high performing and successful leaders have to become more flexible and skillful in managing change, especially as it relates to knowledge and information. Whether working in the public or private sectors, we are coping with knowledge economies, knowledge centers, and knowledge workers. Leaders are continuously learning within this post-industrial environment, to increase their knowledge base, and to extend their understandings of culture, management, and leadership. To become a high performing leader (HPL) under such circumstances requires us first to improve our conceptual thinking.

The word *concept* is defined as a general idea, understanding, or thoughts about something that is conceived in the human mind. It is like an intellectual hook

EXHIBIT 1.1   Astronauts on the Moon

around which we string together many related ideas. What we have discussed above are all concepts – culture, change, communication, knowledge, management, and leadership. These are the dominant themes of this book, and any leadership programs designed on its contents. Knowledge workers and their leaders are focused upon such conceptual subjects.

Our times call for *thinking cosmopolitans* – leaders and followers who gain influence with their fellows by not being just local, but global in their perceptions and outlook. Such HPLs grow beyond cultural limitations of time and place by thinking and acting holistically and synergistically. Cosmopolitans are able to cross borders and disciplines comfortably, so as not to be constrained by any one sphere of thinking and perceiving, be it intellectual, social, religious, commercial, or political. A cosmopolitan leader is not myopic or provincial in thinking, but comfortable in multiple worlds or groups. Presently, humanity is in a period of transition – from being Earth-centered to becoming more space-centered, we are transforming images of ourselves that we have held for millennia. For example, most thought we were earthbound as a species until the Apollo space missions landed astronauts on the Moon. Now humanity is in the process of changing images about our species – we are not bound to live and work only on Earth. Our future is beyond. Maybe we will develop our potential as humans off-world as we explore, settle, and industrialize other planets. Within that possibility, we must also change our self-image.

On 21 July 1969 NASA's Apollo 11 mission landed the first humans, Neil Armstrong and Buzz Aldrin, on the Moon. A total of twelve spacefarers participated in such lunar landings and research. With Apollo 17 on 19 December 1972, Harrison Schmitt and Gene Cernan departed from the lunar surface at Taurus-Littrow. All these astronauts and their ground support teams were high performing knowledge workers. In the twenty-first century, it will take farsighted HPLs to get us back permanently to the Moon, Mars, and beyond. We are in the process of creating a spacefaring civilization as this artistic rendering envisions our living and working off-world.

Among the myriad images we are changing, including ourselves, none is more significant than our perceptions of our planet as *Spaceship Earth*, orbiting within a vast universe. The advances in space exploration and technology over the past six decades are forcing us to plan for settlements and industries beyond our home planet. Consider how high-tech communications, a spin-off of space technology, has impacted our lives. The space satellite industry opened new possibilities for television, telemedicine, and all kinds of telecommunications. Consider also the global economy – most people think in terms of their national or international economies. Only HPLs can conceive in terms of the emerging Earth–Moon twin economies.

Understanding knowledge and know-how

To understand knowledge workers, we must first comprehend the concept of knowledge. It means a state of *knowing* information, ideas, and data gained through experience, observation, or study. It is the sum of what has been perceived, discovered, or learned. Knowledge, whether explicit or implicit, is learned, possessed, shared, and expanded by knowledge workers. Knowledge workers are engaged primarily in collecting data, massaging it into information, interpreting, and transforming this into knowledge. To them, knowledge today is a resource; an asset for individuals and institutions. Knowledge workers are found in most fields of human endeavors and disciplines – such as science and research, education and training, high and space technologies.

Human evolution is a long struggle from darkness and ignorance to enlightenment and knowledge, but the latter concept is viewed differently by some cultures. For example, in the West, knowledge is seen as rationalism and empiricism, whereas in the philosophic tradition of the East, knowledge is perceived as a *quest* for harmony, complementarity, and oneness. Knowledge, created by individuals or in groups, is stored in the mind and traditions, as well as in data banks and libraries. Knowledge is power only when accompanied by *know-how*. That is, the ability to put knowledge to work in the real world. Thus, scientific discoveries can become routine medical treatments. Similarly, inventions like the internet have to be transformed into products and services that facilitate the way we learn, work, and play. Social networks are examples of this knowledge combined with know-how. Such innovation enables HPLs to think strategically in coping with human challenges and problem solving.

Knowledge also has been explained as:

- being able to understand a cognitive system;
- a capacity for effective actions;
- validated information;
- a fluid mix of framed experience, values, contextual information, and expert insight;
- operational understanding about the why, how, and who;
- intuitive or acquired learning through others, books, and research.

To be a high performing leader and worker, knowledge has to be shared with others, such as through broadcasting, publishing, lecturing, teaching, or other means of dissemination. Today's communication technologies provide a range of opportunities for distributing knowledge through the mass media, the internet, and networks, whether interpersonal or electronic. Since knowledge is also stored in people's minds, HPLs encourage their associates not only to continue education, but also to share wisely of their information and insights. Yet, even knowledge can be dangerous when it is shared indiscriminately or with the wrong people.

Organizational knowledge can be disseminated in various ways from research and development (R&D) reports, archives, libraries, data banks, and training, to reports, meetings, marketing, and customer services. This whole volume deals with innovative ways to share knowledge – the new currency of our times. Within human systems today, leaders value and support high performing knowledge workers. With them, a leader is able to transform an organization into a productive business. Such systems innovate and out-think their competitors. Then operational excellence becomes the norm that engenders a continual high performing environment.

EXHIBIT 1.2 The Indomitable Dean Lipp

PROFILE OF A HIGH PERFORMING DEAN

In the 1960s, Dorothy Lipp had the reputation among her peers nationally of being the best dean of women in the USA. For a decade, she was an innovative administrator at The Pennsylvania State University's main campus in State College. As the only woman at that time in the University's top administration, she had to cope with male chauvinism. With a doctorate in psychology, she managed the professional development of some ninety women on her staff who were pursuing Master and Doctorate degrees at Penn State. With a $2 million budget, she and her staff were then responsible for some 18,000 female students scattered at various campuses throughout this large state. In those days, male students could live off campus, but women were required to live on

Continued

---

campus in university residence halls. Dean Lipp's strategy was to concentrate on the development of her staff by releasing their potential. She modeled the behavior that she expected them to employ with their volunteer student leaders working with other female collegians. Thus, she involved her staff, volunteers, and students in formal leadership development. This began at the opening of each academic year when consultants from the National Training Laboratories in the Applied Behavioral Sciences came on campus to conduct leadership workshops. The whole learning strategy created such a vibrant staff and women's program that alumni still remember and discuss it decades later. Many became HPLs because of this experience. Dean Lipp's competence was recognized internationally when she was appointed chair of a US Delegation to UNESCO in Paris.

However, this high performing professor had still other strategies for capitalizing on human assets. When I, then her husband, inquired why she was so effective in motivating people, I got an unexpected answer. My wife replied, "I always treat others as if they are one step beyond where they presently function. In other words, I indirectly convey my expectations of them, and usually they respond by striving to reach that level of my perception – one step beyond their current performance."

After she left Penn State, Dr Dorothy Lipp Harris went on to become a professor and associate dean at United States International University in San Diego. There she designed the research program for the Doctorate of Business Administration. Subsequently, this behavioral scientist joined the faculty of the Command College in the State of California's Department of Justice, where she designed a futures research program for law enforcement executives. In addition, she engaged in a global consulting practice with her spouse. Right up until her death in 1997, she continued to inspire subordinates and trainees to peak performance. There are two techniques reported in this profile that may also help you to become a HPL.

Source: P. R. Harris, *The Indomitable Lady* (for copy, philharris@aol.com).

Input

Leadership in a knowledge culture

For over sixty years, behavioral scientists have been researching, writing, and lecturing about the subject of leadership. But now we need HPLs because we are living in a knowledge culture. So begin by asking the fundamental question, what is leadership?

My mentor at Fordham University, Dr James J. Cribbin, defined the term decades ago: leadership is an action–oriented, interpersonal process that influences the thinking, attitudes, and behavior of those people who are being managed or who lead.[1] Today, as then, there are a number of antagonistic forces buffeting leaders and their institutions. To cope now, HPLs need the assistance of a variety of knowledge workers who usually think "out of the box"; people who are capable of confronting the new realities by developing strategies that solve problems and take advantage of opportunities. In our transnational and turbulent times, effective leaders focus on developing their own and other peoples' potential. We are all underdeveloped, and the successful leader taps into and releases those possibilities, as highlighted by the next exhibit.

Professor Cribbin believed in knowledge-based leadership. So he frequently asked managers at all levels to reveal what effective leaders did. Here is a summary of their replies:

- teach personnel to be critical of their own work;
- have respect for and confidence in your own people;
- be open to new ideas, and encourage such input from others;
- give credit to your associates and teams when they come up with innovative ideas;
- demonstrate professional competence, and help people to reach your standards;
- model your expectations regarding communication and organizational skills;
- give personnel freedom in their own work space, while being available for mentoring and consultation;
- help people to feel important, and convince them their work is important.

One of the pioneers in research on leadership, Michael Maccoby, noted that leaders today have to think in new ways about markets, aggressive use of new technologies, and leadership in human resource management.[2] Dr Maccoby astutely commented that the United States has a very costly system of adversarial relationships. This Harvard University professor called for more charismatic leadership that promotes greater cooperation and collaboration. This is what I would describe as *synergistic leadership*, a quality lacking in too many contemporary managers and executives.

How can you increase your HPL competencies? To become more effective as a leader, search within yourself for answers to the following ten questions:

1 How do you stimulate those you lead to do willingly what must be done in a better than ordinary way?
2 What changes can you promote in the organization's culture, especially with reference to philosophy, goals, traditions, norms, and work environment?
3 What can you contribute to work groups and teams that will help them become more cohesive, homogeneous, and productive?
4 How can you better understand and satisfy the needs, wants, goals, and potential of your associates?
5 What can you and your associates do to improve your technological and managerial competence?

6 What can you and your associates do to improve work relationships, especially relative to encouraging greater self-confidence, and self-esteem among colleagues?

7 Have you shared with your associates what you are trying to achieve both in the short term, and in the long term?

8 What are your colleagues learning from you that makes them better human beings, and more able to develop their potential?

9 Are you patient with yourself and others in matters of changing attitudes, behaviors, and practices within the system?

10 What are you doing outside the organization to enhance your own capabilities, and to prepare for another stage of personal and professional development?

The right answers to such questions may help a HPL to create a learning organization. Today's leaders also need to understand how to motivate and manage knowledge workers (Davenport 2005). In the Western world, an increasing number of workers are engaged in using their brains, not their brawn. These knowledge workers are centered in high-tech and service industries, as well as in academia, research institutes, and the helping professions. These then are the creators of wealth, the inventors of new products and services. HP leaders know how to ensure their productivity. Such leaders provide these valuable human assets with an environment that helps knowledge to be applied in useful and profitable ways. They function best in a flexible, fluid, and informal workplace that allows concentration and stimulates creativity. This is today's reality in knowledge-based economies.

Houses of wisdom

Within civilizations and societies, there are places that promote development of individuals and their potential. Over twelve centuries ago, the poet-scholar, Al-Ma'mun, used the term *house of wisdom* to describe an institution he founded in Baghdad. This learning center was a combination of library, academy, and translation bureau. It became legendary, attracting great mathematicians, scientists, engineers, architects, and thinkers from beyond the borders of Iraq. Its founder dispatched his librarian, Bayt al-Hikmah, as far away as Constantinople to track down and procure every book of classical learning he could find. Then, these written words of Greeks and Romans were translated into Arabic. In that way, knowledge was preserved for use by subsequent scholars of future generations. During the "dark ages" of early Medieval Europe, *the houses of wisdom* were the Irish monasteries where monks preserved and translated the insights and information obtained from previous generations, especially from the Greeks and Romans.

In today's knowledge culture, we need more *houses of wisdom* as knowledge incubators. HPLs can start doing this in the home and school systems that can be transformed into centers of wisdom, with the help of new educational technology. Similarly, HPLs are challenged to participate in updating and renewing higher educational institutions, from community colleges and technical institutes, to colleges and universities. Sometimes these are called "knowledge factories." Furthermore, global corporations should also become *houses of wisdom* by means of information technologies and HRD programs. Knowledge workers need the means to continuously expand their own data base and perceptions. Continuous, lifetime education for all should become the world's standard.

With globalization, and communication technologies, there is no room for pockets of ignorance and backwardness. If allowed to exist, such places become the breeding laboratory for criminals, dullards, extremists, and terrorists. When regions suffer culture lag, falling behind main stream advances of civilized societies, they become places of discrimination, conflict, and war, so evident in too many parts of the world. Reflection on Exhibit 1.3 gives readers both hope and models for human progress. No nation can afford to let an underclass grow because such people lack the necessary know-how and skills to contribute to the common good. Consider the millions of homeless or deprived children who are denied learning opportunities, and the price the human family will pay in wasting such precious resources. The cost is too high when people are allowed to remain for generations in ignorance. HPLs are challenged to capitalize on all human assets everywhere. Their mission is to promote an educated population. By creating more *houses of wisdom*, such as described in the next exhibit, leaders advance human progress and potential.

EXHIBIT 1.3 Middle Eastern transnational houses of wisdom

In the Middle East, there are many ancient institutions of advanced learning, such as the University of Cairo in Egypt. In the last two centuries, modern higher education was introduced by French, British, and Ottoman rulers, as well as by Christian missionaries who started schools and colleges in the region. Some of these evolved into universities such as the American University of Beirut, in Lebanon, the American University, in Cairo, and Bogazici University, in Turkey. A new mercantile class arose in the twentieth century with the growth of the oil and gas industries. Some of their children began to go overseas to get degrees, principally from North American and British universities. National governments also responded to the educational needs of more affluent populations, thus, the establishment by Saudi Arabia of the Alfaisal University in Riyadh and King Abdullah University of Science and Technology (KAUST). Both are based on Islamic values that seek knowledge "to develop ourselves and our societies." When the latter opened in 2009 north of Jeddah, the King expressed the hope that this new house of wisdom would become a forum for science and research; a beacon of knowledge for future generations. KAUST is a graduate level university with a vast complex of high-tech research laboratories, classrooms, and

Continued

libraries. Its streets are lined with modern houses and apartments – the whole campus overlooks the Red Sea. It is typical of a growing number of institutions of higher learning spreading throughout the Gulf region, based upon international models, particularly American. The former CEO of Saudi Aramco which built KAUST, Abdallal Jum'ah, warned, "the knowledge gap separating Arabs and Islamic nations from the advancement of contemporary societies is becoming deeper and wider." Yet consider these counter measures underway that inspire the region's youth with hope.

Parent pressures are a major force behind these changes in Middle Eastern higher education. The more innovative institutions focus on scientific and technical curricula, with emphasis on R&D teaching in English, and critical thinking. Schools of business, medicine, engineering, and design predominate as well as courses in economics, poetry, history, and liberal arts. Many administrators and faculty are expatriates from Western countries. Although co-education is a sensitive issue, many of the students and faculty are women.

The most spectacular innovation is Education City in Doha – the 15-year-old enterprise of the Quatar Foundation. Its 2,500-acre campus represents a learning conglomerate of buildings and branch campuses from well-regarded American universities, such as Cornell, Carnegie-Mellon, Georgetown, Northwestern, Texas A & M, and Virginia Commonwealth. Again there is another HPL behind this academic venture – Quatar's dynamic shaykhan, Mosh bint Al Missned. The foundation that he chairs provides the financial incentives that attract American institutions to this educational undertaking. Thus, its faculty and students have access to state-of-the-art educational technologies and facilities, often unavailable on the parent US campus. However, Education City is also open to foreign students from abroad.

A wider movement, from Morocco to Qatar, seeks to recapture past Islamic intellectual glory, while establishing new knowledge-based economies. The American University of Sharjah (AUS) in the United Arab Emirates is one example. Its 5,200 undergraduates come largely from Jordan, Egypt, and Palestine. The HPL and ruler behind its founding in 1977 is 71-year-old Shaykh Sultan, a member of the United Arab Emirates (UAE) Supreme Council and a passionate scholar himself. AUS has a 313-acre campus featuring palm trees, tranquil pools, monumental domed buildings, columns, and arches.

Other Gulf states have similar strategies, such as Dubai with its International Academic City where Michigan State University is the centerpiece for a bevy of smaller international educational institutions. Nearby in Abu Dhabi, New York University has a branch campus on the Emirates $27 billion Saadiyat Islands, not far from a branch of New York's Guggenheim Museum. All the graduates of this new higher education model are learning how to think and learn differently

Continued

from traditional ways, so that they may transform their commodity-based economies into knowledge-based ones. The alumni of these new universities will be on the leading edge of artificial intelligence, computer, and robotic technologies. There is an interplay of cultures going on in these new university models. For example, Alfasiai University uses online MIT's open software program, while Carnegie-Mellon researchers ponder uniquely Middle Eastern solutions to technological problems. American values about democracy, women's role in society, and freedom of the press obviously are evident in these classrooms.

Imagine the outcomes when Effat University in Jeddah, an institution for Islamic women, partners with Swathmore, Mount Holyoke, and other US universities; or, in Kuwait, where the American College of the Middle East has signed an agreement with Purdue University; or the Gulf University of Science and Technology, which opened in 2002, in a partnership with the University of Missouri in St Louis. This is truly the globalization of higher education. You have to admire the vision of Middle Eastern leaders who bring scholars from around the world to their region, so as to discover, solve problems, and think about humanity's future. Yes, the Middle East is in the process of preparing tomorrow's high performers and cosmopolitans.

Source: Based on Tom Verde, "Houses of Wisdom," *Saudi Armaco World*, May–June 2002: 24–37 (www.saudiaramcoworld.com).

Knowledge management and leadership

In the emerging work culture, effective management of information and knowledge is the critical skill required of HPLs. Knowledge management may be conceived in two ways. In the general sense, there are those who manage this resource as part of their professional career. Librarians and curators are obvious examples. Among the many others who manifest this capability are presidents of colleges, especially business school deans, and faculty who teach business courses or information technology.

With the increase and improvements in computers and information technologies, a specialty has also emerged called knowledge management (KM) in the narrow sense of that terminology.[3] This subset in the field of general management has been defined as a discipline that focuses on enhancing knowledge processing. Such processing accounts for the organizational production and integration of knowledge for business enterprise. It has to do with managing transactions between workers, customers, suppliers, and other agents in the value chain or network. KM aims to satisfy the needs and demands for products and services. The outcomes are the KM specialists who help HPLs to track and supervise the knowledge cycle within organizations. This prevents the loss or misuse of information and insights, such as those obtained from R&D, market research, and other data gathering mechanisms or projects. KM personnel may be located in various divisions, whether R&D, IT, or HR. They are an organizational resource who pre-serve intellectual capital. To capitalize better on organizational assets, KM specialists usually practice at three levels – operational, tactical, and strategic.

KM projects may include activities, such as:

1 designing, for a corporation, a fully integrated database to assist agents at a customer service call center;
2 assisting a telecommunications center with a "digital repository" of solutions for technical problems;
3 building an online forum to facilitate broader personnel participation. The prob-lem with this specialization is that projects have to be individually customized and carefully monitored, especially after a successful pilot project. Its practition-ers need to learn from such experiences, as to what went wrong, as well as from what went right.

Global organizations vie for such intellectual resources to ensure high performance and profitability which sustains the system. In a knowledge-based economy of this Information Age, new paradigms, frameworks, and technologies are necessary. The nascent KM discipline is made up of internal or external consultants who have formed a knowledge management consortium (KMC).[4]

In this knowledge culture, with its changing technologies and knowledge work-ers, we create new, more innovative ways to ensure global leadership in learning organizations.

Interaction

GEO leadership development

Eileen Sheridan Wibbeke did her doctoral research on leadership for global business, and in the process developed a new model which she named "GEO leadership." From this beginning, Dr Wibbeke has created an outstanding book and system for preparing HPLs.[5] For this scholar and online professor, industrial age is leading others across geographies and cultures. In the global marketplace, she argues for leadership that is cross-cultural in perspective, so that both the leader and the led respect one another in the management of resources. To this end, Dr Wibbeke's model of leadership has seven dimensions as illustrated below in Exhibit 1.4.

Group direction. In using the model (Exhibit 1.4) for HPL training, divide up the learners into seven teams of 2–6 persons. Instruct each team to discuss for 20–30 minutes one aspect of the GEO leadership model. For example, those assigned "capability" would exchange observations and information as to why each one believes "intercultural experience and competence" is essential today for a high performing global leader. Each group then summarizes its thinking and chooses a spokesperson to report on their conclusions. The teams then form in a cluster session, so each may report on their dialogue about the seven GEO leadership dimensions.

EXHIBIT 1.4 The GEO leadership system. This is based on the premise that all communication is intercultural. This strategy for developing HPLs is centered upon improving the seven qualities explained in the above visual: capability, care, communication, consciousness, context, contrast, and change (from E. S. Wibbeke, *Global Business Leadership*. Oxford, UK: Routledge/Taylor and Francis, 2012)

Instrumentation

Self-assessment inventory on effective leadership

Instructions. The purpose of this exercise is to "mind stretch." Six types of "leaders" are described below. Which type or combination is presently your leadership style? Evaluate yourself against each point on the right side by checking one of these three choices as to your perceived leadership practices. Use letter "Y" for yes, "N" for no, and "S" for "somewhat."

	yes	no	somewhat
1 I am an *entrepreneur* type. That is, I am self-confident, forceful, and innovative with an extraordinary achievement drive. I follow my own instincts and perceptions to find a better way of doing things. With my teams, I am loyal, protective, and generous.	☐	☐	☐

	yes	no	somewhat
2 I am more a *cooperative* type. I tend to be dominant, but not domineering with my colleagues. Though I can be quite directive, I do allow my associates considerable freedom at work. I can size up people well, without getting too personal with them. I can be consultative and participative with my people. Though I am cordial with my associates, I keep them at a distance.	□	□	□
3 I am a *developer* type. I consider people as human resources or assets. I have excellent human relations skills and win people's support and loyalty. In developing human potential, I am an effective coach, counselor, and mentor within a climate of achievement.	□	□	□
4 I am more an *artisan* type. I am amiable, conscientious, but conservative. I am known as self-reliant, principled, analytical, and knowledgeable. I perceive myself as competent, straightforward, but task oriented. I am independent, while very work and family oriented.	□	□	□
5 I am an *integrator* type. I am egalitarian, supportive, and a coordinator. I am skilled in interpersonal relations, and able to judge people accurately. I seek to be a team and consensus builder, a unifier able to facilitate group decisions. I am known as a subtle leader and catalyst.	□	□	□
6 I am more a *gamesman* type. I am flexible, mobile, fast moving, and knowledgeable. I tend to be a risk-taker, intent on winning, but I learn from defeat and failure. I am not petty or vindictive in life's games.	□	□	□

Conclusions. As you gain insights into your leadership behavior, you may discover that you possess a variety of the above qualities. The *entrepreneur* does well in start-up enterprises, or turning around a venture that has come upon bad times. The *cooperator* has qualities important within large, complex, global organizations. Cordial, but impersonal, this type is valued as tough-minded, but rewarding of achievers. The *developer* increases productivity by helping personnel to achieve better. However, they tend to engender more personal than organizational loyalty. The *artisan* is more often found at middle or front line management levels. Their motivation is the work itself and the desire to see a job well done. Lacking some-what in political skills, this type does not understand corporate complexities. The *integrator* functions well in a collegial management environment. This type is good at creating teams in an egalitarian work climate. Their role is catalytic and their goal is creating synergy. The *gamesman* has a compulsive drive to win, to be where the action is. This type tends to judge people as to what they can contribute to a winning team. The *gamesman* does well in knowledge industries and high-tech companies with rapid change in strategies, technologies, and markets. Such a person needs to realize that life is more than a game, and no game is unending.

By now you have figured out that high performance leadership is complex. There are no pure types of leaders. People behave with a variety of behaviors they think suitable to each situation. Yet, we do manifest a dominant behavior pattern. By considering various leadership behaviors and tendencies that you manifest, you may even discover your *real* self in the process.

Note: The above and other instruments in this volume may be reproduced in single copies for the benefit of the readers only. For multiple copies, use P. R. Harris' *Twenty Reproducible Assessment Instruments* available from www.hrdpress.com.

2

LEADING IN A HIGH PERFORMANCE WORK ENVIRONMENT

Introduction

High performing knowledge leaders

Again, we consider what leadership is, but now within a productive work environment. Leaders are more than excellent executives or managers: they make things happen to achieve organizational goals and influence planned change and organizational renewal. Some leaders may be found among the rank and file without an important title. And not all high performers are leaders. But what makes a HPL is the first question we address in this chapter – in the form of a briefing that offers only an overview. Next, we look at what contributes to a creative and productive work environment – one that "turns people on" and stretches their capacities. What can leaders do with the organizational climate and culture, as well as their own management style, to stimulate high performing workers? Finally, what are the ethical responsibilities of leaders? These are the key questions to be addressed in the Input section of this learning module. Examination of HPL profiles show how real people exercise leadership, so another example is provided below in Exhibit 2.1.

The interactive segment of this chapter will review two strategies that foster peak performance among workers. One is a problem solving session with top performers, and the other is a way to encourage "intrapreneurialism" in the organization. Intrapreneurialism is a type of entrepreneurial policy and practice that innovative corporations or agencies promote within their system. It fosters risk-taking, creativity, autonomy, and enterprise within existing institutions or systems.[6] Finally, the instrument provided is the high performance management inventory (HPMI), a self-analysis tool that can be used by a leader or by the managers and supervisors who report to that leader. The information and insight that the HPMI provides can really maximize performance.

EXHIBIT 2.1   Profile of a high performing business leader

When he graduated in 1991 from St. John's University in Jamaica, Long Island, Mike Repole knew he wanted to work for himself. Being a sportsman, he capitalized on the competitive nature of the business world through his entrepreneurial skills. From the start, he assumed a leadership role by co-founding Energy Brands, Inc. and, as its president, worked vigorously to make its products successful. Its concept of enhanced, vitamin-enriched bottled water appealed to his health consciousness. Having acquired trusted friends throughout his school days, he assembled a team of like-minded individuals who propelled the brand to unimagined heights. His first company was sold to Coca-Cola for $4.1 billion.

Then "Mike from Queens," as he dubs himself, gained stakes in other health centered enterprises – Pirates Brands, a manufacturer of all-natural snack foods; Energy Kitchen, a chain of healthy-eating restaurants in New York City; and Kind Healthy Snacks which produce all-natural nut and fruit bars. While in college, Mike took a course in race horse management, and eventually became an avid, flourishing owner of thoroughbred race horses. In 2009, Repole Stables had fifty-one wins, which propelled this modest, likeable man into a leading racehorse owner not only for NYC, but at Monmouth and Meadowlands in New Jersey.

From his younger days, when he was a coach-counselor at the Forest Hills Community Center, Mike continued that role with his colleagues and employees. Leading by example, he still inspires loyalty and respect. He and his associates work hard, having fun in the process, while he brings out the best in all of them. This high performer is an authentic communicator who tells it like it is. His wife, Maria, says her husband is a good listener, and people are not afraid to disagree with him. In her words, "I've always believed in him, because I could see he had a way of making his dreams come true."

Throughout his career, Repole has maintained an open-door policy with employees, encouraging the sharing of their ideas, suggestions, and concerns. Success for him is not about making money, but in earning the respect of others, finding the best in others, and leaving the world a bit better for his efforts. He is very loyal and supportive to his family, friends, companies, his Alma Mater, and even his horses. No wonder St John's bestowed its Presidential Medal upon him at a recent commencement – recognition of an individual who has achieved exceptional personal and professional success while rendering outstanding service to the University and society.

Continued

Source: This profile is based on "A Personal Definition of Success – A No-Frills Son of Alma Mater," *St. John's University Magazine,* Spring–Summer 2010: 22–7.

Note: The author hopes you will use HPL profiles in this book to inspire yourself and others to higher performance, and development of your potential as a human being.

Input

The Random House dictionary says that to lead is to go before, to show the way, to guide or influence, to take the initiative, and to demonstrate how something can be accomplished. The various meanings of the term include to precede, to persuade, to excel, and to be in the vanguard. Perhaps we should settle for the interpretation offered in the Prologue's conceptual model; namely, that leadership is the generation and direction of people's energies toward the achievement of personal and organizational goals.

Our concern here is, in general, creating a new work culture; more specifically, designing a high performance environment within an organization. The new management theory is that those who lead are attuned to the changing natures of societies and organizations, of the economy and market, of work and the worker, of leadership, and of management. To transform an industrial mindset and environment into a high performance, "meta-industrial" work culture calls for innovative leaders who lead by example and by learning. The principal characteristics of the unique transformational leadership called for by the emerging post-industrial scene are summarized below. They epitomize what a HPL is all about.

New work culture leadership[7]

Leading in:

- Providing improved, more open communication and information to personnel, customers, and suppliers. This is accomplished both personally and electronically, such as through effective utilization of communication and computer technology. Because work is increasingly information-oriented, data needs to be distributed and differentiated more rapidly, then shaped and pared into information that, when refined, becomes knowledge.
- Creating more autonomy and participation, so that workers have increasing control over their own work space and opportunities for involvement in the enterprise. This is achieved in a variety of ways that offer employees psychological or actual ownership in the business. The democratization in the workplace ranges from sharing in planning, problem solving, and decision making to team management and profit sharing.
- Promoting an entrepreneurial spirit in innovative ventures, especially of a technological or service nature. This can be done through encouragement

and funding of new start-up, fast-growth enterprises or by fostering "intrapreneurial" activities within existing organizations.

- Enhancing the quality of work life, so that it is more meaningful, fulfilling, and psychologically rewarding. This incorporates the above strategies but builds into human systems, wellness programs, sabbatical leaves, incentives, and other entitlements that strengthen loyalty and morale, as well as peak performance.
- Generating innovative, high performing norms and standards that foster competence and excellence, a means to productivity and profitability. This is attained by cultivating work attitudes, agreements, and policies that develop a new work ethic of professionalism in which personnel strive to give of their best, to offer quality service at all cost.
- Utilizing more informal, synergistic organizational relations, so that cooperation and trust are reinforced among the workforce. This can be furthered by resisting hierarchical and status relations in preference to adaptive, temporary, cross-functional, or interdisciplinary collaborative activities and networking.
- Advancing technology transfer and venturing, as well as research and development. Because work is becoming more technically oriented, this trend involves more than the introduction of automation and robotics. It means investing more in R&D by the private sector, more technical training and the use of technology for education of people, seeking more applications of new technologies to improve productivity and performance.

Many examples of these characteristics of tomorrow's organizational culture are at work today, particularly among some of the high-tech, take-off companies. James Treybig, president and principal founder of Tandem Computers, Inc., described such a work environment. Among the principal features of his Silicon Valley firm:

- Fast growth by high performers. When only ten years old, Tandem was already listed in the Fortune 500. Since then, it has grown from zero to half a billion dollars in sales, and from four to 5,000 employees.
- High productivity and creativity. These traits come from competent people who continue to learn, especially about customer satisfaction. *Datamation* magazine once rated Tandem first in customer satisfaction because of outstanding, motivated, dedicated personnel.
- Open-door policy toward workers, visitors, and customers. Managers are responsive to their employees and treat them as equals. These attitudes are demonstrated in the weekly "Friday Popcorn," where employees from all levels meet and mix for two hours of unstructured communication.
- Self-management and peer management emphasis. Tandem employees are expected to take on responsibility and are held more accountable; as a result, they

are involved in the computer business, they feel like a part of the corporation, and they enjoy working.

- Information and technology. Tandem prides itself on being a "paperless factory"; personnel not only build computers, they also use them exclusively to conduct their business. The computer is every worker's tool – before it was common practice, each employee had a terminal for setting personal quality standards and reviewing personal quality production; everyone controls quality, not members of a separate department. Electronic mail connects personnel globally from California to Switzerland. Tandem encourages all employees to use the system to help one another, especially in global problem solving. The company also has used its electronic network to produce a daily, real time, internal newspaper that combines print, graphics, and media; employees from all over the world submit news. Other innovations include a journal that discusses corporate strategy, a TV network of forty-three locations to promote organizational communications and trust as well as marketing, and a program of training through computer business simulations.
- Participation – everyone is part of the management process. Everyone shares supervisory responsibility through membership in various manufacturing committees concerned about everything from quality to asset management. Worker democracy extends to voting on corporate policy. As workers contribute to the success of the enterprise, they earn reward in the form of bonuses, stock, sabbaticals, or other forms of recognition. All concerned, including worker families, know where the company is going; the five-year corporate plan is shared, even with spouses of employees.

The Tandem case. Organizational relations at Tandem are such that its knowledge workers have the ability to influence the decision process through systematic representation (Chapter 6 will examine this subject in detail). When Tandem's chief executive gave the speech that included the above information, I was amazed at how well their corporate culture paralleled my own research findings on the subject. The following quotation by Jim Treybig not only summarizes his management philosophy, but the principal message of this book:

> The key to productivity in our business, and in fact in 90 percent of the jobs in our company, comes from its emphasis on people. We develop people concepts; we involve people in what we do. . . . The bottom line for business is that the major change facing companies in the United States today is the shifting roles of managers and individuals. Managers must integrate several functions – caring about people, working on strategy, expanding communication, generating creativity and innovation, raising organization. In essence, HPLs are agents of planned change.

The next exhibit underscores the lesson to be learned.

EXHIBIT 2.2   The leadership continuum

The graph below examines the function of leadership as a continuum in which the leader moves back and forth to exercise a style to fit the situation. This would range from autocratic on the left, to democratic, to participative, and, finally, to abdicratic on the right. In this view, leadership is a delicate balance between the leader's authority and the group's freedom to act. Thus, leadership from this perspective involves a delicate balance between the leader's authority or responsibility, in contrast with the work group's freedom. An autocratic leader reserves complete authority and allows subordinates or followers little freedom.

A democratic leader equally shares authority with the group and seeks consensus. An "abdicratic" leader abdicates authority to the work unit; by total delegation, he or she permits the group to exercise complete control or freedom over decision making and other managerial activities. Abdicrats totally delegate their authority and power to the group.

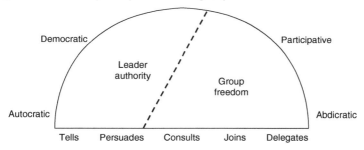

The issue in the illustration is how much authority the leader shares with members of a work unit or team; during an emergency or crisis, the line moves to the right and the leader makes rapid decisions to facilitate the safety of all or quickly resolve problems. On the other hand, with knowledge workers, such as those in an R&D laboratory, a project manager may let the line move considerably to the left, so that team members have more freedom of action. In this conceptual model, leadership is perceived as responding flexibly to the time, place, situation, and people involved.

Changing concepts of leadership

Scholarly research on the subject of leadership has been going on among social scientists for over sixty years. Four schools of thought have emerged. One tries to explain leadership in terms of general traits or characteristics practiced. The second looks at behavior, especially in terms of managerial or administrative style. The third theory explains leadership in terms of situational traits or effective response in specific circumstances with subordinates. The fourth, more recent, theory focuses also on situational behavior, but emphasizes learning a repertoire of responses to varied circumstances, and people believe that a functional analysis of the leader's performance is helpful. The leader's function has been categorized in two ways:

Task. Getting a job done well. This includes setting the direction for subordinates and influencing peers. Task oriented functions may be formal activities, such as making work assignments, or informal endeavors, such as when an unofficial leader of a group of workers determines the group's direction.

Maintenance. Supporting or influencing behavior. The leader affects group morale, performance, and results. Executives, for example, can influence a corporate or team culture so that it motivates and sustains top performance by the group members.

Hersey and Blanchard developed a learning system, for managers, that is centered on situation leadership.[8] These consultants describe a leadership style with varying emphases on task accomplishment and maintenance activities. This model envisions a manager developing leadership skills in understanding, diagnosing, and influencing human behavior at work. The purpose of this approach is to develop personnel so that they contribute to achieving organizational results and success. These contemporary concepts of leadership are performance and result oriented, so that effort is usually measurable and can be evaluated in terms of outcomes. We have read of many CEOs, such as Lee Iacocca at Chrysler or Jack Welch at GE, who were HPLs in turning around a failing enterprise or transforming a world corporation. Such corporate leaders spent their efforts increasing profitability or promoting products, ideas, and values. That is, they have been persuading people. It is a quality of leadership sometimes described as *charismatic* – providing a strategic vision which motivates employees to achieve ambitious goals.

Some writers on leadership complain that management theory focuses on the transactional, rather than transitional or transformational leadership. The latter is the kind of leadership that most institutions need today. In the past, too much leadership research has been too focused on the issues of autocracy and democracy or participation, so that a new paradigm of leadership is required, one that transforms individuals and systems. A high performance leadership model, for instance, seeks a leader who has innovative or revolutionary ideas and offers a vision of future possibilities. Exhibit 2.2 contrasts the two styles of leadership.

A transactional leadership approach can work for managers, but is dependent upon giving positive or negative reinforcement. However, contingent rewards do not necessarily lead to above average performance, and may fail or lead to unintended consequences because of employee contrariness. On the other hand, transformational leadership, especially at the executive level, is needed to supplement such a style, primarily because high performing, charismatic leaders model behaviors that motivate followers to make the transition into a knowledge work culture. Transformational managers provoke extraordinary effort among knowledge workers, inspiring them to work extra hours and produce outstanding results. Leaders who have a personal approach to people, and can instill in them a sense of larger mission, create a high performance atmosphere; one in which the manager becomes a coach, cheerleader, facilitator, and consultant.

According to Bernard Bass, the secret is that high performing, transformational leaders:[9]

- give followers a sense of autonomy, while fostering their self-development;
- treat associates in a friendly, informal, and equal way, being always accessible for consultation;
- provide a model of integrity, fairness, and high standards while being capable of formality and firmness, even capable of reprimanding or correcting when it is appropriate;
- encourage subordinates with advice, help, support, recognition, and openness, while sharing their knowledge and expertise;
- promote reactions of trust, enthusiasm, admiration, respect, pride, and loyalty.

Thus, transformational leaders are role models who offer followers individualized attention and consideration – the opportunities for inputs of information and inspiration. Thomas Watson, of IBM, and Akio Morita of Sony were corporate examples of transformational leadership. Walt Ulmer, former president of the Center for Creative Leadership, also demonstrated the validity of the above observations when, as the commanding general of the US Army's Fort Hood, he implemented a leadership program based on such "power down" concepts. In an era of knowledge workers, such leaders transmit intellectual stimulation by getting people to think and stretch their minds – to visualize the future and what might be done to arouse awareness. HPLs help groups to restructure their constructs or mindsets for more timely and relevant responses. But, this type of leadership also has a reputation for technical and managerial competence, and conceptual and people skills, as well as good judgment and character. They are also known as moral leaders, able to reach down to people and express fundamental values and enduring needs.

Certainly, this kind of leader is in stark contrast to those executives who wish only to assemble or rearrange portfolios of assets – "number crunchers" who forget that their companies are human systems to be developed. Only a HPL is able to transform an economy, an industry, or a corporation by innovating with new products and processes or services. Behavioral science researchers confirm that transformational leadership implies leading in change, creativity, and entrepreneurship; especially by empowering personnel. Such leaders demonstrate persistence, self-knowledge, willingness to take risks, and acceptance of loss or failure. They manifest commitment, consistency, and ability to create a high energy and productive organization so essential in an information-based or "knowledge" society.

This Input review of leadership theory and research summarizes the qualities to seek and cultivate in HPLs. Perhaps Exhibit 2.3 best visualizes the dramatic challenges facing HPLs in this twenty-first century.

High performance work environment

We have seen that leadership which establishes a creative organizational environment can boost performance and productivity, as well as the quality of customer service and profitability. The next chapter will go into detail on improving individual behavior and performance. Now we wish to concentrate on some specific organizational strategies that have been successfully employed to encourage top performance in both public and private sectors. Two companies that are models of corporate cultures that inspire outstanding performance are Intel Corporation and People Express (before its acquisition).

Intel Corporation is a high-tech firm in Northern California. Its president, Andrew Grove, authored a book in 1983, *High Output Management*, on how they produce. Intel adapts its management style to its personnel by structuring decision making to enlist employee support. The company works hard at forecasting and resolving potential problems; enhancing meeting performance and productivity; systemizing performance indicators and reviews; encouraging high performance through raises, bonuses, and promotions; and improving employee career interviewing.

People Express was a "high flying" company before its acquisition by another airline. This enterprise had taken advantage of deregulation in its industry and flourished for a short time. Yet, even though the company eventually fell on hard times, there is something to be learned from its founder, Donald Burr, and the innovative people he assembled. They created a "performance culture" that was totally organized toward people and cutting costs. All employees were owners of stock, and, as such, were designated "customer service managers." All were dedicated to lifestyle improvement and becoming better people by doing their work better. Such ideas and values deserve to live on.

So what really works for high performing organizations? A search of management literature reveals the following:

- Joint goal setting by managers and workers; objectives and targets are always a bit beyond current levels, so that people stretch themselves and strive toward greater achievement.
- Installing and sustaining norms of competence and high performance in the system; accomplished with worker cooperation and consensus, these standards of excellence are incorporated into corporate culture (for instance, with a company slogan such as "we aim to be the best").
- Continual reinforcement of positive behavior and accomplishment, particularly with support services.
- Constructive feedback to redirect worker energies from ineffective to effective work habits and activities, so that people learn from failure.
- Capitalizing on human assets and potential by giving individuals and work groups more flexibility, responsibility, and autonomy while maintaining accountability for top performance and results.
- Encouraging, by managerial example (including risk-taking and experimentation), a spirit of innovation and entrepreneurialism.
- Recruiting, selecting, promoting, and rewarding top performers, and highlighting them as role models to all employees.

- Fostering synergy among personnel, so that individual competition is replaced by teamwork and group achievement.
- Using training, education sessions, and self-learning methods to develop people's potential for success and meta-performance; these methods include personal growth input, self-image building, and achievement counseling.
- Eliminating underachievers who do not respond positively.
- Altering organizational structure so that it is more decentralized, mission-oriented, and responsive.
- Making work meaningful and fun by cultivating informality and fellowship in a context of production achievement and joyful accomplishment.
- Leading by staying close to personnel, suppliers, and customers, so that managers respond quickly to market and employee needs.
- Providing a mix of benefits, rewards, and incentives to encourage talented performance.

These are successful strategies for achieving maximum performance at work; Imaginative leaders translate them into concrete programs in their company or agency, and then devise even better ones. For instance, relative to the last point above, Robert Cawley, when a senior manager at Price Waterhouse, proposed:

1 incentive awards based on achievement over last year's performance goals, or in comparison to peer accomplishments – balanced as to both short and long term goal achievement;
2 compensation ranges for executive performance with appropriate minimum, midpoint, and maximum money amounts;
3 achievable targets and performance standards, measurable both quantifiably and qualitatively;
4 evaluation of performance based on defined goals and business strategies.

Reinforcement of high performance can be accomplished by other rewards in addition to money, but designed to suit individual personality. For some, a leave from regular duties to pursue research, further education, or enriching travel can be more significant and prevent burnout. For others, psychological rewards are more desirable; these may come in various forms, including assignment to leadership positions, or membership in elite groups. People are "turned on" by different rewards, and it is the responsibility of management to discover which "button to push" and to treat everyone as an individual.

Futurist researcher James O'Toole surveyed 200 top performing managers in successful companies to ascertain characteristics in their work environment that accounted for that success. A summary of those findings underscore what is different about a high performance work environment:[10]

- a careful balance of, and attention to, the interests of the various stakeholders;
- a dedication to high purpose vision, concern with long-term performance, and forward-looking;

- a commitment to continual learning, including the fullest development and utilization of human resources;
- an orientation toward technology to improve both product and service;
- a passion for free enterprise, and the dictates of the market;
- an openness to new ideas and willingness to experiment.

Notice how these various research reports confirm over and over certain values and behaviors in high performing work environments.

Capitalizing on knowledge workers

As business adapts to the new work environment, organizations use strategic self-analysis, restructuring, and other mechanisms for survival and renewal. How many, though, turn to their high performing employees to share their leadership in these processes? How many managers really channel the energy or power within their workforce? In the information society, jobs and employment contracts today reflect a wholly different type of employee–employer relationship. A major force behind this change is the emergence of knowledge workers. Such trends are part of what has been designated the *human resource revolution*.

Today's workers are more often paid for their brains, rather than their brawn, as was the case in the industrial age of human development. According to Thomas Davenport, the primary tasks of knowledge workers involve the manipulations of information and knowledge.[11] Such people are creators of wealth in the global economy, so their productivity is important. In essence, the challenge is to make knowledge itself more relevant and productive, but it takes high performing personnel to turn data and information into knowledge.

Everything described in the two previous Input summaries are ways to better motivate workers in today's knowledge culture. A practical means for doing this is to call upon top performing personnel as internal consultants, something discussed in the next section. Hewlett-Packard, for instance, has created an electronic "yellow pages" of the corporation's workers with special expertise. HP leaders build the framework for encouraging people to think about how to make their processes and endeavors more productive. These may range to the best technologies for certain activities, to better ways of sharing findings and results, and to improvements in the workspace itself.

In essence, the HPL challenge is to make the most of intellectual capital.[12] This is where the new IT specialization of KM can be helpful. KM provides tools, techniques, and strategies to retain, analyze, organize, improve, and share business experience and expertise.

Too many organizations forget their own history, and fail to capitalize on their own innovative findings. Too often, especially in the public sector and the military, the turnover of personnel contributes to this loss and the continuing re-learning or discovery of knowledge already present within a human system. To avoid that pitfall, HPLs design methods for evaluating and protecting intangible assets and intellectual capital. The wasting of organizational resources is hazardous in our rapidly changing economies. That is why there is a reformation in our thinking about the utilization of human assets.[13]

Interaction

To exercise leadership in the application of this chapter's insights, there are many opportunities to share this learning with colleagues. For example, some of the issues and strategies we have reviewed here could be placed on the agenda of staff meetings. Among the possibilities for group action about performance improvement through the work environment, here are two approaches known to succeed.

High performance management workshop (HPMW)

At one time in my career, I had been engaged in research with top performing employees that paid off with results.[14] The model has been successfully tested with Navy pilots, savings and loan personnel, public utilities supervisors, and moving company managers. The HPMW process goes like this:

1 *Preliminary data gathering.* The first step in this phase is identification of five critical management concerns, such as performance, productivity, or communications. Then executives define a top performing employee by listing what is required for high performance and describing how such people are to be selected. Finally, managers, HRD specialists, or the workforce nominate the high achieving employees capable of effectively resolving the targeted issues. Written reasons for the individual choices are suggested.

2 *Designing and conducting a workshop.* Participants schedule and plan a two-day session to deal with the problems they have identified. Ten to twelve high achieving personnel participate in each session, with a facilitator. The entire session is videoed in color. Groups are assigned to produce handouts and instruments to help in data gathering and analysis. The focus of this problem-solving session is narrowed to two subjects:

   a. How did these participants become top performers – what are their success stories?

   b. How will they solve the five critical problems presented to them by management?

   Round table discussions are then held on proposed solutions to the target problems. The creation of visual reports with flip charts or laptop computers is encouraged.

3 *Analysis and reporting.* The consultants present during the problem-solving sessions play back the videos to participants for analysis and recommendations of the most feasible solutions and organizational insights. Later they should give key management a briefing on high performance findings and proposed solutions through video synopsis or review. The video provides powerful feedback for management, either by summary or a full playback.

4 *Implications and applications.* This organizational development strategy seeks input on special management concerns or problems needing solutions by outstanding personnel. First, the process recognizes the high achievers within the enterprise and uses them as behavior models for ordinary workers. Also, the videos can be edited and excerpted for use in employee training sessions. For example, high performing expatriate managers can be recorded and the DVDs shown to newly assigned managers and technicians who are being prepared for foreign service.

High performers are today's innovators who help to establish tomorrow's organizational standards. They are vital to any system, yet in two such workshops with field and customer service supervisors at Michigan Consolidates Gas and Electric Company, I learned that many of the participants had never been told before that they were outstanding workers. Selection for the workshop was the first recognition of their better than average performance (see Exhibit 2.3, The high performance management inventory). By using one of the two strategies discussed here, leaders give acknowledgment and confirmation to personnel who excel at work.

The outstanding people seminar (TOPS)

An annual conference of an organization's highest achievers and their spouses or significant others helps maintain high morale and productivity, while rewarding their extra effort and sacrifice for the past year. Slow business periods can be used for this purpose. The occasion can be used to present awards or other forms of recognition for extraordinary service to the organization, as shown in the following case.

A how to case: Tandem Computers, Inc. does this through the program called TOPS. Those invited represent about seven percent of their workforce, the outstanding performers for that year. They assemble in a nearby resort for a holiday with their personal companions. Groups of about seventy include guest managers, so that there is a mix of every level and function of the company. Because they all are outstanding workers, special relationships are formed that engender professional respect regardless of status or education, and thus strengthens a family atmosphere. Executives are convinced that this group socializing builds mutual respect and creativity, as well as an effective and unstructured communication network that contributes to further business success.

(For more information, contact Tandem Computer Corporation, Office of the President.)

Instrumentation[15]

Note: All of the instruments in this book were developed by the author for his clients, and the norms and other data are proprietary. Readers are urged to develop their own validation data by using the Harris instruments with their own organizations.

EXHIBIT 2.3   The high performance management inventory

Directions

This instrument is useful for assessing your own management competencies for higher performance, and provides indicators for continuing professional development. The inventory can also be used for more objective performance appraisal when a supervisor or colleague employs it to evaluate your managerial proficiency. The comparison of ratings obtained between its administration by yourself and by others can provide valuable insights for further learning and growth as an effective global leader. Finally, HPMI can be used as an assessment instrument with those who report to you, or by project managers with team members.

HPMI not only helps to identify one's professional management strengths, but also to focus efforts for career development. The term work unit refers to the organizational group this person supervises from a team to a larger entity. Relative to management or leadership skills, the evaluation utilizes a nine point scale in which you rate yourself or another (or someone else rates you) from low to high proficiency or competence. This is done by locating a number from left to right which best describes the current state of achievement, and then recording that category item with a circle around the number selected. For example, a selection in the range of 7–9 indicates a high performer:

0	1	2	3	4	5	6	7	8	9

NO COMPETENCY	BASIC COMPETENCY	INTERMEDIATE COMPETENCY	ADVANCED COMPETENCY

This analysis will be on 105 items which have been divided into twelve categories of management functions. These cover a range of activities and responsibilities in a leadership role. Kindly review below the meaning of the classifications before beginning the rating process:

1 *Cultural awareness.* Being conscious of and up-to-date on organizational culture, policies, priorities, and power issues (micro-culture); in relation to external issues, trends, and development (macro-culture – economic, political, social, technological conditions, and trends).
2 *Communication.* Internal organizational communications and information exchanges, such as keeping subordinates informed, interpreting work unit activities and priorities, information interface with other units, teams, or divisions.
3 *Public relations.* Work unit relations with its internal and external publics, or stakeholders in its professional activities; this involves representation of what the unit or team is doing to other managers or units within the organization, and to persons/groups outside in the community, industry, or government.

Continued

4 *Coordination.* Performing liaison functions and integrating work unit activities so as to create synergy with other organizational units, or with externals, such as suppliers, contractors, consultants, consumers, regulatory officials, etc.

5 *Planning.* Developing and deciding upon long-term objectives/goals, strategies, and priorities; planning for change or alternative courses of action.

6 *Implementation.* Converting the above plans into short-term targets and activities by sequencing/scheduling, and appropriate decision making.

7 *Financial management.* Inaugurating and monitoring financial controls, such as budgeting which includes preparing, justifying, and administering funds invested in unit activities.

8 *Materials resource management.* Assuring availability of adequate raw materials and/or supplies, equipment, and facilities to carry on the unit's activities; overseeing procurement/contracting functions of the unit.

9 *Human resource management.* Projecting number/type of staff requirements for the unit, and effectively using the human resource development (HRD) systems of the organization or community for recruitment, selection, promotion, training, performance appraisal, and improvement.

10 *Supervision skills.* Providing continuous monitoring, guidance, and coaching of subordinates so that unit activities are accomplished, while recognizing and rewarding high performance, as well as correcting low productivity situations.

11 *Unit monitoring and scanning.* Keeping informed on overall status of unit culture and activities, identifying problem areas for corrective actions (e.g. rescheduling or relocating resources, using external consultants of resources); then being able to compare unit activity with performance or trends among comparable organizational units and industry or foreign competitors through environmental scanning and forecasting.

12 *General performance evaluation.* Action research to critically assess the degree to which the unit is achieving program/project goals and targets, as well as its overall effectiveness in work operations; also evaluation of miscellaneous practices of the manager which affect both personal and unit performance at home and abroad.

Note: These, then, are the twelve dimensions of management, which, when performed very well, contribute to a HPL and work environment. Within the context of these defined categories, now proceed with the judgments. No one else is to see these results unless you decide to share them. Remember, if you are to advance your personal and professional development, or that of others, through this exercise, be discriminating and authentic in your ratings. Recall that you are assessing individual proficiency in a range of managerial activities

Continued

and responsibilities relative to a work unit or team – that is, the part or level of the organization that you or the individual under consideration manage or supervise (a project team, an office, plant, branch, division, bureau, regional or national territory, subsidiary, etc.). If a colleague or supervisor is using this instrument to assess the performance of another person, follow the same procedure).

Record the most appropriate rating from the nine-point scale on the blank space to the left of each numbered item. Thank you for your cooperation. Please begin the assessment process.

Part 1: Cultural awareness

___1 Involved in the transition to the new work culture for myself and my unit by planning change.

___2 Keep up-to-date on the socio-economic developments that affect my work unit.

___3 Keep up-to-date with technological changes and developments affecting areas of expertise for myself and the work unit.

___4 Keep aware of changes in corporate or organizational culture.

___5 Keep up-to-date on changing organizational objectives, roles, norms, activities, priorities, and politics.

___6 Develop a strong work unit or team culture that enhances high performance and excellence.

___7 Be aware of and sensitive to the varied cultures, both macro and micro, in which the unit operates.

___8 Develop cultural empathy/sensitivity to differences in unit members/colleagues, customers/clients, contractors/suppliers.

___9 Have knowledge and language skills for the host culture in which the unit operates.

___10 Apply understanding of roles, expectations, or regulations relative to unit performance from the perspective of *officials* in this organization, its unions, its industry association, or the government.

Part 2: Communication

___11 Explain/clarify changing organizational culture, policies, priorities, and procedures to unit members.

___12 Extract and apply organizational communications pertinent to unit members (e.g. information and directives from higher management).

___13 Keep unit members informed of pertinent external issues and developments that impact their work.

___14 Ensure that work unit activities reflect organizational goals, policies, and directives.

Continued

___15 Prepare required written and oral communications for unit with conciseness, accuracy, competence, and cultural sensitivity.

___16 Communicate respect for the recipient/listener by transmitting both verbally and non-verbally positive concern, interest, and encouragement, especially by trying to get into the receiver's world or life space.

___17 Communicate reciprocal concern and non-judgmental attitude by a dialogue which shares interaction responsibility, promotes circular communication, and avoids moralistic, value-laden, evaluative statements.

___18 Communicate flexibility and capacity to tolerate ambiguity by adjustments to the receiver's mindset and needs, as well as being able to cope with cultural differences and uncertainties.

___19 Communicate changes in organizational policies, procedures, and programs to external clients, suppliers, and stakeholders.

Part 3: Public relations

___20 Identify work unit's diverse publics or stakeholders in its activities and performance.

___21 Represent/promote work unit before groups and individuals within and without the organization.

___22 Respond effectively to inquiries and requests for unit information and service.

___23 Explain work unit programs and functions to non-experts in terms they can understand and which are culturally appropriate.

___24 Persuade other interested parties to "buy into" and support a desired course of unit action.

___25 Use formal and informal resource networks effectively to achieve unit objectives and targets, or to obtain information.

___26 Resolve conflict within unit or with other units by negotiation and compromise, so energies can be constructively channeled.

___27 Develop positive unit image for performance excellence, resourcefulness, and cooperation.

___28 Create unit reputation for innovation and adaptability to varied circumstances, results that are usually on time and within budget, and synergistic relationships.

___29 Demonstrate unit respect for host country or area locals, culture, and work habits.

___30 Maintain concern for environmental or ecological impact of unit activities.

Part 4: Coordination

___31 Maintain helpful, supportive, productive relationships within the work unit.

Continued

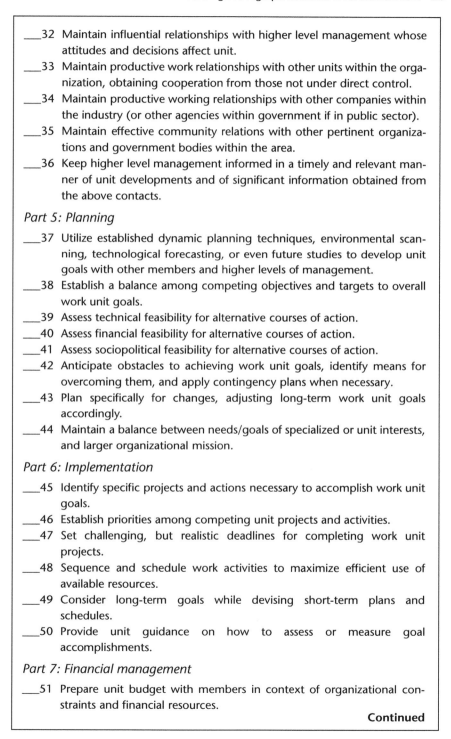

___32 Maintain influential relationships with higher level management whose attitudes and decisions affect unit.

___33 Maintain productive work relationships with other units within the organization, obtaining cooperation from those not under direct control.

___34 Maintain productive working relationships with other companies within the industry (or other agencies within government if in public sector).

___35 Maintain effective community relations with other pertinent organizations and government bodies within the area.

___36 Keep higher level management informed in a timely and relevant manner of unit developments and of significant information obtained from the above contacts.

Part 5: Planning

___37 Utilize established dynamic planning techniques, environmental scanning, technological forecasting, or even future studies to develop unit goals with other members and higher levels of management.

___38 Establish a balance among competing objectives and targets to overall work unit goals.

___39 Assess technical feasibility for alternative courses of action.

___40 Assess financial feasibility for alternative courses of action.

___41 Assess sociopolitical feasibility for alternative courses of action.

___42 Anticipate obstacles to achieving work unit goals, identify means for overcoming them, and apply contingency plans when necessary.

___43 Plan specifically for changes, adjusting long-term work unit goals accordingly.

___44 Maintain a balance between needs/goals of specialized or unit interests, and larger organizational mission.

Part 6: Implementation

___45 Identify specific projects and actions necessary to accomplish work unit goals.

___46 Establish priorities among competing unit projects and activities.

___47 Set challenging, but realistic deadlines for completing work unit projects.

___48 Sequence and schedule work activities to maximize efficient use of available resources.

___49 Consider long-term goals while devising short-term plans and schedules.

___50 Provide unit guidance on how to assess or measure goal accomplishments.

Part 7: Financial management

___51 Prepare unit budget with members in context of organizational constraints and financial resources.

Continued

___52 Project long-term financial needs and resources of work unit.

___53 Explain and justify persuasively the unit budget requests both orally and in writing.

___54 Apply financial systems reports and mechanisms in managing work unit costs and/or income.

___55 Seek entrepreneurial opportunities to supplement unit budget or expand its income production.

___56 Consider national or community financial situation relative to pricing and compensation recommendations, expenditures and contributions, as well as other manifestations of unit social responsibility.

___57 Consider return on investment in unit activities, especially if in the private sector and stockholder dividends are involved or loans are to be repaid.

Part 8: Materials resource management

___58 Plan for the acquisition of needed equipment, facilities, supplies, or services to carry out unit mission.

___59 Apply organizational contract and procurement rules and regulations in managing the work unit.

___60 Oversee or participate in procurement management of key unit material resources, including lease of purchase decisions on equipment and contractors.

___61 Oversee or participate in managing and evaluating contractor or supplier activities for the unit.

___62 Ensure that local and minority contractors or suppliers are given equal opportunity for unit business.

___63 Ensure that illegal, unethical or unjust financial practices are not practiced within or by the work unit.

Part 9: Human resource management

___64 Plan for needed changes in size and composition of work unit staff and supplementary personnel.

___65 Take an active role in recruiting, selecting, and retaining staff for the work unit.

___66 Seek and maintain competence as performance criteria, regardless of sex, race, or other factors in worker's background.

___67 Apply personnel policies and regulations, particularly regarding equal employment opportunity and affirmative action to prevent job discrimination.

___68 Seek synergistic labor/management relations and high performing work culture which enhances people's potential.

Continued

___69 Develop meaningful performance standards, and conduct helpful performance appraisals.

___70 Capitalize on human assets by appropriate training and development programs, especially in new technologies.

___71 Take corrective and constructive actions with work unit members whose behavior or performance is inappropriate.

___72 Consult with unit members and higher management for meaningful reward and recognition program.

Part 10: Supervision skills

___73 Clarify roles and relationships, so all unit members understand work assignments and expectations.

___74 Encourage participative and team management approach.

___75 Delegate responsibility with commensurate authority and resources.

___76 Provide positive re-enforcement for high performance through appropriate recognition and rewards.

___77 Coach and counsel unit members on technical problems, productivity, career development, and appropriate changes in performance or behavior.

___78 Maintain equal concern for task accomplishment and people maintenance within the unit.

Part 11: Unit monitoring and scanning

___79 Establish systems for monitoring work progress, so as to ensure unit excellence.

___80 Adjust to changes in workload, resources, priorities, or schedule in dynamic and timely manner.

___81 Use cooperative relations, direct observation, or informal contacts with general management, users, customers, and suppliers to ascertain needs and unit effectiveness – manage by walking or moving around and staying in touch with unit publics.

___82 Anticipate trends, changes, needs and problems, readjusting and reallocating as appropriate.

___83 Encourage innovation and entrepreneurial spirit within the work unit, and especially in relation to externals.

Part 12: General performance evaluation

A: Unit assessment

___84 Evaluate unit effectiveness in a systematic and objective manner, emphasizing both quantity and quality.

___85 Assess unit climate in terms of cooperative actions that enhance people performance and potential.

Continued

___86 Identify specific ways for improving unit's procedures, processes, structures, and cost effectiveness.

___87 Identify specific ways for improving the unit's culture, morale, relationships, and achievement level.

___88 Develop strategies toward achieving unit long-term goals by continuing system refinements and improvements.

___89 Utilize individual member performance appraisals and input as means for improving unit productivity and excellence.

B: Personal assessment

___90 Evaluate personal effectiveness as a unit manager in a systematic, objective and periodic manner, so as to identify strengths, limitations, and plans for improvement.

___91 Conduct unit meetings to achieve desired objectives by improved skills as a facilitator.

___92 Present ideas clearly and persuasively in both oral and written communication by improved skills as a communicator.

___93 Share helpful feedback with members by improved skills as a listener, observer, and constructive critic.

___94 Practice diplomacy, tact, and consideration of others by improved human relations skills.

___95 Practice leadership in a results-oriented and proactive, rather than reactive, way by improved planned change and strategist skills.

___96 Take responsibility, exercise initiative, and seize opportunity by improved entrepreneurial skills.

___97 Manage information resources for wider input and applications by improved skills in communication technologies and informal networking.

___98 Exercise power by influencing others to get things done through improved skills in negotiations, bargaining, and coalition building.

___99 Apply imagination and creativity by improving problem solving and decision making skills.

___100 Implement and sustain a wellness program which reduces stress and tension, while improving the quality of life and the management of time and leisure.

___101 Manage for transition, ambiguity, uncertainty, and differences by improved transformational management skills.

___102 Act to personalize knowledge and perceptions by improved cross-cultural management skills, so as to recognize the influence of one's own culture on values, perceptions, attitudes, communications, and management practices.

Continued

___103 Endeavor to function in the knowledge or technological work culture by improving technical skills and scientific comprehension.

___104 Endeavor to function in global economy and marketplace by improving skills and understanding of international economics, global regional markets, international management and business protocol, and foreign languages.

___105 Practice synergy by improving skill development in cooperative and collaborative actions, cultural sensitivity and open-mindedness, team building and joint ventures.

___ Total score

Scoring procedure

Add up the ratings provided for the 105 items.

1 Determine an overall evaluation of high performance management proficiency by comparing the total score with these approximations – a score between 210 and 315 would indicate basic competency; between 420 and 630 would be intermediate competency; and between 235 and 945 would be advanced competency.
2 Go back and analyze the implications of any scores rated below 4. Such items are targets for immediate improvement. Those with ratings in the 5–6 range would be secondary targets for professional development if one aspired to become a high performing manager.
3 Observe the twelve parts and the ratings provided within each category. Any selection with a preponderance of scores in the 2–6 range would seem to be an area to focus upon for further career development.
4 If one's supervisor or a colleague were asked to provide a more objective performance appraisal of you on the 105 items, then compare the total score supplied by that observer in contrast to one obtained through self-evaluation. Furthermore, note discrepancies in scores for individual items and categories. A conference with that observer on such matters may offer additional self-knowledge and career guidance.

Scoring

The assessor simply adds up the total of the management proficiency ratings to ascertain whether the evaluation indicates basic, intermediate, or advanced competency. A rating on any item below four identifies areas for performance improvement. The same instrument can be used during performance evaluation sessions by an individual and the supervisor to whom he or she reports; discrepancies in ratings can serve as a basis for discussion on how to increase performance.

3

INCREASING PERFORMANCE AT WORK

Introduction

Performance improvement

To improve performance and productivity in the workplace, the high performance leader does more than shape a creative environment. Managers must endeavor to understand and motivate people, beginning with themselves. Thus, our first objective in this chapter will be to better comprehend human behavior, then to learn how to energize personnel, especially by one's managerial or leadership style.

The second purpose will be to examine individual performance and the factors that contribute to high achievement. The leader who is concerned about performance management should become a behavior model for other workers to emulate. Then executives or managers have a responsibility to hold those who report to them accountable, by developing mechanisms that objectively appraise the work effort and encourage top performance.

Like institutions as described in the Prologue, individuals are also energy exchange systems in themselves. As HP leaders, we must energize ourselves and others in goal achievement. Motivation becomes the mobilizing of our own and others' energy forces, both physical and psychic, toward achieving specific goals, objectives, and targets. A HP leader does not seek workers who are submissive, passive, and dependent. Instead the HPL stimulates personnel who grow personally and professionally by optimizing their talents and resources.

Mothers in their role as housewives are an example of people who are under-appreciated, underutilized, and unpaid, for these women often exercise considerable creativity in their managerial and organizational skills as homemakers. Increasingly, more of these talented females pursue careers or even public office. Furthermore, many of them are becoming outstanding professionals and executives. To illustrate the possibilities, the next profile of a high performance leader is offered for review and analysis.

EXHIBIT 3.1   Anne Millians-Roche is President/Broker of Owens Realty Network

PROFILE OF A HIGH PERFORMING MOTHER AND EXECUTIVE

Anne Millians-Roche of Orlando, Florida, is an energetic, results-driven, hands-on management professional. In her work career, she has distinguished herself by successful marketing strategies and a management style that focuses on customer requirements and satisfaction. She has demonstrated leadership in human relations, strategic planning, administration, accounts development, organizational start-up, training, and HRD. No wonder, in 2010, she became president and co-founder of Owens Realty Network in Florida's Winter Park. It was a personal triumph for this high performer who progressed from housewife to the executive suite.

Born in Georgia, she was raised on a farm until college and her first marriage more than forty years ago. Then she began to hone her managerial expertise as a stay-at-home mom, with the usual involvement in her two sons' football, baseball, and PTA activities. She started a catering business to help her husband through law school. By 1982, she was a divorced, single mom who, in order to support her children, got her first outside job as a clerk-typist for Mezario Maritime Agency. Thus began her initial career in the shipping industry when this Italian firm, impressed by her competency, sent her to Europe for extensive training in steamship operations, documentation, customer service/sales, and cross-cultural relations. She set goals for herself and continually achieved them. Thus, Anne rose with successive shipping companies from customer service representative, to district manager, to regional manager, to vice president, and finally senior vice president. Having put her sons through university, she now found herself alone in New York City as a key executive headquartered in the World Trade Center. There, when VP at Blue Star Lines, her career was nourished by their marketing and sales vice president. Before terrorists destroyed the Twin Towers, that executive, Bill Roche, further developed her self-confidence and abilities. Eventually, her personal relationship with him would grow until they both would retire, relocate to Florida, and get married.

Anne's father had set the high performance model and instilled in her that there was nothing she could not do if she had the right mindset. After two decades of successful experience in the maritime industry, this dynamic female created a second career as a realtor in 2004. Working for Coldwell Banker she obtained her broker's license, and sold over $4 million in property. One of her clients was so awed with her professionalism that he eventually offered her a position as vice president of his company, OR&L Facilities Services, based in Connecticut. Together they co-founded, in Winter Park, Owens Realty Network for property management where Millians-Roche serves as President/Broker. She also has an active role as parent and grandmother (five of her own grandchildren, plus four more of her husband's offspring and their three children). Anne is grateful for her many mentors, but still lives by a simple motto that she got from her own father and mother: do the right thing – always.

Input

HPLs demonstrate greater comprehension of human behavior and motivation – simply, what makes people "tick?" The way leaders answer this question influences how they structure an organization, their philosophy and practices of management, and their strategies to influence personnel and improve performance. For many decades, behavioral scientists have contended that the best way for leaders to maintain a competitive edge is to develop the organization's human assets. To take advantage of the human potential in a corporation or agency, management must deal with complex issues of human nature and achievement.

Behavioral science management theory

Twenty-five years ago, Douglas McGregor produced a seminal book on the human side of enterprise. In it, he described two kinds of managers. One has a view of human nature that is quite negative but prevalent in the industrial age. These *Theory X* types, as he labeled them, believe that the average person has an inherent dislike of work and avoids it and responsibility when possible because most individuals have relatively little ambition. According to Theory X managers, workers prefer to be directed and must be controlled, coerced, and even threatened with punishment in order to make them perform effectively. McGregor (2006) maintained that this type of management was replaced in the post-industrial period with a management style based upon very different assumptions about human nature, which he called *Theory Y*. Its premise is that the expenditure of energy in work is as natural as play or rest, and high performance depends on self-direction and self-control. From this perspective, commitment to organizational objectives is a function of rewards associated with their achievement. Given the right organizational environment, the average worker learns to accept and seek responsibility. The leader's task is to create those conditions that unleash the human capacity for imagination, ingenuity, and innovation.

Other behavioral scientists have rejected what can be called *pull approach* to worker motivation, which depends on external controls used in an almost punitive way. Like Rensis Likert (1961) and Bernard Bass (2008), these theorists did not conceive behavior as dependent solely upon forces in the environment, responding only to demands and pressures, rewards and punishments, and deprivations and inducements. Their research in industry during the last half of the twentieth century has demonstrated dynamic possibilities of human growth when workers are given meaningful work, are permitted to participate with management, and challenged to achieve. Frederick Herzberg (2008) for instance, proved to managers that it is not enough to take care of the needs of employees relative to pay, benefits, and working conditions; instead, the real motivators are to be found in achievement, growth, recognition, responsibility, and advancement. The manager's job, then, involves more than manipulating the work environment to induce and channel human energies. Workers themselves are changing in terms of their education and economic income, and they have a new set of needs and requirements for motivation.

The knowledge-based world of today's business rejects imperial chief executives in favor of low-key leaders who are competent and resolute in creating new futures through people and their potential.

Maslow's hierarchy of needs

One of the most helpful contributions toward understanding human motivation came from the humanistic psychologist, Abraham Maslow. He said that human needs vary according to immediacy and can be arranged in a hierarchy, or graded rank, according to the order in which they must be met. Exhibit 3.2 reproduces his conceptual model for us.

The foundation of Maslow's motivation theory is that we humans must satisfy certain needs before we can act or achieve. In other words, we first seek to satisfy our basic survival or physiological needs, such as food or sex. When these are sufficiently satisfied, we become concerned with another level of need related to safety and security, either physiological or psychological behaviors such as locking homes, organizing neighborhood watch programs, building up bank accounts, and striving for the right job classification and tenure. Once these lower needs are provided for, according to this theory, we are freed for higher level concerns, such as belonging and love. Thus, we satisfy this need and find expression in yearning to be loved by someone, or in membership in some group, and in general acceptance

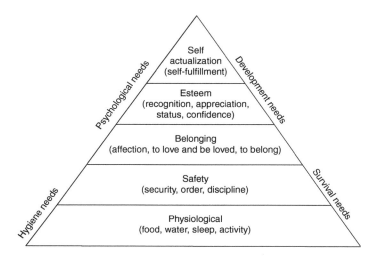

EXHIBIT 3.2 Maslow's hierarchy of needs

Source: Refer to Abraham Maslow, *Toward a Psychology of Being*. New York: John Wiley, 1998; *Maslow on Management*. New York: John Wiley, 1998; and *The Maslow Business Reader*. New York: John Wiley, 2000.

by others. Finally, near the top of the hierarchy are such "esteem" needs as self-respect, recognition, and prestige. Such ego needs can be prime movers toward self-determination, control over one's fate, and achievement. People operating at this higher need level work in order to have others acknowledge their capacities and power. If such needs are thwarted, such a person may feel weak, inferior, and even helpless. For some who distort the satisfaction of these needs, human drive may lead to excessive demands for power and control.

At the pinnacle of human needs in the Maslow model is the inner drive for self-fulfillment or actualization of one's potential. This drive propels some people, such as HPLs, to strive to become what they are capable of becoming and to seek excellence through achievement. At its best, it motivates the search for ultimate value, perfection, justice, truth, beauty, and other non-selfish ideals. It is manifest in high achievers, superior athletes and peak performers, accomplished artists and writers, and outstanding scholars and researchers. It leads to the highest expressions of human creativity and nobility of actions. In the sports world, for instance, Magic Johnson is such a person. Born poor, he used proficiency in basketball to help him climb up the Hierarchy of Needs. By becoming the best player in the world, this high performing sports star went into other successful business ventures. A self-actualized man, he is a model to youth, especially among African Americans.

Maslow theorized that we all have all the varied needs, but that people may focus on one level or another. Thus, the homeless urban dweller of necessity concentrates on survival, while the suburban middle class person may be centered on security needs, trying to preserve what he or she has attained. The theory allows that humans may move up and down on the need hierarchy as time and circumstances dictate. For instance, a young urban professional who loses his or her job may suddenly have a reordering of priorities, especially during a global recession. A second example is that citizens of a First World, affluent society have the luxuries of time and means to be concerned about the environment and ecology, and to strive to prevent pollution or eradicate disease. Those in emerging economies, on the other hand, must focus on fighting to stay alive and on counteracting the effects of drought, plague, starvation, and other disasters. Bill Gates, the Microsoft co-founder, retired from business to devote full time with his wife, Melinda, to their family foundation that combats health and environmental problems, especially in Africa. Now they are joined by Warren Buffet in urging the new high-tech billionaires to devote more time and assets to philanthropy everywhere.

Another example of a self-actualized person is Dr Edwin Aldrin, the second man to step on the Moon.[16] Buzz, as he is known popularly, was a fighter pilot, MIT doctorate, astronaut, and author. But as a senior, he has spent his energies helping humanity realize its future off-world. Buzz has an ebullient space vision, and provides national leaders with a synthesis and strategy for achieving our human potential beyond Earth. So, those at the top of the needs hierarchy have the capacity to stimulate great explorations that transform us as a species and society.

Dr Maslow also maintained that there was a reverse side to his hierarchy; all the needs had associated complaints, which he labeled "gripes or grumbles." Humans perpetually seek fuller lives; their complaints also rise in a hierarchy that corresponds to their needs. Thus, as we have corrected some of the past abuses of the factory system, such as child labor, we become more concerned about higher issues of social justice, such as the employment of minorities or equal opportunities in management for women. If an employer takes care of personnel needs for cleanliness and safety in a plant, then the employer can expect workers' gripes or demands to move up the scale; perhaps they will demand child care centers or sabbatical leaves.

Maslow actually applied his research to the work environment of a small California plant and wrote a book in 1965 on what he termed "Eustachian Management." His point was that a more productive work situation would result when management created a corporate culture that emphasized satisfaction of the three higher levels of needs. In a sense, he anticipated what today is termed the *new management* or the *knowledge work culture*. Leaders who hope to design a high performance corporation or agency would do well to analyze and apply these concepts.

Human behavior in the workplace

Psychiatrists, psychologists, sociologists, and other social scientists have propounded many theories for explaining why humans behave as they do. As a management psychologist, I have synthesized a viewpoint from that myriad research that made sense to me in counseling or consulting with different people and systems. Below is a summary under a series of sub-headings, which can be applied to problems of management – coping with co-workers and attempting to lead them toward higher performance.

Life space

Each of us lives within his or her own life space, which is as unique as a fingerprint. This space has both psychological and physical dimensions. Behavioral scientists call it our *perceptual field*. Each individual views reality from within this space or perspective, and so develops a unique way of reading meaning into it.

Think of life space, for a moment, in terms of concentric circles. At the core is the sense of self – how we view ourselves as persons, positively or negatively. From that core, moving outward in ever larger circles, next comes our systems of needs, values, standards, expectations, and ideals. Together, these influence our perception of what happens outside of ourselves – it is the mindset that ultimately affects our acts or inaction. Thus, we are each different, so that we may disagree as to what is real, true, beautiful, right, or wrong. Perception is relative, and explains why disagreements or arguments may occur, for instance, between fellow workers and ourselves. Knowing this makes a good case for being more tentative, less absolute, in our expression of opinions and viewpoints.

Being a part of a cultural group can further influence and reinforce an individual's perception and behavior (see Chapter 5). Suffice it now to recall that just as our life spaces or private worlds are unique, so is each of our need systems. As we

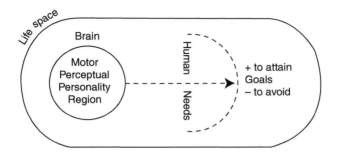

EXHIBIT 3.3 Analyzing human behavior at work

seek to satisfy these needs, we are motivated or energized toward certain targets, objectives, and goals for ourselves, as visualized in Exhibit 3.3.

We motivate ourselves or get aroused when we direct and sustain effort to attain or to avoid something, so as to satiate a need (see Exhibit 3.4). When we are hungry, for example, we are moved to seek food to satisfy that need. Behavior is largely motivated, but there are several different forces within each person's life space that move us to act or avoid in a certain way.

Furthermore, behavior can be affected by habit, culture, or the activities of others. Although originally a course of behavior may have been a conscious choice, over a period of time people may act whilst unconscious of the forces in the past or the culture that dictate their behavior. I was jolted at lunch one day when I was asked why I never used pepper; mulling over the question, I eventually remembered that my grandmother often told me as a child, "pepper puts holes in your heart." Since I consciously recalled the reason for this foolish behavior, I now regularly use pepper, especially as a healthier substitute for salt.

The point is that our behavior can be conditioned by others, by past experience or cultural guides, and by the circumstances in which we find ourselves. But behavior can also be modified toward what increases performance. This knowledge allows us to correct abuses in terms of smoking, alcohol, drugs, and other unhealthy or undesirable practices. In addition, effective leaders learn to reinforce positive or desired behavior in employees, especially through some form of reward or recognition.

The above conceptual model suggests that as we seek to satisfy needs and make adjustments so as to achieve goals, a complex situation occurs when more than one motive pulls us, possibly in different directions, or when a need/goal is frustrated or unattainable.

Exhibit 3.4 below amplifies the behavior model we are proposing for consideration. In striving to meet our goals or objectives, we sometimes meet barriers, physical or psychological, that can frustrate the satisfaction of needs. We may cope with such realities by an adjustment that permits us to circumvent the obstacle or by engaging in conflict within ourselves or with others, such as blaming someone

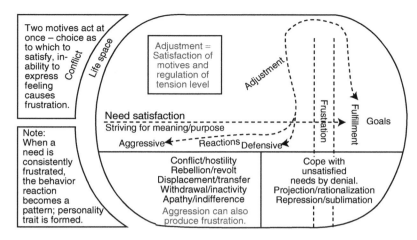

Two motives act at once – choice as to which to satisfy, in-ability to express feeling causes frustration.

Conflict

Life space

Adjustment = Satisfaction of motives and regulation of tension level

Adjustment

Frustration

Frustration

Fulfillment

Goals

Need satisfaction

Striving for meaning/purpose

Aggressive ◄ - - - Reactions Defensive ◄

Note: When a need is consistently frustrated, the behavior reaction becomes a pattern; personality trait is formed.

Conflict/hostility
Rebellion/revolt
Displacement/transfer
Withdrawal/inactivity
Apathy/indifference
Aggression can also produce frustration.

Cope with unsatisfied needs by denial. Projection/rationalization Repression/sublimation

EXHIBIT 3.4 Motivation and behavior responses: achievement or adjustment

else for the problem. This type of negative reaction to frustration may lead to finding a "scapegoat" who is preventing our satisfaction. That unhealthy approach can result in racism and other forms of bigoted behavior – blaming our inabilities or inadequacies on others because of their race, color, or creed. Other responses to frustration range from withdrawal and apathy to rebellion and revolt.

Within a work context, consider this situation. A supervisor and subordinate formulate some career objectives for the latter during the course of performance appraisal. The plan calls for the employee to take courses that will lead to better job performance and enhance career advancement. Frustration may arise when the person discovers a barrier to attendance, for instance, by lack of time, money, or qualifications. The employee is in conflict. One positive adjustment would be to take the program independently using audiovisual media, or going online to teach oneself. A negative adjustment would be to deny the need for the training, project the problem on the company, or even blame the supervisor for suggesting the idea in the first place. The healthy response to frustration is to channel one's energies in constructive, instead of destructive, ways. Frustrated energy in this situation, for example, can be sublimated into service. Repressing that energy, for example by dropping the course and blaming someone else, undermines one's position. Seek-ing alternative solutions to problems, on the other hand, contributes to personal growth, for we develop coping skills.

The late Mother Teresa of Calcutta, as an illustration, was once frustrated as a teacher of science to elite students in a Calcutta private academy. Sensing the needs of the poor surrounding her in India, she sublimated her energies into a new form of service by founding an order and movement dedicated to the most needy humans. Her global achievements and leadership in serving the poor resulted in world acclaim and the Nobel Prize.

Positive reinforcement

Undesirable behavior may sometimes result in a worker being ignored, criticized, or unrewarded by the manager. Punishment is a less effective way of altering people's behavior over the long run. It may for the moment stop the negative actions, but does not permanently change the delinquent. This is, in part, why our criminal justice system, based solely on punishment, is so inadequate. My own experience has proven that deviant behavior can be altered through a positive re-enforcement system. As part of a leadership style, confirm and encourage positive behavior and actions by your associates.

Behavioral deviancy

Deviant behavior occurs when the action differs from what is considered normal by a group. Deviant behavior can be *creative*, as in the case of those who advocate change of obsolete laws and regulations because the norms or standards are no longer appropriate, or it can be *delinquent* behavior, as in the case of a worker who is frequently tardy or absent, or who undermines order on the job. Creative deviants alter the status quo and promote renewal. Delinquent behavior may range from the abnormal to the illegal – it is always disruptive to the family, organization, or society. Sometimes, with counseling or re-education, a delinquent deviant will change behavior; if not, the employee may have to go.

On the other hand, some deviant behavior is pathological – the individual's personality has been so damaged by genetic inheritance or early childhood experiences as requires special mental health therapies. For example, a psychopath's behavior is chronically immoral social behavior – one who gratifies needs by violence, abusive sex, or aggressive impulses. Generally, there are two classifications of this personality type, according to Dr Robert Hare:

1 those who maintain a socially deviant or parasitic lifestyle to overcome boredom; such persons lack realistic goals, have trouble controlling themselves, and are perceived as irresponsible;
2 other psychopaths manifest aggressive narcissism, and are often perceived as superficially charming, pathological liars, cunning and manipulative, shallow and lacking in empathy, unable to take responsibility for actions which hurt others, and lacking in remorse or guilt.

Scientific research today recognizes that some individuals are genetically predisposed to criminality and violence. James Wilson and Richard Herrnstein, authors of *Crime and Human Nature*, reported studies that confirm that some criminals have low regard for the feelings or values of others and are prone to pursue immediate gratification of their own needs at the expense of others. Behavioral differences between the sexes have also been linked to hormonal differences, which, to some, partially explains the tendency for males to be more predisposed toward criminal deviant behavior than are females. Dr Wilson believes that the time is coming when we can provide more effective therapy early in life to those with such unwanted predispositions, and who presently become menaces to society. This may occur by genetic modification and therapy.

Healthy personalities

The best management strategy is to focus on healthy behavior, so that the group will usually exclude those whose behavior is unacceptably disruptive. What are the criteria of healthy behavior that a leader seeks to encourage and develop in organizational members? Here are some characteristics of mentally healthy persons that leaders would do well to cultivate in themselves and in their work force:

- Healthy persons have a strong sense of self; they have resolved the fundamental questions "Who am I?", "Where am I going?", and "How do I get there?"; they are self-accepting and comfortable with themselves and not in perpetual conflict with themselves.
- Healthy persons have a unifying purpose or philosophy of life and realistic views of the world around them.
- Healthy persons have self-esteem balanced with a realistic assessment of their own abilities and skills.
- Healthy persons are able to experience warm and meaningful relationships.

High performers normally have healthy personalities. It has been observed that top performers are usually among the healthiest, happiest, and most enthusiastic people. HPLs learn to develop healthy personalities, starting with themselves.

Cultivation of high performance

Our second concern in this learning module is to identify the behaviors that contribute to high achievement and the ways to foster it on the job. A five-year study of 150 top performers by Benjamin Bloom, an education professor at the University of Chicago, concluded that drive and determination, not great natural talent, led to the outstanding success of the high achievers interviewed. These leading artists, athletes, and scholars expressed an early interest in their fields and experienced continuing encouragement from parents and other adults. Bloom's findings show how moral support and training contribute to extraordinary performance levels. Leaders should bear this in mind when considering how work and organizational culture contribute to this process of achievement.

Various researchers on high performers have concluded that:

- meta-performance is linked to a strong self-concept and self-esteem; average persons will improve their performance when they are helped positively to visualize themselves as achievers and winners;
- creative, top performers seem to be more whole-brained – they use both right-brain capacity of perception and intuition along with left-brain logic;

- high performers are flexible, not rigid, and learn to get around bureaucratic obstacles and obsolete and ineffective policies, rules, or regulations in order to get a job done well;
- high achieving executives care about their employees as well as about profits, and tend to seek advice from subordinates;
- peak performers demonstrate unusual qualities of creativity, risk-taking, and commitment to both their work and change;
- managers who encourage employees to do their very best and to upgrade their performance are usually rated high by workers;
- employees exhibit high internal motivation, work satisfaction, and performance when their work is meaningful and given larger purpose, when they feel responsible for its outcome, and when they have a continuing knowledge of the results of their work activities;
- high performance can be increased through HRD methods.

Research on self-actualized leaders

Dr Thomas Brennan's doctoral investigation at Northwestern University built upon the description of the characteristics of self-actualized people developed by the humanistic psychologist, Abraham Maslow, as well as the theories of emotional development set forth in the prior research of K. Dabrowski and M. M. Piechowski. Brennan conducted in-depth interviews with self-actualized people and eventually composed four case studies. Among the traits common to these high performing individuals were:

- a strong desire to accomplish for the benefit of mankind; focus on problems outside oneself; a life mission;
- a strong philosophy of life; guiding principles or transcendent values; a spiritual or religious orientation;
- a concern for personal growth or change and self-acceptance;
- a sense of responsibility; fairness; concern for ethics, justice, and the growth of others;
- the ability to make decisions; autonomy; self-control;
- an ability to establish exclusive relationships combined with a need for solitude in order to be productive; ability to use contemplation to cultivate inner harmony;
- a high level of energy and physical well-being.

This study not only provides insights about high performance by examining such self-actualized lives, but offers an efficient method for selecting and interviewing people who have achieved higher levels of self-development. This research contributes to a consensus emerging from investigations into meta-performance. High achievers are generally people who are self-disciplined, in the sense of being oriented toward self-caring and self-development. Such individuals cannot only set achievable goals for themselves, but delay gratification of pleasure in order to attain objectives. This discipline involves making tough choices as to what they will do and will avoid in order to reach the target or gain the prize. It is, however, a self-generated and self-maintained discipline; balanced and not rigid, a joy, and an incentive toward positive change and accomplishment in one's life. In another doctoral dissertation on the experience of top performers, D. Yates discovered that the 10–20 percent of the work force in this category were effective because of the vigorous manner in which they applied their skills and energies in the right tasks. These high achievers gained knowledge from success and continually refined their experience and perpetuated their success. In today's knowledge-based economy, such attitudes and skills are critical to a high performance organization.

Too many companies or agencies permit their norms to degenerate to the lowest common denominator, instead of using the top performers to help set standards so that everyone is stretched. Top performers often devise their own systems, which work better than those already in place, and ordinary employees should be encouraged to emulate them. Today's high performer frequently sets tomorrow's norms, procedures, roles, and goals. Learning experiences, therefore, should be designed so that the high achiever's insights can be shared with co-workers.

For almost three decades, the most outstanding research on human achievement and motivation had been done by David C. McClelland when he was Harvard University professor of psychology and founder of Boston's McBer and Company, a consulting firm specializing in job competency analysis based on the high performers. In his 1967 book *The Achieving Society*, and other volumes (1984), McClelland maintained that people can learn to achieve. His research confirmed that achievement-oriented personalities achieve success because of their need to experience success or avoid failure. From school to workplace, people can be taught or trained to achieve. McClelland suggests six steps for doing this:

1 Study your own achievements, strengths, and weaknesses, and examine the characteristics of achievers.
2 Get ideas on what goals to achieve, especially through brainstorming with others.
3 Set a realistic goal that is both challenging and achievable.
4 Develop a plan that outlines the tasks to be undertaken in order to accomplish this goal; include a needs and resource assessment, a self-inventory relative to the goal and the problems to be resolved, and a look at the implications of the proposed actions upon yourself and others.
5 Carry out the plan and check on your progress regularly; according to your results, seek advice or help or even change the plan or the goal.
6 Evaluate your effort, including the reasons for success or failure, and list improvements to be made in accomplishing the next goal.

Behavioral scientists have long advocated goal setting as the key to peak performance. Consultants, such as Maria Arapakis of Software Resources, Inc., in Oakland, California, have attempted to provide guidelines to translate such research into effective management practice. Once a leader defines his or her goals in writing, Arapakis proposes seven steps for improved performance:

- Identify the obstacles preventing the accomplishment of these goals.
- Determine the principal barrier to achievement of the main goal.
- Identify the choices for overcoming this obstacle and write down these potential solutions.
- Make a schedule to meet deadlines for obtaining results in goal achievement.
- Reward self for accomplishing mini deadlines, and share this sense of accomplishment with others.
- Check-up on progress in attaining goals daily, and make necessary modifications to keep moving ahead.
- Create mental images on final results, and be flexible on how you will achieve these goals.

EXHIBIT 3.5 Four competencies in HRD

There are four basic competencies required in high performing leadership:

1 managing your role, including prioritizing and time management, setting goals and standards, planning and scheduling;
2 thinking clearly, including analyzing situations, making plans and decisions, identifying and solving problems;
3 building a team, including training, coaching, and delegating, plus performance appraisal and disciplining with counseling;
4 relating to others, including obtaining unbiased information, giving clear information, plus listening and organizing. At the core of a leader's responsibilities is one's style of communicating, personalizing, and managing.

Finally, self-actualized leaders are skilled at people interactions, establishing relationships, and social networking according to Mark Pincus, CEO of Zynga.[17] He maintains that research confirms that people who are well balanced are more productive, more emotionally satisfied, and have higher self-esteem. The digital generation of leaders will vastly increase their social relationships and information access. They do not distinguish between the real and virtual worlds, or online versus offline friends.

High performance organizations

Finally, studies of successful contemporary corporations have more than demonstrated the impact of organizational culture on human performance. Exhibit 3.6 offers a summary of these findings in terms of leadership style – what an executive or manager should emphasize and avoid in order to cultivate a high performance work environment.

Leaders in high performance management create a corporate culture that excites people and makes work both joyful and productive. The experience can be joyful because it encourages informality, fellowship, and teamwork, as well as productive behavior. Exhibit 3.6 suggests organizational strategies to pursue to maintain a high performance work culture.

EXHIBIT 3.6   The high performance organization

The high performance organization emphasizes:

- workers as assets to be fully used and developed;
- personnel involvement in the management processes of goal setting, problem solving, and decision making;
- fostering innovation, creativity, and a futuristic orientation by all involved;
- open, circular, authentic communications, networking, and information systems;
- alternative strategies and solutions and the search for unconventional answers or markets;
- calculated risk taking, brain storming, the use of decision trees and simulations;
- energized management who serve as behavior models, who are informal, and who are open to creative deviancy;
- tentative and temporary groupings and solutions that permit flexibility and fluidity of response;
- consistent reinforcement of worker goals and achievements, with constructive feedback;
- competence and high performance as behavior norms;
- recognition and reward of productive behavior and merit;
- entrepreneurial spirit and personal commitment to projects;
- capitalization on personnel differences and unique talents, especially through teams;
- wellness programs that continuously support a healthy lifestyle, stress management, safety programs, and multiple insurance options.

The high performance organization avoids:

- under-utilizing, manipulating, and exploiting employees;
- autocratic, unilateral, and secretive approaches that exclude subordinates from power and authority;
- perpetuating the status quo, the tried and true, and advocating the safe "way we have always done it";

Continued

- downward communication, shielding top management from unpleasant news and telling them what they want to hear;
- simplistic solutions and clinging to only proven strategies and markets;
- insistence on orderly and traditional decision making, limiting input and participation;
- managerial vacillation and inertia; overreliance on hierarchical policy-making; slavish adherence to all norms;
- rigid scheduling, solid structures, chain of command, and precise procedures;
- annual performance evaluation and the formal checklists in evaluating employees; focus on corrections and punishments;
- use of average performance standards according to contract;
- recognition and reward based on status and tenure;
- becoming corporate autocrats that control everything;
- encouraging conformity; striving for organizational unity and a "corporate look";
- reliance on standardized health and accident insurance benefits, such as inadequate care for personnel or the policy of annual physicals only.

The high performance organization does:

- offer new challenges and opportunities to relate to other professionals whom they respect;
- reinforce their enormous pride in the results they achieve by demonstrating respect for them;
- provide independence for workers to do tasks assigned without frustrating interference from supervisors;
- give them more freedom by making occasional exceptions to rules and dress codes, being flexible about work hours and working at home, and supplying necessary equipment and support services;
- remove organizational obstacles to their performance on the job, allowing them to maintain intensity while maintaining a balanced control.

Managerial don'ts and dos based on my behavioral science research. Chapters 6 and 7 will provide further insights on how to create a high performance organization.

Some insight into future organizational leadership and performance has been provided by Vineet Nayar, of HCL Technologies.[18] In the next twenty-five years, he envisions more organizations built on trust, based on transparency, and with cultures that emphasize constant innovations. Such enterprises foster manager accountability to employees, and vice versa, while pushing change down to the level of young workers. These new organizations consider employees first so as to push innovation to the bottom of the pyramid. Top management's concern is that of enabling and encouraging all their associates. Leadership then becomes more collective and dependent upon the situation where those with special talent step in to lead.

Interaction

HP leaders always want to be fully involved in their organizations' HRD efforts. Continued, shared learning with colleagues is one way to sharpen leadership skills. The following group dynamic process can be used in a staff meeting, in formal management development sessions, or in informal get-togethers, such as in the lunch hour. As a starter, the group can use this process to share learning with some of the topics in this book. In any HRD or training effort, a variety of inputs, methods, and forms of participation are essential. This strategy has that advantage, plus it keeps stretching people's minds with fresh input and discussion. Start by using the insights offered in the next case study of Exhibit 3.7.

EXHIBIT 3.7   "She beat the SEC team over sex harassment"

WORK ENVIRONMENT MINICASE

To illustrate how managers can influence a work environment in a way that undermines productivity, consider this news report of a negative work culture:

> Attorney Catherine Broderick worked for five years in a Washington regional office of the Securities and Exchange Commission. In a suit against the SEC, she described the work environment as a "brothel," a place where senior managers had affairs with their secretaries, gave them cash awards and promotions in return for promiscuous relationships, and encouraged an atmosphere of drinking, jogging, and little work – the accepted behavior for those who were part of their "team." Broderick testified that she was trapped in that office and could not get out; it took away her spirit, causing her to experience hopelessness and powerlessness. By not cooperating, she experienced severe harassment, her outstanding work went unrecognized, and she was blackballed from transfer or promotion by the "good-old-boy network of the securities bar." After struggling against the situation for nine years, justice finally triumphed ... In June 1988, US

Continued

District Judge John H. Pratt II ruled in her favor after finding the SEC's regional office was a work environment permeated by sexual harassment and discrimination in which managers retaliated against complainers. Pratt ordered that Broderick be granted three promotions with retroactive pay plus interest, and all negative evaluations be removed from her file. The Judge also ordered an end to the sexually hostile environment, and initiated investigations and reforms within the agency.

Source: Based on *Los Angeles Times,* June 17, 1988, Part V: 22–23.

Input bombardment (IB)

In this process, the first step is the formation of a small group, usually between six and twelve. This might be a natural work unit, a group of buddies interested in professional development, or a project team. The approach can also be used with a large audience divided into smaller groups (in that case, each group should be given a different reading, for instance each covers a different article on the general subject of motivation).

Second, the group selects or is assigned a reading for review. This may be a book chapter, an article from a technical or professional journal, or newspaper feature article. The internet is also a source of such discussion material. Then each person has a copy of this reading. For example, the group could reproduce and distribute the two short essays on human behavior in the Input section on our previous pages; or an article on high performance or productivity from a popular business magazine or a trade or technical journal. Choose content that is timely, interesting, stimulating, and relevant to the theme under review.

Third, each member of the group is assigned to cover a portion of the material. This can be done quickly by going around the circle and assigning paragraphs or sections to each person in order, until all the article is assigned (a variation on this procedure, time permitting, is to give each person a separate chapter or article on the same theme to scan on behalf of the whole group).

The fourth step to follow in the IB process is Read, React, and Report (RR&R). Everyone reads his or her assignment individually, reacts to its message in terms of the group or the organization, and reports to the group his or her findings. The reading is a rapid scanning, so that the essence of the writer's ideas are extracted. The report is an overview of the major points in the assigned reading and that individual's reaction to its implications here and now. That is, can the input be adopted, adapted, or applied within this group for personal and organizational improvement? After each member has provided input to the total group, the group together discusses the insights obtained from all the reports. At the end, group members should study, at their leisure, the complete reading in greater depth. Another possibility is to give out the assigned reading before the IB session, so that people have an opportunity to study a larger portion of data in greater detail.

Normally, this process can be accomplished in forty to sixty minutes, or more as time permits. Let us assume that there is an hour and fifteen minutes available for IB during lunch, a staff meeting, or a training session, and that we have an ideal group of eight persons. One person – the manager, trainer, consultant, or someone elected by the group – assumes the role of facilitator. The facilitator is both timekeeper and discussion leader. The material in question is divided into eight parts, and each group member is allowed three minutes to read privately his or her assignment. Each then, in topical sequence, takes three minutes to react to what he or she has read. The process at this point will have taken up to fifty minutes. This leaves about twenty-five minutes for the general discussion, which might also include some action planning to apply this input back on the job.

Many variations can be made on this group dynamic technique. The facilitator can use a blackboard, overhead projector, flip chart or PowerPoint to outline the principal points of the material as it is reported by each person. If there is a large audience of say, sixty-four, provision can be made for eight group reports to the total assemblage; each group chooses a reporter to summarize that unit's findings.

I have used this method successfully hundreds of times with managers and professionals throughout the world, from small teams to audiences of 2,000. Its values are:

- a lot of information is covered in a relatively short time;
- the stimulation of new ideas can prompt one to read the material more critically;
- the opportunity to learn together and share in group communication furthers professional development.

Thinking managers will find IB an ideal mechanism for exposing peers and work groups to research and developments that might not normally be discussed. Readers who wish to share the insights in this volume with their co-workers can use the Input sections in this book for that purpose. The process can be used to cover the latest trends and concepts in your field or industry, marketing, manufacturing, and public and community relations.

Not every manager has the time to read the many new books on the new management techniques. IB is a chance to divide and conquer this database by having various groups or individuals in a group RR&R on a specific title. Readers may wish to start with the further reading list at the end of this volume. Or go on the internet to identify current management books available for purchase. You also can request publishers of management books to put you on their mailing lists for new book announcements and catalogs. A representative sample of suggested titles and publishers will be found at the end of this book, along with recommended periodicals and journals.

Contemporary periodicals range from business magazines and international publications such as *The Economist*; to management journals such as those of the American Management Associations, the *Harvard Business Review* and *Academy of Management Executive*, and all the many management journals of Emerald Group

Publishing in the UK, such as the *European Business Review*. You might also ask a work team to look for articles relating to productivity and performance. Then reproduce these articles for a monthly IB session. Remember that the very definition of the word "productivity" has changed in the new work culture: these days, productivity involves things like product reliability, customer satisfaction, and quick response to market demands.

The group dynamic technique of IB is not limited to printed material, but may also be used in a training session by using PowerPoint downloads, and audio or video media purchased from publishers.

Managing responsibility

When people clearly understand what is expected of them and are held accountable for fulfilling these expectations, performance improves and productivity increases. Clarifying roles and relationships among personnel is a continuing responsibility of leadership. The instruments provided in these chapters also facilitate this clarification among a manager and work unit. Now, consider an interaction process for the same purpose contributed by Dr Woodrow Sears, a management consultant now in Vilnius, Lithuania. Author of *The Front Line Guide* series on management, Sears (2007) designed this group exercise especially for use in team building. "Expect/inspect" is his way of summarizing the leader's charge to monitor and manage work performance. Exhibit 3.7 summarizes this process. Note that this interaction works best in groups that work together on a regular basis. If it is a large work unit, break it down into smaller teams of six to eight workers. The facilitator will require slide presentation software, or simply a flip chart with newsprint paper, large colored marking pens, and masking tape. The exhibit suggests a way to help workers in understanding what are the most important activities in which they engage while at work.

EXHIBIT 3.8 Critical pay-off functions exercise

Critical pay-off functions. Group members are asked to make a list of the things they do on their jobs. Then subgroups are formed to share the data, note common activities from each list, and draft a consensus report for their group. The manager or trainer then drafts a master list on a whiteboard or newsprint sheets composed of the information supplied by the sub-group.

The various groups meet a second time to come to agreement on what they perceive as the "critical pay-off functions" on that master list, activities which must be performed if they are to succeed on the job. The facilitator underlines or stars each item that the groups report as critical.

Continued

Self-assessment. At this point a break should be taken for individual work, or the task can be given as a home assignment. Next, participants are asked to review their personal lists, and the comprehensive list compiled by the group, and decide upon four to seven key elements of their jobs which they see as essential to the proper performance of their jobs. After this review and evaluation, they are asked to write down these functions in detail making one copy for them and one for the facilitator. Now responsibility for job performance can be pin-pointed in the written word of the individual doing the work. It would be ideal if that person's supervisor could review the list for feedback to the individual on whether his or her manager perceives such activities as critical functions. To stimulate the trainee in the assessment process, questions might be raised, such as: Are you doing things you are not paid to do? Is your daily work schedule filled up with busy work or tasks with which you are most comfortable *because* you are unsure of the nature and scope of your job?

Synthesis. During the next group session, the small groups meet again to share their assessments, and to develop a total group report on major categories of job functions which are critical in their work. This data is again visually displayed as the reports come in from the sub-groups. They might include such topical headings as planning, communication, budgeting, etc. Then the trainees are given another management model to aid them in becoming more responsible in carrying out their job duties.

Need/problem. Group members are asked to identify either individually or in groups the needs they are seeking to satisfy by doing their jobs, or the problems they are trying to resolve through job performance. The data is then recorded on a blackboard or newsprint sheet under the major heading: Need/Problem. The same procedure is followed for the next four categories.

Objectives/goals. Based on the results of the above exercise, the participants are invited to set down one or more principal objectives/goals which they should have for adequate performance of their jobs. They are encouraged to describe these aims with an action verb, to include a key outcome, to qualify and quan-tify, to set a time frame, and budget dimension. Again, the results are collected and visually recorded.

Resources required. To accomplish the above objectives/goals, what help or assis-tance is required? The individuals or groups are then requested to note the human/material/financial resources which are necessary for them to carry out their job purposes and perform the critical functions.

Action steps. To satisfy the needs or resolve the problems identified above, to achieve the objectives/goals set, what actions must be undertaken? The trainees

Continued

are asked to develop a set of steps, phases, or stages to be followed in accomplishing the critical job functions.

Evaluation. To assess what has been done, particularly in terms of cost, the participants are asked to indicate some quantifiable standards or criteria or performance. How do they plan to measure the results of their efforts?

Finally, as a home assignment the trainees are asked to refine the above data in terms of their own job. Using the model provided, they are to write on a computer their personal plan of action in terms of the categories or processes presented in the training session. One copy should eventually get to the participant's supervisor. How effectively the latter uses the information will influence the degree of pay-off on the learning experience.

Source: Based on Woody Sears, *The Front Line Guide to Mastering the Manager's Job.* Amherst, MA: Human Resource Development Press, 2007 (www.hrdpress.com).

Dr Sears often introduces the above procedure with this astute observation:

> The continuing reality is that in most organizations, many employees are vague about the exact nature of their duties, the goals of the organization, and the specific objectives which must be reached to make possible goal achievement by the total organization. In short, most people who go to work still don't know what their jobs really are about, and how the functions they are supposed to perform relate to work done by others ... Furthermore, most supervisors and managers cannot describe what it is they are supposed to do in specific terms that are tangible, achievable and measurable. Instead they talk in generalities about motivating people, seeing that the work gets done and even getting the work done through others.

> (www.woodysears.googlepages.com)

Instrumentation

Leadership motivation inventory (LMI)[19]

This simple instrument may be used by a manager for personal assessment of his or her own need pattern or to ascertain the motivations of subordinates or a work team. It is based upon the research of Dr Abraham Maslow described above in the Input section. The thirty items are arranged in five categories that match his Hierarchy of Needs (Exhibit 3.2). Needs are grouped under these classifications: P (physiological or survival); S (safety or security); B (belonging or affiliation); E (esteem or ego); and A (actualization or self-fulfillment).

The respondent is asked initially to place an X next to five items on the list that most energize that person to perform or do better work. These first selections are considered to be the pattern of primary motives. The next task is to review the choices again, excluding those already picked, and to place a check next to one's secondary motives from among the remaining items.

Transfer this information to the pyramid diagram provided so that one can see his or her major needs in the context of the Maslow paradigm. If the leader is working with a group using the same inventory, then a PowerPoint, flip chart, whiteboard, or overhead projector can be used to draw a large version of this exhibit. Each person then inserts his or her primary motives on that display at the proper level by marking Xs where they appear on one's individual inventory sheet (or the facilitator can simply take a hand count of those in the group who had a primary motive marked for each of the levels). In this way, members can see the total group motivational picture and can be encouraged to discuss the implications in terms of performance and productivity.

EXHIBIT 3.9 Leadership motivation inventory

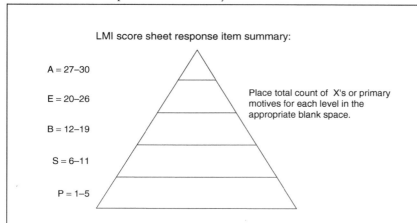

LMI score sheet response item summary:

A = 27–30

E = 20–26

B = 12–19

S = 6–11

P = 1–5

Place total count of X's or primary motives for each level in the appropriate blank space.

Part A. Personal motivators

Please place an X next to the five items below which you believe are *most important* in motivating you to do better work:

1 Assurance of regular employment

[Physical Needs]

2 Satisfactory physical working conditions
3 Suitable rest periods and coffee breaks
4 Adequate vacation arrangements and holidays
5 Good pay

[Security Needs]

Continued

  6 Having an efficient supervisor who tells me exactly what is expected
  7 Clear organizational objectives so that I know where I stand
  8 A good performance rating so I know where I stand
  9 Pensions and other fringe benefits (insurance, *et al.*)
10 Written job description which tells what is expected of me
11 Maintenance of adequate living standards for my family
12 Means for knowing what is going on in the organization (inclusion)
13 Being told by my boss that I am doing a good job
14 Getting along with others on the job by being cooperative

[Belonging Needs]

15 Participation in management activities (e.g. attending staff meetings).
16 Receiving appreciation feedback when work is well performed
17 Being kept informed on what is happening in the organization
18 The support received from fellow workers in a work unit
19 Means for promotion and advancement
20 Feeling my job is important

[Ego Needs]

21 Respect for me as a person and/or as professional at my job
22 Chance to turn out quality work
23 Opportunity to gain status in the organization
24 Means of achieving and proving myself
25 Obtaining more freedom and independence on my job
26 Opportunity to do challenging and meaningful work

[Actualization Needs]

27 Opportunity to experience sense of accomplishment
28 Others

Scoring part A. Please take the Maslow pyramid above and write down the *numbers* of your *primary* motivations (those marked X in each category). You may also wish to compare your own results with those of your team by inviting the group to take and score this LMI. Finally, compare your own and your group motivators with a national survey reported next.

Part B. Job motivational factors

Summary of 1,522 responses from both government and private business to the following request:

> Please indicate the five items from the list below which you believe are important in motivating you to do your best work.   **Continued**

Rank order	Number of responses	Percentage
1 Feeling my job is important	920	61
2 Opportunity to do interesting work	863	57
3 Opportunity for self-development and improvement	757	50
4 Respect for me as a person	665	44
5 Chance for promotion	654	43
6 Good pay	651	43
7 Chance to turn out quality work	494	32
8 Knowing what is going on in the organization	423	28
9 Large amount of freedom on the job	356	24
10 Steady employment	315	21
11 Being told by my boss when I do a good job	294	20
12 Getting along well with others on the job	251	16
13 Chance to do work not under direct or close supervision	225	15
14 Having an efficient supervisor	179	12
15 Agreement with agency objectives	162	12
16 Good physical working conditions	137	09
17 Getting a good performance rating so I know how I stand	94	06
18 Pensions and other security benefits	64	04
19 Miscellaneous	34	02
20 Attending staff meetings	16	01
21 Having a written description of duties of my job	16	01
22 Fair vacation arrangements	15	01
23 Knowing I will be disciplined if I do a bad job	9	06
24 Not having to work too hard	6	04
25 Adequate rest periods and coffee breaks	5	03
26 Having an employee council	3	02
27 Having a local house organ, employee paper, bulletin	3	02

Note: By comparing your results of your group's profile with the above study responses you get a basis for self-analysis as to your motivations and that of others. This data gathering and comparison raises people's awareness of their own needs and that of others associated with them. When a manager has some insight as to what motivates an employee or team, it may be possible to lead in meeting those needs better. How can one lead without knowledge of what "turns these people on" to achieve more?

Continued

> Remember also that Maslow also maintained that one's gripes or grumbles vary with the need level. Humans are ever seeking for the fuller life, so one's complaints are satisfied at the level of basic needs, and then one becomes more aware of other concerns, such as social injustice.
>
> Response items summary:
>
> A = 27–30
>
> E = 20–26
>
> B = 12–19
>
> S = 6–11
>
> P = 1–5

Human resource inventory (HRI)

This instrument (Exhibit 3.10) was designed for personal and career development. Because life is a dynamic process, individuals should periodically assess their progress and growth. Recall in the Input section that psychologist David McClelland (1984) proposed six steps in achievement learning, the first of which is self-study, that is, systematic analysis of past achievements, strengths, and weaknesses. HRI enables a person to do this in terms of aptitudes, competencies, skills, and experiences. There are fifty opportunities for respondents to record their self-evaluation and accomplishments.

The inventory is divided into three components for analysis – life values, individual competencies, and human relationships. The first section of twenty-eight items uses a ten-point rating scale on such matters as self-awareness, leadership, affection, independence, and self-appreciation. Respondents mark a capital P to indicate present self-estimates, a small p to indicate past rating over a five-year period, and an F to reveal their aspirations for future growth. Provisions are made for re-examination of each rating. In the next competency section, respondents examine their professional and educational attainments in the context of intellectual, judgmental, social, physical, aesthetic, actualizing, and personal competencies. In the last part, respondents rate the quality of their human relationships as *unsatisfactory, adequate*, or *very satisfactory*; a final review is offered as to objectives to seek and obstacles to be anticipated.

Developed by me as part of an Office of Naval Research project, HRI is a one-hour exercise in personal review and reflection. It can also be used in a group setting. This examination yields maximum benefits when results are shared with a trusted friend or family member who knows the person well or are discussed with a counselor or mentor. The HRI is intended to release some of the untapped human potential within every individual and organization. It advances personal and professional growth because it aids the respondent to improve self-insight and image. As a means for continuous life planning, HRI is a mechanism for pointing out those performance possibilities that need to be developed. An honest self-appraisal, checked out with others, can help the person to become a more effective worker, team member, and leader.

The basic assumptions of this instrument are that staying well gives one greater control over life, increases performance, and is less costly than rehabilitation. Wellness is critical to high performance.

EXHIBIT 3.10 Human resources inventory

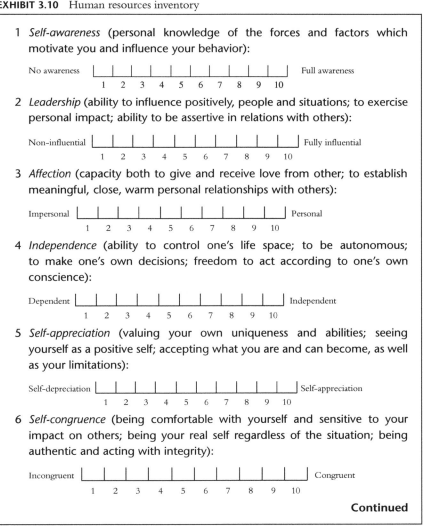

1 *Self-awareness* (personal knowledge of the forces and factors which motivate you and influence your behavior):

No awareness | 1 2 3 4 5 6 7 8 9 10 | Full awareness

2 *Leadership* (ability to influence positively, people and situations; to exercise personal impact; ability to be assertive in relations with others):

Non-influential | 1 2 3 4 5 6 7 8 9 10 | Fully influential

3 *Affection* (capacity both to give and receive love from other; to establish meaningful, close, warm personal relationships with others):

Impersonal | 1 2 3 4 5 6 7 8 9 10 | Personal

4 *Independence* (ability to control one's life space; to be autonomous; to make one's own decisions; freedom to act according to one's own conscience):

Dependent | 1 2 3 4 5 6 7 8 9 10 | Independent

5 *Self-appreciation* (valuing your own uniqueness and abilities; seeing yourself as a positive self; accepting what you are and can become, as well as your limitations):

Self-depreciation | 1 2 3 4 5 6 7 8 9 10 | Self-appreciation

6 *Self-congruence* (being comfortable with yourself and sensitive to your impact on others; being your real self regardless of the situation; being authentic and acting with integrity):

Incongruent | 1 2 3 4 5 6 7 8 9 10 | Congruent

Continued

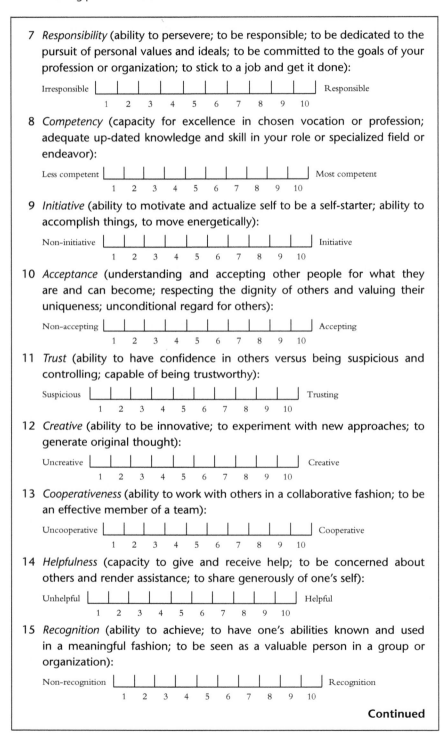

7 *Responsibility* (ability to persevere; to be responsible; to be dedicated to the pursuit of personal values and ideals; to be committed to the goals of your profession or organization; to stick to a job and get it done):

Irresponsible |__|__|__|__|__|__|__|__|__|__| Responsible
      1   2   3   4   5   6   7   8   9   10

8 *Competency* (capacity for excellence in chosen vocation or profession; adequate up-dated knowledge and skill in your role or specialized field or endeavor):

Less competent |__|__|__|__|__|__|__|__|__|__| Most competent
      1   2   3   4   5   6   7   8   9   10

9 *Initiative* (ability to motivate and actualize self to be a self-starter; ability to accomplish things, to move energetically):

Non-initiative |__|__|__|__|__|__|__|__|__|__| Initiative
      1   2   3   4   5   6   7   8   9   10

10 *Acceptance* (understanding and accepting other people for what they are and can become; respecting the dignity of others and valuing their uniqueness; unconditional regard for others):

Non-accepting |__|__|__|__|__|__|__|__|__|__| Accepting
      1   2   3   4   5   6   7   8   9   10

11 *Trust* (ability to have confidence in others versus being suspicious and controlling; capable of being trustworthy):

Suspicious |__|__|__|__|__|__|__|__|__|__| Trusting
      1   2   3   4   5   6   7   8   9   10

12 *Creative* (ability to be innovative; to experiment with new approaches; to generate original thought):

Uncreative |__|__|__|__|__|__|__|__|__|__| Creative
      1   2   3   4   5   6   7   8   9   10

13 *Cooperativeness* (ability to work with others in a collaborative fashion; to be an effective member of a team):

Uncooperative |__|__|__|__|__|__|__|__|__|__| Cooperative
      1   2   3   4   5   6   7   8   9   10

14 *Helpfulness* (capacity to give and receive help; to be concerned about others and render assistance; to share generously of one's self):

Unhelpful |__|__|__|__|__|__|__|__|__|__| Helpful
      1   2   3   4   5   6   7   8   9   10

15 *Recognition* (ability to achieve; to have one's abilities known and used in a meaningful fashion; to be seen as a valuable person in a group or organization):

Non-recognition |__|__|__|__|__|__|__|__|__|__| Recognition
      1   2   3   4   5   6   7   8   9   10

Continued

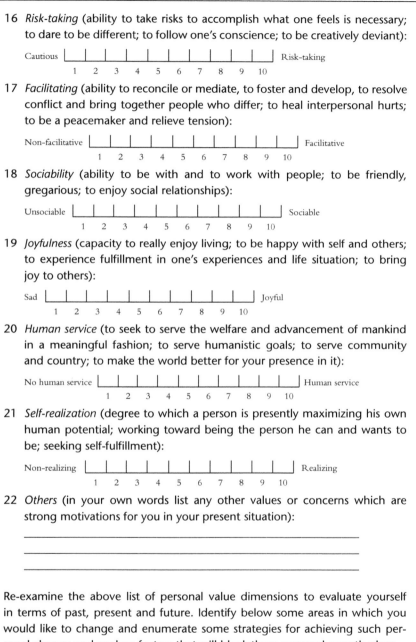

16 *Risk-taking* (ability to take risks to accomplish what one feels is necessary; to dare to be different; to follow one's conscience; to be creatively deviant):

Cautious |　|　|　|　|　|　|　|　|　|　| Risk-taking
　　　　　1　2　3　4　5　6　7　8　9　10

17 *Facilitating* (ability to reconcile or mediate, to foster and develop, to resolve conflict and bring together people who differ; to heal interpersonal hurts; to be a peacemaker and relieve tension):

Non-facilitative |　|　|　|　|　|　|　|　|　|　| Facilitative
　　　　　　　　1　2　3　4　5　6　7　8　9　10

18 *Sociability* (ability to be with and to work with people; to be friendly, gregarious; to enjoy social relationships):

Unsociable |　|　|　|　|　|　|　|　|　|　| Sociable
　　　　　1　2　3　4　5　6　7　8　9　10

19 *Joyfulness* (capacity to really enjoy living; to be happy with self and others; to experience fulfillment in one's experiences and life situation; to bring joy to others):

Sad |　|　|　|　|　|　|　|　|　|　| Joyful
　　1　2　3　4　5　6　7　8　9　10

20 *Human service* (to seek to serve the welfare and advancement of mankind in a meaningful fashion; to serve humanistic goals; to serve community and country; to make the world better for your presence in it):

No human service |　|　|　|　|　|　|　|　|　|　| Human service
　　　　　　　　1　2　3　4　5　6　7　8　9　10

21 *Self-realization* (degree to which a person is presently maximizing his own human potential; working toward being the person he can and wants to be; seeking self-fulfillment):

Non-realizing |　|　|　|　|　|　|　|　|　|　| Realizing
　　　　　　1　2　3　4　5　6　7　8　9　10

22 *Others* (in your own words list any other values or concerns which are strong motivations for you in your present situation):

_____

_____

_____

Re-examine the above list of personal value dimensions to evaluate yourself in terms of past, present and future. Identify below some areas in which you would like to change and enumerate some strategies for achieving such personal change and analyze factors that will block these personal growth plans.

Continued

Areas

_____

_____

_____

_____

_____

Strategies

_____

_____

_____

_____

_____

Obstacles

_____

_____

_____

_____

_____

Individual competencies

Each person possesses unique skills and accomplishments. Identify some of these special strengths and talents as revealed in the past in your relationships, your work, your family, or your hobbies. Also list those areas in which you find you have personal limitations. Such enumeration may help you group your personal assets and liabilities.

A *Professional attainment* (list major vocational and professional successes, and then your objectives or potentials, both in terms of wishes and opportunities, based upon life experiences to date):

Attainments

_____

_____

_____

_____

Objectives

_____

_____

_____

_____

Continued

B *Educational attainment* (list here educational accomplishments and needs; major areas of interest you wish to pursue; ask yourself if further or continuing education is desirable or necessary):

Attainments

_____
_____
_____
_____

Objectives

_____
_____
_____
_____

C *Intellectual competencies* (analyze your unique rational or mental abilities – intelligence or capacity to apply knowledge; ability to conceptualize and to perceive relationships, etc.):

Attainments

_____
_____
_____
_____

Objectives

_____
_____
_____
_____

D *Judgment competencies* (ability to abstract essences and make reasonable decisions; capacity to differentiate between fact and fiction; ability to weigh ideas, discriminate and to solve problems):

Attainments

_____
_____
_____
_____

Objectives

_____

Continued

_____
_____
_____

E *Social competencies* (skills in interpersonal and human relations; capacity to deal with people on a one-to-one, group or organizational level, etc.):

Attainments

_____
_____
_____
_____

Objectives

_____
_____
_____
_____

F *Physical competencies* (physical prowess and appearance; athletic/outdoor abilities; skills to construct with hands, etc.):

Attainments

_____
_____
_____
_____

Objectives

_____
_____
_____
_____

G *Aesthetic competencies* (responsiveness and appreciation of beauty in art or nature; good taste; capacities in arts, crafts, music, literature, etc.):

Attainments

_____
_____
_____
_____

Continued

Objectives

_____

_____

_____

_____

H *Actualizing competencies* (ability to make decisions and to perform; to act effectively upon judgment; to cope effectively; to motivate self beyond present level of accomplishment; opposite to procrastination; apathy and immobilization by fear):

Attainments

_____

_____

_____

_____

Objectives

_____

_____

_____

_____

I *Personal competencies* (security within self, confidence and congruence; emotional strengths; personal integration, character, etc.):

Attainments

_____

_____

_____

Objectives

_____

_____

_____

Now that you have examined your present and past situation, your strengths or assets, and your personal directions for growth, you can examine strategies to maximize your potential. Analyze those factors in yourself, in others, and in the work situation which both *support* and *block* your personal growth goals. Secure feedback on your self-evaluation from others to check for discontinuities. Experiment with new behaviors to maximize your own personal growth tendencies and then seek continuous feedback to assess how you are doing.

Continued

Hopefully, this instrument may emphasize that you are a unique, dynamic, changing person. There is no one else alive now – or in the past or future – quite like you.

Note: This and other inventories utilized in this book may be reproduced in quantity by purchase of P. R. Harris, *Twenty Reproducible Assessment Instruments* (www.hrdpress.com).

4

IMPROVING LEADERSHIP COMMUNICATION SKILLS

Introduction

Effective communication is essential to high performance. Yet in several surveys of corporations conducted by the American Management Association during recent decades, management communication was consistently identified as the number one difficulty in business life. This chapter will focus upon the important issue of human interaction at work. Our capacity to communicate in diverse and complex ways sets humans apart from other species. Since communication is the key to organizational excellence and high performance, special attention will be paid to this subject.

Our primary objective is to understand better what is involved in the process of human exchanges so that we can improve our interaction skills. By comprehending, for example, what is involved in perception, co-workers should become more sensitive to each other's viewpoints and meanings in their interactions. Ideally, better relations and exchanges will result. Specifically, we will analyze the all-important matter of self-image and how it impacts communication (i.e. the concept of behavioral communication). Our second major aim here will be to examine organizational communication and how it affects performance and productivity. We will review some of the physical and psychological barriers to such communication, as well as some of the characteristics of effective communication within human systems. The impact of new communication technologies will also be discussed. To help readers appreciate the scope of changes in communication technologies, we begin with the next profile of a leader in Exhibit 4.1.

Information age leadership

EXHIBIT 4.1 Profile of an electronic HPL

In 1972, computer scientist, Bob Metcalfe, created a new wireless network technology known as Ethernet. As a result of this invention, he was able to pursue his PhD at Harvard, become a multi-millionaire, and revolutionize computing. Although his doctoral dissertation in applied mathematics was initially rejected because it was not theoretical enough, he went to work at Xerox writing innovative software for a machine that would become the inspiration for Apple's Macintosh. While in Palo Alto, he also taught at Stanford University and finished his doctorate by adding theories on how computers communicate using a common transmission medium. When he adapted his ideas to wired networks based on coaxial cable, it led to his creation of Ethernet which became the world's most widely deployed electronic network. It was his standardization and commercialization of that idea that promoted his success. As he says decades later, "Nothing happens until something gets sold."

All this highlights his remarkable ability to observe, synthesize, and improve things. Since then Dr Metcalfe has progressed through multiple careers as academic, entrepreneur, and venture capitalist, all because he can detect opportunities and follow up on them while taking risks. Although he overlooked the possibility of linking networks together, rather than computers, he succeeded when he became the publisher of *InfoWorld* and the author of a widely read column, "From the Ether." This HPL admits he has made mistakes, especially relative to industry predictions, but it does not deter him. Now he is off on his latest Polaris Ventures, where he is trying to apply lessons from the computer industry to clean energy start-ups. As a communicator, Bob Metcalfe is valued for his authenticity and ability to argue, as well as to see other points of view.

Source: Based on "Beyond the Ether," *The Economist Technology Quarterly*, December 2009: 23–24 (www.economist.com/specialreports/technology-quarterly).

Input

Human interaction is the linking of two different life spaces or perceptual fields.

As humans, we all see our worlds differently. Reality is so distinctive for each of us since we were not raised in exactly the same way, and our communication occurs from each individual's life space. In our interactions, we share our life experiences, and factors make each person unique. Apart from the general differences inherent in our cultural backgrounds, we each have had special inputs, imprints, and experiences. This realization helps to explain the differences between the generations, and why sometimes people have difficulty communicating with each other even

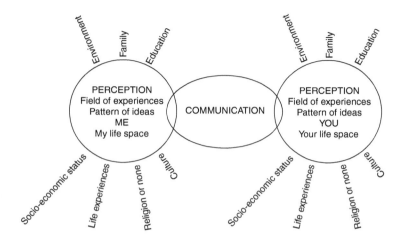

EXHIBIT 4.2 Communication and perception

when they are raised in the same family. Consider the complexity of interpersonal communication in terms of two partners in business or marriage, or two people who are brought together on the job and begin to interact for the first time.

Humans are symbol-using creatures with the power of abstraction. That is, the developed human brain permits us to ascribe meaning and value to words, gestures, actions, experiences, and things, so that we have a rich capacity to exchange with other human beings, and even other species. Although some communication symbols are universal, as with marriage, meaning for "another" differs by culture, including as permitted by religion or law. Even sex symbols vary in cultures, such as the significance of female breasts or nape of the neck, or hand-holding by those of the same gender. Furthermore, within a specific culture, agreed upon symbols are subject to continuous updating as the culture changes. The point is that communication, especially in business, is a complex process. Would-be leaders have to increase their awareness of what is involved, so they may improve their cross-cultural communication skills. During the past fifty years we have probably doubled our communication capacities in comparison with the prior 5,000 years. With new technologies offering unlimited opportunities for global exchanges through mass media, computer interaction, communication satellites, electronic networks, and other such innovations, we are truly forming an information society within a global knowledge culture.

Communication is our most important tool and is at the heart of all organizational operations. Communication can be the basis for understanding, cooperation, and positive action; without it, such capabilities would be undermined. The vitality, creativity, and productivity of organizations depend on the content and character of their exchanges, both verbal and non-verbal. Through the interaction process, information and knowledge are transferred between people. When the process is inadequate, messages are distorted, frustrations develop, and people or their organizations are rendered ineffective. Failures in communication contribute to management problems, and the cost of miscommunication may be incalculable.

Communication as a human process

It may help to consider the communication process in terms of circular interaction between a sender and receiver of messages. The message is the what of communication, the content. The media is the how of the communication, the means or mechanism used to convey that message. The reason, or why, may be personal or professional, social or organizational. The sender may or may not be consciously aware of the motives for initiating a conversation or exchange. Although humans are able to communicate with animals or commune with nature, let us focus now upon our formidable talent to interact with other people. There are some general observations to note before we get into details.

Every person operates from within his or her private world or perceptual field. As defined in Chapter 3, this perceptual field is our life space, and we can view it from within a personal or organizational context. Every individual or institution communicates from that perspective. We take in and give out information through the filter of our perceptions. These influence both the context of our messages and the media utilized to send them. From time to time, effective communicators examine whether their perceptions of reality generally match what is commonly and currently held "outside" in the larger world or collective reality – is our subjective view in synchronization with objective actuality? Although two generations may share the same "outer world," their "inner worlds" may be vastly different. The more we are aware of our past conditioning and understand the forces influencing our own behavior, the more successful our communication will be.

Every person projects self into human communication. Each of us communicates an image of self, including a system of needs, values, standards, expectations, and ideals, as well as our perceptions of people, things, and situations. We can sense this self-concept in others if we pay attention to their body movements, bearing, tone of voice, and choice of language, as well as the content of their message. The more we can understand their "world," where they are coming from, the better our chances for improved communication.

Every person is a medium or *instrument of communication.* We are not just senders and receivers of messages, but the medium can be a message also. Thus, if an individual is uncomfortable with self, then others are likely to become uncomfortable with that person. The more self-confidence or congruence is conveyed by the communicator, the more likely the receiver is to accept the message.

Every person is a versatile communicator. We communicate verbally and non-verbally; orally and in writing. Our communication capacities are more than language – we communicate through gestures, signs, shapes, colors, sounds, smells, pictures, and other communication symbols. The artist, for instance, expresses thought and feeling in paintings, sculpture, music, dance, and architecture. Business communicates through its products and services, as well as through systems and procedures. Technologists communicate through their systems and ever changing creations, be it hardware or software. The diversity of our communication media is evident in the past use of smoke signals, drum sounds, and telegraph. But in the present, we use satellites for communications by television and computers, mobiles and webcams. Progress in technology only increases our abilities to communicate and the diversity of our media.

Exhibit 4.3 illustrates the process of circular interaction – the sender and receiver exchanging messages. Both occupy unique psychological environments, or perceptual fields, in which they receive, translate, and analyze input, and from which they send information to another. In technical terms, each *decodes, interprets*, and *encodes*. Essentially, we selectively perceive new data and determine if it is relevant and consistent. That is, does it fit into our perceived way of thinking? Two people may receive the same message at work, but derive two entirely different meanings from it because of perceptual background differences. Each decodes and interprets the same input differently.

Consider a manager communicating to a colleague or subordinate about work performance. The messages are simultaneously being *transmitted* at different levels, intended and unintended. Thus, we transmit information at a conscious, verbal, level and subconsciously, through a so-called silent language. At the same time, messages are being *received* at two different levels, cognitive and affective; that is, thinking and feeling, the intellectual and emotional.

Our simultaneous, multilevel nature of transmission and reception often results in mixed messages – the words, for example, do not always match the feelings being conveyed. When the message is incomplete or ambiguous, the receiver has to try and fill in the meaning. The receiver's interpretation of the sender's intentions or motivations may or may not be accurate. The complexity of this process increases with the amount of input. For example, technology today provides us with the means for instant global communications via the internet. Whether it is electronic mail and attachments, websites or blogs, we deal today with much more input than our grandparents.

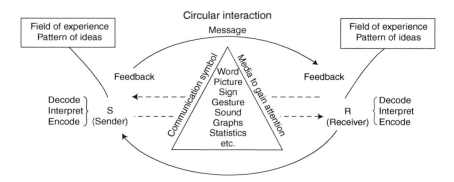

EXHIBIT 4.3 A model of interactive communication

Understanding communication is important to everyone, but particularly to those who would exercise high performance leadership. Because we transmit our self-image in the course of human interaction, we can influence – more often than not – the kind of reception we get from others. Usually, if we have confidence in ourselves, people sense this and respond more positively to us and the messages we send. On the other hand, if we lack confidence and convey inferiority feelings, we undermine the reception of our messages. Similarly, if a sender has a distorted self-perception, such as unwarranted feelings of superiority, these can be communicated intentionally or unconsciously and can produce hostility or resentment in the receiver. Talking down to fellow workers can lead to rejection of both the sender and the message.

So, if we wish to improve our human relations and communications, let us begin by examining our self-image. How do we answer the big question, "Who am I?" Filling out the Human Resource Inventory and the Leadership Motivation Inventory (Chapter 3) can help. These provide data for revising or improving our concept of self. The better our self-appreciation, the better our chances of improving our communications with others. Again, more often than not, we influence the response of others to us. If we are loaded with inferiority feelings, others will probably "dump" on us. If we project a positive image, people will be more likely to accept us and our messages.

One exception to this rule occurs when the receiver has prejudice against some kinds of people – tall or short, white or black, native or foreigner. Thus, an Eskimo meeting someone for the first time might project a very positive self-image yet be rejected. The problem is in the bias of the receiver against Eskimos. There are some persons we may never effectively communicate with because they close their minds to us, dismissing us as women, intellectuals, or whatever group in which they place us in their mindset.

Usually, though, we can influence others positively by the way we communicate ourselves. Thus, it is vital for communicators to be comfortable within themselves and congruent, that is with the inner and outer selves in harmony. Even if we have paid public relations or image consultants to improve our dress, appearance, and message delivery, people will eventually sense if we are inauthentic – not true to our own selves and beliefs. In real communication, two people share themselves – their way of thinking, their values, their hopes, and their aspirations. That is why communication, in the deepest sense, is both the establishment of a relationship and an exchange of human energy.

Organizational communications and human performance

These insights on interpersonal communication can be applied to people in groups and organizations. Those who would exercise leadership in both personal and team communications need to take a systems approach; that is, analyze the communication systems within their organizations. The instrument provided later in this chapter is one means for making such an analysis.

There are usually both formal and informal communication systems within a corporation, association, or agency. The former involves the official lines and media of communication. Information is sent or received in the form of letters, memoranda, reports, briefings, meetings, and conferences. The media employed include word processors, computers, telephones and teleconferencing, bulletin boards, newsletters, manuals, and posters, as well as by e-mail, websites, and blogs. In this manner, corporate policies, plans, programs, and procedures are transmitted. The formal aspects of what an organization wants to communicate may be seen both in its management information system for data processing, analysis, and distribution, and in its public information programs for communicating outside the organization.

There is also the unofficial system of communication. It is evident in work relationships, where people come together because they labor in the same organizational unit or because they are members of a project team which may be made up of employees from various departments. Sometimes these occupational relationships also occur because people share a carpool, sit together in the cafeteria, attend the same union meeting, or serve on the same company recreational team. These interactions become opportunities for workers to exchange information, to spread rumors, to affect productivity. People within organizations may group together informally for a variety of reasons – they have compatible line or staff positions, they graduated from the same college, they share the same profession, they have the same interests or skills. It is in these relationships and settings that one can study the informal communication system of an organization – at the refreshment breaks, hobby or sport meetings, and even in the rest or fitness rooms. However, technology is constantly providing new ways for personnel to communicate informally with one another about corporate business or personal matters. We are well aware how e-mail, blogs, and Twitter messages can be used for such purposes. With rapid change in communication technologies, it is vital that a leader keeps informed of what is next in media possibilities.

To be HPLs, we should be not only aware of both formal and informal communication systems, but be able to use them as appropriate. To rely on one and to ignore the other can be fatal. The two systems overlap and intertwine.

Another way to examine organizational communication is to classify it as internal or external. There are many messages and media that are intended only for use within the enterprise, for instance corporate handbooks, in-plant closed circuit TV, and reports of task force meetings or field visits to factories and offices. External communication may include executive participation in community organizations, press releases, advertising, websites, and marketing strategies. The internal system is directed to the stakeholders in the organization – owners, stockholders, management, employees, and sometimes suppliers and contractors. The external system is aimed at the public at large, government officials, customers, competitors, investors, and the media. Of course, many kinds of communication are not clearly external or internal, such as those aimed at workers' families, corporate bankers, and suppliers.

Perhaps managers can best appreciate the interplay between these four systems in the matter of organizational image. The behavioral communication concept described above applies equally to institutions and individuals. Since the organization is a collection of people, how does it see itself? If a company's perception of itself is inadequate or distorted, its representatives may behave inappropriately and cause negative reactions in others outside the organization. If a corporation really knows what business it is in and has energized its people to carry out the organizational mission, it is likely to positively influence its clientele.

Many executives are concerned that the firm portrays the proper image through its logo and letterhead, its annual report and other such publications, and its advertisements or commercials. Leaders sometimes seek to generate good will and positive community relations by demonstrating corporate social responsibility. Are they equally aware, however, of the effect on corporate image made by the appearance of corporate buildings, offices, and employees? They should be concerned about the informal communications about the corporation transmitted by:

- employee attitudes, manifested, for instance, in the way telephone operators or receptionists treat callers;
- the quality of service by employees to customers;
- product appearance, packaging, and quality;
- the appearance of company-owned vehicles and their operators;
- the facilities made available for the safety and comfort of employees and visitors;
- the creativity and tastefulness of illustrations used for media advertising and promotion.

Global corporations are beginning to appreciate how their policies and concerns influence public perception of them. For example, do they demonstrate corporate social responsibility by their ethical behavior, or by real programs to enhance assets – human, natural, material, and otherwise? Organizations perform well and gain credibility with their own people and the public when they make effective use of all four communication systems. Organizations must involve all personnel and their families, as well as board members and stockholders, in projecting a positive organizational image; it is not enough to rely on specialists in public relations or employee relations. Effective leaders should think of the four systems described as a matrix of equal parts. All of them – formal, informal, external, and internal – interact and together make up the full range of organizational communications.

For high performance, leaders make it easy to receive their messages. They can do this by helping their hearers broaden their perceptions or fields of experience as a result of new information. If the communication symbols are obsolete or inadequate, substitutes must be found so the message is more relevant and better received. If the media does not reach or inform for maximum coverage, then perhaps new communication technologies should be used. Leaders are sensitive communicators, capable of listening and meeting the needs of their receivers. Leaders are flexible in their communication styles, shifting to accommodate differences in time, place,

THE HOW OF COMMUNICATION

CLOSED	Communication channels	OPEN
Evaluative	vs.	Descriptive
Controlling	···	Problem-oriented
Strategic	···	Spontaneous
Neutrality	······································	Empathetic
Superiority	···································	Accepting
Dogmatic	································	Provisional
Threatens ego		Promotes collaboration

EXHIBIT 4.4 The how of communication

Source: Reproduced from Jack R. Gibb, "Defensive Communication Model." Reprinted with the permission of the International Communication Association and its *Journal of Communication* 11:3.

and audience. Leaders accept the responsibilities of communication – to enter into the private world of the other by trying to see things as that person does.

Leaders understand that communication may fail not because of the message's content or because of the choice of media, but because of the manner in which the message is delivered. Psychologist Jack Gibb developed a helpful communication model for this purpose which is replicated in Exhibit 4.4. Managers would do well, for example, to avoid words and behavior on the left side of the model, while speaking and acting in a way more like the descriptions on the right side. It is not just oral language which convey our feelings, but also our body language. People can sense when another does not accept them or disrespects them because of skin color, national origin, religious or political beliefs, and even dress or level of sophistication. Without words, they know when you disapprove of them without really knowing or understanding them.

The organization assigns roles and often defines work relationships in order to accomplish its mission. Since we may have outdated images of ourselves and our organizations, we need continually to revise our images of ourselves and our roles. For example, what is the contemporary role of manager in a corporation, agency, or association, particularly in relation to a work unit or team? If a manager acts according to the image of management developed in the disappearing industrial age, that person will increasingly be in difficulty with today's knowledge workers. If, on the other hand, we create an image of a meta-industrial manager, such as I have previously described (Harris 1983, 1985), communications will be effective now and into the future.

In the twenty-first century, the role of leader is increasingly one of coach, consultant, coordinator, facilitator, mentor, and, above all, sensitive communicator. The latter role requires the practice of listening skills, as well as the giving and receiving of feedback with subordinates, colleagues, and others. The how of such communication will in part determine whether the message is perceived as offensive or inoffensive, acceptable or unacceptable, meaningful or irrelevant, helpful or hurtful. Managers who hope to have a high performing unit, therefore, adopt the strategies listed on the right side of the above Gibb model so that their feedback promotes collaboration. If we are sensitive to the subtle cues and feedback others give to us, then we will adapt our behavior and modify our messages accordingly.

Managers who would like to be HPLs also communicate acceptance of their people, rather than rejection. We can respect an associate or colleague worker's inherent dignity as a person, even when the performance may be less than adequate. In our human exchanges, we can recognize other's being, rights, needs, and feelings. We can demonstrate capacity to separate the unique person from actions that may displease us. We can convey this acceptance by demonstrating confidence in our people and their performance potential, thereby permitting them to have confidence in themselves. High performance managers not only provide behavior models, but encourage others to emulate them through continuing positive reinforcement. A spoonful of honey still produces more with people than does a barrel of vinegar.

For the manager to fulfill the role of sensitive communicator, there are barriers to be overcome or pitfalls to avoid. Exhibit 4.5 below lists ten such hindrances to effective organizational communications.

EXHIBIT 4.5   Hindrances to effective communications

Communication is a complex process, especially because different perceptions of those involved in human interaction may cause difficulties in the transmission of thoughts and ideas. However, there are some roadblocks to communications which managers or professionals can avoid or try to minimize. In this way, the message can be sent or received more effectively.

1 Overload: a barrier to communication may exist when talking is too long, too complex, or even too loud – present the message so people can process it.
2 Bias: distortions can creep into communication when the message is not authentic, edited, or reflects the prejudice of the sender – be authentic and tell it like it is.
3 One-sided: that is interpreting the message from your own point of view, without trying to put yourself into the frame of reference of the receivers, so as to promote dialogue.

Continued

4 Passive: merely sending or passively receiving the message undermines two-way or circular communication – only an active, dynamic process involves people.

5 Assumptions: communication cannot be based solely on the sender's assumptions about the realities connected to the message. You must scrutinize your assumptions and inferences to see if they are shared by others in the meeting. You must also explore what assumptions may underlie the message from their perspective.

6 Suspicion: avoid expressing, verbally or non-verbally, suspicion and dislike. Instead endeavor to build up trust among the audience.

7 Imposition: people are alienated when the meeting coordinator tries to impose personal ideas and values on them, failing to take into consideration their opinions and feedback.

8 Inattention: both leaders and participants may not get their message across when their attention is not focused upon the subject of the communication or if they listen selectively. Keep minds on the message, and avoid preoccupation with outside interests or concerns.

9 Bad timing: acceptance may be blocked when an important message is presented inappropriately or at a poor time, such as just prior to lunch. People must be prepared and "psychologically" ready to receive a vital communication.

10 Insufficient explanation: people are inclined to reject proposals or messages when they are not given adequate facts or reasons for the desired course of action. Gather data, present the case with the necessary information on its validity and allow for questions.

Some barriers to communication may be of a physical nature – such as poor hearing on the part of a receiver, faulty microphone or audio system, inadequate chair arrangements, or too much noise. Other obstacles may be psychological in either sender or receiver – such as emotional handicaps, mental illness or inferiority feelings. All the leader can do is to be aware of such possibilities and minimize as many as is feasible.

The communication doors, on the other hand, can be kept open by the manner in which the communication is delivered – the "how" body language may facilitate human interaction, or hinder it. If people are threatened, literally or psychologically, they may close the communication channels. When one is judgmental or evaluative, such as when giving feedback or discussing another's performance, the individual may get defensive. When the communication is given in a way that is descriptive and objective, the message is more likely to be accepted. When one attempts to control or dominate the conversation, for instance, the receiver may become resistive. But the cooperation is likely to be forthcoming if the communication is problem or issue oriented, and allows for exploration and exchange of ideas.

When meeting coordinators engage in "game playing" with participants, in the negative sense, the group becomes wary of being manipulated. But when the communication is spontaneous and authentic, they react favorably. When communicators are cold, neutral, or equivocal, they turn the receivers off. The expression of empathy can reverse the situation. When you indicate superiority in the communication, people may become resentful or hostile. However, if you treat others like equals they are more likely to respond.

If communicators are dogmatic or distorted, people do not want to engage in conversation; but when those same individuals are tentative or provisional in communication, they are more apt to enter in an exchange of ideas or views, as the next exhibit indicates. Thus, the "how" of the communication can also distort the message, no matter how valid its content may be. Exhibit 4.6 suggests six ways to aid human interactions and exchanges.

EXHIBIT 4.6 How to further leadership communications

In effect, a leader should be like a consultant or facilitator. A sensitive communicator should consider these factors that promote dialogue:

1 Availability: involve as many human senses or powers as possible in the process.
2 Contrast: let the message stand out, be vital and relevant, not colorless or indifferent.
3 Reward: meet people's needs; let them know "what is in it for them" if they act on the message.
4 Appropriateness: use communication symbols and content that are suitable to the people and circumstances.
5 Efficiency: give maximum information in minimum time; be concise and precise.
6 Flexibility: be resourceful, creative, and able to adapt your message to the changing situation and people.

High performance leadership is demonstrated when the above communication guidelines are observed.

High-tech communications

Since the Second World War, the computer and myriad advances in communication technology has spurred a revolution in human interaction and exchange. Communications satellites, a spin-off of space technology, contributed mightily to this process. ViaSat of Carlsbad, California, planned to launch, in 2011, a broadband satellite, with more bandwidth than all existing satellites combined, that offered internet services all at above average delivery speeds. Today, the internet provides us with electronic mail, websites, blogs, and instant messaging, as well as global television, mobile phones, and much more to come. Communicating with other human beings has become both easier and more complex, especially within organizations. A space-based internet is transforming human communications capabilities. One outcome is that electronic communication advances are literally fulfilling the prophesy of the old media philosopher, Marshall McLuhan. Namely, our world is shrinking into a "global village."

This communication revolution is not only producing new industries, such as wireless technology, but numerous new global corporations to capitalize on them. Social networking has radically improved, including Facebook with its 500 million users promoting a more collective identity in the human family.[20] Its founders endeavor to promote greater "connectivity" by combining software programming skill with successful entrepreneurship and commendable advisors. Facebook, for example is developing its own online governance, economy, and currency. Online communities are continually growing in their worldwide participants. For example, MySpace has 300 million users, while Twitter has 124 million – these online services are larger than the populations of many nations. Many such entities are becoming social utilities, as well as giant transnational movements. They are producing new businesses, including web security firms whose products counteract intruders and invasions.

Our era requires social media competence that demonstrates transparent and authentic communications, especially with consumers, and suppliers. World corporations are learning hard lessons about controlling distant ends of their supply chains which can leave them vulnerable politically, environmentally, and commercially. Computer and communication technologies are even transforming the military and their role in society. The emerging "cyber war" depends on such technology to counter terrorism and to combat more effectively through "cyber security" weapons. Computer viruses can bring down e-mail systems not only of government, but undermine whole industries, such as oil and gas pipelines, railway networks, air-traffic control systems, electrical grids, financial data storage and transfer, and even orbiting satellites. Much internet traffic is dependent on fiber optic cables under the sea, and are vulnerable to attack by unknown wrong-doers. Cyberspace is not only open to disruption and distortion, but to crime and corruption. Information technology (IT) is already being used for national and corporate espionage by "cyber spies." So for every good use of these technologies, there can be a bad use. "Smart grids," for example, are used for data acquisition, control, and waste prevention in energy utilities; but they can also be manipulated to falsify bills and deter services. Therefore, HPLs keep themselves aware of such changes and dangers, so they may plan strategies and make decisions that optimize the former, and minimize the latter. They seek to advance asymmetry, while avoiding the apocalypse that threatens both business and society. As a case in point, what are the implications of Exhibit 4.7?

EXHIBIT 4.7 Internet effects

THE INTERNET AND THE BRAIN

Consider the impact science, and especially the computer, have on human cognition. Does the use of PowerPoint, for instance, not only change how a presentation is made, but also the thought process of the presenter? Do we really control the tools we make, or do our creations alter the way we perceive and think? Our frequent use of modern hypermedia does seem to impact long-term memory, the basis for true intelligence.

We combine data stored deep within our brains to forge new ideas. Now neural networks can be rapidly reorganized in response to new experience, such as going on the web. So there is concern that digital technology can enable us to rewire our brains. There is some evidence, apparently, that it may damage long-term memory. Humans seem to be moving toward a socially constructed mind that values speed and group approval over originality and individual creativity. Yes, the new machines do improve eye–hand coordination, pattern recognition, and multi-tasking skills. But does constant scanning of the net for fun and work result in a shallow, scattered mindset? Is overuse of the internet addictive, like a drug? Does online "bingeing," particularly by the young, need an antidote, like self-restraint? Perhaps reading Carr's book may provide some answers to these questions.

Source: Based on Nicholas Carr, *The Shallows: What the Internet is Doing to Our Brains*. New York, NY: Norton, 2010.

Managing information in an era of instant and comprehensive data requires leadership to transform data collection into meaningful information and useful knowledge. Data bases built on digital information make it possible to do many things – such as spot business trends, prevent diseases, combat crime, and improve education.[21] When properly managed, the results may be applied to unlock new sources of economic value, provide fresh insights into science, and improve governance. Today we benefit from these new technologies to capture, process, and share information by computers, cameras, sensors, mobile phones, and the like that almost exceeds our storage space. Software to analyze and manage this abundant data is now a $100 billion industry. Scientific researchers in all disciplines have unparalled data on which to work. Internet traffic flow almost grows faster than the ability of electronic networks to carry it all. Information surfeit is leading to social and quantitative change that is making a qualitative difference in our "global village." Information created by machines talking to other machines is generating some 2,000 exabytes annually, while consumers are being bombarded with some 3.6 billion gigabytes per person per day. We are literally developing a data–centered economy and civilization. Thus, business decisions are becoming more sophisticated based on computer algorithms. That means leaders have to have understanding of statistics and correlations.

To appreciate the significance of these developments, consider how new companies are capitalizing on real time information. China's Li & Fung, for instance, has become one of the world's biggest supply chain operators by orchestrating a network of 12,000 suppliers in forty countries that source goods for a variety of brands. To accomplish this smoothly, the company uses a web-service platform that speeds up processes from bids and orders, to delivery and audit. Improved video conferencing is another example of communications innovation. It moves the brain, rather than the body, at much less cost. Now vendors, buyers, and manufacturers can exchange from their own offices as if they were physically sitting opposite one another. Further, real time images make change happen more quickly. And new communication technologies are constantly being discovered to increase the uses of data – like cloud computing and open source software. This leads to new enterprises, as Amazon, Google, and Microsoft found when they made their massive computing infrastructure available to clients. Similarly, firms like Hadoop take advantage of free programming language called "R" to help ordinary PC users analyze huge quantities of data that formerly required a supercomputer. Other companies are compiling masses of data on people, their activities, preferences, and relationships with others – while this is good for marketing, it raises issues of personal privacy. Data is becoming the "new coin of the realm." You can see it in corporations, like Amazon and Netflex, which make recommendations to users on the basis of collaborative filtering, using what others say about a product to increase sales.

Information search engines also continuously improve data mining and applications. A case in point is Matthew Maury of the US Navy who, back in the 1800s, developed the aggregating of ship logs to find routes that offered the best winds and currents for ocean travel. Today Google uses the same principle for translation and voice recognition by book and document scanning, feedback loops, and statistical inferences. No wonder Google is able to answer 35,000 queries every second. Not only is data becoming more accessible, but we are learning to display massive amounts more effectively, such as by better data visualization. And the organizational cultures of these new communication entities, like NetScape, are different because of the processes and technologies they use. Even governments are beginning to apply such innovations to use their massive records to develop a more open society. The new communicators are learning to appeal to our brain functions for improved information processing – the right hemisphere recognizes shapes and colors, while other parts identify patterns, proportions, and relationships, even making subliminal comparisons. High performance leadership will be needed to develop new regulations and administration of big data flows and processing to ensure the integrity of information's use, so it is not used to cause harm or invade privacy.

In this twenty-first century, words are migrating from wood pulp to computer pixels on computers, phones, game consoles, televisions, billboards, and tablets. Printed letters or words on paper have moved to glass surfaces in a rainbow of colors and can be read as fast as the eye can blink. Since the fifteenth century, we have used the printing press to transmit words and thoughts. Now, with digital technology, we do more of our reading on screens. As a result, the number of people reading has vastly expanded, and we have added over a trillion pages to the web. Book and newspaper reading has shifted to screen reading, a communication platform that is visual; merging words with images. Visualizing data and reading charts is an art HPLs have to acquire to succeed. While book reading strengthens our analytical skills, screen reading encourages rapid pattern making, and increased thought – it nurtures, rewards, and enriches thinking in real time, according to Kevin Kelly, author of *What the Technology Wants*, "Screens will be the first place we look for answers, for friends, for news, for meaning, for our sense of who we are and who we can be."

Vern Cerf, the internet pioneer who helped design ARAPnet, considers the World Wide Web a collaborative medium unlike any before it. Through it, people work, play, and interact together – today some 4.5 billion digital screens illuminate our lives. The problem, as in all media, is to be able to sift valid information, from that which is distorted or false. This requires critical thinking on the part of those who would become HPLs. The space-based internet will soon become galactic in scope, providing communication links not only to orbiting space stations and hotels, but to space settlements on different planets, beginning with the Moon.

Yes, knowledge is power, but the issue is how to make more knowledge safer and available, so that it leads to wisdom. A positive indicator is the not-for-profit venture called the "Internet Archive." Here entrepreneur, Brewster Kahle, records all the content on the web, as well as software, films, audio recordings, and scanned books. Another project is trying to record electronically every book written since we began to document human activity. Our present data and information cornucopia is a resource that has to be managed, so as to actualize our potential as a species.[22]

To all this add the communication possibilities now unfolding with advances in virtual reality. In the next quarter century, Don Tapscott, chairman of Geneva Insights, forecasts an economy based on networks, as well as new principles and ways of creating value.[23] The new organizational model is business webs based on partnership with others who create innovation and value through social networking. The key is collaborative learning and active citizenship which is transforming traditional social institutions.

Interaction

The leader who wants to improve a group's performance should take time out from task achievement to work on group maintenance, for example by proposing that a project team examine the communications among its members, or with other units in the organization. A staff meeting or a training session might be devoted to such issues. To stimulate discussion, a training film on organizational communications might be shown. The following two group techniques have also been found useful for this purpose.

Analyzing meeting behavior

When personnel gather for a group encounter, for instance at a project meeting, they operate at different levels of communication, as previously noted. Two such patterns of communication are called task behavior and maintenance behavior. Some of the members' input, actions, or activities contribute to the accomplishment of the team's mission; this is task behavior. Others' actions contribute to improving interactions and building morale; these are maintenance behaviors.

It is beneficial to show the distinction between these two behaviors while demonstrating the value of each. To do so, the leader may sit as an observer, rather than a participant, at a group meeting. Alternatively, the group may choose two of its own to assume the observer role, or invite two persons from outside the group to attend the session as observers. The observers use check sheets, such as those shown next in Exhibits 4.8 and 4.9, to track the communication patterns during the session. One check sheet lists five categories of task behaviors; the second sheet lists five categories of maintenance behaviors. The observers place the names of each participant at the top of the columns, so as to be able to check under that person's name, the observed behavior. This method works best when the group consists of eight or fewer members, and there is one observer to note task behavior and another to note maintenance behavior. During the session, the observers record their checks of each participant's behavior. With a laptop computer and PowerPoint software, these evaluation sheets can also be recorded.

Before the meeting is concluded, a break is taken from the normal business of the day, so the observers may total the number of checks in each category for each person. For the last ten or twenty minutes of the meeting, the observers share their findings with the group and members discuss the implications of this data on their meeting performance. Another variation is to visually record the whole session, then distribute the check sheets to the members. During the replay, members could then analyze the pattern of their group's communication with the aid of the task/maintenance forms. A video camera is another way for recording and reviewing the observations.

What emerges from this exercise is a profile of individual interaction in the group that can then be used by a facilitator for diagnostic or feedback purposes. Team members then become more aware of what they have been doing in meetings to help or hinder participation or performance. Those who have been too task oriented should be encouraged to experiment with some maintenance functions in future sessions, and vice versa. Actually, both functions illustrate something of the person's leadership style. Chapter 9 fully covers issues of high performance leadership at meetings.

Improving listening skills

Another group process can increase communication skills and member participation. The technique is best used with a large audience, such as at a major conference, annual meeting, or training session. Members of a team can also use

EXHIBIT 4.8 Meeting functional analysis: task behavior

Name of group:_____ Date:_____

Instructions. You are observing the behaviour of an individual in a group. Write names or initials of each team member at the top of one of the columns on the right side. As the session progresses, put check marks on the right hand under the person's name whose communications best fit the five categories listed on the left side. When the group or team has completed its work, the chart of check marks provides an overview of how each individual contributed to the group or team task.

Member behavior during group discussion

	Names/initials of individuals observed			
1. *Initiating*. Proposing tasks or goals; defining a group problem; suggesting a procedure or ideas for solving problems.				
2. *Information or opinion seeking*. Requesting facts; seeking relevant information about a group concern, asking for suggestions and ideas.				
3. *Information or opinion giving*. Offering facts; providing relevant information about group concern, stating a belief, giving suggestions or ideas.				
4. *Clarifying or elaborating*. Interpreting or reflecting ideas and suggestions; clearing up confusions; indicating alternatives and issues before the group; giving examples.				
5. *Summarizing*. Pulling together related ideas; re-stating suggestions after group has discussed them; offering a decision or conclusion for the group to accept or reject.				

this approach while listening to a formal presentation at a technical or professional meeting. In the first step, group members assume assigned listening roles. Each individual (or group) listens to the speech or the information being transmitted from a specific perspective, such as: agreeing, disagreeing, seeking clarifications, and seeking applications. After the presentation, these "designated listeners" present their perspective to the total group. As an alternative, the listening teams meet separately to arrive at a consensus on what they have heard (for example, those listening from the perspective of *seeking applications* discuss how to apply the speaker's ideas to their own work situation).

EXHIBIT 4.9 Meeting functional analysis: maintenance behaviors

Name of group:_____ Date:_____

Instructions. Write names orinitials of group or team members at the top.
Then check the behaviors observed during the session that are closest to acting
out those items listed when the group has completed its work; the chart
can give them a picture of how each individual contributed to the group task.

Member behavior required for building and maintaining the group as a
working unit

	Names of individuals observed			
1. *Encouraging.* Being friendly, warm and responsive to others; accepting others and their contributions; regarding others by giving them an opportunity or recognition.				
2. *Expressing group feelings.* Sensing feelings, mood, relationships within the group; sharing one's feelings with other members.				
3. *Harmonizing.* Attempting to reconcile disagreements; reducing tensions through "pouring oil on troubled waters"; getting people to explore their differences.				
4. *Compromising.* When one's own idea of status is involved in a conflict, offering to compromise one's own position; admitting error, disciplining oneself to maintain group cohesion.				
5. *Gate-keeping.* Attempting to keep communication channels open; facilitating the participation of others; suggesting procedures for sharing opportunity to discuss group problems.				

A variation that permits greater audience participation is "buzz groups." The
audience is encouraged to listen carefully to the speaker, taking notes or outlining,
because later they will be asked to join a small group to discuss the speaker's ideas
in greater depth. Following the presentation input, the audience divides into sub-
units of six to twelve people who had sat near one another. These sub-units meet
for ten or fifteen minutes to react to the speaker's ideas. If time permits, each group
selects a spokesperson. The spokesperson presents to the group reactions as a whole,
expressing the consensus achieved by the sub-unit, or perhaps a question for the
speaker (sub-unit reports should be kept to 1–5 minutes). If a speaker has divided
his or her address into logical themes or parts, sometimes the sub-units are chosen

in advance and assigned to report on specific topics. With imagination, a leader can do much with group dynamics to stimulate both attention and involvement of the audience and achieve a meaningful learning experience for all.[24]

Instrumentation

Management communications inventory (MCI)

This check list is for appraisal of yourself or another person as a communicator.

EXHIBIT 4.10   Management communications inventory

Name of person being evaluated or observed:

- -

   Simply place a check mark next to the category which best describes the individual's typical approach to the communication process. You may wish to share your evaluation with a colleague to ascertain if your assessment is confirmed or not. When you have identified areas of improvement, develop a strategy to increase that person's communication skills.

1   In communicating, this person projects a positive image of self (e.g., voice, bearing, appearance, etc.)
   a. Seldom   ☐
   b. Occasionally   ☐
   c. Often   ☐
   d. Always   ☐
2   This person tries to understand and enter into the receiver's frame of reference (e.g. empathetic, restate his point of view, etc.)

   a. Seldom   ☐
   b. Occasionally   ☐
   c. Often   ☐
   d. Always   ☐

3   This person establishes eye contact with the receiver

   a. Seldom   ☐
   b. Occasionally   ☐
   c. Often   ☐
   d. Always   ☐

4   This person communicates respect for the receiver of his/her message (e.g. listening carefully, not making the other person feel inferior, etc.)

Continued

---

a. Seldom ☐
b. Occasionally ☐
c. Often ☐
d. Always ☐

5 This person uses different media or means as necessary to get his/her meaning across (e.g. communication symbols that appeal to several senses)

a. Seldom ☐
b. Occasionally ☐
c. Often ☐
d. Always ☐

6 This person seems aware of his/her own inner state which conditions communication (e.g. feelings, needs, motives, assumptions, prejudices, etc.)

a. Seldom ☐
b. Occasionally ☐
c. Often ☐
d. Always ☐

7 This person tries not to use emotionally loaded words to distort responses

a. Seldom ☐
b. Occasionally ☐
c. Often ☐
d. Always ☐

8 This person tries to listen not only to facts and ideas (cognitive data), but to be sensitive to the feelings which the others reveal

a. Seldom ☐
b. Occasionally ☐
c. Often ☐
d. Always ☐

9 This person tries to be open to new ideas and constructive criticism regardless of the source

a. Seldom ☐
b. Occasionally ☐
c. Often ☐
d. Always ☐

10 This person is willing to share ideas with others to the point of personal change if it is warranted

a. Seldom ☐
b. Occasionally ☐

Continued

c. Often ☐
d. Always ☐

11 This person tries to be authentic in his/her communication and levels with others when it is appropriate

a. Seldom ☐
b. Occasionally ☐
c. Often ☐
d. Always ☐

12 This person tries to reduce the physical and psychological distance between himself/herself and listeners

a. Seldom ☐
b. Occasionally ☐
c. Often ☐
d. Always ☐

13 This person checks to ascertain if his/her real meaning is understood

a. Seldom ☐
b. Occasionally ☐
c. Often ☐
d. Always ☐

14 This person allows the other person to ask questions and seek clarification regarding the message being sent

a. Seldom ☐
b. Occasionally ☐
c. Often ☐
d. Always ☐

15 This person asks questions and seeks clarification during the communication exchange

a. Seldom ☐
b. Occasionally ☐
c. Often ☐
d. Always ☐

16 In speaking, this person tries to project their voice clearly and avoids mumbling

a. Seldom ☐
b. Occasionally ☐
c. Often ☐
d. Always ☐

Continued

17 In speaking, this person tries to vary their tone of voice

    a. Seldom   ☐
    b. Occasionally   ☐
    c. Often   ☐
    d. Always   ☐

18 In speaking, this person tries to say what they really mean

    a. Seldom   ☐
    b. Occasionally   ☐
    c. Often   ☐
    d. Always   ☐

19 In speaking, this person tries to use a vocabulary that is understandable to the receiver

    a. Seldom   ☐
    b. Occasionally   ☐
    c. Often   ☐
    d. Always   ☐

20 In speaking, this person tries to be concise and precise

    a. Seldom   ☐
    b. Occasionally   ☐
    c. Often   ☐
    d. Always   ☐

21 This person follows up on the communication to see if agreements or instructions are carried out

    a. Seldom   ☐
    b. Occasionally   ☐
    c. Often   ☐
    d. Always   ☐

    Observer's initials

Organization communications analysis (OCA)

Exhibit 4.11 offers a way to analyze competence in the four systems of organizational communications. Respondents (managers or employees) check the items appropriate to their company or agency in each of the quadrants related to the four interacting communication systems – formal, informal, internal, and external. The first purpose is to create awareness of the scope and subtlety of these systems, but the real learning occurs as an individual or group seeks to provide "other" examples in each category. In a work unit, this part of the exercise can lead to interesting discussion as to what is the appropriate classification for such matters as facsimile or text message, e-mail, and other forms of communication technologies. In addition, there are five sections dealing with questions of organizational image, publics, communication flow, relations, and environment. These require descriptive statements to be written. When a team, for instance, has completed individual analysis, members can compare their opinions and attempt to arrive at some consensus on the issues.

EXHIBIT 4.11 Organizational communications analysis

Analyze the communication systems in your organization by checking the appropriate boxes if you utilize the practice.

System A	Formal	System B

External organizational communication

- ☐ letters
- ☐ telephone
- ☐ advertising
- ☐ mass media
- ☐ press releases
- ☐ publications/reports
- ☐ public relations/marketing
- ☐ community relations program
- ☐ visits/field work
- ☐ teleconferencing
- ☐ websites
- ☐ products/services
- ☐ blogs

- ☐ plant/office appearance and atmosphere
- ☐ employee contacts (outside participation in person) or electronically (online via)
- ☐ e-mail, blogs, Twitter, etc.
- ☐ grapevine/rumors
- ☐ visitor/guestrelations
- ☐ networking in person or online
- ☐ other _____

Internal organizational communication

- ☐ letters/forms
- ☐ memoranda/reports
- ☐ signs/posters
- ☐ bulletin boards
- ☐ telephone
- ☐ computer/electronic mail
- ☐ closed circuit TV/radio
- ☐ office visits
- ☐ staff or other meetings
- ☐ organization chart for "hierarchy" communications
- ☐ task forces/committees/teams
- ☐ other _____

- ☐ work relationships
- ☐ social relationships/memberships in external organizations
- ☐ geographic/project relationships
- ☐ union trade/professional relationships
- ☐ client/customer relationships
- ☐ economic/status relationships
- ☐ cultural/religious relationships
- ☐ grapevine/gossip orally or electronically
- ☐ internal networking in person or electronically (iPod, iPhone or other forms of smart phones and tablets, telephone)
- ☐ other _____

System C	Informal	System D

The previous conceptual model is simply a useful means of quickly reviewing the diversity of your organization communications. By completing the following questions, you may gain a greater understanding of the status of its communications system and what you can contribute to its improvement.

Continued

1 Image

a. What is your perception of your organization's image?

_____

_____

b. What is your perception of your division's (department or work unit) image?

_____

_____

c. What do you feel is the perception of your unit's image by those *outside* your immediate organization/division?

_____

_____

(Consider this from the viewpoint of those people outside the organization, such as the public, as well as those who are in the organization but are not a part of your unit – for example, members of other divisions or departments.)

2 Publics

a. Who are the various publics to whom you communicate your organizational messages? (Remember to include such varied recipients as suppliers, politicians, family, etc.)

_____

b. What could be done to project a better organizational image?

_____

3 Communication flow (Describe the direction of your formal communication systems)

a. External:

i. Downward (one way)_____

ii. Upward_____

iii. Circular (two way or part participative)_____

b. Internal:

i. Outward_____

ii. Inward_____

iii. Circular_____

Continued

4 Organizational relations

    a. List the names (titles or categories) of those people with whom you are in *most* frequent communication in the course of your work week:

    _____

    _____

    _____

    _____

    _____

    _____

    b. Review this list and put a check next to the person or groups with whom it is vital you maintain good relations to do your job effectively.

    _____

As a result of your insights learned from this chapter, what steps can you take next week to improve your relations/communications with these people? Be specific.

1 _____

2 _____

3 _____

4 _____

5 _____

6 _____

7 _____

8 _____

9 _____

10 _____

Continued

5 Organizational environment

   a. The improvement of both formal and informal communications can contribute significantly toward bettering the organizational atmosphere. What other recommendations can you make to management in this regard next week?

   _____

   _____

   b. What strategy or procedures will you utilize to accomplish this? (To whom and how will you direct your observations?)

   _____

   _____

For those who wish to improve skills as a mentor or coach, consult Dr Robert R. Carkhuff, *The Art of Helping, 9th Edition* (www.hrdpress.com).

5

INFLUENCING WORK CULTURE AT HOME AND ABROAD

Introduction

Culture is a concept that enables leaders to gain insights and knowledge. It is like a jewel – hold it to the sunlight, and turn it slowly for myriad applications. Culture has a critical effect on the behavior and performance of people, individually and in groups. International traders appreciate this. Only in the past four decades, however, have executives and managers begun to appreciate the significance of corporate culture. This chapter will offer insights to would-be HPLs about this vital subject in the context of the work environment, so that we may better understand ourselves and provide leadership in a more diverse work force.

What is Culture? Culture is a coping mechanism, a tool of survival to deal with the circumstances in which people find themselves. People create a social environment out of the biological, physical, historical, and other aspects of our surroundings. This "culture" is the "communicable knowledge" that is transferred from generation to generation to help group members live in a time, place, or situation. Culture is the human "tool" that separates our species from other animals. In conjunction with biological evolution, culture has not only helped the human species to survive, but to grow and develop on this planet, and to begin to develop its potential beyond Earth.

Culture is learned behavior and knowledge that are integrated by a group, shared among its members, and passed along to descendents. These group beliefs and practices become customs, traditions, and guidelines that distinguish one people (civilization, country, or organization) from another. Certain behaviors, for instance, arise from peculiar circumstances of climate, geography, danger, ignorance, or discovery that at one time conditioned group members. Although the reason behind the behavior is forgotten, the behavioral pattern persists – it is part of the culture: "the way we do things around here."

In this chapter we will look at culture and its diverse ramifications, especially in terms of the work environment.[24] We will also examine *cultural conditioning* and see how it affects communication and performance. Finally, we will review the influence of culture on work and organizations. We will show that the role of leadership is to design and sustain a more creative and productive work culture, one that helps personnel to achieve their human potential. In Exhibit 5.1 we begin with a profile on a HPL who demonstrates extraordinary cross-cultural skills.

EXHIBIT 5.1 Profile of an international HPL

In the last century, business increased efforts to move manufacturing to places where the cost of labor would be cheaper. But in the twenty-first century, there has been an explosion of electronic outsourcing of work from a home base to a place, at home or abroad, where it can be accomplished at less cost, so as to be competitive in the global marketplace. In either case, such operations call for considerable cross-cultural expertise on the part of executive, managers, and other professionals.

A pioneer in outsourcing, Donald L. Conover, founded CBay Systems in 1998, and several other international IT firms. Skip, as he prefers to be called, built CBay's business around medical transcriptions for hospitals and physicians. In his Annapolis, Maryland plant, he would gather dictation from medical professionals, and ship it electronically to India. When transcribed, the health reports would be sent back by computer for distribution to US clients who consistently gave the company superior ratings in customer satisfaction surveys. As the corporation grew to the third largest in the healthcare services industry, it went public in 2007. In the process, Skip developed close working relations with numerous Indian professionals and investors in this and other enterprises abroad, including real estate development. As an international lawyer, he also did extensive travel for investment projects in the Middle East and Asia which led in 2008 to the "International Entrepreneur of the Year" award presented at the United Nations' headquarters, as well as a cover story in the magazine *Global CEO*.

To be a high performing global leader requires learning foreign languages and cultures. Conover not only speaks Mandarin Chinese and Japanese, but has the right credentials. A graduate of Hamilton College (BA), Defense Language Institute, State University of New York-Buffalo (JD) and the University of Rochester (MBA), this humanitarian has always been concerned about promoting international business relations. His early career in Vietnam as an intelligence officer for the US Marine Corps (Lt Col), prepared him to do business in Asia. Raised in his youth in Japan, he returned there later to serve for five years as country director for Schlegel Engineering. His varied career demonstrates high

Continued

performance, whether as an Associate Dean in the University of Maryland Graduate School or a promoter of IPOs (Initial Public Offerings), such as with his current undertakings as President of GCI Systems and Chairman of Bhavana Developers in India.

Skip Conover, a gifted painter, also seeks to build bridges between Islam and the West, so he initiated media projects like "Words Matter" and wrote an electronic book, *Tsunami of Blood*. In an interview with *Global CEO*, he described his HPL evolution as a process of change in pursuits, roles, and perspectives – from a lone ranger to team player, from entrepreneur to growth partner, from being an American citizen to a global human being. He wishes to bring more comfort and happiness within reach of the world's multitudes who deserve better. Skip believes the latter goal can be accomplished through improved management of resources, especially by wise investments in infrastructure.

(www.gcinfosys.com/pages/aboutUs.html; www.linkedin.com/in/donaldconover)

Input

Human performance is dependent upon culture – that is, the social environment which strongly influences people either to strive and excel or to be resigned and apathetic. Some cultures are dynamic and spur members to be creative and productive. Other cultures inhibit creativity and trap the mind or spirit, repressing human aspirations and efforts to improvement. Such cultures, whether national or organizational, overburden people with ritualism, legalism, defeatism, and fatalism. Leaders can change their group's culture so that it enhances worker productivity by removing obsolete norms, practices, and procedures and by introducing more relevant standards, operations, and technologies. Leaders can induce a society or a company to capitalize on its human assets.

Cultural influences on behavior

Culture provides us with a framework for analyzing human behavior, especially in terms of people in groups. Because human beings are so complex and diverse, what we know of the effect of culture on their performance is relative and tentative – a series of generalizations subject to many exceptions. Furthermore, each of us tends to view others' behavior in terms of his or her own background, so that actions that may appear to us as bizarre or reprehensible may be acceptable and normal in another part of the human family. For example, some affluent societies find extreme poverty appalling and seek to eradicate it, while others in the economically emerging nations accept being poorer as their way of life and wait for their circumstances to change. A society's shared values determine individual response on many issues. Brazil, for example, had a rural population in 1990 in which fifty percent of the population lived below $1.25 a day. A new Presidential administration with better anti-poverty programs reduced that figure to only ten percent by 2010. Thus, the culture is being altered in numerous ways.

Anthropologists have called culture *created designs for living*. In addition to the customs and traditions mentioned, culture is manifested by a tribe, an organization, or a nation in the group's beliefs, rites, myths, symbols, morals, habits, thought patterns, language, standards, laws, art, architecture, artifacts, and technologies. In these manifestations of a culture, its guidelines may be rational or irrational, explicit (spelled out and evident) or implicit. The tenets of a culture – its "truths" – are expressed in its behaviors or its taboos; what members do and do not do. Thus, members strongly identify with their culture's beliefs and practices. They are usually reluctant to question or change those which are commonly held within their society. Traditions evolve as to what are proper behavior and dress, what foods or people are to be considered desirable or to be avoided. In traditional or simple societies, daily life is somewhat smooth and predictable because of such observances – peasants, for instance, do not question the validity of these beliefs or practices which became tradition. Unfortunately, culture can also be the means for perpetuating ignorance and misinformation, as well as prejudices and bigotry. Some suffer from culture lag, and are backward as fundamentalists or ultra-conservatives in orientation.

Culture is marked by both diversity and unity. Although we all belong to a culture, its expressions differ by place and circumstances. Cultural differences are so wide, and so compelling, that what one person considers desirable food in one culture, can be perceived as poison in another. There are numerous universals, however, behaviors common to all cultures and human nature everywhere. They include age-grading, body adornments, language, law, sports, luck, magic, marriage, mourning, visiting, weaning, and predicting the weather.

Different human groups, however, fluctuate even in the ways they practice the above universal behaviors. Hand-holding, for instance, occurs in almost all cultures, but in some societies it is only permitted between men and women, while in others also between people of the same sex. The marriage customs and laws of certain societies favor monogamy, while in other circumstances polygamy or polyandry is preferred. We must be sensitive to these differences in cultural universals – whether in humor or hygiene, greeting or gift-giving – and, when outside our own cultural group, respect and observe (if possible) local custom. In seeking to interpret the behavior of a worker from another culture, be careful not to be fooled by appearances. What we consider phlegmatic others may think of as respectful. For example, Americans are normally expressive, while Asians generally cloak their feelings – a matter of cultural conditioning.

Actually, it is cultural differences that add spice to life and make people so interesting. If we were all the same, life might be quite boring. When we are sensitive to the differences in meaning attached to communication, we watch for subtle signs, such as body language, gestures, symbols, even color. In India, for example, people shake their heads back and forth to say "yes" and nod their heads to say "no" – exactly the reverse of Western practice. Similarly, in the West, black is usually associated with bereavement and white with joy; doing so in an Asian nation could result in a faux pas. Mourners wear white in Japan, blue in Iran, and purple in Latin America. A sensitive leader should check local customs when abroad, as well as be aware of minority cultures at home.

To raise cultural awareness, look for patterns and themes in whatever culture you are studying. Some Asian cultures, India for instance, instill in their members a belief in reincarnation, and their people are very fatalistic. Anthropologist Ruth Benedict pointed out that the Pueblo Indians of the American Southwest have an integrative culture that could be described as "middle of the road" – that is, they avoid any form of excess or conflict in order to obtain harmony. In the Far East, there are many cultures in which people follow a similar, consistently summative theme in their lives. We could search for distinctive themes in American culture in general, or with its many minorities within its society (such as Latino and African American micro-cultures). Such world views, declared or implied, usually control behavior or stimulate activity within that group. In the American business sub-culture, one such theme is the importance of profit – the "bottom line." Many corporate cultures in our society differ, however. Some now place the emphasis on profitable service, quality, excellence, or even environmental sensitivity. This is called corporate social responsibility.

Within a group, organization, or nation, there are majority and minority cultures. The behaviors and attitudes shared by most members can be said to make up the *mainline* or *macro-culture* (the term I prefer). Within any society, regardless of size, there are distinguishing characteristics that differentiate people by sex, age, race, class, or some other classification. Anthropologists call groups made up of people who share these distinguishing characteristics *subcultures* or *micro-cultures*. Thus, within the macro-culture of the United States, there are many micro-cultures, that is, segments of American society (such as criminals, drug users, defense establishment, teenagers, surfers, senior citizens, blue collar workers, college students, yuppies, Jews, Chicanos, immigrants, and refugees. In terms of business, a Canadian company represents the macro-culture of that country and the micro-culture of that particular corporation. For example, within the organizational culture of the Canadian Broadcasting Company (CBC) there are micro-cultures grouped around sub-entities (such as subsidiaries, divisions, or departments, as well as Anglo–French orientation). The offices of CBC operating in the province of Quebec differ somewhat from those in other provinces because of the dominance there of the French-speaking inhabitants.

People within national cultures, such as Mexicans or Ethiopians, may share a common micro-culture of Catholicism or Communism. Similarly, countries may share the sub-cultural traits of poverty, their particular stage of agricultural or industrial development, or of being urbanized or rural. So, too, groups of people across the world may share the traits of a micro-culture with which they have more in common than they do with their fellow citizens. Thus, globally, this could prove true within the micro-culture of managers, police officers, rock musicians, or computer addicts. A Japanese and an American manager often share more with each other in terms of occupation and class than they may share with a fellow national on their company's assembly line. Realizing that we are all members of many cultural groupings, both macro-cultural and micro-cultural, can help us understand behavior in ourselves and others. As a result, we become more tentative in our judgments, more tolerant in our attitudes, and more effective in coping with the peculiarities of cultural differences. Perhaps awareness of culture can make us less simplistic and more sympathetic, for instance to a micro-culture of alcoholics, unemployed people, or welfare recipients.

By appreciating the impact of cultural conditioning on people, we may be less inclined to blame, to castigate, to express hostility toward those who are different from us. Instead, we may be more inclined to enrich life experience by including in our relationships those who are less like us in terms of ethnic background, customs, dress, thought patterns, or communication. The more we comprehend the concept of culture, the more able to develop cross-cultural skills and to manage change we become.

For the past fifty years, human beings have begun to explore, live, and work beyond Earth. Humanity is now in the process of creating a spacefaring civilization, and an entirely new space culture suitable for a microgravity environment. As a result our species is likely to develop two kinds of people – Earth kind and space kind.[25]

Today's global leaders are high performers who manage cultural differences, promote cultural synergy, and become more cosmopolitan. They are not terrestrially biased, but open to business and industrialization off-world. They are already leaders in space communications, commerce, transportation, and tourism.

The characteristics of culture

Leaders need a relatively simple method for analyzing a culture. That is, a logical way when going abroad or aloft to do business. They are able to examine the various dimensions of a national culture, or, when at home, to consider minority and organizational cultures. Anthropologists have many schemes for studying the various parameters of cultures. One, for example, is a systems approach by which the investigator examines the many sub-systems that make up the whole of a society, such as kinship, education, economics, politics, religion, health, recreation, and associations (Miller 1978).

One way to analyze any macro-culture or micro-culture is to consider the way the group works. During the course of human development, societies and institutions have been created around the dominant work prevalent at that point in time. Early human culture, for instance, was organized around hunting and gathering food – there are aboriginal tribes still living that way today. The mainstream of humankind moved beyond that stage of development to a work culture built around farming or ranching – this agricultural lifestyle still lingers on in pre-industrial nations or in rural communities where agriculture is still the main occupation. For the last three hundred years, the dominant work style has been industrial, centered around the factory system and an urban way of life. Now we are undergoing a transition to a post-industrial work culture focused on "information processing and services." Today we live and work in a "knowledge culture" (Harris 2005).

An easy way to analyze the varied dimension of any culture, both macro or micro, is provided in the next section.

Ten characteristics of culture

Note that, in each category, there are two related but distinct features of culture to be observed. These features can serve as ten benchmarks to categorize the various aspects of a culture, whether a national or organizational culture, a work or team culture. For each category, we will provide an illustration in terms of human behavior and performance within one of the following aspects of culture:

- a national culture (NC): either a foreign country or a minority in another country.
- an organizational culture (OC): a corporation, agency, or association.
- a work culture (WC): specifically the meta-industrial society now emerging.
- a team culture (TC): either athletic or corporate.

Here are ten other classifications to examine or analyze any culture:

1 *Identity and purpose.* Culture helps to give people a sense of identity with reference to a group, and to some extent determines their life space (both physical and psychological). The borders that mark off and define the group can be concrete or abstract, explicit or implicit; drawing the lines is the way the group defines itself and exercises its territorial imperative. Culture also contributes to the group's rationale for being together: its sense of mission and goals.

   NC: The people of some nations express pride and confidence, while those of other nations are of humble bearing and more respectful of others. The American sense of space requires more physical distance between individuals, while people of some other countries tend to get much closer during interpersonal interaction.

2 *Communication and language.* A group distinguishes itself by its communication systems, both verbal and non-verbal. Unique interaction processes develop, with special vocabularies, terminologies, and codes. Within the major language groupings, further differentiation occurs through dialects, accents, slang, jargon, and other variations.

   OC: For example, the US Department of Defense (DOD) employs acronyms extensively, not only with its own members, but with its many contractors, so as to facilitate communications with the myriad DOD components. It also employs much of the jargon common to a bureaucratic government agency.

3 *Dress and appearance.* Whether as a whole or through its members, a culture delineates itself through garments, decorations, and other adornments or the lack thereof. Hair length or the lack of it, facial markings, jewelry, and body markings can set a tribe or unit apart – remember the pirates of old or the terrorists of today. Think of the Japanese kimono, African headdress, British

bowler, Polynesian sarong, and the military or police uniform. The appearance of its members, equipment, and institutional look sometimes conveys the nature of a culture or its business; consider the appearance of an airlines flight attendant, an IBM computer consultant, or a McDonald food server.

WC: In the new, knowledge work culture, high technology firms often require workers to wear white sanitary garments to prevent contamination (e.g. in computer microchip production). These knowledge-centered factories often look like college campuses – they are usually set in modern industrial parks that feature eye-catching buildings, attractive landscaping, and open spaces, as well as recreational facilities for worker fitness programs. The dress of workers inside the plant or laboratory tends to be informal.

4 *Food and feeding customs.* The manner in which food is selected, prepared, presented, and eaten differs by culture, as every visitor to a Chinese or French restaurant knows. One person's pet hate may be a delicacy to someone in a different culture. Religious observances forbid certain foods, such as beef or pork, and dictate the manner of preparation (e.g. kosher food preparation and cooking distinguishes Jewish food). Feeding customs may determine the use of hands, chopsticks, or cutlery – an American uses a knife in the dominant (usually the right) hand to cut food, then puts down the knife to wield the fork with the same hand; Europeans do not switch implements. In some subcultures, ladies prefer the tea room, soldiers use a mess, executives have separate dining rooms, and vegetarians have their own restaurants. Feasts and banquets in various forms, from luau to retirement dinners, are used to celebrate important events.

TC: NASA permits astronauts to order or choose their food preferences (e.g. steak, fish, vegetarian, or whatever), but then has to package everything in special plastic containers to deal with the reality of eating or drinking in zero or low gravity when in outer space.

5 *Time and time consciousness.* The study of this aspect of human behavior called "time" is *chronomics* – keeping, telling, and measuring the duration of intervals. Our biological and circadian rhythms are affected by nature, climate, and speed – air travelers through time zones know of this and experience "jet lag." Cultural factors cause some people to have a more exact or relative sense of time. In some cultures, time is told by sunrise or sunset, rain, its lack, or other seasonal variations. Consider Daylight Saving Time. In the far north and on the lunar surface inhabitants cope with time disorientation caused by extreme variations in the periods of light and darkness.

WC: Consider that the military use the twenty-four hour time system; or the new technological work culture often functions on a round-the-clock schedule, either as standard operating procedure or to meet special project deadlines. The industrial age approach to a twelve-hour day with an eight-hour work day is disappearing. Chronobiologists are concerned about drastic changes in time and labor schedules, such as those brought on by night-shift work, which alter both performance and personal life and may contribute to accidents and illness.

6 *Relationships and sexuality*. Cultures fix human and organizational relationships by age, sex, status, and degrees of kinship, as well as by wealth, power, and wisdom. Studying sexual practices (clan, sibling, marriage, and familial groupings, as well as sex roles) is one way to map a culture. The family is a key manifestation of this characteristic. Families vary widely in size and in form. There are nuclear families, as in the West, or extended forms, such as the Hindu joint family. In these households, membership extends from parents and their children to uncles, aunts, and cousins, but the living areas separate the sexes. Depending on whether the culture is patriarchal or matriarchal, the authority figure is male or female. In some cultures, the elderly are venerated; in others, youth holds supreme. Culture can dictate equal opportunity for women, or force females to wear veils, appear deferential, and give up many rights to the dominant males. Some cultures decry homosexuality, while others accept gay rights, even in marriage. In addition, in human systems, customs and policies, organization charts and structures, role definitions, and even security clearances determine relationships. Protocol and rank can inhibit human interaction, even segregating minorities or the non-commissioned.

OC: In a successful global corporation, Schlumberger, multicultural relationships are that of international engineering and technical fraternity, male-dominated until recently, and family-oriented. Among the largely knowledge-based workers, personal and electronic networking is normal behavior. However, there are contradictions: outside of North America, the company discourages assignments to their remote sites of engineers who are married; wives of employees find it difficult to pursue their own careers because of their husbands' frequent transfers, often to Muslim countries. Customer relations are prized, and the emphasis is on service and honesty with clients. Relations with people in developing countries are deliberately cultivated in a company spirit of equality. Human–machine relations are encouraged through the widespread corporate use of automation, robotics, and artificial intelligence. In their global relationships, Schlumberger personnel tend to be more cosmopolitan and less ethnocentric, valuing human relations.

7 *Values and norms*. Culture influences what people perceive as their needs, and, as a result, what they set as their priorities. Those functioning at the survival need level value such basics as food, clothing, and shelter; those at the security need level value material things, law and order, titles, and other symbols that maintain their position; those with higher ego and actualization needs value recognition, quality of life, and self-fulfillment. Thus a HPL competes against self rather than others.

Based on what the culture values, behavior norms are overtly or covertly expressed in that society. The acceptable standards of behavior may take the form of a work ethic, principles of etiquette, codes of conduct, regulations, and laws. The process begins in the family, and the norms range from absolute obedience to permissiveness; the process continues into organizational life, where employee standards are formally or informally stated (sometimes in a booklet of organizational regulations).

NC: Macro-cultures start from different sets of premises in setting down what behavior is pleasing, annoying, embarrassing, punishable, or rewardable. In some countries, one is expected to be truthful only with one's friends and family but not with strangers. These conventions differ – consider that in some Pacific Islands the higher status one has in the community, the more one is expected to share personal belongings. An extreme example of culture-based norms can be seen in the fundamentalist Islamic movement in Iran, which today encourages some inhabitants to value and seek death through martyrdom for their cause.

8 *Beliefs and attitudes*. Every cultural group has beliefs that shape member aspirations and attitudes, regardless of their rationality or objective truth. In national cultures, this can take the form of belief in the supernatural or a god and can be associated with the adoption of a religious system, so that the country and its people may be described as Christian, Jewish, Muslim, Buddhist, or Hindu. In this way, the culture seeks to provide guidance to fundamental life questions – the character of human nature; the relationship of humans to nature; the temporal focus of life (past, present, or future); the modality of human activity (spontaneous expression, self-development, measurable accomplishment); the relationship of one person to another. Some cultures provide equal opportunity for all people, others have restrictions because of gender, class, caste, or whatever.

Within organizational cultures, the dominant business philosophy permeates policies, procedures, personnel, and publications. Corporate beliefs, for instance, may originate with a founder or company hero; that person's ideals and principles affect employee attitudes, so that they all want to make profits, innovate, provide service, or excel. Organizational beliefs and attitudes determine recognition and reward systems – rites and rituals that range from parties and ceremonies to prizes and the establishment of clubs for excellent performers. Furthermore, the culture's beliefs and attitudes are incorporated into its myths, those traditional or legendary stories about the group's heroes and events of exceptional character.

WC: The beliefs of a culture are manifested in many ways, such as its position on the role of women in that society. In some societies, women are revered, in other societies they are considered equal to men, in still other cultures they are subservient and sometimes treated as chattel. In the disappearing industrial work culture, women were frequently denied entry or promotion to certain job classifications or activities, relegated to performing what was considered "women's work," or paid less than men for doing the same work. In the emerging knowledge work culture, competence, not sexuality, is the issue. Therefore, women (and minority members) are to be given equal employment opportunities. Organizations are expected to take affirmative action to aid, not interfere with, their career development. Today, compensation should be based on performance and results, not on gender, race, religion, or other such irrelevant factors.

9 *Mental habits and learning*. Because the mind internalizes culture, the way people think, learn, organize, and process information is unique and often different. Some

cultures may emphasize whole-brain thinking, others right- or left-brain development. For instance, in some countries logic is prized, while in others intuition is emphasized. As one travels abroad, it becomes evident that some people excel in abstract thinking and conceptualization, while others prefer rote memory and quantification. Although reasoning and learning are cultural universals, education and training are manifested in diverse and distinctly different ways.

TC: Many aerospace companies involved in space programs use *matrix* or *project* management. Engineers, for instance, are trained in both technical and interpersonal skills for effective performance on project teams. This instruction makes use of modern communication and educational technology, with the latest media combinations, such as computer-assisted learning, video, CDs/DVDs, and teleconferencing. Too often, the behavioral aspects and group dynamics involved in team building are neglected or de-emphasized by those with an engineering education. NASA technicians, in preparing crews for assignments on the International Space Station, are now focusing on the human dynamics involved in that off-world work environment.[26]

10 *Technologies, work habits and practices.* Cultures differ in the perceptions of, and attitudes toward, work and its tools or technologies. They vary in the types of work favored; manner of dividing work; in work practices; and even the technologies employed. Hall (1985)[27] examined both the horizontal (division of labor) and the vertical (occupational gradations) dimensions of work. Cultures, especially through economics, determine what work is considered necessary and valuable to that particular people. In some cultures all members are expected to engage in desirable and worthwhile activity, but their members do not measure the work's value in terms of money; instead, they focus on the work's value to the community. In some traditional cultures, the females are expected to do most of the ordinary work. Culture defines the terms, scope, and segmentation of vocational activity – labor or toil, laborer or professional, job or career. Today we are experiencing a change from a "work" ethic to a "worth" ethic, which emphasizes the quality of work life. More advanced, technical work cultures use technology, such as automation, to assist or replace workers, to share work through team management, to value informal and comfortable work environments. Work also is the context for exercising power, authority, and leadership. Some organizations are formed as hierarchies with power concentrated at the top, while other work cultures distribute power and authority, encouraging member participation and collaboration. Work also helps to define roles and relationships – for example, in advanced cultures, both genders are welcome and compensated equally, while in other work cultures, women may be excluded or relegated to inferior positions.

NC/WC: In the American culture, the orientation is toward the future, free enterprise, and achievement. The emphasis is focused on innovation, entrepreneurialism, and high performance. Contemporary corporate recognition and reward systems support people who demonstrate such qualities in their work.

Given the complexities and subtleties of culture, it should be obvious why HPLs must excel in their knowledge of cultures and languages.

Synergy and high performance cultures

Twenty-first century leaders want to do more than cope with cultural differences. Domestically or internationally, it is more appropriate and profitable to promote cultural synergy. That requires HPL skills in promoting cooperation or collaboration, so as to capitalize upon cultural differences or produce something that is more than merely the sum of its parts. Thus, when Japanese (Theory Y) and American (Theory X) management philosophies and practices (McGregor 2006) are combined in "Theory Z" management, the result can be better than either approach can achieve individually (Ouchi 1981). Another example is the success of a bi-cultural manufacturing process when Toyota partnered with General Motors' management thinking in a joint venture at Fremont, California. For a time, their New United auto plant demonstrated the "best of both worlds" – an operation with state-of-the-art technology and high productivity achieved by adapting the Japanese approach to quality, employees, and effective management. With the enormous trade shift to the Pacific Basin, greater synergistic relations are desirable not only with the Japanese, Korean, Indian, and Chinese, but also with many other Oriental peoples.

A joint venture between First and Third world corporations based on principles of synergy, rather than on exploitation of one at the expense of the other, can prove mutually beneficial, with each organizational culture adding to and supplementing the other. This was evident when a Canadian consulting firm entered into an agreement to assist a Mexican company to use advanced technology; the agreement is but part of a larger deal between the governments of both countries in which Mexico supplies energy, facilities, and labor, while the Canadians provide capital, information, know-how, and equipment. Such international undertakings fuse both national and organizational cultures so that both peoples are enhanced in the exchange. Synergistic relations help companies to avoid strikes and labor disputes. Another case to consider – Japanese companies were among the first foreign firms to open factories in China. But as the Chinese work force became better educated and sophisticated, Japanese managers in that country failed to alter their management style to these work culture changes. Their expectations for Chinese employees of loyalty, docility, sacrifice, and lower wages were rudely upset with recent labor unrest and demands in the People's Republic. To cope in China now, Japanese managers have had to increase pay, alter their management practices, and shift more labor-intensive work to other Asian countries where the work situation is less demanding. It might have been better if they had introduced more responsive strategies and policies that ensured worker cooperation abroad.

Synergy is combined action in which diverse or disparate peoples or groups work together, and it is a norm of the new work culture. The objective is to increase effectiveness by sharing perceptions, insights, and knowledge, so as to build on the strengths of each cultural entity. The very complexities of global problems and markets demand such cross-cultural collaboration, as is evidenced in the European

Union or its Airbus venture involving several companies and countries on that project. The latter is a European consortium, a synthesis of national and corporate cultures which produces a successful and profitable series of jet airplanes. It involves French, German, and Spanish firms working together to create a superior aircraft that utilizes either an American or British motor. Technocrats have jumped traditional trade and cultural barriers in Europe, and choose personnel not on the basis of passport color, but on the basis of ability to do the job. Many global corporations reflect such synergy, especially in its top management of mixed nationals and their combined cultures.

Whether leaders are dealing with reorganization or relocation, acquisition or merger, or structural or environmental changes, synergistic strategies improve performance and promote productivity. The overly competitive and individualistic approaches of the disappearing industrial work culture are giving way to teamwork and team management. Within the context of national, organizational, or team cultures, synergistic groups are found to be more friendly, helpful, secure, and comfortable with themselves, and higher in morale and performance.

Today, many global corporations outsource work to another part of the world, and this implies cross-cultural issues requiring the practice of synergy. For example, legal work from the UK is now being contracted for completion by lawyers in India. The primary reason is costs – a lawyer in London can charge up to eight times more per hour than an Indian counterpart. Legal process outsourcing (LPO) is growing fast with the global economic slowdown. Despite worries about confidentiality and quality, Western firms are increasingly utilizing those trained in the same legal system but living in different nations. This is especially true for document review and proofreading.[28] The same international business trend is expanding in the field of book, journal, and magazine publishing. The point is that such activities call for intercultural cooperation and collaborations on the part of those so involved.

Personal and electronic networking is another example of how synergy pays off, especially when intercultural interactions are involved. Such global networking may be either in person or through electronics. International networks are being established among practitioners of the same occupation or profession. Material-handling or training managers within the same multinational corporation or within the same industry group together in cooperative exchanges to enhance both knowledge and skill. Leaders would do well to use such networks for their own professional development and to accomplish tasks and objectives. The network concept is based on shared super-ordinate goals, power, and self-interest; influence is by competence, not by position. It is an open system featuring not only collaboration, but changing and participative leadership, consensus decision making and goal setting, and multiple use of multicultural resources.

Synergy, then, is an idea whose time has come because it builds upon cultural uniqueness while promoting peaceful cooperation instead of divisiveness and conflict. Learning about cultural differences and synergy should be a part of all management development, but is essential for those going abroad (Moran and Harris 1982). Leadership researchers Leonard Sayles and Robert Wright maintain that cultural awareness is a managerial instrument for reshaping an organization. They remind us that behavioral scientists have known for decades what today's executives are rediscovering: namely, what employees do, in contrast to what they are told, depends on the norms, values, and unstated beliefs of the corporation, as well as on the infrastructure of procedures, incentives, and division of labor. An organization's culture can be the key to high performance, as so many world corporations are discovering. Vibrant work cultures are marked by diversity and synergy, not necessarily homogeneity.

John Sherwood, a San Francisco-based organizational consultant, was among the first to write about high performance, high commitment work cultures.[29] Sherwood makes a compelling case for such a strategy, citing many progressive companies, such as General Electric, Procter and Gamble, Digital Equipment, and Ford, who are innovating in the redesign of work and organizational structure. As a result, he maintains their personnel exhibit energy because work is more challenging and significant; in such firms, continuous "learning" is emphasized and rewarded to produce quality performance. He recommends, as a tool for this purpose, establishing design teams to redesign sociotechnical systems. Sherwood believes that management will only succeed in gaining a competitive advantage when leaders change their views about people and the design of work, linking human and technical resources in a collaborative work *system*. He advocates many of the same approaches suggested in this text, emphasizing that leaders inspire and articulate the organization's vision – that is, its mission and a set of values for achieving its goals. This is the foundation of an organization's work culture that anticipates the future and encourages high performance.

Succeeding through high performance organizational cultures

Leaders influence whether their organizational cultures are high or low performing, ethical or unethical. Corporations, agencies, and associations can create a work culture that motivates and inspires personnel, or undermines their morale and productivity.

For decades, behavioral science management has confirmed what will turn workers on or off, what will promote their civil or uncivil behavior and their legal or illegal activities.

The organization's culture can promote harmonious team relations, or overwork and overstretch its people. A Hay survey of employees reported that sixty-three percent of workers think their employers do not appreciate their extra efforts, while fifty-seven percent reported feeling their bosses treated them like dispensable commodities.[30] The implication is that for the majority, their work culture is negatively affecting performance, possibly by too many reorganizations and reshufflings, as well as by an overload of memos, meetings, and cut-backs. Such conditions disturb the output of high potential workers or "HiPos" – they are doubly frustrated by the disproportionate share of a growing burden of work they must undertake, while senior positions dry up during recession.

Personnel are disheartened and disillusioned when executives get greedy and push for profits at any cost and in any way. Two sad examples of this were recently revealed in global corporations, such as Enron and BP. The former was guilty of unethical and illegal behavior, while the latter cut corners, allowed sloppy or inadequate maintenance of facilities, and ignored government regulations and warnings. When an American commission studied a huge BP oil well failure in the Gulf of Mexico, it concluded that the corporation had a culture of complacency along with neglect and insufficient concern for safety. An investigative report on the collapse of the financial giant, Lehman Brothers, a global investment banking house, revealed management failures, a destructive internal culture, reckless risk-taking, and financial manipulation.[31]

A more positive organizational culture seeks innovative ways to hire adequate staff and value their performance. Better than mere symbolic awards, HPLs discover ways to empower employees so they have more control over their work lives, such as by more flexible working hours. The aircraft maker, Bombardier, encourages managers to act as consultants to other divisions, while most companies give their personnel 3G devices, so they can accomplish administrative tasks while traveling. Creative organizations adopt strategies which promote high performers or those workers with high potential. Proctor & Gamble supports workforce "stars" to undertake "crucial roles" in solving difficult problems, while Hewlett-Packard invites them to attend high level corporate meetings and suggest solutions. Smart systems find unique methods to reward their "superstars" or "high-flyers."

Interaction

Leaders who wish to increase the cross-cultural effectiveness of work units can employ a variety of group processes, including case studies, critical incident analysis, role playing, and dramatics (see Chapter 8). Four sources of helpful learning materials for this purpose are the Intercultural Press (www.interculturalpress. org); Human Resource Development Press (www.hrdpress.com); Emerald Group Publishing (info.emeraldinsight.com); and Simulation Training Systems (www.simulationtrainingsystems.com). Here we will focus on two interactive techniques useful to managers – simulation and the quality circle.

Simulations for cultural understanding

Simulations are powerful training tools involving role playing with actors, or the use of computers or games. In this way, what might happen on a job in days or weeks can be telescoped into one or more hours. During a management or sales game, a life or work experience is recreated in a shorter time frame, according to established rules. People can practice behaviors in a simulated experience, just as a pilot trainee might do in an aircraft simulator. As people get more involved in such intensive learning experiences, their reactions are akin to their behavior at work. Simulation uses trial-and-error experimentation for problem solving, learning, and research – it is better to fail in a job simulation than in real life.

Simulations, for instance, can be used to prepare a group of managers assigned overseas to deal with the culture they will face. Simulations can also be used to better human relations among minority groups in the workforce. Simulations can be purchased in the form of games or software or created to meet specific needs. Exhibit 5.2 summarizes an interview I held with Dr Garry Shirts, founding president of Simulations Training Systems about the most popular of the simulations he has created. This game about cultural understanding comes in a box containing a facilitator's manual, audio CDs, and learning materials for practicing two simulated cultures, an imaginary Alpha and Beta.

EXHIBIT 5.2   BAFA BAFA – a cross–cultural training simulation

What happens in BAFA BAFA?

Participants live and cope in a "foreign" culture and then discuss and analyze the experience. There are two cultures in the simulation. The Alpha culture is a warm, friendly, patriarchal society with strong in-group out-group identity. The Beta culture is a foreign speaking, task oriented culture. Once the participants learn the rules, customs, and values of "their" culture they visit the other culture. The visitor is generally bewildered and confused by the strangeness of the foreign culture. Bewilderment often turns to intolerance and hostility once the visitor returns home. "They're strange, real strange, that's all I can say. They're making funny sounds and weird gestures. Just be careful when you go over there." But in the post-simulation discussion they come to understand that there were reasons behind the behavior they observed. With this realization, their attitudes change from one of hostility to understanding. Through discussion this experience is then generalized to attitudes towards other groups in the real world.

Who is it for?

Anthropologists, sociologists, psychologists, instructors of communication skills, minority studies, language, women's studies, as well as any training program, course, or situation in which it is important for the participants to have an experiential understanding of the meaning of culture. For example, the game is used by the Peace Corps, the Civil Rights Commission, American Field Service, the Census Bureau, and many other government and business organizations.

What is the unique feature of BAFA BAFA?

Probably the most unique feature of BAFA BAFA is that the interest and involvement reaches a climax in the discussion after the simulation rather than during the simulation itself. It is during this follow-on discussion that the mysteries

Continued

of each of the cultures are unraveled and the participants compare perceptions of one another's culture.

What does BAFA BAFA teach?

BAFA BAFA simulation is often used to introduce the notion of cultures, then followed up with a discussion and analysis of specific cultures and the way they are formed. "Betans" speak a "foreign" language made up of combination of vowels and consonants. It is easy to learn and use but difficult to understand if one does not know the rules governing its use. When "Alphans" hear the language, they often will not even believe that anything is being said, "It's gobbledy gook." Others feel intimidated by it and withdraw from the culture, creating an impossible communications barrier. Some are able to make themselves understood very easily with gestures, sign language and facial expressions. Each of these reactions creates excellent opportunities to discuss and analyze the communication process: the use of body language, feelings created by language, language snobbishness, and the attitudes one must have to learn a foreign language. Many instructors use BAFA BAFA to help trainees or students understand how stereotypes of other groups and cultures get formed and perpetuated. "They're cold, greedy, all they do is work," are some of the words Alphans use to describe the Betans. The Betans, on the other hand, come to believe that the Alphans are "lazy, unfriendly to outsiders, and don't like females."

As in life, these stereotypes become so strong and useful during the game that many students do not want to give them up. Unlike life, however, there is an opportunity during the analysis and discussion of the simulation to examine the stereotypes in a non-threatening and constructive manner. The fact that the students are not only the perpetrators of stereotyping but also the victims, makes it possible to confront the students with a mirror image of their own behavior. This mirror image allows them to see and understand the negative effect of stereotypes in a way that is not possible with lectures, films, and readings.

By the end of the discussion on stereotyping, the participants understand better the value of description over evaluation. The importance of asking, "In what ways are they different from us?" and "In what ways are they the same?" rather than "What is good or bad about their way of life?" After playing BAFA BAFA, participants report that they learned that:

1 What seems logical, sensible, important and reasonable to a person in one culture may seem irrational, stupid, and unimportant to an outsider.

Continued

2 Feelings of apprehension, loneliness, and lack of confidence are common when visiting another culture.

3 When people talk about other cultures, they tend to describe the differences and not the similarities.

4 Differences between cultures are generally seen as threatening and described in negative terms.

5 Personal observations and reports of other cultures should be regarded with a great deal of skepticism. It requires experience as well as study to understand the many subtleties of another culture.

6 Understanding another culture is a continuous and not a discrete process.

7 Stereotyping is probably inevitable in the absence of frequent contact or study.

8 The feelings which people have for their own language are often not evident until they encounter another language.

9 People often feel their own language is far superior to other languages.

10 It is probably necessary to know the language or a foreign culture to understand that culture in any depth.

11 Perhaps a person can accept a culture only after he or she has been very critical of it.

12 One should make up one's mind about a culture through observations and experience, rather than rely on what others say or write about it.

How long does it take?

It can be played in one fifty minute period and discussed the next. It is best, however, to allow one and a half hours for playing the game and a half hour minimum for discussion. Approximately 30–40 minutes should be devoted to preparations before the game is played.

How many participants does BAFA BAFA accommodate?

The lower limit at which the simulation can successfully be played is six people in each culture, but it probably would work, although with less impact, with five or even four. The maximum number is less fixed, but it would probably become unmanageable when the number gets larger than forty.

Are any consumable forms or special equipment needed?

Everything is included in the kit with the exception of the two cassette players and a chalkboard or newsprint pad. It is necessary to have an additional space besides the classroom such as a hallway, another classroom, a stage or patio.

Source: R. Garry Shirts PhD, Simulation Training Systems, PO Box 910, Del Mar, CA 92104, USA; Sales@SimulationsTrainingSystems.com.

Virtual reality simulations

The computer is a powerful tool for creating simulations through video games and social media that promote positive multicultural relations. One such is the Second Life simulation invented by two attorneys, Michael Carey (his real world identity (RI)), and Rose Springfield (her simulated identity (SI)).[32] This is an imagined community of Al-Andalus on the online 3D digital platform run by Linden Labs. It is a graphically rich, photo-realistic world which creates the illusion of being in medieval Spain on the southern Iberian Peninsula. The virtual world features Muslims, Christians, and Jews who live together harmoniously as they did in the real world of the Islamic caliphate.

Al-Andalus is a combination of history and fantasy, a metaphor for our multicultural future. The architecture is a virtual version of Alhambra's buildings and gardens, including a Grand Mosque. In its bazaar, virtual goods are sold for Linden currency, including furnishings and attire. Users explore the interaction modalities between different languages, nationalities, religions, and cultures within an Islamic social, political, and juridical environment. Within six virtual islands, accommodations may be rented by its avatar inhabitants, and real world visitors go there as tourists.

Second Life has more than seventeen million registered accounts with participants who average thirty-five years in age, seventy-five percent of whom live outside the USA. SI residents are primarily female, perhaps a result of a design for an open-ended social world with neither rules or tasks defined. Users chose their SI names, communicate in multiple languages using text or voice chat. SI populations function within a virtual economy in which they may purchase goods, services, land, and buildings. Some 770,000 customers from the real world visited this virtual world Al-Andalus in 2009, and using credit cards transacted $55 million in cash earnings via a PayPal account. While no one is required to buy or rent anything in Second Life, most sign up to have a simulated experience and exchange with other global members of the human family.

Simulation moon – Apollo 18

A leader can create a simulated situation from real life, from fiction, or from a likely future event that will promote learning among a work team, such as in the following example. This is a popular training game that can be used to instruct participants not only about cultural influences, but also about decision making.

All members are informed that they have been appointed to a NASA Task Force to assist with an emergency related to the first work crew to return to the Moon since the last Apollo mission in 1972. However, the trip is now made in two stages – Spaceship 3 to the International Space Station (ISS), then a transfer to second orbiter vehicle, called Apollo 18, to the lunar surface. All this is to prepare for the construction of a base on the Moon where the Global Space Administration expects to establish a permanent human presence off-world. This is to be the stepping stone for exploration of the universe, so that people will be less Earth-centric.

The incident. The crew of six departed successfully to the ISS, transferred to Apollo 18, which then landed them safely on the Moon. However, the vehicle developed a power problem and the crew is stranded on the lunar surface. Because this is the early stages of the lunar return, there is only one other functional orbital transfer vehicle (OTV) now docked at the space station. Another is nearing completion on Earth, and two others are in production. However, the second OTV in lower Earth orbit at the space station is still experimental and being tested. Its chances for a successful lunar mission are calculated by Houston Control at one in six. The six lunar astronauts have enough food, water, and support services to last them for only two weeks. If a rescue attempt is made and is successful, six lives will have been saved, as well as the prestige of the world space agencies involved. But if an attempt is made and fails, then the lives of the second OTV crew may also be jeopardized. If no other solution is forthcoming, and no attempt is made, the whole plan to return to the Moon permanently will be a failure, and the lives of the six lunar spacefarers are likely to be doomed.

The problem. Should the second experimental OTV be launched to recover the Apollo 18 pioneers? To ensure optimum conditions, the timing of the rescue orbit requires a decision within the next thirty-five minutes.

The analysis. When the group or sub-groups have reported their decision and their reasons, the facilitator should then raise these issues for further learning:

How do the cultures of the seventeen nations sponsoring this mission influence this decision? Were this to have been a decision of only the Russians regarding stranded cosmonauts, would the outcome be the same? The same question might be re-phrased for missions under the sponsorship of the space agencies of Europe, Japan, China, or India.

Would the decision change if two of the lost lunar astronauts included two women?

Did the group really explore other alternatives for solving the problem? For example, did this NASA Task Force consider seeking assistance from the Russians?

What process did the group go through in making this decision or arriving at a consensus? Was this culturally influenced? How does one's culture affect the choice-making process, especially when the outcome involves the value of human life?

Quality circles and work cultures

The concept of a quality circle was developed originally in the United States and transported to Japan by an American consultant. The Japanese adapted the technique so successfully that it was imported back to North America with further application and refinement. Westinghouse, for example, used the strategy to transform its corporate culture. Quality circles are useful to bring about planned change in a work culture, to promote worker participation, to increase performance, and in general to improve the quality of working life. Quality circles have been used by human resource specialists as a strategy for organizational renewal; a whole professional society has developed around the method explained below in Exhibit 5.3 by the International Association of Quality Circles (www.asq.org).

EXHIBIT 5.3   What is a quality circle?

Quality circles are voluntary groups of workers who have a shared area of responsibility. They meet together weekly to discuss, analyze, and propose solutions to quality problems. They are taught group communication process, quality strategies, measurement and problem-analysis techniques. They are encouraged to draw on the resources of the company's management and technical personnel to help them solve problems. In fact, they take over the responsibility for solving quality problems, and they generate and evaluate their own feedback. In this way, they are also responsible for the quality of communications. The supervisor becomes the leader in the circle and is trained to work as a group member and not as a "boss."

Quality circles consist of small groups of employees or teams doing similar work who voluntarily meet for an hour each week to discuss their quality problems, investigate causes, recommend solutions, and take corrective actions. A circle is primarily a normal work crew – a group of people who work together to produce a part of a product or service.

Circle leaders go through training in leadership skills, adult learning techniques, motivation, and communication techniques. The quality circle itself is trained in quality strategies, including use of cause and effect diagrams, histograms, and various types of check sheets and graphs. More advanced circles move on in their training to learn sampling, data collection, data arrangement, control charts, stratification, scatter diagrams and other techniques.

A typical quality circle includes five to ten members. If the department requires more than one circle, then a second leader is trained, and a second circle is formed. The circles then call on technical experts solving problems. Circle meetings are held on company time and on company premises. Where companies have unions, the union members and leaders are encouraged to take an active role in the circle, to attend leader training and to become fully aware of circle principles.

Source: Reprinted with permission of American Society for Training & Development, 1630 Duke Street, Alexandria, VA 22313 (www.astd.org).

This interactive process could be inaugurated by having the quality circle groups examine the existing work culture and propose what changes the participants would like in their work environment. Then management would be challenged to cooperate with their own personnel in planning, enhancing, and implementing these changes with quality circle members as leaders in the process.

Instrumentation

The two data gathering instruments presented next can be used by leaders to deal with cultural issues from two different perspectives. With the first, Cross-cultural

Relations Inventory (CRI), Exhibit 5.4, an individual may contrast his or her cultural background with another person of a differing culture. The second, Organizational Culture Survey Instrument (OCS), Exhibit 5.5, may be used by a leader or consultant to analyze the cultural dimensions of a particular human system.[33]

EXHIBIT 5.4 Cross-cultural relations inventory (CRI)

This CRI can be used for culture contrast purposes in two different ways, depending on whether one wishes to deal with a macro or a micro-culture. It can be employed to contrast one's own national heritage with another foreign culture, such as when an American is sent abroad as a manager, technician, or professional and wishes to analyze similarities and differences of home and host cultures. Or it can be used by an administrator or supervisor to compare their own cultural influences with a person they supervise or serve who comes from a distinctly different sub-culture. Thus, a white manager might utilize the instrument for self-learning about African American or Hispanic workers who report to that individual. Or, a Canadian health professional of English heritage might employ the process to better understand clients of the same nationality who come from a French–Canadian background. The instrument may even be used as a basis for contrasting cultures between institutions or organizations, especially during mergers or acquisitions. Within a company, for instance, it can be used to contrast the cultures of subsidiaries, plants, divisions, departments, and teams. The aim is to increase cultural awareness and sensitivity, while stimulating the respondent to obtain more accurate information about the two cultures under study.

This inventory is based upon the ten principal characteristics of culture suggested in the Input section. Although the inventory is filled out on an individual basis, it is best employed as a learning experience in a small group situation. For example, a project manager of a multicultural work team might have the members complete the form in terms of each other's cultural backgrounds; then they could share and discuss their analysis with the group as a whole. Or perhaps a group of engineers is being relocated into an Asian country – as part of their pre-departure training, a valuable learning experience could be conducted by comparing the engineers' national culture with that of the target land to which they have been assigned.

When working with a group or team, the facilitator may wish to follow this procedure:

1 Everyone fills out the Inventory privately as directed.

Continued

2 Individuals then share their insights on each of the ten principal characteristics of culture and try to arrive at some consensus as to the accuracy or
inaccuracy of their perceptions.
3 Summarize the consensus visually for the group by means of two columns
with ten classifications which may be displayed on a whiteboard, flip chart,
or overhead projector.
4 After editing, have this information transcribed and reproduced for distribution to participants and their supervisors.

(Note: If you are doing this learning exercise with other members of a group,
allow no more than thirty minutes to complete the form. Then participants will
be asked to share their information and insights with the whole group, correcting any gross inaccuracies in the process, and trying to arrive at some consensus
for each of the key categories.)
Directions. In the blank space provided, contrast your understanding of your
own culture (left column) with the one under review (right column) on the
basis of the ten principal characteristics below. Please be brief and only outline
with words, your ideas and illustrations on each point in terms of your relations
with people from the target culture.

Your name
_____

*Date of administration*_____

Name of your culture (this may be your own home majority or minority culture (e.g. Canadian, African American, etc.), or an organizational culture, as
desired).

_____

Name of target culture (this may be a host culture in a foreign country, a differing minority culture within your own society, or another organizational/team
culture).

_____

1 *Identity and purpose* (generally speaking, how do these people envision and
project themselves as a group; how do they express their sense of space
and purpose?)
_____
_____
_____

Continued

2 *Communication and language* (generally, what are the styles and systems for interacting, transmitting, and exchanging messages, both verbally and non-verbally? For example, what is the language of business and do any special media dominate the society?)

_____

_____

_____

3 *Dress and appearance* (generally, what is the look, style, and appearance of this group of people, both in terms of adornments, as well as image or reputation created? For example, is there anything distinctive about their clothing and its color, especially at business or work?)

_____

_____

_____

4 *Food and feeding customs* (generally, what distinguishes this people in terms of what, when, and how they eat, including food preparation, serving, and eating habits? What is distinctive about their diet or their use of meals to express themselves?)

_____

_____

_____

5 *Time and time consciousness* (generally, how do these people measure duration intervals, or differ in their time sense? Is there anything different about meeting times and arrivals?)

_____

_____

_____

6 *Relationships and sexuality* (generally, how do these people differentiate their associations with one another and strangers, whether in terms of kinship and gender, age and rank, position or status, rewards or recognition? Is there anything different about their family and marriage arrangements? Particularly note matters of bisexuality, and the status of either male or female in the group or society.)

_____

_____

_____

Continued

7 *Values and norms* (generally, what distinguishes the need and priority systems of this people in terms of importance? And, as a result, what behavior standards or expectations do they establish, explicitly or implicitly? For example, what about business ethics?)

_____

_____

_____

8 *Beliefs and attitudes* (generally, what is the philosophy of life of this particular group? What is the dominant force, such as religion or myths, that affect their outlook and possibly is expressed in various attitudes, rites, and rituals?)

_____

_____

_____

9 *Mental habits and learning* (generally, what distinguishes the thought processes of this people – such as the method of learning, emphasis upon logic and intuition, rote learning, whatever? Is there anything special about their systems of educating and training?)

_____

_____

_____

10 *Technology, work habits, and practices* (generally, what is the primary vocational focus of this people – hunting, agriculture, industrial, post-industrial, or high technology? What is the level of technology widely used? Is there anything distinctive about their view of the nature of work and the ways of organizing themselves for work, such as patterns, policies, and procedures? For example, are there peculiar attitudes or arrangements about caste, color pigmentation or race, gender, minority or majority personnel, foreign workers?)

_____

_____

_____

Participants are encouraged to add any other dimension of culture which is considered significant to distinguish the two cultures being analyzed.

EXHIBIT 5.5 Organizational culture survey instrument (OCS)

The ninety-nine items in this survey can be used by a leader to assess the culture of one's own organization, including one's own managerial perceptions. (With adaptation, the instrument can be used to study another organization's culture. Further, with slight changes, the survey can also be extended to a managerial group or the whole workforce so as to obtain more comprehensive data for analysis.)

Unless instructed otherwise, the respondent generally provides an effectiveness rating for the items by selecting a number on a seven point scale from one (lowest) to seven (highest). The inventory is divided into seven major sections – overall analysis, organizational communication, management team, work group, managerial self-perception, organizational relations, and organizational change.

The results can then be used to diagnose the health of a system and its need for change. If used with others, such as among various sub-units (e.g. a department or division), the findings can be tallied by section and group comparisons made. Within an organization, local norms may be developed. Among a management group which has filled out this form, individual results and differences in perception can be a basis of discussion, further action planning and learning.

Directions. This questionnaire should be as complete and authentic as possible. It provides you with an opportunity for: (a) giving feedback *anonymously* to foster your organization's development, (b) evaluating its key management, including yourself, and (c) understanding better your organizational environment, whether at home or abroad.

There are seven major sections to this inquiry, and a total of ninety-nine items seeking your opinion. A maximum of fifty minutes is being allowed for thoughtful completion of this inventory. Please consider your answers carefully for each point. Your first effort at responding should reflect your spontaneous reactions and thoughts on how you view your organization's culture from your position. If time permits, review your replies and make changes if necessary.

Name of organizational culture being analyzed:

Overall analysis

1. The goals/objectives of this organization are clearly defined and regularly reviewed.
   Effectiveness   1   2   3   4   5   6   7
2. Managers and supervisors at all levels have the opportunity to participate in this process of setting goals/objectives.
   Effectiveness   1   2   3   4   5   6   7

Continued

3. The organization has mechanisms for periodic evaluation of its achievement of goals/objectives.
   Effectiveness   1   2   3   4   5   6   7

4. Key management devotes adequate time to advanced, dynamic planning and involves subordinates in the process as appropriate.
   Effectiveness   1   2   3   4   5   6   7

5. Key management in this organization supports high achievers among employees.
   Effectiveness   1   2   3   4   5   6   7

6. Management regularly reviews the assignment of roles and responsibilities, as well as the delegation of authority for performance.
   Effectiveness   1   2   3   4   5   6   7

7. Key managers ensure that adequate personnel development and training are available for employees to carry out assigned tasks.
   Effectiveness   1   2   3   4   5   6   7

8. Management has an adequate system for regular and meaningful performance evaluation of employees.
   Effectiveness   1   2   3   4   5   6   7

9. The organization emphasizes cooperation as an operational norm.
   Effectiveness   1   2   3   4   5   6   7

10. The organization demonstrates commitment to providing satisfactory service to its clients/customers.
    Effectiveness   1   2   3   4   5   6   7

11. The organization utilizes well the human energies of its work force.
    Effectiveness   1   2   3   4   5   6   7

12. The organization rewards personnel on the basis of merit and performance, encouraging competence.
    Effectiveness   1   2   3   4   5   6   7

13. The work climate encourages employees to do their best and perform well.
    Effectiveness   1   2   3   4   5   6   7

14. The atmosphere in the organization encourages people to be open and candid with management.
    Effectiveness   1   2   3   4   5   6   7

15. The organization treats employees equally, regardless of their sex or race.
    Effectiveness   1   2   3   4   5   6   7

Organizational communication

16. Are you satisfied with the present state of organizational communications?
    Effectiveness   1   2   3   4   5   6   7

17. Do you think the communication between management and yourself is adequate?
    Effectiveness   1   2   3   4   5   6   7

Continued

18. Do you believe that organizational communications between central headquarters' staff and field personnel are satisfactory?
    Effectiveness   1   2   3   4   5   6   7
19. Do you believe that in your area of responsibility, communications is satisfactory between you and your subordinates?
    Effectiveness   1   2   3   4   5   6   7
20. Do you think there is adequate written communication in the organization?
    Effectiveness   1   2   3   4   5   6   7
21. Do you think there is adequate oral and group communication?
    Effectiveness   1   2   3   4   5   6   7
22. Are your satisfied that adequate communication is provided about organizational changes?
    Effectiveness   1   2   3   4   5   6   7
23. Your communication with various levels of management around you is *largely*
    downward ( )   upward ( )   circular ( )

Management team evaluation

In terms of upper-level management, the emphasis as I evaluate it is:

24. Clear organization objectives and targets.
    Effectiveness   1   2   3   4   5   6   7
25. Competency in themselves and their subordinates.
    Effectiveness   1   2   3   4   5   6   7
26. Providing a leadership model for subordinates.
    Effectiveness   1   2   3   4   5   6   7
27. Continuous, planned organizational renewal.
    Effectiveness   1   2   3   4   5   6   7
28. High productivity standards.
    Effectiveness   1   2   3   4   5   6   7
29. High service standards.
    Effectiveness   1   2   3   4   5   6   7
30. Experimenting with new ideas and approaches.
    Effectiveness   1   2   3   4   5   6   7
31. Encouragement of human resources development.
    Effectiveness   1   2   3   4   5   6   7
32. Coordination and cooperation in and among the organizational work units.
    Effectiveness   1   2   3   4   5   6   7
33. Conducting meaningful and productive meetings.
    Effectiveness   1   2   3   4   5   6   7

Continued

34. Confronting conflict directly and settling disagreements rather than avoiding or ignoring it.
    Effectiveness   1   2   3   4   5   6   7
35. Promoting creative thinkers and innovative performers.
    Effectiveness   1   2   3   4   5   6   7
36. Always *trying* to do things better.
    Effectiveness   1   2   3   4   5   6   7
37. Equal employment opportunity and affirmative action.
    Effectiveness   1   2   3   4   5   6   7
38. Creating a motivating environment for employees.
    Effectiveness   1   2   3   4   5   6   7
39. Open, authentic communications with each other and their subordinates.
    Effectiveness   1   2   3   4   5   6   7
40. Seeking suggestions and ideas from employees and the public (feedback).
    Effectiveness   1   2   3   4   5   6   7
41. Clarifying organizational roles and responsibilities so there is no confusion or overlap.
    Effectiveness   1   2   3   4   5   6   7
42. Teamwork and collaboration within and among upper-level management.
    Effectiveness   1   2   3   4   5   6   7
43. Effective concern for training subordinates to perform competently.
    Effectiveness   1   2   3   4   5   6   7
44. Willingness to consider innovations proposed to increase organizational effectiveness.
    Effectiveness   1   2   3   4   5   6   7
45. Sharing of power, authority, and decision making with lower-level management.
    Effectiveness   1   2   3   4   5   6   7
46. Policies and procedures that counteract absenteeism, slackness, and unproductivity.
    Effectiveness   1   2   3   4   5   6   7
47. Management of responsibility on the part of employees they supervise.
    Effectiveness   1   2   3   4   5   6   7
48. Problem solving and confronting issues.
    Effectiveness   1   2   3   4   5   6   7
49. Constantly improving working conditions, both physical and psychological.
    Effectiveness   1   2   3   4   5   6   7
50. Consistency in organizational policies and procedures.
    Effectiveness   1   2   3   4   5   6   7

Continued

Work group assessment

Please answer this section in terms of the work group you manage. That is, respond in terms of personnel who report to you or for whom you are responsible.

51. The atmosphere and interpersonal relations in my group are friendly and cooperative.
    Effectiveness   1   2   3   4   5   6   7
52. The members encourage one another's best efforts, reinforcing successful behavior.
    Effectiveness   1   2   3   4   5   6   7
53. The group organizes and problem-solves effectively.
    Effectiveness   1   2   3   4   5   6   7
54. The members maintain adequate standards of performance.
    Effectiveness   1   2   3   4   5   6   7
55. The group is open to and ready for organizational changes.
    Effectiveness   1   2   3   4   5   6   7
56. The members work effectively as a team.
    Effectiveness   1   2   3   4   5   6   7
57. The group communicates well within our work unit.
    Effectiveness   1   2   3   4   5   6   7
58. The group communicates satisfactorily with other work units.
    Effectiveness   1   2   3   4   5   6   7
59. The members provide group input and may participate in the management process as appropriate.
    Effectiveness   1   2   3   4   5   6   7
60. The group makes effective use of available equipment and resources (both material and human).
    Effectiveness   1   2   3   4   5   6   7
61. The members generally demonstrate pride in themselves and in their work.
    Effectiveness   1   2   3   4   5   6   7
62. The group actively seeks to utilize the skills and abilities of its members.
    Effectiveness   1   2   3   4   5   6   7
63. The members do not feel constrained by rules, regulations, and red tape in accomplishing their work.
    Effectiveness   1   2   3   4   5   6   7
64. The group is dynamic in its approaches and activities, that is, the work environment "turns people on."
    Effectiveness   1   2   3   4   5   6   7

Continued

65. The members of this group are not characterized by conformity and dependency.
    Effectiveness   1   2   3   4   5   6   7
66. The group has a record of consistent accomplishment in the organization.
    Effectiveness   1   2   3   4   5   6   7
67. The members in my work group generally exercise responsibility and achievement.
    Effectiveness   1   2   3   4   5   6   7

Managerial self-perception

68. As a leader in this organization, check the words or word combinations that best describe your management approach:
    ( ) idealistic   ( ) realistic   ( ) innovative   ( ) pragmatic
    ( ) cooperative   ( ) individualistic   ( ) task-oriented   ( ) sensitive
    ( ) change maker   ( ) change reactor   ( ) hard-nosed   ( ) imaginative
    ( ) inspiring   ( ) participative   ( ) traditional   ( ) futuristic
69. Do you seek out and use improved work methods?
    Rarely ( )   Sometimes ( )   Usually ( )
70. Does your managerial performance demonstrate sufficient skill in:
    administration   Rarely ( )   Sometimes ( )   Usually ( )
    human relations   Rarely ( )   Sometimes ( )   Usually ( )
    obtaining results   Rarely ( )   Sometimes ( )   Usually ( )
71. Do you reinforce and support positive behavior and performance in your subordinates?
    Rarely ( )   Sometimes ( )   Usually ( )
72. Do you actively encourage your subordinates to make the most of their potential?
    Rarely ( )   Sometimes ( )   Usually ( )
73. Are you willing to take reasonable risks in the management of your work units?
    Rarely ( )   Sometimes ( )   Usually ( )
74. Do you take responsibility to ensure that the employees you manage make their best contribution toward achieving organization goals and production targets?
    Rarely ( )   Sometimes ( )   Usually ( )
75. Do your key subordinates really know where you stand on controversial organizational issues?
    Rarely ( )   Sometimes ( )   Usually ( )
76. Do you demonstrate by example personal standards of competence and productivity?
    Rarely ( )   Sometimes ( )   Usually ( )

Continued

77. Are you generally objective, friendly but businesslike in dealing with employees?
Rarely ( )   Sometimes ( )   Usually ( )

78. Are you doing something specific for your own personal and professional development?
Rarely ( )   Sometimes ( )   Usually ( )

79. Do you take responsibility to seek change in organizational norms, values, and standards when these are not relevant and need updating?
Rarely ( )   Sometimes ( )   Usually ( )

80. Please read back to yourself the above 12 statements. In light of the demands of modern management and employee expectations, how would you rate the above evaluations of your leadership role?
Please check one: Inadequate ( )   Adequate ( )

81. A study by Michael Maccoby describes the new post-industrial organizational leader in this way: a gamesman, "in contrast to the jungle-fighter industrialist of the past, is driven not to build or to preside over empires, but to organize winning teams. Unlike the security-seeking organization man, he is excited by the chance to cut deals and to gamble." The author also states that such new leaders in top management are more cooperative and less hardened than the classical autocrats, as well as less dependent than the typical bureaucrats. This sociologist suggests that the new leader is more detached and emotionally inaccessible than his predecessors, yet troubled that his work develops his head but not his heart.
How does this description of the emerging executive fit you? (check one)
This is comparable to the way I am/feel.   ( )
I do not identify with this new type of manager.   ( )

Organizational relations

Please check the category that best describes the situation for you.

82. Employees generally trust top management.
Effectiveness   1   2   3   4   5   6   7

83. Employees usually "level" in their communications with management, providing authentic feedback.
Effectiveness   1   2   3   4   5   6   7

84. Employees are usually open and authentic in their work relations.
Effectiveness   1   2   3   4   5   6   7

85. If employees have a conflict or disagreement with management, they usually work it out directly or seek mediation.
Effectiveness   1   2   3   4   5   6   7

Continued

86. When employees receive administrative directives or decisions with which they do not agree, they usually conform without dissent.
    Effectiveness   1   2   3   4   5   6   7
87. Older managers are psychologically threatened by younger, competent staff members or subordinates who may have more knowledge, information, or education.
    Effectiveness   1   2   3   4   5   6   7
88. Managers are able to interact effectively with minority or female peers or subordinates.
    Effectiveness   1   2   3   4   5   6   7
89. Managers really try to b fair and just with employees, using competence only as their evaluative criterion of performance.
    Effectiveness   1   2   3   4   5   6   7
90. Many managers have "retired" on the job and are indifferent to needs for changing organizational renewal.
    Effectiveness   1   2   3   4   5   6   7
91. Employees have opportunities to clarify roles and relationships.
    Effectiveness   1   2   3   4   5   6   7
92. Is organization concerned about the needs of people as well as getting the task done?
    Effectiveness   1   2   3   4   5   6   7
93. Organization encourages and assists employees in the development of community relations.
    Effectiveness   1   2   3   4   5   6   7

Organizational changes

94. The organization is able to adapt to the dramatic shifts and changes under way in society and the larger culture.
    Effectiveness   1   2   3   4   5   6   7
95. The organization is able to handle the new demands made upon it as a result of the changes in top administration and management emphasis.
    Effectiveness   1   2   3   4   5   6   7
96. The organization does not seek adequate input from employees on those changes that affect them, or that they are to implement.
    Effectiveness   1   2   3   4   5   6   7
97. The organization is able to deal effectively with the new kind of person coming into your work force and management.
    Effectiveness   1   2   3   4   5   6   7

Continued

98. The organization has changed its management priorities and approaches with regard to scarce resources, as well as environmental and ecological concerns.
    Effectiveness   1   2   3   4   5   6   7

99. The organization is innovative in finding ways to improve the institutional environment.
    Effectiveness   1   2   3   4   5   6   7

Total the rating received in each category to summarize and gain insight into the contemporary culture of the organization or system being evaluated.

Note: Please recognize that cultural factors influence the way the above questions were constructed, and the way in which you responded. However, this evaluation can provide insight into your organizational culture in terms of Western perspective and future trends.

6

ENHANCING ORGANIZATIONAL AND TEAM RELATIONS

Introduction

Human relations affect the performance of the people in an organization. Such relations can be viewed from three perspectives: interpersonal (between individuals), intragroup (among members of a group), and intergroup (among groups that make up the organization or with external groups). Leaders should be aware of how these relationships affect their own behavior and may be used to enhance or undermine productivity. Awareness of and skill at human relations, applied to clients, customers, suppliers, and contractors, as well as government and community officials, increase goodwill and profitability. Finally, in the global marketplace, these insights have cross-cultural applications to improve the organization's international relations. Our first objective in this chapter is to understand relationships in terms of human systems in general and of organizations in particular. HPLs who truly appreciate the importance of organizational relations in achieving increased productivity devote time and energy to the following concerns:

- group characteristics, space, and change;
- group goals, norms, and values;
- group style, leadership, and influence;
- group roles, relationships, and responsibilities;
- group image, communication patterns, and feedback;
- group decision making and problem solving.

We will now examine organizational relations, focusing on the team. Because team management is one of the characteristics of the new work culture, leaders have to become more skilled in team formation and building. We will determine how to make teams productive, how to promote a helping relationship, and how to use conflict to achieve objectives. Many of the previous chapter insights can be applied here to a team's culture. We begin with a profile of a high performer in terms of team relations.

EXHIBIT 6.1   Profile of a HP scuba dive master and manager

Jason Winter Belport has always lived his dreams with a passion. Since his days at La Jolla Country Day School, and later at San Diego State University, he has consistently demonstrated leadership as a team player in a variety of sports and dramatics. At the age of six, he envisioned himself as a skin diver playing with dolphins, and he fulfilled that ambition as a young adult in the Caribbean when an orphan dolphin adopted Jason as his buddy for over a year. Certified as a scuba diver at the age of twelve, he gradually transformed his love of the seas and its creatures into a career as a high performing dive master, ship captain, and resort manager in the Cayman Islands.

Along the way, Jason mastered photography and became an aquatic artist as well. His undersea pictures were featured in national dive and travel magazines. In addition, he graduated from the US Coast Guard's Maritime Institute licensed to command ships up to one hundred tons. Today he is captain of a nine-ship fleet for the Reef Divers Corporation. In 2007, the world's most elite water explorers acknowledged his superior qualities as a diver and photographer by bestowing on him their Platinum Pro award for 5,000 successful dives. Belport's skill in team and customer relations was first manifested on Cayman Brac where he served for a decade as dive master and assistant operations manager. Now as manager of Little Cayman Beach Resort, he further demonstrates his unusual people talents, and is responsible for dive operations on both islands. He also demonstrated his leadership in the West Indies environment, business, and associations.

This multi-talented professional has battled numerous hurricanes, rescued boats and people in distress, and charmed clients. But it is his ability to develop staff teams that gains the support of top management. Jason and his Reef Diver teams share their ocean joys, wonders, and adventures with clients from all over the world. In the Cayman Islands, their guest divers experience a hundred different species, and five hundred types of fish.

(www.littlecayman.com; www.blueoceanart.com)

Input

Once again relationships are the key to successful individual and institutional performance. Career development, increased productivity or sales, and organizational effectiveness all depend to a great degree on positive human relationships. The Random House dictionary describes *relationship* as a connection, such as that of an individual with another individual or group. Apart from kinship through birth or marriage, relationship can refer to a special affinity, alliance, or association with one's fellows, such as with co-workers or professional colleagues. In a deeper sense, however, people confirm and express themselves in terms of their relationships with other human beings and creatures. The profoundest expression of relationship is love – between parent and child, husband and wife, friends, and even business partners. Our focus here will be on work relationships.

Two primary forms that relationships can take are:

- *Dyad*. Two people interacting (e.g. two peers working together or a supervisor and a subordinate). The dyad is the basis of interpersonal relations. Partners are important, for example, in police work.
- *Triad*. Three people interacting; the beginning of group or team relations. Triads affect morale and performance. Work teams may be three or more in number.

Systems approach to organizations and groups

In the Prologue, I described the organization as an energy exchange system. A *system* is defined as the regular interaction or interdependence of parts in a more complex, unified whole. It can be an ordered and comprehensive assemblage of facts, principles, and doctrines. For instance, a system may be manifest in a philosophy; tissues and organs of the human body; a perceived arrangement of heavenly bodies associated and acting together as a solar system; or a coordinated body of methods, schemes, classifications, and procedures as a management system.

In his classic book, *Living Systems*, James Grier Miller (1978) described seven levels of living systems: cell, organ, organism, group, organization, society, and supranational. We will consider here two of these systems, the group and the organization. Dr Miller offered helpful explanations of these terms. A *group* is a set of single organisms, commonly called members, that over a period of time or multiple interrupted periods, relate to one another face-to-face, processing matter, energy, and information. An *organization* is a system whose components and sub-systems may be subsidiary organizations, groups, and people; it is also a sub-system of one or more societies.

We can use a systems approach to analyze functional interrelationships in a group or organization. People in organizations enter into a "psychological contract"; they contribute their energy and information in return for role definition and compensation, which may take the form of money, benefits, or other types of rewards. In the modern corporation, for example, management is permitted to exercise power and authority over workers, but the employees enforce their expectations by giving or withholding work effort and energy. It is the quality of management relationships with personnel that influences performance and determines the success of organizational outcomes such as products and services. When workers find conditions in an organization unsatisfactory, they may withdraw their services, and even go on strike.

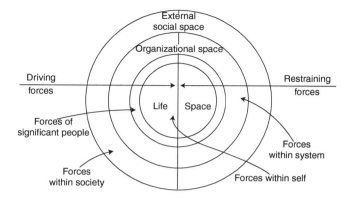

EXHIBIT 6.2   Conflicting forces affecting work relationships

In Chapter 3, we discussed the concept of life space, and in Chapter 5, we examined how culture contributes to the sense of space experienced by a whole people. Organizations, and their work units or groups, are also set apart by and identified by physical and psychological space. Again, organizational culture contributes to this process of delineation and demarcation. Individuals who belong to a group must integrate their life space with their divisional, team, or organizational space.

There are forces in both the individuals and institutions that influence behavior, including our image, needs, values, ideas, principles, standards, and expectations. Sometimes these may be in conflict and cause "binds" or frustrations for members – for instance, when individual values conflict with organizational values, or when employee norms are not in harmony with group standards. When leaders act as facilitators, they lead in resolving such conflicts and in promoting synergy between people and the enterprise. When organizational or group change is sought, these same forces may be seen as driving or restraining. Exhibit 6.2 shows this interplay of forces on behavior and relationships in terms of the system, the individual, and other significant people (e.g. co-workers, family, customers, suppliers). It is based on an analogy of taking pictures with a camera where we may get different images, so the operator seeks to bring these into focus by adjusting the lens. The four circles represent four differing life spaces and images which need to be synchronized.

The leader, like all group members, has a self-image and an image of the organization. The system, too, has an image of itself and of the individual. Other significant people related to the organization, such as managers or consultants, also have images of both the institution and its employees. As these images and spaces become more compatible or focused, performance is likely to improve. Thus, if an organization is committed to the value of quality work and excellence, the role of the leader is to focus the energies of followers so that they will be equally committed to that value, individually and as a team. By understanding organizational and group dynamics, leaders can synthesize differences and create consensus. For example, the *esprit de corps* and training system of the US Marines has made it possible for countless drill sergeants to weld raw recruits from diverse backgrounds into successful fighting units.

The interplay of organizational relations influences the attitudes and behavior of members. Leaders learn not only how to cope with these forces in every individual or institution, but how to control and manage them, so as to actualize the potential of both person and the organization. Leaders must do more, however, than exercise human relations skills to improve organizational relationships. The challenges for group leaders today are:

1 to provide for role enlargement, so that individual participation in the group and organization becomes more meaningful and effective;
2 to create temporary and supportive networks, groupings, and arrangements that cut across traditional divisions to promote cross-fertilization of ideas, knowledge, and specializations;
3 to increase the span of control, by increasing employee participation in management controls, in order to enhance individual initiative and responsibility;
4 to decrease distance between people at various levels within the organization, removing barriers to organizational communications.

In essence, HPLs aim to dismantle hierarchies and to decentralize, so as to increase membership participation. With regard to organization relations, they behave as facilitators rather than as order-givers.

Characteristics of effective groups

As social beings, humans take readily to group affiliation and formation. Some groups come together naturally out of common interests or concerns. Others are formed because of a common task or assignment; for example, a product team. It is possible to study a group's behavior – that is, its personality, culture, interactions, relationships, and performance. Our discussion of groups will be in terms of such work units and teams, A successful leader should understand his or her behavior in relation to groups, being able to observe the process and activities operating within them.

Groups have ten characteristics that leaders may analyze. For instance, to assess a project team performance, a manager can ask the questions suggested in each category below:

• *Group background*. Every group develops a history. Individually, members contribute to the group's character by reason of their own attitudes, interests, feelings, and competencies. When a group forms, each member has preconceived ideas and attitudes that influence directly the life and work of the group until that individual leaves it. What a group has experienced in the past affects its present and future. For example, technicians who work on a project team develop over time some unwritten agreements as to who does what and when. Observers must discover these arrangements by getting answers to: What is the team's history? What traditions has it developed? How does this affect relationships within the team and with other groups or the total organization?

- *Group participation patterns*. Participation in group activities and accomplishments is one way in which power is exercised – members influence the behavior, direction, and work of the team. Teams develop patterns of member interaction, which frequently change. Some of these patterns show the high emphasis placed on status, politics, forcefulness, and competence. Participation patterns affect what members do in a group; for instance, an overly dominant member who talks eighty-five percent of the time reduces the participation possibilities for the others. On the other hand, when there is free and democratic exchange within the group, the opinions and input of all are sought and expressed equally. Observers should seek to know: Is there sufficient opportunity for participation in this team, so as to bring out what various members are able to contribute? How do leader and members share participation and involvement?

- *Group communication patterns*. The system of verbal and non-verbal communication within a group can be objectively analyzed. Who talks to whom? What do they say? What are the effects? In analyzing oral communication, leaders should look for clarity of expression, common vocabulary, and the results. The body language of members – posture, facial expression, and gestures – can also be studied. Top management should communicate quickly and easily with employee groups. In analyzing group communications, seek answers to these questions: How clearly are the group's leader and members expressing their ideas? Does everyone understand the group's mission and what is going on? Are the verbal and non-verbal messages the same, and do they both aid communication?

- *Group cohesion*. When a group is working well together, it is attractive to members. Usually, cohesion is evident when elan or morale is high, members like one another, and are interdependent. Teamwork happens when people feel free to invest themselves in the group and contribute fully to the accomplishment of its tasks. Cohesion means that members work as one or as a unit for the common cause, and are concerned about the welfare of each member, as well as that of the whole team. Observers ask: How well does this collection of people work together as a team? Do members help each other? How willing are members to accept and act readily on group decisions?

- *Group atmosphere*. Cohesion depends in large part on atmosphere. To what degree does the group permit informality, freedom of expression, and acceptance of individual differences? In an unfriendly, formal, and rigid situation, members are unwilling to be open and to express themselves, especially when authentic feelings and ideas may seem to be in conflict with the group's directions. Instead, members tend to say what authority figures want to hear, and group energies may be wasted. When the group climate encourages frankness and participation, it facilitates sharing, leveling, and creative exchange. Observers analyze: Do members really feel free to express themselves in this group? How willing are members to listen and to share personal feelings or beliefs? How would you rate the group on its friendliness and informality?

- *Group standards.* As a group, members adopt, formally or informally, norms of behavior. This results from the need to coordinate group effort and activities toward a common goal. Such standards provide a guide for adjusting individual needs and resources to the group's requirements. These norms stabilize group energies and contribute to cohesiveness and improved performance. Observers analyze: Has this group developed standards on member responsibilities or team discipline? Are group expectations clear on such matters as ethics, operational behavior, protocol, and dress (i.e. what distinguishes this team's culture)?

- *Group procedures.* Every group needs to define ways to get its work done. Whether formally set down or just commonly understood, procedures should help team effort; they should be adequate and appropriate, not burdensome. The job is made easier when process allows for flexibility and innovation. For example, procedures that allow quick and effective group decision making are critical for high performance. Observers ask: What kinds of procedures does this group use to get its job done? How appropriate are these in relation to the type of this job?

- *Group goals.* Members must agree on and accept the group's primary purpose. This is necessary whether management has assigned the mission or the group has established its own objectives and priorities, and whether the goals are long-range or immediate. When goals are clear and all endorse them, members tend to be more supportive and committed. Goals must also be realistic; when they are, group members are more enthusiastic. Group goals motivate the membership when they are compelling, offer mutual advancement, include interim objectives that are attainable, and are subject to alteration when the situation requires it. Observers analyze: Do members have a clear understanding of the group's goals? Are the goals attainable given the group's resources? Are members supportive of these goals?

- *Group leadership.* A group may have an appointed leader or an elected leader, or group members may share leadership functions. Sometime the designated leader, such as the project manager, is not the real leader; a "natural" leader may emerge. The trend today is toward democratic and participative, rather than top down or authoritarian leadership. Group leaders should be flexible and responsive to situations and people, able to use both formal and informal structures and communications. With knowledge workers, for instance, those in leadership roles must be helpful, open to experimentation, and capable of resolving conflict and attaining consensus. Much of what we discussed about organizational leadership in Chapter 2 also applies in terms of group leadership. Observers analyze: How is leadership influence exercised in this group? How are leaders chosen and held accountable?

- *Group alignments.* Groups usually have sub-groups and affiliate with other groups with similar concerns. How many and what kind of sub-groups form depends on the group's size and make up. Sub-groups form because members have mutual needs or interests or because of shared friendship or antipathy toward other members or the group's direction. These sub-groups change as tasks, forces, or issues change. Although sub-groups are a normal occurrence, in the interest of healthy group relations, leaders should be aware of them and ready to respond creatively. For example, the formation of cliques based solely on race, gender, sexual preference, harmful habits (e.g. substance abuse), or resentment of some perceived exploitation, may undermine group effort unless confronted. Similarly, groups interface with other groups, and may form coalitions or working relations, so as to be mutually helpful. Thus, observers analyze: What sub-groups exist? Do they tend to work together as a whole, or do they dissipate group energies? What are the needs, issues, or forces behind the formation of these sub-groups? How does this group deal with other groups, and for what purpose?

The above ten categories provide a handy way for leaders to assess group performance; later we will provide instruments for this purpose.

Improving group performance

In the emerging high-tech work environment, executives and those in leadership positions will have to know more than finance, marketing, and technology. They will be leading workers into uncharted waters and places requiring special people skills. We have already indicated what some of these competences will be, including understanding group dynamics. Group relations are especially important in isolated, confined, extreme environments, for example, the special group challenges facing oil platform workers, scientists and contractors in Antarctica, or forest fire workers in remote locations; as well as spacefarers in an off-world environment.

Consider, as a case in point, the challenges to group interaction and group leadership that are posed by establishment of space stations and settlements colonies. NASA's report, *Living Aloft: Human Requirements for Extended Spaceflight*,[34] examined such issues as habitability, performance, organization, and management. What concerns us here is the section on small groups. Space crews are becoming larger and more heterogeneous, and space missions are longer. Living together in what amounts to a micro-society, astronauts depend for survival on cooperation. The isolation and confinement spacefarers must face has prompted leaders to study the findings of behavioral science research literature about group process and performance.

The following summary of some of the insights that Connors, Harrison, and Akins (1985) provided for that NASA report on NASA small group behavior may prove useful to managers on Earth concerned about high performance teams:[35]

- *Social compatibility* is a key ingredient in group member selection because incompatibility severely hurts morale and performance; members need interpersonal as well as technical competence.
- *Mixed gender groups* are the advantage of greater social diversity, but may face conflict on issues such as gender stereotyping and sexual harassment. These and other issues involving sexual prejudice and gender roles, such as leadership and command, must be resolved beforehand.

- *Diverse groups* with a broader age range and mix not only can work together effectively, but may possess greater human resources and experience.
- *Multicultural groups* may have a broader outlook and a wide range of skills, but they present special challenges for consideration in training regarding differences in perceptions and communications.
- *Work groups benefit* when members possess task competence, emotional stability, and cooperativeness (sensitivity to other people's needs, and concern for other people's welfare).
- *Work group members* should be selected and trained for such desirable attitudes and skills; an important goal of selection and training is member compatibility (members have different but complementary needs and skills).
- *Work groups composition* shows concern for acceptable size and homeostasis (group equilibrium). The balance between group responsibilities and the number of members may even favor slight understating, so that people stretch themselves to perform, as long as health and safety are not jeopardized in the process.
- *Group leadership and followership* involves mutual influencing and task-sharing, and social and emotional interaction.
- *Group cohesiveness or solidarity* results from the rewards and satisfactions of group membership; it is high when members experience intrinsically satisfying group activities, goals of importance, social support, and emotional gratifications.
- *Group harmony* should not be sought at the expense of performance; "group think" may lead to undermining critical thought and result in poor decisions, false optimism, fear of disapproval for expressing new alternatives, denial or rationalization of warnings or ill omens, and illusions of unanimity.
- *Group conflict management* should include dealing with deviancy, including reintegrating deviants into the team.
- *Group performance* involves an interaction process dependent upon three variables: the knowledge and skills of members; the amount of energy and effort members apply; and performance strategies and procedures followed (e.g. manipulating social standards – norms favoring conformity might undermine problem solving, while those favoring innovation might favor creative risk-taking).
- *Group continuity* depends upon whether goals are long-term or short-term; effective long-term group relations require strategies and methods for introducing and assimilating newcomers so that they are not disruptive but learn to share the group's history and knowledge base.
- *Group high performance* depends on developing a delicate balance between the independent action of individual members and the social influence of the group.

Leadership in high performance teams

In the industrial age, organizational relationships tended to be long term; today, the new work culture often features intense, temporary relationships with colleagues. The high performance business environment, for example, emphasizes team management and ad hoc relationships formed for task forces, product teams, and other time-limited work arrangements. Such groups come rapidly into being, function for a period, and then are phased out. Personnel must, therefore, learn to jump quickly into such task oriented situations, establish connections and communications with co-workers from different disciplines or work units, and then disengage when the mission is accomplished. All this may happen while one maintains a dual relationship with another group that serves as one's base in manufacturing, marketing, finance, or information systems. This type of matrix management system may involve a worker reporting to two supervisors, one from the functional group and another who coordinates a special project. Once the special project is over, the worker may be assigned to another temporary group, and the cycle repeats itself.

Organizational realities such as these make new demands upon leaders and knowledge workers to develop team skills. In the Interaction section of this chapter we will deal with the need for team building, but what should our aim be in any team development?

My research indicates that there are certain behaviors practiced by team members that help their relations with others in the group and with others in the organization. These behaviors include:

- taking an interest in both individual and team accomplishments;
- tolerating ambiguity and the seeming lack of structure at times;
- giving and receiving feedback sensitively and non-defensively;
- creating a team atmosphere or culture that is informal, comfortable, and non-threatening;
- encouraging team participation, joint decision making, and consensus seeking;
- being open to planned change, risk taking, and innovation
- valuing listening and circular communication;
- being concerned about strengthening team morale and commitment;
- clarifying roles, relationships, and responsibilities;
- fostering trust, supportive norms, and shared leadership;
- resolving conflicts and using this energy constructively;
- promoting cooperative and collaborative relations (synergy) among members and with other work units;
- being (as a team) goal oriented, self-evaluating, and linked to other organizational groups.

Such behaviors not only improve organizational relations, but also effectiveness as an enterprise. A culture in which people act in this manner encourages positive social exchange and interpersonal interactions. HPLs ensure that groups do not waste time and talent on useless conflict and competition. The very differences in the perceptions of group members can become a source of strength for the team, enriching the mix of the inputs and insights. Realistically, individuals may disagree on such issues as team strategies, problem solving, accountability, resources, and scheduling. But with synergistic attitudes, such differences can be resolved and built upon. As Andre Van Dam, former director of planning for Corn Products Company – Latin America, once said to me: "Admittedly, cooperation requires trade-offs between rival ideas or interests – trade-offs imply negotiation. Cooperation hinges upon the recognition of common as well as conflicting interests."

The above characteristics can enhance team relations and performance particularly in regard to two critical factors, decision making and conflict management. Leadership ensures that such collaborative teams function in this manner (Parker 2010).

Improving team decisions

The character of a group is influenced by the way the group makes decisions; this process can foster or undermine the entity's progress. Ideally, decision making should be integrative, that is, it should advance the common good of the group. Psychologist Eric From maintains that the more one learns through making choices, the more one becomes truly free (instead of being limited by acting upon instinct, cultural conditioning, or provincial interests). When people are given the opportunity to exercise control over team choices, the group becomes a democratic laboratory for people to grow in decision making skills. When those who must implement the decision are involved in the choices, not only is the decision likely to be better, follow-up on the decision is likely to be more thorough.

If freedom of choice is a prevailing norm, personal growth takes place as group members become aware of possibilities, alternatives, and consequences of following a specific course of action. Teams now have added technological resources to help with this process, for instance, improved information retrieval, system and program analysis, computer simulations, and decision-tree methodology.

Team decisions are further enriched when other, previously discussed characteristics of effective groups are present, such as competent members, mutual trust, and shared leadership. Poor communications within the team, conflicting loyalties, and internal ego struggles, on the other hand, weaken a group's resolve and undermine the decision process. A too-rigid decision making procedure may also inhibit imagination and thus group problem solving. Premature decisions based upon inadequate information can also prove fatal.

If team decisions that improve performance are to be made, then members have first to consider the quantity and quality of the information available upon which to base a choice. Obviously, if it is inadequate, further data gathering and analysis are called for. The next step is the adoption of the problem solving method. This may range from the (less desirable) parliamentary procedure to (more useful) consensus approach. Scientific and computer models, such as PERT (Program Evaluation and Review Technique), can be effective for this purpose. When involved with project management of a global team composed of varied national cultures, then special skills are required.[36]

Exhibit 6.3 discusses strategies for problem solving in groups devised by the late behavioral scientist, Gordon Lippitt. It is an eight-stage procedure for team members to follow when major decisions are at stake. As people increase in awareness and knowledge through the group decision experience, their potential grows for making better, informed, intelligent choices. When leaders are autocratic and make the decisions for the followers, they cut off these development prospects and endanger the organization's future growth.

EXHIBIT 6.3   Team problem solving strategies

1 *Clearly define the problem.* Set the limits of group responsibility and provide necessary clarifications. Analyze resources available for solutions and conditions involved in the problem.

2 *Define the responsibility for decisions.* Who has the ultimate authority to make the decision? If the group is to assume this responsibility, then the degree of its freedom to act should be understood.

3 *Communicate ideas and alternative solutions.* Consider a wide variety of creative and innovative ways to resolve the problem without evaluation; here is where brainstorming may be an effective technique.

4 *Examine the group size.* Should the group be too large for effective decision making, it may be preferable to break into sub-groups to consider the problem and then reassemble to consider the data developed in the smaller groups.

5 *Test alternative solutions.* Through simulation or projection into the future, the group can imagine results based on certain courses of action; trials or pilot projects may be made of selected alternatives, to provide data for appropriate decisions at a later time. Consider the demands various solutions will make upon individual and group resources.

6 *Specify responsibility and delegation.* During the planning, the group needs to think about how various decisions are to be carried out. What commitment will be required of various members for a decision to become effective?

7 *Agree on methods of decision making.* Before the issue is resolved, the group must first reach agreement on the procedures to be used in arriving at a decision. What criteria and standards will be used in choosing one alternative over another?

8 *Concur on actions and evaluation.* When the group has made final its choice, then it must organize itself to carry out the decisions. Individual, committee, or project assignments need to be made and accepted. Perhaps a report is to be written with management recommendations. Finally, a means to evaluate the action planning is necessary in case it should prove to be unwise.

Source: Based on G.P. Likert, P. Langseth and J. Mossop, *Implementing Organizational Change.* San Francisco, CA: Jossey-Bass, 1985.

Team conflict resolution

There was a time when leaders considered conflict a negative factor within organizational life, something to be avoided at all costs. This "happy ship" approach to conflict has given way to a more balanced strategy, in which a reasonable amount of conflict is permitted, to maintain a healthy tension and excitement in the group. Conflict management should be considered in the context of corporate industrial relations policies, and should become part of a "win-win" strategy of negotiations. When conflict is viewed as energy, to be used instead of abused, its proper management can stimulate group action in place of boring conformity. Limited conflict among team members, for instance, may contribute to optimizing satisfaction and performance efforts.

When properly managed, it may bring more input, wider consideration of alternatives, and improved solutions. In its positive aspects, conflict can identify issues that have not been confronted or problems that are not recognized. Had the crew of the orbiting Skylab 4 not got into conflict with their ground controllers, those astronauts might have remained saddled with a work schedule that could have undermined their morale and impaired their performance (Harris 2009). If conflicting views with other groups or within a team are synthesized, not only may a better solution emerge, but participants are more committed to making it work. Such disagreements, when professionally handled, can force the contending parties to identify mutually beneficial goals or arrangements. Obviously, conflict, whether in an individual or institutional situation, can prove dysfunctional and can undermine peak performance. To contain the destructive elements in conflict energy, social scientists have developed two models of conflict management – structural and process (Schein 1985).

The structural model traces conflict to four sources:

1 *Behavioral predispositions* related to individual inadequacies, in turn related to attitudes, needs, motivation, competence, and other personality qualities. Conflict can arise when the person with these problems projects them onto the group.
2 *Social pressures* from within a group or with other groups, or from outside persons or systems.
3 *Incentive structures* where the distribution of rewards to both cooperative or noncooperative actions, or the existence of a conflict of interest, can cause conflict.
4 *Procedural arrangements* manifested in rules, regulations, customs, and conventions which may be open to differences in interpretation or become inoperative and ineffective.

The process conflict model, on the other hand, focuses on five variables related to specific episodes of disagreement:

1 *Perceived frustration* in the satisfaction of a need or achievement of a goal.
2 *Conceptualizations* based on individual perceptions that may be distorted and magnify one's frustrations.

3 *Behavioral practices* that maximize or minimize the conflict.
4 *Behavior by the other party* (reaction) that may escalate, contain, or de-escalate conflict.
5 *Outcomes* including resolution and future cooperation, compromise and accommodation, and mistrust and hostility.

As we understand more about conflict and its causes, team members can learn to cope with it better and not to react with panic. A staff meeting or group training session can be devoted to examining this issue. Exhibit 6.4 provides eight points for stimulating meaningful analysis.

EXHIBIT 6.4 Dimensions of conflict

(This material can be used for IB when each group member is assigned one point to read, react to, and report upon to the whole team.)

The following ideas are presented to stimulate small group discussion about the subject of conflict, whether it is between individuals or groups.

1 *Conflict is a relationship.* It takes at least two people, groups, or even nations to have a conflict. Do we permit the experience to develop so that issues, not personalities, can be confronted? Exploring differences can result in useful insight and information if we do not cut off the relationship before data is sufficiently generated for analysis.

2 *Conflict is energy.* Human effort is necessary to maintain it, so the critical question is whether we can use this energy constructively or permit it to be wasted. Conflicts cannot always be resolved when their source, for example, is a sick sense of self. Sometimes the individuals have to be honest with one another and "agree to disagree" while respecting one another.

3 *Conflict can be defused.* If we do not deliberately seek and promote conflict, there are strategies which a leader can pursue to minimize unnecessary conflict in the organization or community. When the situation that can lead to conflict is not yet critical, when it is still simmering, an innovative supervisor can "head it off at the pass." Like the bomb detection squad that deactivates weapons, a manager can confront or resolve situations that might end up in serious conflict. He or she can keep combustibles apart and can deal with differences of opinion before they get out of hand.

4 *Conflict is aided by hardening of positions.* When people become inflexible and rigid out of a sense of fear or threat, they tend to set hard boundary rules, to draw lines and dare anyone to step over, to polarize in their positions. In periods of profound transition, like today, conflict seems to be growing as people experience "future shock." Pluralistic societies require cooperation rather than dogged adherence to past traditions and positions.

Continued

5 *Persons are in conflict.* Human relationships are strained, tension is increased, and emotions run high during conflict situations. Reason can work only when the situation is "cooled," objectified rather than subjectified. Keep in focus that "feelings" are involved, and try to shift discussion to the issues. Yet it is just as bad to over-emphasize the interpersonal elements in conflict as it is to depersonalize intergroup conflict.

6 *Conflict involves perception.* The apparent conflict may sometimes be caused by misunderstanding or misperception of the situation. Clarify each person's true position, and you might discover that there is no real conflict, or at least it is not so great that it cannot be handled.

7 *Collaboration is the opposite of conflict.* One way to reduce undesirable conflict in organizations is to encourage team building, consulting skills, and the development of a "helping relationship" among staff.

8 *Conflict happens because people are different.* People come from diverse cultural, social, and educational backgrounds, which form or condition their unique life spaces or perceptions.

Conflict can be managed, rather than denied by flight-or-fight behavior. When conflict in groups is not confronted so that differing viewpoints and opinions are considered, the individuals may resort to delusion or fantasy. HPLs not only understand the nature and causes of conflict, but use mediation resources to resolve it. HPLs minimize conflict by promoting organizational and team relations that are positive and supportive.

Interaction

Among the many group process opportunities for improving organizational relationships, team building is among the most valuable. Team building is most effective when it uses an internal or external consultant familiar with the process, although a concerned manager who is a good facilitator can conduct such sessions with the help of management development texts, instruments, and films. Team building can improve team relations among group members, and promote positive intergroup relations among various teams or work units. Team building meetings aim at group maintenance and consider such performance issues as:

- How do we work together?
- How do we resolve conflict?
- How do we solve problems and make decisions?
- What are our roles and relationships on this team?
- What are our relationships with other groups?
- What changes are needed in how we function?

Team building conference

- *Who?* Members of a work team or teams who must relate to each other and a facilitator from outside.
- *What?* A series of intensive learning experiences about team structure, process, and relationships.
- *When?* With the start-up of a team, when a group's performance level declines, or when the group is having difficulties with other teams.
- *Where?* If feasible, begin away from the work site (for instance at a conference center or weekend resort), then continue with monthly meetings in an on-site company meeting room or training facility.
- *Why?* To improve team collaboration and performance by clarifying team expectations, goals, resources, and potential:
  - analyzing interpersonal dynamics;
  - confronting and clarifying issues that block mission accomplishment;
  - examining team relations with other work units or external groups;
  - developing leadership skills in communication, cooperation, problem solving, and conflict resolution.

- *How?* By structured exercises, role playing, data gathering, and analysis, as well as problem solving, the group learns how to work together more efficiently and effectively. Members are urged to:
  - be experimental – test out new styles of behavior, communication, participation, and leadership;
  - be authentic and open – tell it like it is and avoid game playing, while considering others' viewpoints;
  - be sensitive and empathetic – express feelings while empathizing with others; be attuned to non-verbal cues and communication;
  - be spontaneous and helpful – respond creatively to here-and-now data shared in the group, warmly receiving people's revelations of themselves, and sharing yourself while assisting other members.

The team building conference not only develops meaningful relations among members, but enables them to become more trusting and congruent (comfortable with themselves and their capacities). It is a challenge to participants to revise their self-images and to actualize their potential through personal and group change. The learning experience aids members to gain control over their own team space and to risk becoming what they are capable of becoming. If a company or agency does not have a competent facilitator on its staff to conduct the team building, external consultants in organization development or transformation are available.

The helping relationship exercise

People have many opportunities to promote organizational effectiveness by practice of the "helping relationship," for example when a manager gives feedback to a subordinate, when a co-worker seeks assistance in solving a problem, or when a customer or supplier needs information or service. Despite the best of intentions, our "help" is seldom really helpful, particularly with colleagues or team members. To enable people to grasp this important concept and become skillful in its application, I recommend the S/H/O method. This method involves a triad of team members – a seeker of help (S), a helper (H), and an observer (O). They decide among themselves who takes what role, and they may later switch roles until all members have played all three. Although this strategy can be used with actual or simulated issues, I urge the "seeker" to bring a real problem related to a team or work unit. The manager or facilitator sets the ground rules for the process, such as a time schedule (e.g. five to fifteen minutes for each role – for S to present the problem, H to counsel on solutions, and O to offer analysis and comments upon observations made). If the length of the staff meeting or training session permits, then the process can be repeated twice more until all three experience all roles.

While S presents the problem, H carefully listens to comprehend its scope and may ask questions for clarification purposes. When the sequence shifts to the helping time frame, H then assists, consults, or counsels. The observer is both a time-keeper and note-taker for the process. Exhibit 6.5 provides the criteria to be read and used by O in his or her evaluation of the helping relationship underway. Later, when O shares findings with the other two, a copy of these guidelines can be distributed and discussed among the triad. O can begin the feedback session by asking S if that person actually received any help from H. The principal learning outcomes for the members involved should be to learn the nature and importance of an interpersonal relationship, which are:

- accepting: an unconditional, positive regard of the other person's worth is manifested.
- authentic: the helper is genuine in approach and does not play games at the expense of the seeker of help.
- empathetic: the helper expresses understanding, is neutral, and places himself or herself in the other's life space.
- non-evaluative: the helper avoids being judgmental of the person with a problem and making that individual feel defensive.

EXHIBIT 6.5   Criteria for a helping relationship

GUIDELINES FOR OBSERVERS

The helper is in effect a consultant who provides added resources and a means for permitting the one in need to reflect more objectively upon his problem. The helper seeks to assist the other person to mobilize his own capacities to resolve the issue at hand or to develop his potential. The helper must first check

Continued

his own reasons for wanting to give help; is it merely to gain recognition? to demonstrate superiority? to exercise power over another? to be a do-gooder? or to make the other person dependent upon him? Whose needs does he seek to serve – his own or the other person's? Furthermore, he should be able to listen and to let the other person exercise some responsibility in developing solutions.

On the other hand, the receiver of help must be ready and willing to accept assistance from another; he must face up to those inadequacies which make it necessary for him to obtain outside help. The receiver must be able to lower his own defenses if help is to be effective and to offer an open mind to the communication of the helper. The receiver must avoid undue dependency on the helper while realizing that the particular competence of the helper may enable the receiver to tap unused inner strengths in resolving the problems he faces.

Individuals can best give help to one another when the atmosphere in an organization permits expression of true feelings, when intimacy and flexibility are possible in behavior and when change is an accepted norm. Unfortunately, many systems today are in need of renewal, and such an organizational environment is more ideal than real. One of the greatest means for personal growth within organizations is the process of feedback. It is a manifestation of real help when feedback or authentic communication is given and received freely in a sensitive, caring manner.

Feedback is that aspect of the communication process, verbal or non-verbal, which allows for the expression of feelings, attitudes, and thoughts so the communicator may be more effective. The feedback process is a means for improving behavior and performance. Feedback, in a sense, is a system of messages or cues which are sent and received. When a message has been sent from the originator and received by another, and a second message returned to the originator, and the originator reacts to the feedback, the process has been completed. The implication in human relationships is that "feedback is a way of helping another person to consider changing his behavior." It can be seen as a mechanism for helping a person to learn how one's behavior matches one's intention. Thus feedback is more than just a mechanical process but rather a means to learn, to grow, and to "become." It can aid or abort organizational relations. The following exercise encourages members to seek help from one another and to be collaborative.

Instrumentation

The next two data gathering instruments enable a leader to assess an individual or team's performance in group meetings:[37]

Individual behavior analysis (IBA)

This instrument is designed to help in the diagnosis of the level of a person's interpersonal performance skills within a work unit, team, or group. The range of inquiry goes from ascertaining the extent to which that individual helps others express their ideas in group communication, to determining how conflict is managed. The inventory is for self-assessment or for evaluation by another. A five-point rating scale is employed on thirty-six items in which the respondent is to choose the word which best describes the individual's performance – always, often, occasionally, seldom, or never. With the exception of items 10, 12, 18, and 22, selection of the last three rating possibilities usually indicates a need for improvement. The instrument can be used for self-improvement purposes, for use during performance evaluation between a leader and team member, or for group discussion during team building (refer to Exhibit 6.6).

EXHIBIT 6.6   Individual behavior analysis (team member)

Group_____

Date_____

Name of person you are describing:_____

The person you are describing is: (check one)

myself   ☐
my superior   ☐
my subordinate   ☐
my peer   ☐
other   ☐

_____

_____

_____

Instructions. Following are listed thirty-six descriptions of ways in which people participate in group meetings. For each item, choose the alternative which comes closest to describing how the person performs in this group meeting. Answer the items by marking an "x" on the line in front of the alternative that best expresses your feelings about the item. Mark only one alternative for each item. Keep in mind that you are evaluating this person's behavior in this meeting, and not how you have seen him/her perform in other settings.

1 Helps others express their ideas.

always   ☐
often   ☐
occasionally   ☐
seldom   ☐
never   ☐

Continued

---

2 Tries to understand the feelings (anger, impatience, rejection) which others in the group express.

always	☐
often	☐
occasionally	☐
seldom	☐
never	☐

3 Shows intelligence.

always	☐
often	☐
occasionally	☐
seldom	☐
never	☐

4 Sympathizes with others when they have difficulties.

always	☐
often	☐
occasionally	☐
seldom	☐
never	☐

5 Expresses ideas clearly and concisely.

always	☐
often	☐
occasionally	☐
seldom	☐
never	☐

6 Expresses own feelings (for example, when he/she is angry, impatient, ignored).

always	☐
often	☐
occasionally	☐
seldom	☐
never	☐

7 Is open to the ideas of others; looks for new ways to solve problems.

always	☐
often	☐

Continued

occasionally ☐
seldom ☐
never ☐

8 Is tolerant of other people's feelings and beliefs.

always ☐
often ☐
occasionally ☐
seldom ☐
never ☐

9 Thinks quickly.

always ☐
often ☐
occasionally ☐
seldom ☐
never ☐

10 Is angry or upset when things do not go his/her way.

always ☐
often ☐
occasionally ☐
seldom ☐
never ☐

11 Is persuasive, a "seller of ideas."

always ☐
often ☐
occasionally ☐
seldom ☐
never ☐

12 You can tell quickly when he/she likes or dislikes what others do or say.

always ☐
often ☐
occasionally ☐
seldom ☐
never ☐

Continued

13 Listens and tries to use the ideas raised by others in the group.

always ☐
often ☐
occasionally ☐
seldom ☐
never ☐

14 Helps others in the group to express their feelings (for example, when they are irritated or upset).

always ☐
often ☐
occasionally ☐
seldom ☐
never ☐

15 Demonstrates high technical or professional competence.

always ☐
often ☐
occasionally ☐
seldom ☐
never ☐

16 Is warm and friendly with those with whom he/she works.

always ☐
often ☐
occasionally ☐
seldom ☐
never ☐

17 Is able to get the attention of others.

always ☐
often ☐
occasionally ☐
seldom ☐
never ☐

18 Communicates feelings. He/she does not have a "poker face" front.

always ☐
often ☐
occasionally ☐
seldom ☐
never ☐

Continued

19 Is quick to adopt new ideas.

always ☐
often ☐
occasionally ☐
seldom ☐
never ☐

20 Encourages others to talk about whatever is bothering them.

always ☐
often ☐
occasionally ☐
seldom ☐
never ☐

21 Comes up with good ideas.
always ☐
often ☐
occasionally ☐
seldom ☐
never ☐

22 Pride is hurt when this person feels he/she has not done his/her best.

always ☐
often ☐
occasionally ☐
seldom ☐
never ☐

23 Pursues his/her points aggressively.

always ☐
often ☐
occasionally ☐
seldom ☐
never ☐

24 Usually know where you stand with him/her.

always ☐
often ☐
occasionally ☐
seldom ☐
never ☐

Continued

25 Encourages others to express their ideas before he/she acts.

always   ☐
often   ☐
occasionally   ☐
seldom   ☐
never   ☐

26 Tries to help when others become angry or upset.

always   ☐
often   ☐
occasionally   ☐
seldom   ☐
never   ☐

27 Tries out new ideas.

always   ☐
often   ☐
occasionally   ☐
seldom   ☐
never   ☐

28 Is competitive. Likes to win and hates to lose.

always   ☐
often   ☐
occasionally   ☐
seldom   ☐
never   ☐

29 Presents ideas convincingly.

always   ☐
often   ☐
occasionally   ☐
seldom   ☐
never   ☐

30 Responds frankly and openly.

always   ☐
often   ☐
occasionally   ☐
seldom   ☐
never   ☐

Continued

31 Is willing to compromise or change.

always   ☐
often   ☐
occasionally   ☐
seldom   ☐
never   ☐

32 If others in the group become angry or upset, listens with understanding.

always   ☐
often   ☐
occasionally   ☐
seldom   ☐
never   ☐

33 Offers effective solutions to problems.

always   ☐
often   ☐
occasionally   ☐
seldom   ☐
never   ☐

34 Tends to be emotional.

always   ☐
often   ☐
occasionally   ☐
seldom   ☐
never   ☐

35 Talks in a way that others listen.

always   ☐
often   ☐
occasionally   ☐
seldom   ☐
never   ☐

36 When feelings run high, deals directly with them rather than changing the subject or smoothing the problem over.

always   ☐
often   ☐
occasionally   ☐
seldom   ☐
never   ☐

Team performance survey (TPS)

TPS can be used for data gathering before or after a team building session. Members of project teams or other work units can use the survey to evaluate a group's progress and problems from a team perspective. Then the participants can compare their selection on the twenty-five items for further discussion, clarification, and learning.

To record total group scores, a matrix can be presented by PowerPoint software, drawn on a whiteboard, flip chart, or other screen projection, containing four columns on which the headings or choices are written horizontally across the top (yes, sometimes, no, uncertain). Vertically on the left side, insert the numbers 1 to 25. Each team member would then be invited to place their personal rating checks for all items on the display matrix for other members to see. By tallying up the results for the group on each item, trouble spots in team relations then could be identified. For example, with reference to item 1, in a team of eight persons, if four of them marked "no" and one checked "uncertain," the majority indicate that the group's goals are uncertain. In this way, a leader and team can diagnose the healthiness of the group's development and where improvements are desirable for increased performance (refer to Exhibit 6.7).

EXHIBIT 6.7 Team performance survey

Name of the group you are describing:_____
(e.g. a project or product team, or a task force).

Date:_____

Instructions. Please consider each item relative to the above work unit or team during a meeting in which you are participating or observing. Kindly check for each item in the box which best describes your evaluation or opinions about this group at this session:

	Yes	Sometimes	No	Uncertain
1 This group's goal or mission is quite clear to me.	—	_____	—	_____
2 The group's charter in terms of mandate parameters, and time frame is evident to me.	—	_____	—	_____
3 My role and relationship to team members and other functional units is clearly understood by members.	—	_____	—	_____
4 The team shares a sense of being accountable individually for the group's results.	—	_____	—	_____

Continued

---

5 From my perspective, the material and human resources available to the group's tasks are adequate.

6 Member competencies are sufficient to help this team accomplish its goal.

7 In my opinion, this team lacks some members in the organization who are vital to its success.

8 The team works well together and has cohesion.

9 The members of this group do not feel free to level with one another, hiding true opinions and feelings.

10 Some members of this team seem to be psychologically threatened by me.

11 To be effective, this group has to deal with the differences within it, instead of ignoring or smoothing over them for task accomplishment.

12 This group has the skills within it to deal effectively with its differences and disagreements.

13 This group communicates at both the cognitive (I think) and affective (I feel) levels of interaction.

14 This team provides individual support to members when needed.

15 This group regularly gives recognition and encouragement to me.

16 This team facilitates member involvement and seeks their opinions.

17 This group fosters my participation and positively re-enforces other member contributions.

18 The leadership in this team is shared.

19 Members play a variety of roles in this group, and no one person dominates.

Continued

20 This group welcomes input and feedback from members. — ———— — ————

21 This team is committed to cooperation and collaboration among members and with other groups. — ———— — ————

22 This group values competence and high performance. — ———— — ————

23 This team inspires members' best efforts. — ———— — ————

24 The members work well together. — ———— — ————

25 This team pauses occasionally from pursuit of its tasks to improve group maintenance and functioning. — ———— — ————

7

LEADING IN THE MANAGEMENT OF CHANGE

Introduction

In these turbulent times, we are transiting to a high performance work environment within a knowledge culture. As a result, management is involved in continuous planned change of the organization and its people. Change must be built in to both institutional and individual systems, so that we learn to operate on the basis of a new work norm – ultra-stability. Whereas the maintenance of stability was characteristic of the more static industrial age, the meta-industrial work culture demands a more dynamic leadership, which establishes innovation as standard operating procedure. This is especially true with reference to the practice of management.[38] For example, the field of human resource management is changing its focus on a people function to one of organizational effectiveness. The shift in HR mindset is toward business activities, such as reorganization, mergers, and acquisitions; transforming organizational culture and leadership succession; health and global HR delivery services; and partnering with organizational leaders and colleagues. Changing labor demographics calls for internal and external consulting skills attuned to such issues, as well as innovation in developing human capital in terms of knowledge building and professional development. The economic downturn alters perspectives on engaging employees so as to retain high potential and performing employees, overcome their resistance to change, and develop talent.

Coping effectively with alterations within social, economic, political, and organizational systems is one of the most important skills required of modern management. Change happens at all levels – social, technological, financial, and individual forces are transforming the way we live and do business. Consultants such as Tom Peters maintain that tomorrow's winners learn to deal with chaos, and learn to thrive on it, while other consultants focus upon renewing institutions so they can better serve human needs. To meet the challenge, transformational high performance leadership is essential.

Our first objective in this chapter is to look at the why and what of planned change. Managers need the "big picture" of what is happening to work and culture as we create a new information society as part of twenty-first century life. As management expert Peter Drucker (1985) warned, "If the big companies and big institutions do not innovate, change, and acquire entrepreneurial competence, the social costs of their obsolescence and eventual failure may be unbearable to society." Thus, we next examine the transitional experience connected with major life changes and the relationship between culture and change. Then we will look at some of the new methods of future research and technological forecasting.

This chapter's objective is to consider planning for change: how to develop the skills of a change agent. It is impossible to review all of the various techniques for managing change, so we will focus on force field analysis, a strategy for analyzing the driving or resisting forces of change within the organization or individual. We will also discuss organizational development (OD) and organizational transformation (OT), strategic planning and management, and ways to renew systems and position a company on the competitive edge. The outcomes should include some definite action plans for both organizational and personal change, or, to use the current term, "re-engineering" the corporation, agency, or administration. We begin in Exhibit 7.1 with a profile of a HP thinker who promoted much organizational change through his writings and teaching.

EXHIBIT 7.1 Profile of a HP thinker

C. K. Prahalad was one of the most creative management thinkers of his generation. He revolutionized thinking on business strategy, economic development, and innovation by global organizations. In 1989, this agent of change burst on the scene with two path-breaking articles for the *Harvard Business Review*, "Strategic Intent," followed the next year by "The Core Competence of the Corporation." In his publications and lectures, this superstar from India urged leaders to capitalize on their advantages, while re-defining their markets. By that he meant identifying and developing organizational strengths that cannot be easily imitated by competitors. Thus, he advised stretching a firm's skills and talents to the maximum, and setting industry-transforming goals that galvanized their own workers. Prahalad was impressed by those corporations who harnessed the ideas of humbler employees. This professor and board member promoted innovations which should emphasize "co-creation," so that companies collaborate both with customers and business allies. Thus, he challenged corporate titans to "compete for the future."

Continued

In his homeland, this pragmatist fostered a self-help group called Indus Entrepreneurs. In analyzing the gap between the rich and poor worlds, he produced a thought-provoking book, *The Fortune at the Bottom of the Pyramid: Eradicating Poverty through Profits* (2009). There he argued that the global poor, the bulk of humanity, were being ignored as a market, and represented trillions of dollars worth of pent-up spending power. He cited a legion of innovative businesses in emerging economies who were profiting in the process of providing the natives with goods and services. Such ideas drew praise from philanthropic foundations, and brought him membership on the UN commission for the private sector and development. With the intellectual restlessness of an "outsider," "C. K." advocated that big corporations develop a "portfolio of competencies." No wonder his death in 2010 was widely mourned within the worlds of both top management and the developing peoples.

Source: Based on "Schumpeter – The Guru of the Bottom of the Pyramid," *The Economist*, 24 April 2010: 69. Refer to C. K. Prahalad and M. S. Krishna, *The New Age of Innovation*. New York, NY: McGraw-Hill, 2008.

Input

Managers struggle to adapt in a new business climate in which traditional procedures of managing, manufacturing, and marketing give way to applications technology such as automation and robotics. Contemporary executives are confounded by such trends as the corporate mania for mergers, takeovers, and joint ventures. Leaders in established industries try to cope with the forces unleashed by deregulation and divestiture (McManus and Hergert 1988). In the new work culture, innovation and creativity are now norms of organizational behavior (Harris 1998).

The meaning for management

Nowhere is accelerating change more evident than in the field of modern management itself. A product of the twentieth century, it is being totally transformed in the twenty-first century. Management guru, the late Peter Drucker, once remarked that "management is the organ that converts a mob into an organization, and human efforts into performance."[39] This foresighted thinker first noted that the world is moving into an economy of knowledge where the most important resource is brainpower. He advocated that organizations set long-term goals/objectives, and empower workers. Replacing the "creative destruction" of the bureaucratic organization is an emerging model attuned to the marketplace – more flexible, agile, and able to adjust to new realities. Thus, today's management push power and decision making down to the knowledge worker who becomes more entrepreneurial.

Alan Murray attempted to describe the response of leaders to "gale-like market forces" of change – rapid globalization, accelerating innovation, relentless competition.[40] As deputy editor of the *Wall Street Journal*, he identified these changes altering the practice and policies of management:

1 new communication technologies such as desktop and laptop computers; mobile telephony and internet innovations (e.g. websites, blogs, iPods, iPads, Facebook, digital photography, online stock markets).
2 responsiveness to the marketplace by listening to customers and suppliers, identifying trends, and allocating capital to investments in innovations that open new markets and foster block-busting products and services.
3 creating synergistic relations through collaboration and team formation which enable people to work together in facilitating productivity.
4 resource allocation which quickly realigns high-value enterprises so that investment is made not in what is, but what might be (e.g. Google allowing engineers to spend twenty percent of their time on corporate projects not assigned to them).

Exhibit 7.2 summarizes behavioral science research on coping with the contemporary whirlwind changes.

EXHIBIT 7.2   Leadership in the management of change

The challenge

Because of acceleration in the rate of change, critical factors in modern management are to:

- be proactive rather than reactive to change;
- develop the means for continuing planned change;
- utilize proven procedures for controlling change;
- invest regularly in innovation.

The definition

Since change is characteristic of all life and growth, it is:

- dynamic – the word is synonymous with "evolution" and the opposite of "static";
- an alteration in relationships because of new information, inventions, situations, people;
- a shifting in the present equilibrium or balance (the current status quo);
- a reallocation of resources.

Continued

The organization

The organization is a system, and relative to change, it:

- allocates and plans changes in energy efforts by human and material resources;
- innovates to survive and develop – this involves retooling, redesign, re-engineering, re-assignment, re-training, and review;
- is neutral, in that change is neither good nor bad in itself, but depends on surrounding factors and circumstances;
- promotes collaboration or synergy, flexibility and adjustments to new market realities.

The leaders of change

The managers of change:

- stimulate innovation and creativity in the achieving of goals;
- are concerned with being proactive in regard to both personal and organizational actions;
- anticipate needed, constructive changes for increased effectiveness;
- always subject goals, objectives, and targets to continuous re-evaluation and possible change;
- continuously plan and control change by creating norms and mechanisms for ongoing, dynamic change;
- make choices about which changes can be realistically undertaken, given the imitations of time and resources;
- initiate the selected changes with the maximum of employee cooperation and the minimum of destructive disturbance.

For further insights, refer to P. R. Harris, *Toward Human Emergence; Managing the Knowledge Culture*. Amherst, MA: HRD Press, 2009; 2005.

The case for change to gain or restore an organization's competitive edge can be made best by key executives who are HP leaders themselves. They seek to comprehend the baffling changes in the business environment which require them to rethink every aspect of their operations – from how many workers are needed, to where to invest hard-earned profits. Some companies shrink while others expand; some dump unprofitable activities while others invest in automation or entrepreneurial ventures. The acceleration of change demands speedy critical decisions and unprecedented risk-taking. To meet these demands, leaders must foster a faster-reacting, entrepreneurial culture in the organization. Consider the following observations of corporate leaders about their "forced strategic self-analysis," reported recently in the *Los Angeles Times*. Then you may be willing to utilize the insights suggested in this chapter.

- "Corporations are going through wrenching change because you are experiencing a revolutionary era when critical decisions are being made to preserve the future of American industry" (Richard M. Cyert, President, Carnegie-Mellon University).
- "The company has to be concerned about future life of the institution ... You either make strategic adaptations or go the way of all flesh ... The transformation of Motorola has made the company more dependent upon technology and less on human labor, particularly in the United States" (William J. Weisz, Vice Chairman, Motorola Corporation).
- "Restructuring is a euphemism for struggling to adapt. This is business Darwinism – the dinosaurs didn't survive because they couldn't adapt" (Irwin Kellner, Chief Economist, Manufacturers Hanover Bank).
- "The smart managers are redeploying assets and cutting their costs ... They're taking advantage of emerging technologies because they realize if they don't plan and invest for the future, there won't be one" (Carl Shrawder, management consultant, Coopers & Lybrand).
- "Companies have always been interested in the new venture. But what makes the romance so much more serious is that all the pieces – entrepreneuring, decentralizing, venturing, restructuring are finally coming all together" (Rosabeth Moss Kanter, Professor, Yale University and author of *The Change Makers*).

Such insights into global industry result in the abandonment of the pyramidal and paramilitary style of organizations. Corporate giants like GE, for example, are becoming leaner as they cut layers of management. Simultaneously, new venture incubators are "in," along with many other forms of creative transformations. Other CEOs are aligning their partnerships with great universities – knowledge factories. It is important, however, to put this transition into some context, and for leaders to have the larger perspective. It is necessary to understand the why and what of such change.

Implications for HP leaders

Exhibit 7.3 provides a visual overview of changes in human development, illustrating activities at various evolutionary stages of our species. The diagram includes my forecasts of the post-industrial or meta-industrial stage of development now underway in this twenty-first century. The latter stage is summarized in the description of the Cybercultural Person. I foresee a dramatic increase in time spent in creative

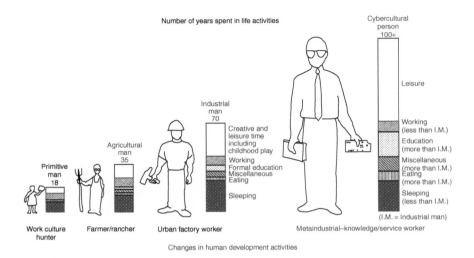

Changes in human development activities

EXHIBIT 7.3 Human development – changes in activities
Source: US Bureau of Labor Statistics.

leisure, social networking, and lifelong continuing education. Not included in this model is the phenomenon of our going beyond Earth as we create a spacefaring civilization which includes extraterrestrial travel, industrialization, and settlement off-world.

The term "cyberculture" was coined by MIT physicist, Norbert Weiner, to describe the emerging society dominated by cybernation (the science of communication and control in man and machines). Cyberculture is the unfolding knowledge culture; an information society centered around advanced automation and communication technologies, including the widespread use of computers, robotics, and artificial intelligence.

The HP leader's challenge is to help people make the transition from a rural or industrial mindset into that needed to be effective for a super industrial lifestyle. The "industrial age" management philosophy, assumptions, policies, practices, and technologies, as well as rules, regulations, and traditions must undergo scrutiny and some elimination. They must be replaced by more tentative, relevant approaches that speak to the more informed, technologically/ecologically oriented worker. The vocational shift is away from involving people in the production of things to more involvement in research, education, service, new careers, and recreational activities. Further, with improved capabilities in global transportation, communication, and management, this is in a whole new work environment or "ball game." Thus would-be leaders operate today in a radically changed "ballgame and ballpark" with new players, rules, and technologies. Exhibit 7.4 elaborates on the paradigm offered in the previous graphic.

EXHIBIT 7.4   Historical perspective on human progress

THE SCOPE OF HUMAN DEVELOPMENT

One way of viewing work history is to conceive it in terms of five major stages with three significant turning points – all of which impact our culture, society, world, and way of working. Such happenings imprint themselves on human attitudes and thinking processes. Furthermore, human experiences in the past and present provide the input for future planning. Consider the implications of these five evolutionary phases:

- *First stage.* Hunting – survival level of human existence. The primitive hunter operates on a day-to-day basis in tribes and as a nomad. For the mainstream of humanity, this stage took millions of years before the next major turning point took place. But today there are still some "primitive" people locked into this initial stage who did not make the transition into the next phase of human development.

  Agricultural Revolution – first major turning point in human history.
- *Second stage.* Farming/ranching – security level of human needs. The agriculturalist plants seed, domesticates animals, plans and saves up for tomorrow, settles down, and builds villages and civilization. For the mainstream of humanity this transition took thousands of years, but many people are still living in this stage – they have a rural mindset.

  Industrial Revolution – second turning point, from about the eighteenth century onward.
- *Third stage.* Industrialization – produced periods of affluence and abundance. The factory worker uses machines and assembly lines to replace brawn. The population shifts from rural areas to the city; urbanization is largely influenced by the social legislation, new institutions, and mindset. Characterized by greater movement upward on the need hierarchy toward socialization, recognition, and reward, there is expansion of middle class families. This transition took only a few hundred years, and some people still function in this way – they have a factory or industrial age mindset.

  Cybercultural revolution – third major turning point since the end of World War Two; we are now in the early period of impact, but already causing "future shock"; the beginning of the post, meta, or super industrial age resulting from innovation in science, technology, and information distribution.
- *Fourth stage.* Cybernation – links computers to machines to create advanced automated systems. Knowledge workers and technicians displace traditional farmers and factory workers; cybernation speeds up quantity and quality of production, with fewer people and more robots; life is more complex and

  Continued

interdependent; there is a sharp increase in leisure time and in recreational/cultural pursuits; traditional roles and institutions are faced with crises and the challenge of rapid change and renewal; individuals and society are in a state of profound transition to a new state of being; needs, values, norm systems are all in the process of transformation; there is movement toward the highest levels of need hierarchy of self-actualization; humans no longer perceive themselves as "earthbound" and begin to explore and consider colonization of the universe. Cyberculture, or the Information Age, is taking only decades to accomplish. Humankind in this twenty-first century is well into this fourth stage of human development. For those in this mainstream knowledge culture, life is being transformed by advances in biotechnology and genetics. Our species has probed far corners of the universe with telescopes and automated space missions. The creation of commercial space industries is underway, beginning with satellites, aerospace engineering, and tourism.[41] The internet furthers global communications, and promotes social networking. Many, especially the young, have this technological mindset, but most are still earthbound in their thinking.

Spacefaring revolution – the fifth stage in ongoing human development will begin to mature in mid-twenty-first century. Human potential will be realized in off-world developments beyond the cradle of the home planet. Eventually, we may make contact with aliens from other universes.

- *Fifth stage.* Spaceflight and culture – creation of a spacefaring civilization. Humankind is migrating beyond Earth, and is being transformed into spacekind. As we pursue space exploration, industrialization, and settlements, the focus will begin on the Moon and Mars. Most human disciplines for learning and knowledge will be transformed aloft (e.g. astrophysics, astrolaw, astromedicine, astrobusiness, *et al.*). We are in the process of creating a space culture that will alter the species. As we exhaust resources on Earth, many of our agricultural and mining activities will be transferred to the Moon, asteroids, and beyond in our solar system.

The adaptability issue

The acceleration in the rate of change has caused time to condense, so that what once took a long period to accomplish can now be achieved in a far shorter time span. The twentieth century has provided remarkable and intensified growth, development, and expansion in every aspect of human endeavor, but the twenty-first century already shows a faster pace of alterations in life and work styles. Now HPLs must cope effectively with more rapid change as a reality of modern life; develop an open and positive philosophy of life about people's roles; be more foresighted, so as to project ahead and get the "big picture" of what is happening within human society worldwide; provide leadership in innovation and spacefaring.

Ability to cope with such rapid change and to control it somewhat may very well determine our ability to survive as a species. Both individuals and institutions must learn to plan and regulate change so as to ensure growth and development. Among the big changes to adapt to is life control and our traveling, living, and working beyond our home planet.

Change alters our relationships with each other and the world as we perceive it. It is caused by new information and knowledge, by new insights and discoveries, by new situations and happenings. It challenges each person to re-educate self and to modify our psychological constructs – the way one reads meaning into the events and experiences of his or her life. Since the pace of change has risen so astronomically in this century, change must be managed if it is not to cause disastrous dislocation in individuals, organizations, and society. Not all change is good, so careful choices must be made relative to which changes are to be inaugurated. Nor is it advisable to merely react to change, but to be instead proactive – to plan for it. Haphazard change can sometimes be worse than no change. To begin, consider your own attitude toward change. How do we feel about change? Most people fear it, for they are comfortable and secure with the status quo. The real issue is whether we will permit fear of the unknown to paralyze us into inaction or to withdraw from necessary personal change in our lifestyle or approach. The change inventory in the Instrumentation section will help you in this analysis.

If a person or corporation is to survive in the future, three attitudes or outlooks will be necessary:

1 openness of mind to consider new perspectives and more creative solutions to problems and other challenges;
2 adaptability and flexibility regarding the many new changes with which we must cope;
3 development and use of methods for the management of change.

The Force Field Analysis in the Instrument section is a tool that helps in this regard.

Since human interaction is normally dynamic, pressures for change build up in people and systems because of altered relationships. These forces for change can be avoided, resisted, or incorporated into the person's or organization's perceptual field with the result of restructuring one's constructs. Generally, people resist new information, especially data inconsistent with their present constructs, in a way that tends to be resistive. Exhibit 7.5 illustrates the struggle when initiating changes.

When one encounters new information or experiences inconsistent with old constructs, there are times when such inconsistencies cannot be avoided, resisted, or otherwise defended. The resulting pressure or dissonance will usually motivate the individual to alter or update his or her construct system. During this phase there is within the person a temporary confusion or disorganization until equilibrium or order is restored to a relative state of congruence or harmony.

MANAGING THE FORCES OF CHANGE

DRIVING	RESISTING
1. Analyze the type of change and those who would support it.	1. Diagnose the resistance to this change.
2. Respond sensitively and creatively to influences on this change.	2. Constructively channel the resistance.
3. Provide adequate data on the change.	3. Counteract arguments against change.
4. Freeze driving forces at new level.	4. Respect freedom of dissent.

EXHIBIT 7.5 Altering the equilibrium of forces

Factors involved in planning change

Timing: ideally, change should be introduced before the crisis occurs and at a time when the situation is most conducive to implementation. Psychological construct: this is the perceptual or mental system that individuals and institutions construct to read meaning into their life space – to make "sense out of the events and experiences that occur in their private world. Each of us has a set of highly-organized constructs around which we organize the world in which we live. By these constructs, a person mentally puts order into the world as he or she perceives it. This intellectual synthesis of perceptions relates to our images of self, family, religion, nation, job, etc. Each individual develops a system of constructs that serve as anchor points for mental health. This system exerts a pushing/pulling effect upon all other ideas we encounter. It gives meaning and order to the multiple sensations and impressions that bombard us daily.

Not only do all individuals have a unique set of constructs through which they filter experience, but groups and organizations also construct systems through which they interpret information coming from their environment. These result from a set of intense interactions with segments of various populations which are then organized to achieve certain goals. Thus, organizational or group styles emerge as people share themselves and their perceptions converge. In a sense, members of groups and organizations link up their perceptual fields. They act and perceive according to their common, shared sets of relationships. Adjusting to change requires a readjustment of our constructs – a reassessment or review of our traditional way of interpreting situations. Essentially, it involves an "attitude change" before actual change in policy, program, or procedures occur. For example, with the landing of the Apollo astronauts on the Moon, we realized we are no longer "earthbound." We have to change our images of our species – maybe our real home is up and out there.

Change mindset: either one is consistently open to or opposes change, becoming, in the process, a world-maker or world-squatter. To live is to change, and to grow implies changing often. The very word "change" is synonymous with evolution, for the whole universe and all creature life are in a constant flux. Until recently, such change has been slow, almost imperceptible. Today, humans live in a period of accelerating change. We have unprecedented technological and scientific power to alter and shape our own future. We are not only agents of change in the world, but are changed in the process of creating our tomorrows. That implies changing our images of ourselves and our roles. Obviously, there are many factors which influence the acceptance or rejection of proposed changes.

Guidelines for managing change – the how

With some knowledge of the psychological factors affecting human behavior in groups, the change agent is in a better position to inaugurate planned change, as well as to stabilize an uncertain situation. The following guidelines may help in the process of planning change:

- *Create a positive climate for change.* The proper climate for change often makes the difference between successful change and disruptive, stress-producing chaos. A change agent must strive to create an emotional atmosphere in which people feel the situation is non-judgmental and empathic toward their needs. We must make clear our own purposes and the extent of the projected change, then allow those affected to express openly their feelings and resistances with assurance that this input will be taken into full consideration.

  The readiness for change can best be developed by first opening the system of organizational communications. One-way or downward systems of communication need to be replaced by two-way or circular systems, which permit feedback to the person proposing change. Closed channels of communication foster dissatisfaction in a group or organization. Lack of knowledge about the expected change by those affected often creates organizational "paranoia." People throughout the corporation or community express deep anxiety about the change by imagining every possible calamity and raising every conceivable objection as to why the proposed change will not work. Such expression often gives rise to disruptive and vicious rumors which have the potential for creating widespread organizational damage.

• *Involve those affected by change efforts.* People respond well to change efforts only when they have some understanding of the purposes and consequences of the proposed change. Lack of knowledge, understanding, and involvement in planning for change only feed the forces for resistance. Therefore, change agents must allow for some participation by those affected by change in the preparations, decision making, and implementation. This may range from "brainstorming" about the change at a staff meeting, to appointing a task force to make recommendations concerning the change.

People can be persuaded to reduce their objections, but they should not be treated arbitrarily when they initially oppose the change. By practicing human relations skills, the change agent can help people to cope with fear of the change. When they have ample opportunity to comprehend the nature and extent of the suggested change, individuals may become self-motivated toward problem solution. When employees, for example, have some measure of control over the forces that influence their organizational life space, they are more apt to implement the change than to resist it.

Furthermore, participation by those who must implement the proposed change often results in better efforts. It is often with these people that the more creative and realistic solutions lie. Change agents may often assume they have adequate knowledge of what is involved in the problem area requiring change to design its solution. However, those affected by such planning usually share unique perspectives, which more often than not contribute substantially to the overall problem resolution.

• *Develop a change strategy.* If change in individual and organizational lives is to be planned and controlled, the agent of change must employ an orderly problem solving process. However, there are various methods for this purpose. One developed by the social psychologist, Kurt Lewin, has been designated "force field analysis." In this conceptual approach, one proceeds with change on the basis that behavior is the product of a field of interdependent factors, such as action, thinking, wishing, striving, valuing, achieving, and so forth. As previously noted, for each individual, this perceptual field encompasses one's life space or psychological environment. Groups and organizations also have a life space, or unique environment, resulting from the merging of each member's perceptual field. The "private world" or life space involves these factors:

o "existence" – anything having demonstrable effects on the individual or group whether conscious or not;

o "interdependence" – various parts of this life space are to some degree dependent on each other and thus overlap;

o "contemporaniety" – only determinants of behavior at a given point in time are properties of any life space.

With knowledge of these factors in the individual or group, one is able to analyze what forces drive the members in a particular direction and what restrains them (see Exhibit 7.6). A way of analyzing these factors influencing behavior is to consider two sets of forces at work in our life spaces –the forces for and against a change in the current condition. These forces, for instance, may be people within an organization, or economic factors (a recession), or social factors (war or peace). Once the present situation has been determined, then the change agent is in a position to inaugurate the changes and stabilize the new situation.

Now consider a case in point regarding a change in leadership development at IBM and its global consequences.

EXHIBIT 7.6   Case for change in leadership development

> Innovators at IBM sought for a better way to prepare "high flying" managers for executive positions. Thus was born the IBM Corporate Service Corps (CSC), which now has 500 such volunteers annually, with 10,000 applicants. They work pro bono for up to a month outside the firm in six-person, multi-ethnic teams offering new strategies, relative to public needs, in areas of transport, water supply, and food safety to cities in countries from Poland to Vietnam.
>
> This approach to leadership development is comparable to the Peace Corps and is being copied by other organizations – the drug manufacturers, Pfizer and Novartis; Dow Corning; FedEx, and other world-class corporations. The original idea came from trying to implement IBM's vision for a globally integrated enterprise. CSC volunteering is viewed as a way of training corporate executives for that role. As a result, communities from Africa to the Philippines are benefiting from the free problem solving of corporate top performers. The business gains squadrons of more committed leaders with new skills acquired as volunteers.
>
> Source: Based on "Corporate Volunteering – Big-hearted Blue," *The Economist*, 30 October 2010: 73.

Here are some of the questions a change agent must answer in the process of effecting planned change:

1 What kind of change is planned? Is it in attitude, behavior, policy, structure or process? Determine the nature and properties of what is being changed –

customs, beliefs, opinions, principles, operational procedures. Define change in terms of the total system. Spell out the objectives of the change.

2 What are the number and strength of the driving forces in favor of the change? Once ascertained, concentrate on increasing these forces supporting the change; get these forces mobilized to create a climate for change – think of this as a "tug-of-war" game, the center line being the status quo. For example, when these forces are people, interest them in promoting the change and provide them with sufficient information on its purposes. Involve them in the communication of well thought-out reasons for the change, or enlist their help in doing the research necessary to develop a solid case for the change. Thus, the change agent helps to unfreeze the status quo and provide a new basis for growth within the group. Begin with those in the system most open to change who can provide leverage.

3 What are the number and strength of the resisting forces? Diagnose the opposition and the reasons or emotions behind the resistance. Systematically, counteract the arguments against the change; remove or isolate the obstacles to the change. To what degree is the group ready for change and what changes are realistic in the light of the resistance? How much power do the change agents possess to overcome the change resisters? What are the difficulties in inaugurating and maintaining the change? Each person who is a potential resister must be analyzed as to why he or she will take this position. If it is simply a question of ignorance, then adequate information must be supplied to enlist support. If one has a closed mind and is against any change in principle, then that person should be bypassed and effort should be concentrated on those most amenable to change. If one has a vested or conflict of interest, then the reasons for the opposition may have to be exposed. Coercion and repression of opponents of change are not in order; people have a right to disagree.

4 What action do the change agents plan? Who is to do it? How is it to be done? Where is it to be done? When is it most appropriate? (Timing is important in inaugurating change.) A strategy must be developed in the light of the situation and the abilities of the group. This means the change agents must know the resources of the group for promoting and maintaining the change.

5 How can the change agents stabilize the change when introduced? Once a new level of change has been brought about, it must be "refrozen" until it becomes an accepted and habitual practice. This means the change agents must stick with the change before moving on to new projects or changes. It implies "reinforcement" of the new balance established between the driving and resisting forces in the group. A force for stabilization occurs when those who must implement the change are involved in the decision making about the change.

6 Are the change agents open to continuous change, and have they a plan for re-evaluation of the change inaugurated after a trial period? This means that the proponents must be willing to accept improvement and further changes on the plan or program they espoused. Sometimes such follow up studies can be accomplished by the change group itself. Large-scale changes, on the other hand,

may require "action research" by outside consultants to objectively determine standards by which to measure progress. Realistic fact finding and evaluation are prerequisite for any learning from the change experience.

Resistance to organizational change

Need for change is often brought about in situations characterized by high levels of stress or tension within an organization. When organizations cease to function well, when the people in them are put under a great deal of pressure and frustration, the time for planned change may be in order. Paradoxically, these conditions can also mitigate against its success. The overwhelming evidence from the behavioral sciences is that heightened drive, tension, and stress make people more rigid and inflexible in perceiving and interpreting events. Under undue tension, our perspective and foresight may become severely restricted. Individuals tend to see things in terms of our most probable expectations and to decide things along the most habitual lines. Our capacity to solve problems can be severely reduced. If change efforts are to be successful, they must be carried out in an atmosphere most conducive to it. Change efforts must be planned well ahead of any crisis and inaugurated, if possible, in a climate in which stress, frustration, and anger are at a minimum.

In assessing resistance, change agents must be aware of the fears of disorientation because of the unknown factors involved for the people affected by the change. We must be conscious of threats to existing vested interests, power and status ties to existing conditions, as well as the resulting potential for personal loss when conditions change. Proponents must be alert to the defenses of past tradition, standards, values, and beliefs.

Attempts by the change agent to meet resistance with defensiveness, advice-giving, premature persuasion, censoring, controlling, or punishment will only engender greater resistance. Rather, dissent should be valued in its own right as it represents a legitimate point of view. As previously indicated, when the people affected by any given change are involved in its planning and implementation, restraining forces against the change can be reduced and successful change can be accomplished. Recognize that everybody cannot be won over to accept the change – some who resist any change will have to be bypassed or fired. There are people who are against all and every change, and are comfortable with the way it was.

Because of the rapidly rising rate of change within the life spaces of individuals, organizations, and communities, the thesis of this presentation has been that such change must be managed (Exhibit 7.5). Merely reacting or coping with accelerating change is unsatisfactory. Leaders in families, business, and society need to view themselves as potential agents of change. Managers, especially, should not be dragged "kicking and screaming" into this twenty-first century; rather, they should develop the skills now available for planning and controlling change.

Applied behavioral scientists describe change as a process within a system of initiating, diagnosing, implementing, and maintaining a new level of performance in the group or organization. By viewing the organization as a total system and a department or division as a subsystem, one begins to appreciate the interrelatedness of all the parts. Thus, when a change agent attempts to bring about an alteration in one aspect of the system, he or she takes into consideration its effect on the other parts of this whole. Planned change involves the creation of a new environment in which people function, hopefully, more effectively. The force field analysis method can be a powerful means for bringing about changes with a minimum of dislocation and a maximum of collaboration (refer to "Force Field Analysis," in the Instrument section).

Consider that, among scientists, there is a growing belief that many of the primitive hominid species disappeared not because they merged to form one larger human family, but because they failed to meet the challenges of their time and so became extinct. Scientists also think it possible that those hominids may have vanished without having contributed to the evolution of the species that did adapt and survive: *Homo sapiens*. Today, in an information society, the survival of the wisest depends upon managing change.

Organizational transformation
The challenge

Having considered in general *why* it is necessary to plan and control change, the HP leader relates trends in society and the world of work to his/her current experience in an organization. In other words, a leader is challenged to consider why it is vital to become an agent of dynamic change in human systems.

The organization

- defines human objectives, expectations, obligations;
- structures human roles and relationships;
- provides processes, procedures, technologies;
- develops human and material resources;
- goes through growth stages:

  o formation
  o survival
  o stabilization
  o image projection
  o rendering unique products and services
  o cooperating in achieving goals and satisfying needs within the system.

The reorganization

Renewal is necessary when the organization:

- diminishes in its uniqueness or satisfaction of relevant needs;
- begins to operate ineffectively and is financially threatened;
- must redefine its objectives, policies, structures to survive;
- must eliminate traditional roles, procedures, products, services;

- must create *new* roles, procedures, products, services;
- must acquire *new* specialists and markets.

Then it is time again for planned change or redirection. Otherwise, "organization shock" will be experienced in varying degrees.

Organization shock

"Organization shock" is characterized by:

- information age impacting upon traditional modes of operating;
- resistance to organizational change at all levels;
- high degrees of stress, tension, and frustration among its people;
- negative environment, such as increasing job dissatisfaction, or threat and defensiveness;
- symptoms such as a drop in members/clients/customers; declining loyalty, attendance, and productivity; increasing turnover, absenteeism, and tardiness; decreasing income or profit; increasing dissatisfaction and charges of irrelevance about operations; decreasing communication and increasing conflict; increasing alcoholism, drug abuse, nervous breakdowns, and even suicides among workers;
- corporation becomes take-over target by others, or suffers from a merger.

Transforming the organizational model

The organizational model known as *bureaucracy* is disappearing, while a new modus operandi called the *ad-hocracy* is emerging (refer to Exhibit 7.7 in the Interaction section under the heading "Trends in organizational change"). To prevent organization shock or to lessen its impact, management must:

- develop a more positive attitude, a readiness or openness, toward necessary change;
- create mechanisms for continuous, planned change in the system;
- listen more effectively to input from employees, customers, competitors, public;
- manage innovation – that is, encourage creativity and expressions of differences in opinion and perspective, and promote R&D activities.

To avoid organization shock, consider these six factors identified by behavioral scientists as blocking innovation in individuals and institutions:

1 excessive need for order and control;
2 reluctance to use imagination and to play;
3 narrowness of vision and perception, or failure to envision broader connotations;
4 reluctance to risk and excessive concern about failure;
5 reluctance to exercise influence or leadership;
6 overcertainty or absolutism on present position.

Strategies to avoid organization shock

Undertake to:

- Analyze the psychological environment: factors or forces affecting behavior with an individual/organizational life space which may help or hinder the projected change.
- Examine the communication system: evaluate your managerial communication style, as the agent of change, or of the organizational communication system. If the style is open, two way, circular, and participative, then you are ready to promote the change. If it is a closed, one way, authoritarian style, then the communication system must first be opened before the change can take place.
- Encourage participation in the change planning process: identify and involve those who are open to the proposed change and those who must implement the change once it is adopted. Utilize participative management in the very process of planning for the change.
- Develop a case for change: begin by doing the background research and investigation as to why the change is desirable. Assemble data on the reasons the change is advantageous. Build up a file on your projected change. At the appropriate time, communicate this case to all who will be involved in the change.
- Keep a low profile as a change agent: avoid having the change identified with you or your personality. Seek collaborators who can provide the outward leadership in promoting the change, and feed the data to these people. Real change makers are often not visible within their organizations.
- Be prepared for modifications of your proposed change: be open to feedback and to modification, amplification, and revision of the original plan for change.
- Be sensitive to the pro/con forces relative to the change: stay alert to the varied forces at work within the individual or the system that promote or restrict the anticipated change. Assess these driving and resisting forces.
- Unfreeze the present equilibrium: unlock or alter the status quo by eliminating or weakening the restraining forces, and by strengthening or increasing the driving forces.
- Be prepared to take risks: the agent of change must be ready to take wise and calculated risks, to expose himself or herself to ridicule, and to live with the consequences of initiating change. Progress is not made by "playing it safe."

Implications for high performing leaders

Because accelerating change can become unmanageable, HP leaders seek to manage change. To accomplish this, the leader needs to acquire skills to better plan and control change. In human systems, this implies imitating, diagnosing, implementing, and maintaining a new level of performance within a group or organization. Change is an altering of priorities within that energy exchange system called "the organization." This will occur if the above strategies are followed. By eliminating the archaic and obsolete, by experimenting with the innovative and unknown, the agent of change insures the organization's survival so it can develop. Such leadership helps to renew the system by creating a new psychological environment in which people can function more effectively.

Necessary changes occur best within an innovative work culture. That means seeking and implementing creative ideas within an established corporation, agency, or association. Such leadership offers positive reinforcement to those with strategies for improvements, especially by creative types who deviate from the "way it is always done here." Some organizations even establish units or teams to discover innovative ways for better marketing and production to open new territories.

Interaction

The next four exhibits provide an opportunity for a leader to engage in a personal analysis, and to interact with a work unit or a group of managers on issues related to OT. The whole undertaking can be accomplished in four training meetings or staff sessions. There are four separate sections for group discussion. Beginning with organizational change in general, the participants are asked to diagnose the situation in their own company, agency, or association:

1 Examine Exhibit 7.7. Trends in organizational change; compare the two management systems, and discuss their implications regarding your organization – note any instances of bureaucracy being replaced by "ad-hocracy."
2 Fill out Stages of Organizational Growth at Exhibit 7.8 to ascertain by group consensus where your organization is in its development.
3 The third diagnosis, at Exhibit 7.9, comes from systems analysis based on the research of behavioral scientist Rensis Likert. Using six major characteristics of organizational management, the individuals rate twelve items as to whether the organization is still traditionally authoritarian or emerging as participative in its style of management. Then the data is shared with the group, and some consensus on evaluations is sought for all items. When there is no agreement, simply add up the scores of each person, and circle the majority rating.
4 The final instrument is Creative Risk Taking at Exhibit 7.10; an exercise in examining the risks in initiating change within an organization.

Trends in organizational change

EXHIBIT 7.7   Trends in organizational change

Disappearing bureaucracy (industrial age – factory system). The way it was:

1 *Old system* – characteristics: permanence, hierarchy, and a division of labor; traditional organization (called Theory X or Systems 1/2);

   a. workers in sharply defined slots for a division of labor;

Continued

b. narrow specializations – each in own niche;

c. vertical hierarchy – chain of command from top down;

d. permanence of organizational relations and structures; intractable departments and divisions; slow to change, often by external influences static;

e. operates well in stable society when problems are routine and pre-dictable; needs highly competitive, undifferentiated environment;

f. concerned primarily about organizational self-interests, board, and stockholders;

g. vertical, downward authority – power concentrated in a few at the top who make all-important decisions for lower echelons; managers share a monopoly on decisions; organizational communication vertical; information flow slow; delay normal.

2 Old organization man

a. executives and managers are the "brains" and workers are the "hands";

b. people differentiated according to rank and role in hierarchical pyramid, while personnel have more permanent work relationships;

c. organization man looks within the corporation for approval, rewards, and punishment – conditioned to subservience and paid to conform. while deviancy and creativity is discouraged;

d. factory system produces the industrialization of the skills and profession into narrow specializations;

e. free-swinging rugged individuals built vast enterprises unafraid of defeat and adverse opinions became the leaders of industries;

f. focus is on proficiency and profitability, as well as upon plant equipment maintenance and capital expansion;

g. requires masses of moderately educated workers.

Summary: *Old bureaucratic man* employs his skills and energies for the good of the organization to whom he is loyal and committed; is concerned about eco-nomic security and hierarchical status; subordinates individuality for the good of the organization. The emphasis is on competition and quantity production. He fears change and advocates the status quo; by his past orientation he is ripe for future shock. He is usually a white male with females limited in management positions.

Emerging "ad-hocracy" (Post-industrial age – cybernation). The way it is today:

3 *New system* – characteristics: fast-moving, information-rich, a kinetic orga-nization of the future, filled with transient cells and extremely mobile individuals (sometimes referred to as Theory Y or Systems 3/4):

Continued

a. workers' roles more hazy and temporary; convergence of talent and disciplines to accomplish a task;

b. fluid, participative arrangements; organizational redesign is a continuous function;

c. temporariness of organizational relations and structures – disposable divisions, task forces, and teams; ad hoc committees;

d. self-renewing; constantly changing in response to changing needs, dynamic – functions best in a super industrial society;

e. practices social responsibility – concerned about community and ecological implications of organizational actions;

f. authority – horizontal, power disbursed, and decisions shifted downward or "sideways" with responsibility shared at all levels;

g. organizational communications circular or lateral, information flows fast;

h. problem solving mechanism ideal for; routine issues at moderate pace, while staff/line arrangements are supportive – also complex problem solving; capabilities for meeting increasing number of non-routine, novel, and unexpected problems; high speed decisions;

i. specialists and advisors more involved in planning and decisions; convergence of specializations through a team approach;

j. requires limited numbers of skilled technicians and self-regulating cybernetic or robotic systems;

k. emphasis on effectiveness and profitable service;

l. focus on people maintenance and development; human resources development – requires knowledge workers.

4 New super industrial person

a. executives and managers are coordinators of varied and transient work teams;

b. people differentiated flexibly and functionally according to skill and professional training;

c. personnel develop human relations and cross-cultural skills for quick, intense relationships on the job while dealing with diversity;

d. super industrial person looks within one's self and profession for approval and fulfillment;

e. an agent of change and nonconformity; unorthodox, creative and venturesome;

f. operate comfortably in techno-societies fostering information exchanges, networking, professionalization and cooperation that reaches beyond narrow discipline;

g. emergence of entrepreneurial groupings within large organizations with independent colleagues unafraid to rise and venture into new fields.

Continued

Summary: *New associative person* employs his or her skills and energies for self-actualization in temporary groupings committed to personal and professional development; mobile self-motivated people who take economic security for granted; find transience liberating and never permanently submerges individuality while working on the team; emphasis on cooperation and quality service; change is a challenge for new learning, and adaptability is advocated; future-orientated; prevents or lessens future shock; varied; competent people; includes women and all minorities at all levels. Compare these two systems in the context of your organization and diagnose its principal needs for change based on group interaction.

EXHIBIT 7.8 Stages of organizational growth

Step 1: Using the organization that presently employs you, identify in terms of dates in the past and present the stages of growth it has gone through; that is, insert dates or the approximate number of years in the allotted spaces.

Name of the organization:_____

Stages of growth	Approximate time period (dates/years)	Example:
formation	_____	Organization is founded.
Survival period(s)	_____	Organization grows and meets expenses.
Stabilization	_____	Organization makes profit; develops workable systems.
Image creation projection	_____	Organization develops an image with brand/s, reputation, and public relations program.
Products/services	_____	Organization becomes distinctive in its output.
Cooperates in achieving goals and needs satisfaction	_____	Organization matures and is involved with local/world markets.

Continued

Step 2: Your organizational diagnosis

Review Exhibit 7.7. Trends in organizational change. Then, take an objective look at your organization: specifically, your work unit and your subordinates. You need to hear, observe, sense, and apprehend change underway – "the whisper of the future." Only when the manager has such a sensitive inner ear to catch the voice of tomorrow can he/she avoid obsolescence and business decline.

Demonstrate that you hear, observe, sense, and apprehend the need for change in your system: identify some of the symptoms of "organization shock" which might be present in your organization. Note some needed changes that have yet to be considered.

Organizational characteristics: analyze your organization's present state in terms of the following characteristics: rate your organization as *adequate (+)* or *inadequate (−)* for each characteristic.

	Rating	
Competency level	(+)	(−)
Managers	☐	☐
Staff	☐	☐
Subordinates	☐	☐
Training of new entries	☐	☐
Human resource development at all levels	☐	☐
Employment of new specialists	☐	☐
Effectiveness level		
Productivity standards	☐	☐
Useful meetings	☐	☐
Utilization of human potential	☐	☐
Clarity of job roles, functions	☐	☐
Managing change by:	(+)	(−)
Encouragement of creativity/innovation	☐	☐
Resolution of conflict	☐	☐
Motivating work environment	☐	☐
Rewarding of high performance	☐	☐
Job enrichment/redesign	☐	☐
Involvement in problem solving/decision making	☐	☐
Job advancement/mobility	☐	☐
Time management	☐	☐
Organizational relations	☐	☐

Continued

Step 3: System analysis

In light of Exhibit 7.7 with its change diagnosis of the "disappearing bureaucracy" and the "emerging ad-hocracy," now do a more in-depth analysis of your organization based on a systems approach. That is, evaluate your organization's communication, goal setting, control motivation, and leadership style. Decide if your organization is either Traditional Authoritarian (TA) or Emerging Participative (EP) in each of the six areas, rating each of the twelve points below as high, medium, or low in your opinion. For example, if organizational goals are *always* set at the top, the management style is "TA" and you might rate it low. If middle management are permitted input into organizational objectives, then you might mark it high. On the other hand, if a Management by Objectives system (MbO) has been introduced throughout the organization at all levels, it is likely your company or agency is in the "EP" or emerging participative style of management, and you might decide to rate it medium or high. If MbO only exists at the division levels, you may give it only a low rating under "EP"; or if you look at Item 7 on direction of information flow and it is largely downward, an appropriate rating under "TA" would seem to be in order, whereas if it is circular – two way in direction – the mark would be placed under "EP" in the appropriate evaluation, depending on how open you consider the organizational communications to be.

Do the rating for the next twelve items by circling the most appropriate rating. (L/M/H). When finished, you may wish to plot a graph by connecting the points with a line (then turn the page sideways to view your highs, mediums, and lows more graphically). This will indicate the current trend of your organization's management style as you perceive it.

Your system analysis Organizational characteristics	Ratings:	
	Traditional authoritarian	Emerging participative
Goal setting		
1 Establishing organizational goals/objectives	L M H	L M H
2 Amount of resistance or collaboration to goals set	L M H	L M H
Control		
3 Unity of purpose/activity of formal/informal organization	L M H	L M H
4 Use of control data	L M H	L M H
Decision making		
5 Levels of delegation/involvement	L M H	L M H
6 Contribution to worker motivation	L M H	L M H

Continued

Communication
  7 Direction of information flow   L   M   H   L   M   H
  8 Accuracy of information flow   L   M   H   L   M   H
Motivation
  9 Cooperation and teamwork   L   M   H   L   M   H
 10 Human energy productivity   L   M   H   L   M   H
     utilized
Leadership
 11 Confidence shown in subordinates   L   M   H   L   M   H
 12 Freedom to discuss job with   L   M   H   L   M   H
     superiors

Organization shock symptoms
Determine if some of the typical symptoms of organization shock are present
in your institution. Simply check the appropriate box.

	Some	Little	Much
1 Substantial drop in membership, clients, or customers	☐	☐	☐
2 Gradual loss of chapters or local units, plants, or subsidiaries	☐	☐	☐
3 Significant reduction in attendance at professional conference, conventions, external meetings, or exhibits	☐	☐	☐
4 Decreasing financial income or drop in profits	☐	☐	☐
5 Declining loyalty of adherents and productivity	☐	☐	☐
6 Decreasing dissatisfaction with program goals, objectives, and targets	☐	☐	☐
7 Charges of irrelevance in programs, projects, and processes	☐	☐	☐
8 Widening communication gaps between departments and among workers	☐	☐	☐
9 Recruitment difficulties to attract younger, competent workers	☐	☐	☐
10 Polarization of traditionalists and activists	☐	☐	☐
11 Increasing conflict between labor or management; or staff and volunteers	☐	☐	☐
12 Growing dissatisfaction of younger staff with older administration	☐	☐	☐

Continued

Step 4: Action planning

1 As a result of reading the Input section and engaging in this learning exercise, identify two personal changes which you might undertake to promote organizational change and advance your professional development.

   _____

   _____

2 What specific targets will you establish to accomplish these changes and in what time frame?

   _____

   _____

3 What specific steps will you undertake to achieve these targets?

   _____

   _____

4 From the above analysis of your organization, what changes should be planned now?

   _____

   _____

5 What strategies would you propose to implement these changes?

   _____

   _____

6 What personal contribution could you make to fostering these changes in your organization?

   _____

   _____

On the basis of this learning experience, a group or team might engage in joint "Action planning" to identify what organizational changes should be sought immediately and what could be done to accomplish these. Now consider the next exhibit in terms of the risk-taking required in the promotion of a change.

EXHIBIT 7.9 Systems analysis

Regardless of the change being planned, an individual or group may engage in an introspective process to identify the risks involved and to assess what may happen if one does/does not facilitate the change. Weighing the pros and cons in this regard may help in the decision to proceed or not with the innovation or alteration. The following example demonstrates how one management team uses this approach to consider changes in their management style.

Recall that undue resistance to change is caused by fear, particularly hesitancy to take risks. There are two types of people in the world – world-makers and world-squatters. The critical factor distinguishing the two seems to be risk-taking – the former will take reasonable risks, while the latter sit back, play it safe, and observe from the sideline. A reasonable risk-taker weighs alternatives, makes decisions, and assumes responsibility for control of his or her own life. Living involves making changes, many of which are taken unconsciously. Those who accomplish great things in their personal and professional lives are aware of the risks, consider them carefully, and are not afraid to make judgments. In other words, they are not afraid to stick their necks out.

Risk-taking can be creative. To illustrate this creativity, here is a creative risk report by a group of supervisors on the risks involved in adopting a "Theory Y," or an EP approach to management. This example will underscore the insights that can be obtained by a group dynamic approach. Read and discuss implications with your group.

Creative risk taking

EXHIBIT 7.10 Creative risk taking

Risk	Reasons
Lack of time to meet deadlines by using this management style	Personal needs interfere with accomplishing task and prevent lack of mutual understanding
Inability of subordinates to work together and arrive at a timely decision	Perhaps the composition of the group is inadequate and the wrong members are participating
Having to change is painful. The old way is easier	Threat of the unknown, loss of traditional controls, initial confusion in learning new approach
The authority of middle and upper management is compromised	Lack of information and training in new concepts and practices

EXHIBIT 7.10 Continued

Risk	Reasons
Inefficiency because it takes too much time and involves too many	Preliminary inefficiency may result in long-term commitment and greater productivity because of involvement
Some of the traditionalists will resent it, and the dependent types will be afraid to participate	No risk – too big an issue for compromise, those who can't be retrained will have to take their chances

The challenge in the creative risk exercise is to have the whole group examine and weigh the risks, as well as the alternatives, if participative management is not adopted. The above data can be "massaged" and new learning stimulated. Based on this input, these five principal conclusions may be reached:

1 The primary responsibility of the manager is to define the area of freedom relative to the new leadership style. Greater personal growth can be possible in this new participative mode, and this can contribute to greater organizational growth.
2 With proper planning, time problems can be minimized; initial time loss by this method can be regained by improved organizational relations and cooperation.
3 Success is not measured by getting things done but by getting them done better.
4 The new approach permits expression of diversity of opinion in the discussion stage and may prevent costly mistakes.
5 Training is required for subordinates to gain new skills in cooperative group action.

Instrumentation

What is your personal attitude toward making changes in your life? The change inventory below is a two-part checklist for determining a leader's attitude toward accelerating change. There are fifteen statements of attitude, and participants indicate how often they feel that way – "usually," "sometimes," or "never." The first eight items deal with the qualities required in an agent of change – openness, flexibility, sensitiveness, creativeness, person-centeredness, and goal oriented planning. The second part examines the capacity to cope with personal and organizational change relative to changing image, construct, values, role, society, goals, and lifestyle. The inventory takes about fifteen minutes to fill out. If desired, participants may share findings or enter into a group discussion on their significance. The instrument can be used to create self-awareness and to stimulate thinking about planned change, or to delimit "future shock." As an OD survey, it can provide insight into managerial attitudes toward change.

Change inventory for leaders

Do you have a positive or negative attitude toward change? Most people fear change, but the issue is whether you let such concern paralyze you into inaction. Some people merely react to change; others are proactive – they plan and control change.[42]

EXHIBIT 7.11   Change inventory for leaders

Part 1: The following check list includes some characteristics of effective change agents. You may find it useful to analyze yourself as an agent of change in your organization or community by evaluating yourself on these criteria, checking your present lifestyle in terms of one of the following: "usually," "sometimes," or "never."

1 Openness – willing to consider new ideas and people of differing opinions; tentative in communications, rather than dogmatic or closed-minded in one's approach.

   Usually   ☐
   Sometimes   ☐
   Never   ☐

2 Flexibility – adaptable to new people, situations, information and developments; able to handle the unexpected and to shift position; spontaneous in responding to the "here-and-now" data and experiences.

   Usually   ☐
   Sometimes   ☐
   Never   ☐

3 Sensitiveness – conscious of what is happening to oneself and others in the communications about the change and its effects; aware of the needs and feelings of others because of the proposed change; able to respond empathetically.

   Usually   ☐
   Sometimes   ☐
   Never   ☐

4 Creativeness – respond with resourcefulness to new people and situations; avoid stereotype answers and solutions; exercise initiative, imagination and innovativeness.

   Usually   ☐
   Sometimes   ☐
   Never   ☐

Continued

---

5 Person-centered – concerned more about people than task or mere progress; care what happens to the people involved in the change; support, encourage, inform, and involve people in the decisions for change which they will be expected to implement; respect the right of dissent.

Usually ☐
Sometimes ☐
Never ☐

6 Goal oriented planning – develop a case for change with others which takes into account long-range objectives, while developing a plan with different stages or targets and short-term steps to accomplish the planned change; communicate these purposes and plans to all involved; state goals in terms that have positive value to those affected by the change.

Usually ☐
Sometimes ☐
Never ☐

7 Group understanding – possess knowledge of the group process and skills in team dynamics; analyze the driving and resisting forces within the group relative to proposed change; understand the character, structure, needs, and wants of the group or organization to be affected by change; involving entire group in change process.

Usually ☐
Sometimes ☐
Never ☐

8 Communicativeness – promote open, circular interaction; able to analyze and clarify the problem and reasons for change; motivate members to desire to change and to use the available resources; develop a helping relationship with others so they can accept and live with the change.

Usually ☐
Sometimes ☐
Never ☐

Part 2: Relative to your capacity to cope more effectively with rapid change in your own personal and organizational life, indicate your present typical response by checking the category in the right hand columns which is most appropriate for each descriptive item in the paragraphs on the left. Be self-critical in your appraisal, for no one will receive these results but you, and it is intended as an exercise in "mind stretching."

Continued

9 Changing image – possess the capacity to re-evaluate my concept of self-based on new feedback, so as to expand my self-image; fluid in my self-conception, amplifying my sense of identity as a result of new encounters and experiences.

Usually ☐
Sometimes ☐
Never ☐

10 Changing construct – willing to review periodically the way I read meaning in my life; flexible in my attitudes and perceptions, so as to make "new sense" out of added inputs and insights; able to break out of "old mindsets" and to develop new rationale; able to accept, at times, inconsistencies and discontinuity in my life.

Usually ☐
Sometimes ☐
Never ☐

11 Changing values – able to sense new needs in myself and others, to develop new and changing life values, to abandon past, ready-made values and ideals, to revise my expectations of self and others; and, as a result, willing to re-examine the norms or standards which I have set for myself and others and to develop new ones as appropriate.

Usually ☐
Sometimes ☐
Never ☐

12 Changing role – willing to have an unclear, hazy role in life or an organization, one that is dynamic and responds to current relevant needs; able to live with a role definition which is open-ended and subject to continuous clarification; accept new role definitions for women, for parents and spouses, for colleagues, for professionals, and other career people.

Usually ☐
Sometimes ☐
Never ☐

13 Changing society – able to be comfortable with impermanence or a lack of structure; capable of coping with constant alteration and perpetual transition; willing to live in changing times, without the traditional stability and reference groups; able to make the most of the present moment – the "here-and-now" – to be "existential" or to "hang loose," ready to combat

Continued

unwarranted resistance to change in myself and the communities in which I participate.

Usually   ☐
Sometimes   ☐
Never   ☐

14 Changing goals – concerned about actualizing my own and others' potential, as well as increasing the levels of awareness and consciousness in both; seek improvement in my capacity for feeling, and intuitiveness, for creating and risk-taking; desire more knowledge and education for personal and professional development; willing to provide cultural leadership by experimenting with new life styles of adaptation to the demands of rapid change.

Usually   ☐
Sometimes   ☐
Never   ☐

15 Changing lifestyle – willing to be more transient and mobile within and among organizations; able to change jobs and locations when appropriate; capable of abandoning old relationships when necessary, and to search for new, more meaningful ones; willing to reject past stereotypes of other people, especially various minorities or foreigners; able to participate in team efforts to solve increasingly complex problems; able to cope with stress and urban crowding, lack of privacy, noise, pollution, and other modern discomforts, while seeking to improve these situations; capable of enduring discontinuities and disconnections in my life.

Usually   ☐
Sometimes   ☐
Never   ☐

Note: The above inventory items are offered with a view to stimulating your thinking about planned changes within your personal and organizational life space if "future shock" is to be avoided or minimized. There are no "right" or "wrong" answers. Research indicates that people who check "usually" are moving in the direction of developing those qualities which make for a more healthy personality in today's and tomorrow's fast-changing world. Those who check only "sometimes" or "never" are challenged by such items to set new personal goals which enable them to move in the future to a state of mind or behavior whereby they can mark "usually" if they were to retake the inventory. You may wish to compare your answers with others in your group, team, or work unit.

Force field analysis inventory

Force field analysis could be used, for example, with each of the changes identified previously. This instrument helps you or others diagnose driving and restraining change forces in people or organizations. There are eighteen questions, ranging from analysis of the type of change and one's relationship to it, to the resources available to implement the change and the case that can be made to get others to support it. Item 7 requires use of the accompanying worksheet for in-depth consideration of the driving and resisting forces to this alteration of the present equilibrium or status quo. Thirty minutes is required for a thinking manager or professional to answer the inquiries and to delimit the trauma of transiting away from the "way we always did it." The inventory is suitable for group analysis, especially on organizational changes.

For example, suppose a department group has identified likely changes to occur over the next ten years within a specific market. Force field analysis can be applied to study which human or non-human forces push for each change, as well as the forces likely to restrain the driving forces from having their fullest impact. Such forces may be human (some person who is pushing for the change), or non-human (like a drop in the stock market or a natural disaster). Forces may be ideas, principles, other people, or within oneself (self-image, needs, standards, perception). Essentially, human behavior is the product of a field of interdependent factors which motivate or energize individuals and organizations. These have been designated *energy forces* (physical or psychological).

EXHIBIT 7.12   Force field analysis inventory

This exercise requires you to check or write-in short answers to the following eighteen questions:

1 Describe the change you wish to initiate:

   _____

   _____

2 Analyze the type of change (check one or more):

   Policy
   Structure
   Attitude
   Program
   Procedures/methods
   Other

   _____

   _____

Continued

---

3 Self-analysis (describe your relationship to the change and analyze needs and motives for promoting it)

_____

_____

4 Organization analysis (describe briefly why the company, agency, association, larger society will benefit from this planned change)

_____

_____

5 Related effects (describe the other effects this change may have on the socio-economic system in which it may be introduced)

_____

_____

6 Identify potential change agents (note the names of those people who can collaborate with you in the promotion of this planned change)

_____

_____

7 Analysis of forces (use worksheet after item number 18 to list the driving and resisting force in your life space which will promote or retard the introduction of this intended change. Within your perceptual field, analyze these forces which may be persons, events, situations, customs and traditions, etc.)

_____

_____

8 Arguments for/against (anticipate objections which might be raised by those resistive to the change and how you may deflect its force)

Argument for_____

Counter argument_____

_____

9 Analysis of creative dissent (listen to the valid objections to the change as you intend to promote it. If you are satisfied that the change is still worthwhile, what modifications should be made in your plan as a result of

Continued

these observations? How would you revise the plan?)

_____

_____

10 Channel resistance (what steps can be taken to convert some resistance into a constructive force for the change?)

_____

_____

11 Inventory resources (what other resources are present in the organization which can be utilized in initiating and carrying out this change?)

_____

_____

12 Develop your case (summarize the case for change which you will later develop in detail)

_____

_____

(Now do the investigation or research which makes the change worthy of support.)

13 Communicate your case (your reasons for the change must be properly conveyed to those who will be affected by the change; create a climate of readiness).
    How? What media will you use to communicate this message?

_____

_____

To whom will you primarily direct this communication?

_____

_____

(The above should not only include names of individuals, but divisions and departments within the organization.)

14 Other strategies (in addition to what has already been done, what other steps could you take to insure the general acceptance of this change)

_____

_____

15 Project ahead (if you understand your goal in this change, as well as the means for achieving it and your expectations if it is inaugurated, then you are in a position to predict the probable outcomes when this change is under way)

_____

_____

Continued

16 Action plan (list the immediate steps to be taken to get the change accepted and functioning. You may wish to include a testing or pilot project phase)

_____

_____

Use additional sheets of paper if more space is needed. Such a plan should include what is to be done, how it is to be done, who is to do it, when it is to be done. It should include a data gathering stage before communication.

17 Alternative plan (if the plan you propose is rejected, you should have done adequate thinking on other alternatives to the change as described)

_____

_____

18 Participative provisions (if the change is to be successfully introduced, then some provisions must be made to involve those who will be expected to implement the change or who will be affected by it. What have you done with regard to planning and decision making to insure that this has been accomplished?)

_____

_____

Worksheet for Item 7 Analysis of Forces

_____

Driving (D)
(list all the promoting forces for the change)

1 _____

2 _____

3 _____

4 _____

5 _____

6 _____

7 _____

Continued

8 _____

9 _____

10 _____

11 _____

12 _____

Resisting (R)
(list all the restraining forces against the change)

1 _____

2 _____

3 _____

4 _____

5 _____

6 _____

7 _____

8 _____

9 _____

10 _____

11 _____

12 _____

Checklist (in identifying the above sets of forces, did you list those which might be found under these headings? If you missed any, then note them under D or R)

Continued

200 Leading in the management of change

( ) Goal/objectives problems
( ) Power/authority problems
( ) Communication problems
( ) Role/relationship problems
( ) Decision making problems

Change theme review

High performance leadership is achieved mainly through people skills. Certainly, today's executives have to know how to manage technology, to take advantage of scientific advances to reduce costs, and to utilize innovations. But that is not enough to ensure outstanding organizational effectiveness – it is in the arena of human resource management that the real pay-off will come over the long term. To streamline bureaucracies and function well in a high-tech environment, managers will have to exercise judgment and communicate more easily and quickly with diverse employees. The increase in foreign joint ventures and overseas manufacturing also requires managers to deal with someone not only from another company, but another culture. Therefore, our emphasis in this text so far is on leadership development of all human relations, particularly cross-cultural.[43]

The media is filled with stories about global management waking up to the new work realities, especially regarding the critical human factors. The messages of behavioral scientists to management for the past sixty years are finally being heard and practiced. Everybody, from the high level manager to people at the hourly level, like to feel they are participating in the decision making. If people do not feel like they own a piece of the action, then they are not going to act like entrepreneurs; they are going to act like paid help. HPLs value personnel, employee relations, and talents. They resist putting profits before quality products and service. Executives must relearn that their primary resource is people: power and profit reside in personnel, not property.

We have completed our review of the six major human relations themes that dominate the behavioral science management literature. We began by examining the issue of leadership in a knowledge culture with a high performance work environment. We then examined motivation and related factors of human performance at work. Then we concentrated on the communication skills necessary for both personal and organizational excellence. Furthermore, we linked these insights to culture and its impact on behavior at work. We also focused upon human relationships in terms of both organizations and teams, demonstrating their importance, particularly with reference to decision making and conflict management. Finally, we concluded with change and why it is so vital to manage it for personal and OT. Through this volume, so far, the emphasis has been upon these six dimensions for developing human potential.

Throughout the Introduction, Input, Interaction, and Instrumentation sections of our previous chapters, creative ideas and methods have been suggested for the leader to share these learnings with colleagues. However, the next two chapters will focus specifically on presentation skills for managers or trainers who wish to transmit these key insights to co-workers or customers, and the last chapter will provide forecasts about leadership for the remainder of this twenty-first century.

8

DEVELOPING PEOPLE THROUGH LEARNING

Introduction

In an information society, in which knowledge is power, a large part of the work force is engaged in acquiring, analyzing, processing, distributing, or otherwise servicing this precious resource. Data are pieced together to form information, and information is shaped to create knowledge. When knowledge provides enlightenment, it can then be profitably applied to improve performance or to increase productivity. This happens as a result of study, of sharing the knowledge. The process is called learning – the systematic acquisition of knowledge, for instance, as in the mastery of a specific scholarly field or a new technology. In the emerging social environment the new work culture emphasizes lifelong learning, either formally or informally. Today those who would be leaders must first and foremost be learners. They must create a learning environment for the human systems in which they lead, so that learning may be fostered among others.

To capitalize on an organization's human assets, leaders must develop people. In Chapter 1, I described the emerging role of the manager as an agent of change. For career development, such planned change begins with oneself and extends outward to include those for whom one is directly responsible. This human resource management and development function includes the promotion of learning (the Epilogue will develop this theme even further).

Such learning can happen through:

- attendance at classes outside the organization, for instance, universities, colleges, adult education centers, or through conferences and seminars sponsored by professional and trade associations;
- self-learning endeavors, such as by reading or online study, enrolling in correspondence or television courses, using video or audio programs, and even by participating in community service activities;

- in-service training opportunities, such as varied programs for personnel development sponsored by a corporation, agency, or association.

While there are multiple opportunities to learn today, the last method is the one that concerns us in this chapter. HRD – simply put, learning – can occur at weekly or monthly staff meetings, or in formal training sessions, annual conferences or retreats, programmed instruction, job rotation, or exchanges. Even an international assignment makes cross-cultural learning possible. If an organization operates a formal "assessment or educational center," then action learning research should occur there.

As a case in point, take the major themes of behavioral science management that we have discussed in this book. How can a reader share these insights with co-workers? The professional development strategy proposed in this chapter will help the manager or trainer improve HRD skills through:

- the concept of action learning, an approach to adult education;
- planning and designing action learning to improve personnel performance;
- action research in training sessions for data gathering and evaluation;
- action learning methods for group dynamics.

As a role model for lifelong learning by doing, consider the following profile of thought leadership.

Lifetime learning

EXHIBIT 8.1   Profile of a HP inventor

Dean Kamen is best known as the inventor of the Segway scooter, but his career illustrates the difficulty of turning innovative ideas into reality. He has spent over forty years involved in promoting technological change. In the process, this high performer has amassed 440 patents, some of which have saved thousands of lives. Now he promotes FIRST (For Inspiration and Recognition of Science and Technology) aimed at nurturing the next generation of innovators. This is a challenging robotic competition which annually attracts 200,000 entrants from schools in fifty-six countries. He hopes the teams participating, supervised by professional scientists and engineers, will be motivated by his $12.2 million in scholarship prizes.

At his DEKA offices, a design and research company in Manchester, New Hampshire, this entrepreneurial genius seeks to inspire youth with his passion for science and technology. He maintains that he "wants kids to realize that engineering and problem solving are fun and rewarding." He hopes his learning

Continued

project will especially excite girls and minority children. His life is a real role model for youth – from a geeky kid of sixteen who first devised a new, dynamic lighting system that responds to sound, he has helped humanity and amassed a fortune through inventing. These include iBOT, a robotic stair climbing wheel chair; a wearable drug infusion pump for diabetics that evolved into a home dialysis machine; a personal, mechanized scooter for city transport; a Sterling generator for using waste products to make electricity. Kamen maintains that while it is easy to develop new technologies, the challenge is in developing new mindsets that move the culture from one mental model to another. To overcome people's resistance to change, this idea instigator hopes that his FIRST contest of one million young participants will help them become proponents of innovations that will impact our lives in the decades ahead!

Source: Based on "Brain Scan – Mr. Segway's Difficult Path," *The Economist*, 12 June 2010: 26.

Input

Action learning strategies

Action learning is a dynamic means for acquiring and applying new knowledge. The HRD function includes recruiting, selecting, counseling, training, and evaluating people. In regard to the last two concerns, action learning creates a learning environment for new insights and information, changing attitudes, and gaining expertise. To foster high performance and to actualize the potential of knowledge workers, action learning is a rationale system for planning, designing, implementing, and evaluating adult education or organizational training. It is a strategy to promote learning by doing, a means for accomplishing andragogy (the art and science of helping mature people learn). Action learning encompasses a variety of methods of learning and requires maximum participation by the learners (trainees). To make the best use of resources, this approach to learning is organized in modules: instructional units, usually several hours long, that are independent in themselves but can be linked together, for instance in a seminar or workshop. The learning modules provide time for the four I's (undertakings as used in each chapter of this book):

Introduction to the learning module – the purpose of the session, such as objectives or goals, often exemplified in a profile of a HPL.

Input from the presenter, facilitator, or trainer; from the trainees; from computers, audiovisual aids, or printed material. PowerPoint software is often used to convey such input.

Interaction or group process opportunities for a group or team to exchange insights and information on the subject matter. Often the profile from the Introduction becomes a focus for discussion.

Instrumentation in the form of inventories or questionnaires that can be used with learners for data gathering, analysis, and reporting.

Action learning sessions can be a mechanism for engaging in action research through interaction and instrumentation, thus contributing to OD. All told, it is an intensive learning experience, both cognitive and experiential, that encourages active participation by trainees or students. Each day learners are expected to write "action plans" based upon the learning obtained. Sometimes their supervisors are given copies of these plans, so that they may follow up on the outcomes of the learning or utilize them in performance appraisal.

Action learning is a strategy that a leader may use for staff training, team building, or to fulfill any HRD function. Action learning can be employed by anyone with a training responsibility and competence. Action learning can be done within the organization, or outside, for instance, at a conference center or as a volunteer in community activities.

In general, action learning has these characteristics:

Situational. It is in-service education or on-the-job training that has as its target *change* in the work situation or in the person who receives the training in the work or therapy situation. It is most effective when it concentrates on training a work unit or team. By providing time for practice in the meeting session, the learner has an opportunity to internalize knowledge.

Experiential. It makes the prime focus training data gathered by participants in the learning experience or provided by them from previous experience.

Plural. It emphasizes both affective and cognitive learning with two or more people; its concern is for both feelings and ideas; it should be a balance of the "I feel" and the "I think."

Problem orientation. It deals with issues for personal and organizational change and provides practice in problem solving and decision making; it aims for action not only in the learning process, but also in the follow up as a result of training.

Systematic. It envisions the training effort as only a sub-system of a larger system for HRD; it is given as a part of a total program for personal and professional growth; it is viewed as an essential component for broader OD. The systems approach can also be applied to the actual training process itself.

Personalized. Although group process may be utilized, due consideration is given to individualizing the learning so as to make allowance for each trainee's unique needs, perceptions, and expectations. Action learning, furthermore, provides performance standards for the trainee by setting goals, objectives or targets. It also offers a means for self-assessment by using feedback and group evaluation.

Action learning is based on certain assumptions about the learner and educational methodology. Dr Malcolm Knowles (1984), the noted adult education specialist, suggested these assumptions:

> Adults enter a learning activity with an image of themselves as self-directing, responsible grown-ups, not as immature, dependent learners. Therefore, they resist situations in which they are treated with disrespect. Implication for methodology; if adults help to plan and conduct their own learning experiences, they will learn more than if they are passive recipients.

> Adults enter a learning activity with more experience than youth. Therefore, they have more to contribute to the learning activity and have a broader basis of experience to relate to new learning. Implication for methodology: those methods which build on and make use of the experience of the learners will produce the greatest learning.

> Adults enter a learning activity with a different quality of experience and different developmental tasks than youth. Implication for methodology: the appropriate organizing principle for adult learning experiences is developmental sequence primarily and logical subject development only secondarily.

> Adults enter a learning activity with more immediate intentions to apply learning to life problems than youth. Therefore, adults require practical results from learning. Implication for methodology: adults will perceive learning experiences that are organized around subject topics.

Another behavioral scientist, Chris Argyris (1982) proposed that such learning be used by a manager to:

- establish trust and cooperation with new members in a work unit;
- build a cohesive and effective work team;
- educate new people in corporate policies, procedures, and culture;
- deal with ineffective performance and improve productivity;
- encourage managers to change leadership style and accept greater responsibility;
- foster a participative group approach to problem solving and planning.

The essential characteristic of action learning is that it seeks behavioral change in the learner. The impact of this learning experience can lead to a change in knowledge, understanding, skills, values, attitudes, interests, or motivations. The conditions necessary for action learning to be effective are:

- recognition of the learner or trainee's needs, as well as those of the organization;
- ability of the learner to take an active role in the process;
- a threat-free learning climate of acceptance and freedom;
- measurable criteria and means for achieving learning goals or module objectives;
- skill on the part of the learning facilitator.

Planning for action learning

There are many ways to meet the above criteria. First, identify the learning or training needs of a group. One strategy is to bring together several knowledgeable and representative people from the organization to assist in planning the learning program. For example, suppose an executive wished to conduct a high performance leadership institute (HPLI) based upon the content of this book. Having identified those for whom the HPLI project is intended, the executive establishes a planning task force with a representative sample of all those eventually to be involved (e.g. people from different levels or divisions of the organization). If the organization has an HRD or training department, obviously these specialists would provide their professional services.

The task force is asked to:

- determine what the organization and the targeted training group need in the way of human relations skills;
- review this text's ability to provide the information, instruments, and interaction methods needed, and ascertain if additional learning materials are required;
- employ the method described in Exhibit 8.2 to further refine the planning process for the proposed institute;
- finalize the objectives of the program, the number and topics of learning modules to be presented, dates and schedule of the institute, the learning materials necessary (such as audiovisual aids or film/video disk rentals), preferred instructional methods and resources (e.g. case studies or simulations, speakers or trainers), suggested action research during the sessions (e.g. forms of data collection, program evaluation).

EXHIBIT 8.2   Action learning planning model

Planning task force procedure (the initials stand for the major topics or tasks which make up this model: Needs, Goals, Methods, Contents and Resources):

1 The planning group or committee should be divided into five sub-groups for task assignments and formed into small circles.
2 Each group is given several sheets of large newsprint or flip chart paper and a felt tipped marking pen for reporting purposes; it is asked to choose a recorder.
3 Each group is given a specific task as outlined in Exhibit 8.3; each group works on one of the five tasks within a definite time frame (e.g. 30–45 minutes).
4 The consensus of their findings should be summarized on a single sheet of large newsprint or flip chart paper.

Continued

5 This is then posted in sequence (N/G/M/C/R) with the other reports on a wall using masking tape; each task force recorder then provides an oral summary for the group using the outline displayed.
6 When all sub-groups have reported, the entire committee reviews the results in order to modify and integrate the data into a meaningful whole.
7 The committee then decides whether (a) it can accept the information as edited as its training plan or (b) it should return for further group work to refine the reports in each of the five categories or (c) it should appoint an ad hoc coordinating commission to synthesize the information and issue a formal training plan.

The Planning Task Force may prefer to work together as one entity and follow the next model in sequence, or divide up into sub-groups. Exhibit 8.3 provides an overview of the five key steps in this planning paradigm, relating the proposed learning to the organization's human resources development strategies. There are other planning possibilities, such as to formulate a planning flowchart which identifies the target audience, develops a questionnaire for obtaining information from the intended trainees as to their needs on the job, and lists the action learning planning task force and their responsibilities.

EXHIBIT 8.3 Planning model sequence

Needs

The Action Learning Task Force develops a policy statement which summarizes the training needs of the group you seek to serve by this educational program. In your discussion, please focus on the following issues, incorporating the decisions in the group report.

1 What are the overall training needs for this learning experience?
2 What training is presently available to serve these needs?
3 What are the unmet training needs?
4 In terms of priorities, list the most important needs to which this training program should be directed (check the hierarchy of human needs to see if any level has been neglected – physical, security, belonging, recognition, self-fulfillment).

Goals

The purpose of the next meeting is to develop the goals for training in the area of your group's concern. In your discussion, focus upon the following issues:

Continued

1 What are legitimate broad *goals* for divisions or departments in your field and in your institution?
2 What are the *objectives* for training (staff or clients) in the proposed program?
3 How do these relate to organizational goals and objectives?
4 What specific targets should be set in this forthcoming training course?

(Describe behavior changes and consequences desired after training).

Content

The purpose of this session is to develop the content to be covered in the course of HRD. In your discussion, please focus upon:

1 new knowledge to be acquired by the learners;
2 new skills to be developed as a result of the training;
3 new attitudes or insights to be attained by the trainees.

Methods

The purpose of this session is to agree regarding the varied methodologies for the proposed training. In your discussion, focus upon:

1 a general pedagogical approach;
2 specific methods and techniques to be employed;
3 evaluation instruments and procedures to be utilized.

Resources

The purpose of this session is to decide on the educational resources available for the projected training. In your discussion, focus upon:

1 the general support services and resource consultants in your community which could be used to enhance your training effort;
2 the overall resources – human and material – in your organization which could be tapped for the proposed training;
3 the specific resources in your center or training department that would actually be utilized for this training;
4 Check to see if you have neglected any person who can provide valuable assistance, and whether the necessary facility and equipment are available.

Continued

Conclusion

When the total group reviews the five reports and pulls the data together into a comprehensive whole, ask these questions:

1 Have we adequately identified the needs of the organization and the training group?
2 Have we sufficiently detailed the training goals of this program to satisfy those needs?
3 Have we satisfactorily outlined the content to be covered and the methods to be used in the projected training endeavor?
4 Have we sufficiently identified the human and material resources available to conduct this training program?

Now having reviewed the purposes, subject matter, and means for satisfaction of the training needs, consider the following factors relative to *implementation* of these policy statements:

- Action plans: the who, what, when, where, and why relative to the training.
- Research design: how will we evaluate the training and measure its behavioral consequences? What plans should there be for follow up study of the group after training?

Job analysis

Another way to plan for training is a performance oriented job analysis of tasks and functions through interviews with experienced and successful performers in that role. Then, objectives and tests are created for the proposed training with emphasis on specific desired behaviors. The learning experience is designed to ensure such behavior results. The system is described in Exhibit 8.4.

The planning strategy should be appropriate to the specific situation, synthesizing the needs and concerns of both the organizational sponsor and the learners, while ensuring that the presentations and content will accomplish the desired objectives and results. Planning cannot be done in a vacuum and should be participative, including the intended learner.

Designing action learning programs

For leaders who aim to develop high performance personnel, there is an advantage in designing learning programs in terms of needs and functions related to specific job roles. Exhibit 8.5 amplifies the previous systems strategy by proposing ten steps to follow in such a planning process.

EXHIBIT 8.4   Planning interview strategy

STRUCTURED INTERVIEW SAMPLE QUESTIONS

1 Think back to when you first started your present job. What type of training would have helped you at that time?
2 What training would benefit you now in your present job?
3 What training do you need to become a promotable candidate for the next position up? What job is that?
4 What would be the prerequisites for your job? What is the minimum experience level of a candidate for your job?
5 How should you best receive training, i.e. seminars, on the job, computerized-learning, etc.?
6 Where should we have training, i.e. resort hotel, work location?

EXHIBIT 8.5   Ten steps in training needs analysis for a job role

---

1 Analysis of the organization as a human system particularly in terms of its training history, policies, and facilities.
2 Analysis of the particular job in terms of tasks required to accomplish it well and its relationship to other positions.
3 Analysis of job restructuring in terms of other alternatives for doing this activity, or for enriching the work experience on the job.
4 Development of measures for job proficiency, or ways for determining how well the job is being performed if adequate training is provided.
5 Specification of knowledge and skills, or the competencies involved in performing this job well.
6 Determination of training objectives, or what needs to happen in the action learning experience for the trainee to succeed in this job.
7 Synthesizing personnel policies with training objectives by consultation with both personnel and training specialists.
8 Construction of the training program, or design, creation, and conducting of the training for the job for self or group learning.
9 Evaluation of the training, or action research to assess program effectiveness.
10 Consideration for re-training or redesigning; that is, dealing with those who fail to achieve on the job after the training. Is it the fault of the individual? What should be done, if anything about re-training? Are there weaknesses in the training program? How can it be redesigned? Preliminary Program Planning Agreement.

In a sense, all action learning is customized to meet the needs of a client. For an outside consultant, the client is the organization that hires that person, including the people in any training program or meeting. For an internal consultant employed by the corporation or agency, the client is the department, division, or subsidiary seeking that individual's services. In either case, it is valuable to obtain some understanding and agreement as to the program being planned. Exhibit 8.6 is a form which may prove useful for such clarification. The term *trainer* is used to indicate the one with organizational responsibility for planning, designing, and conducting the training; some may prefer *facilitator* or *instructor*. This person can be an HRD specialist or a manager (sales, operations, plant, or safety).

EXHIBIT 8.6   Program planning agreement

Organization/division/department_____

Date_____

Client representative_____

Title_____

Address_____

Telephone_____

Description of proposed services

Program title_____

Purpose of program (goals)_____

_____

Type of trainees (if applicable)_____

Special needs of the group_____

Services training consultant would provide_____

Anticipated number of days:

    Training_____

    Consulting_____

    Research_____

Anticipated number of:

    Trainers_____

    Consultants_____

    Researchers_____

    Trainees_____

Preferred dates for the program_____

Number of sessions to be conducted_____

Number of days to be in session_____

Number of learning modules per session_____

Continued

Materials trainer would provide_____

Materials client would provide_____

Number and type of client staff available to assist with
training/coordinating_____

Place(s) program to be conducted
Facility to be utilized_____
( ) Client to make arrangements
( ) Trainer to make arrangements

Acceptance can be indicated by signing and returning one copy of this agreement
Approved for_____
Accepted by_____
(Trainer signature)_____   (Client signature)_____
Date_____
(one copy is retained by client; one by trainer)

For a manager undertaking such training with his or her own staff, the items may be useful as a checklist for preliminary discussions about the learning with the participants.

As part of the design phase, a leader in learning may wish to prepare a "prework package." Participants receive this handout material prior to the opening session of training. It contains advanced reading materials on the subjects to be discussed, or an inventory or questionnaire to be completed before the first learning module. This could sensitize the learners to issues to be considered and get them interested in the coming sessions. As an alternative, the completed instrument could be collected as part of the registration process for the training course. In that case, the information is feedback on trainee expectations to be used in both the design and preparing for presentations.

Some professional trainers prefer to wait until the initial meeting with the learning group to engage in an "expectations exercise," which is then included in the learning design. Following the general orientation to the program and introduction of the key resource personnel, the exercise is an opportunity to clarify why participants are engaged in this learning as they introduce themselves to the group. Each trainee at the opening session is invited:

- to write down three personal expectations regarding the learning experience;
- to join a small group to share those expectations and to come to some consensus on the principal expectations of that group;

- finally, to put the group's mutual concerns down on newsprint or flip chart paper and share them with the total class or seminar.

The trainer or facilitator then posts these sheets around the room. In this first session, the trainer comments on his or her own expectations of the participants and the program. In the closing session, as part of the evaluation process, the trainer refers to the expectations on display and discusses with the learners whether they were fulfilled, and to what degree.

Previously, we indicated that the planning should include setting forth both the organizational and individual program objectives. Eventually, this statement of objectives is distributed to the participants (along with the program format or schedule). At the same time, the trainer should set down specific behavior and performance changes to be sought through the training. The design of the actual program should be developed with such changes in mind. For example, if the contents of this book were to be incorporated into a HPLI for selected employees, the general program theme, "Increasing Organizational Effectiveness with People," might be included in the announcement or schedule. Each training session or learning module, then, might have a specific theme that aims at a particular behavioral change or performance improvement, such as "Improving Management Communication Skills."

Final planning includes selecting particular learning activities with the participants that contribute to the achievement of program objectives. Trainers or facilitators should limit their "on air" time during the sessions. In place of long lectures, for example, short presentations are preferred, lasting 15–35 minutes. In the Interaction section of this chapter some methods for group process are discussed. Exhibit 8.7 demonstrates some of the possibilities to ensure learning variety that will stimulate the learners.

EXHIBIT 8.7 Selecting alternative learning activities

GENERAL SESSIONS

Platform presentations:

- speeches, research reports, book reviews
- individual or group interviews
- panel discussion, symposium, debate
- audiovisual aids, dramatizations
- powerpoint presentation, demonstrations

Audience participation:

- listening teams, reaction panels
- audience role playing

Continued

- buzz session by sub-grouping
- question and answer session
- group or team reports
- triad consultations on content
- open discussion on presentations

Types of work groups:

- problem solving groups/task forces
- discussion groups
- listening group
- planning groups
- instructional groups
- research and evaluation groups
- skill practice groups
- consultation groups
- operational groups
- leaderless groups

In designing learning topics and activities, the facilitator is concerned about:

- sequence (movement); logic
- continuity (line); build on previous knowledge
- unity (coherence); appropriateness
- rhythm (pace); variety
- color (spirit); excitement
- climate (feelings); atmosphere
- creativity (uniqueness); innovativeness
- involvement (ego-identification); participation

Another critical factor in meeting planning is the selection of the appropriate presenter for live input during the training program. If an in-house leader or trainer is not suitable, then speakers may be sought from elsewhere within the organization. It may be necessary to use an expert from a nearby university, a trade or professional association, or an industrial source. Speakers directories are available from several sources including the National Speakers Association and the American Society of Association Executives. Many national and international professional associations have membership directories that may be helpful in this search. A logical source to start with is the American Society for Training and Development, which offers a national Who's Who in Training and Development. Once a presenter has been chosen, invitations have to be communicated to that person, negotiations undertaken, and speaking dates and expectations confirmed. The program planning agreement shown in Exhibit 8.6 may prove useful in this regard.

During the design phase, the trainer or manager will have to select or create instruments to gather data or to create awareness among the participants. Throughout this book, the Instrumentation sections have shown examples and possibilities.

It is helpful if the participants receive a program schedule or agenda at least two weeks prior to the actual training event. Exhibit 8.8 is a sample of a schedule for a training institute on the contents of this book, and Exhibit 8.9 suggests a form for ensuring that all necessary supplies and materials are on hand for the opening of the training session. Provision is made to include other learning aids, which could range from games to computers.

Preparations also include supervising the reproduction and packaging of the learning materials, from textbooks to workbooks to name tags, to be distributed to participants. It is vital that the HRD planner order films, DVDs, videotapes, slides, and other audiovisual aids in advance so that they are available at the time and place required. Just before the event, it is wise to preview all audiovisual materials. If guest speakers have been invited, double check on their availability as previously scheduled.

Similarly, arrangements must be made for adequate rest period facilities and for refreshments, possibly when trainees arrive in the morning or during the mid-session breaks. Sometimes this may include group meals for participants, which involves menu selection, luncheon speakers, or the showing of a film. In a seven-day program, it is advisable to allow one afternoon for play – such as a golf tournament, or small group discussion for action planning; or even a field trip to a local sight of interest.

Nothing should be left to chance if high performance is to occur during the learning. An organization makes a significant investment when it devotes time, energy, finances, and people to a training program, so HRD planners strive to ensure that people both enjoy and learn while the program moves along smoothly and produces the desired results. When dealing with external facilities, such as hotels, triple-checking with their representatives may ensure that arrangements proceed smoothly. Remember Murphy's Law – if anything can go wrong it will. Then there is O'Toole's Law – Murphy is an optimist!

As we have described the planning process, it should be evident that those who take a professional approach to action learning effectively prepare very carefully and leave nothing to chance before, during, and after the training session. Furthermore, they seek to:

- customize the design of the training to meet both organizational and trainee needs;
- vary the learning experience, so as to maintain interest and involvement on the part of participants;
- use training sessions for data gathering and action research, so as to achieve OD aims.

EXHIBIT 8.8 Schedule for a high performance leadership institute

	First Day	Second Day	Third Day
AM 8:00	Learning Module I Dynamics of human behavior ■ Input: Human motivation ■ Learning aids: slides; "Motivation of Human Resources," handout; "Management Motivation Inventory" ■ Group process: Input bombardment	Learning Module III Improving communication skills ■ Input: A behavioral communication theory; perception and communication model ■ Learning aids: slides; "Communication as a People Process," handout; "Communication Inventory" ■ Film	Learning Module V Creative approaches to conflict resolution in organizations ■ Input: Conflict utilization theory ■ Group process: Anecdotal reports ■ Learning aids: "Analysis of Conflict Utilization," handout ■ Film
12:00 Noon	Learning Module II Understanding deviant behavior ■ Group process: Critical incidents ■ Film ■ Learning aids: "Motivation & Human Resource Development," handout; "Human Resource Inventory"	Learning Module IV Overcoming communication obstacles ■ Group process: Communications laboratory ■ Learning aids: "Organization Communications Analysis"; "Communications Bibliography"	Learning Module VI Insights from client feedback ■ Input: Utilizing feedback ■ Learning aids: audio or videotape playback; administration of client profile – "The Helping Relationship and Feedback in Organizations," handout and exercise
PM 1:00			
5:00			

EXHIBIT 8.8 Continued

	Fourth Day	Fifth Day	Sixth Day
AM 8:00	Learning Module VII Cultural influences on client/staff behavior ■ Input: Concept of culture ■ Learning aids: slides ■ Group process: "Understanding Culture," programmed learning exercise	Learning Module IX Understanding group behavior in organizations ■ Input: Group dynamics and organization relations ■ Learning aids: "Systems Approach to Groups and Organizations" ■ Group process: Task assignment	Learning Module XI Managing change and changing roles ■ Input: Why and how to plan change ■ Learning aids: slides and film; "Management of Change Inventory" ■ Group process: "Force Field Analysis"
12:00 Noon	Learning Module VIII	Learning Module X	Learning Module XII
PM 1:00	Cultural influences on decision making ■ Management game – Moon Twenty or Hollow Square	Interpersonal skills for human resource personnel ■ Simulation exercise: Kerner Commission Report	Behavioral strategies within organizations and with clients ■ Learning aids: Brainstorming ■ Optional programs: Creative problem solving
5:00	■ Learning aid: decision making and cultural influences ■ Group process: "Intercultural Relations Inventory," or "Supervisor/Worker Relations" exercise	■ Learning aid: "Behavioral Science Management," handout; "Organizational Roles & Relationship Inventory" ■ Film	■ Closing ceremony ■ Distribution of certificates ■ Evaluations

EXHIBIT 8.9 Checklist for training materials and supplies

Project manager:	Date:
Client and program:	Shipping/pick up instructions, including dates:
Item	Check if needed To be provided by

A Training aids
  1 Overhead transparency projector
  2 16 mm movie projector/other media
  3 Screen size
  4 Blackboard, eraser, chalk
  5 Newsprint, easel, and paper
  6 Podium type
  7 Computer generated or slide projector
  8 Tape recorder audio ( ), video ( )
  9 Flannel board
  10 Laptop computer/electronic projector
  11 Multimedia accessories
  12 White board connected to personal
      computer or tablet plus digital
      marking pens.
  13 Other: PowerPoint software, etc.

B Training materials
  1 Pencil sharpener
  2 Stapler
  3 Name tents
  4 Lapel tags
  5 Pencils/pens
  6 Yellow tablets
  7 Punched white bond paper
  8 Grease crayons (marking pencils)
  9 Masking tape
  10 Training workbooks (number)
  11 Special handouts (number of items)
  12 Other:

The whole human resource management effort is aimed at making people more productive; this is doubly true for HRD planning and implementation that is intended to develop leaders.

Implementing the training plan

Those who are not amateurs at offering training programs, take steps to make certain that the plan is carried out effectively. That means working assiduously with those in charge of the meeting facilities, whether internal or external (see Chapter 9). The meeting coordinator seeks to provide a comfortable facility with

proper lighting, noise control, ventilation (air conditioning or heating as necessary), seating, equipment, and other amenities to facilitate learning. The details are
important and should be resolved in advance.

Twelve learning modules, as described in Exhibit 8.8, can be accomplished in
six days, perhaps during a one-week session at a residential or resort facility.

Adult workers are not used to sitting for learning purposes for six to eight hours
a day for almost a full week. Even with the best action learning plan, to make the
process more acceptable and to improve performance, the sponsor must do other
things, such as scheduling a recreation hour after lunch, or a hospitality hour at
five p.m. Perhaps the afternoon of the fourth day could be given over to golf or
sightseeing or the evening devoted to a fiesta, luau, or banquet. If the same program
is scheduled for six monthly meetings held in the company training room, such
arrangements are unnecessary. The way the schedule is implemented influences the
choice of site and the other arrangements.

Group size also influences the facility arrangements. Learning groups often consist of from twenty to forty people; the ideal for effective participation is around
thirty. If small rooms are used for such groups, then extra, break-out rooms or out-
door facilities may be necessary for sub-group meetings. A very large ballroom can
also be used, with the training area in the center and circles of chairs on the sides
for smaller group discussions. On the other hand, if there is a large audience of several hundred, or even several thousand, the seats must be movable so attendees can
move chairs to form small groups of from three to six people for short assignments.

Room arrangements depend on program objectives, participant numbers, and
facility possibilities or limitations. Assuming a group of thirty, it is often advantageous to set up the training room with tables forming a U; people can sit along the
outside of the U, and the center is left open for a projection table and for the trainer
to easily move among the participants. That same open area can also be utilized for
role playing or demonstration; a screen for visual aids, a lectern, a table for trainer
supplies, and a blackboard or easel can be set up at the top of the U. Name plates
or cards will help staff members identify participants.

The implementation stage begins at the training site when the trainer arrives
well in advance of the trainees to ensure that all learning materials and equipment
are in place and in working order. If necessary, an information or registration desk
is set up and staffed. Food and refreshment arrangements must be finally checked.
Then the training coordinator warmly greets the participants either informally and
personally, as they arrive, by circulating during a reception or registration hour, or
by welcoming them as a group during the opening sessions. An informal, friendly
atmosphere facilitates learning.

Special guests, such as company officials, speakers, or panelists, have to be
greeted and acculturated, so they integrate quickly and smoothly into the learning experience. Everyone, including learners, guest presenters, and organizational
representatives, should be made to feel wanted and comfortable by the HRD staff
or manager.

Exhibit 8.10 lists some useful guidelines for adult education. The training coordinator needs to be especially mindful of timing and pacing, so that activities occur as scheduled and the program moves along in a lively manner. Learning can be fun as well as enlightening, and boredom can be avoided. Despite all the detailed planning, be prepared not only with contingency plans, but to meet the unexpected, from power failure to a speaker's sudden unavailability.

Worldwide, the curriculum of universities and colleges is often far behind the actual job market needs. Furthermore, too many institutions of higher education still use the traditional lecture system, failing to utilize modern communication technologies in their teaching. Action learning is also needed within institutions of higher education. Schools of Education who prepare teachers, and any form of continuing education would benefit by adopting action learning strategies.

Lifelong learning is also being encouraged by government and organizational subsidies of various types. Grants for further education and training is becoming commonplace in our knowledge culture. People denied such necessary learning often end up in an "underclass" deprived of income and opportunity. Thus, it is essential for leaders to ensure that the learning is relevant and motivating. Learning should be a transforming experience.

Completion of any educational milestone calls for recognition, whether this marks the ending of a formal school or training experience. The closing ceremony indicates that the learner is "graduating" into another learning opportunity or stage. Therefore, we mark such occasions with special ceremonies to celebrate another life success.

It is also an occasion to take a training class photograph or to present a video that encapsulates the whole learning experience.

EXHIBIT 8.10 Guidelines for training adults

Globally, humanity is moving into the age of the "knowledge worker" in contrast to the laborer of the past. Increasingly, authority will be given to those with the information and skill to solve complex problems. Competence is becoming the true criteria for career advancement. Continuous change in technologies also requires new training. Thus, there is a growing demand by adults for continuing education. Large numbers of personnel must be constantly retrained in new skills and occupations. Because of this expanding desire for learning, their instructors, too, must develop more dynamic methods for teaching them. If the interest and commitment of mature learners is to be maintained, then various instructional techniques must be used which personally involve the trainees.

Instructors in continuing education should take into account the following factors in preparing their course presentations:

1 The age, maturity and diversity within the trainee group.

Continued

2 Previous trainee education and the length of time since the trainee was involved in formal instruction.

3 The actual needs of participants for the content of the course (e.g. in adapting a particular course to a trainee group, some subject matter might be eliminated and other topics added).

4 The amount of time the trainees are devoting to an intensive schedule of classes (e.g. sitting for five or six hours over a one or two-week period will cause fatigue and limit efficiency of learning; it also reduces the available time for outside reading assignments which are usually expected).

5 In residential programs, the trainees may travel long distances to a strange location and be separated from their families (this requires extra effort on the part of the staff to help them feel at home, overcome strangeness, facilitate their adjustment, and assist in any problems; each instructor should be concerned about the human factors related to the participants' learning).

6 To make learning a pleasant experience, an informal classroom atmosphere is to be encouraged. The instructors can help the trainees appreciate the value of further education and the need for continuing self-development.

7 Adults are normally very grateful for any help offered and hold trainers in high regard. Frequently, the instructor will have great impact on adult trainees and their organizations. Therefore, flippancy and unsubstantiated generalizations are to be avoided; your words may be quoted to back-home organizations and your behavior imitated.

8 That trainees have interesting and varied experiences which they should be encouraged to share with the group (they may even present their own case studies). The key factors in adult training are variety and participation. It is not always possible to have a variety of places at which the training is conducted (e.g. change of classroom or setting). However, you can use different techniques in the sessions. While the lecture method might be acceptable with the class which meets two or three times a week for a short time period, it becomes wearing to sit in one place for long sessions with only one instructional method.

9 A varied approach to teaching is very helpful in maintaining interest. Furthermore, it is disconcerting to sit several hours simply listening and taking notes. The field of group dynamics provides many worthwhile ideas for improvement of adult training.

Finally, Exhibit 8.11 suggests some strategies for bringing the training program to a fitting and successful conclusion. The purpose is not only to achieve a learning climax, but to send the learner away satisfied and motivated. The training cycle ends with program evaluation, which begins during the closing session, when some time is devoted to filling out feedback forms. At this time, the participants might discuss what they have learned and assess the value of the training program. In the Instrumentation section, several examples of these forms are presented for the reader's convenience.

Typically, this is only the start of several strategies to appraise program effectiveness, so as to determine what changes should be made before offering any future similar training. Ascertain what additional training may be necessary and why and how to undertake applied HRD research.

EXHIBIT 8.11   Strategy for concluding the training program

> During the final session of any learning experience, some time is devoted to filling out feedback forms. At this time, the participants might discuss what they have learned and assess the value of the training program. In the Instrumentation section, several examples of these forms are presented for the reader's convenience. Typically, this is only the start of several strategies to appraise program effectiveness, determine what changes should be made before offering any future similar training, ascertain what additional training may be necessary and why, and how to undertake applied HRD research. However, this is also the occasion when closure is sought for this particular period in the acquisition of knowledge and skills.
>
> **Planning for the closing exercises**
>
> After the last learning module in a training course, some provision should be made for a formal ending to the program. This can be as short as one hour or as long as three hours, depending on how elaborate the trainer wishes to make the procedure. Since the participants have just finished an intensive learning experience, something should be planned which will summarize the course, reinforce the learning, and motivate the trainees to apply their new knowledge and skills. Provision might be made for the following:
>
> 1 *Program evaluation* or feedback from the participants on the total experience (forms as illustrated in the next section might be administered for 15–50 minutes – see Exhibits 8.13 and 8.14). It is also possible to use objective tests for some measure of content knowledge or to ask the trainees to write a short essay on "What was the most important concept I learned in this course," or "My plans for applying this new knowledge." A brainstorming session could be conducted on "What can I do to further the professional development of my subordinates/clients."
> 2 *Guest speaker* – someone of prominence inside or outside the organization can be invited to make a "graduation" address for twenty or thirty minutes. Be sure to confirm the arrangements by writing/telephoning as to when, where, and why the event is scheduled. Brief the guest beforehand on the
>
> **Continued**

type of trainees to be present, the objectives and content of the course and request that his remarks be appropriate to the theme of "human service." Selection of an organizational leader is always recommended.

3 *Certificates of achievement* – prepare a certificate to signify completion of the course; printed, it can be adapted to suit your circumstances. Before writing the trainee's name on the document, have participants check the correct spelling of their names on a roster which is circulated to them prior to the last class. A prominent official in your organization should be invited to sign these and later distribute them personally at the closing ceremonies.

4 *Other possibilities* – planners may wish to invite an inspiring leader to end the sessions with appropriate remarks of encouragement for the trainees; invite spouses and relatives to attend; have the certificates inexpensively framed or placed in a plastic folder; invite the class or training group to elect a spokesman at the closing ceremonies; have the ceremonies video-taped and transmitted to the staff's clients assembled together elsewhere in the building; have some appropriate music played before and after the event (organ, harp, cello, band, etc.); provide some refreshments after the ceremony for all. If feasible, arrange for university or college credit for the course, at either the undergraduate or graduate level.

Should the corporation have its own university or college, then this would be an occasion for formal graduation exercises and the bestowing of degrees upon the participants.

Outline of a "graduation" address

- Congratulations on reaching another milestone in the development of your own human potential – significance of the accomplishment...
- Praise to all those who provided support services to you during this learning experience – faculty, clerical/cleaning/food staffs, family...
- Concept of "professional" development – what sets the "pro" apart from those who take a mechanical approach to a job; the need for continuous lifetime personal and professional growth...
- Concept of "change" as a byproduct of learning – you should not be the same people who came here on the first day of class. As a result of new information, experiences, insights, dialogue, and encounters with people in a new way during this course, you should enlarge your "psychological construct" or the way you read meaning into your life; your ideas, attitudes, needs, and values should change. Most importantly, you should change your image of yourself, your role, your clients, and your organization...
- Concept of action learning – something positive should happen as a result of this training; you are challenged to apply the new knowledge and benefit

Continued

skills which you have acquired to improve the human condition. You learned much about people and what makes them "tick"; hopefully you will by all this and utilize it for the benefit of those you seek to serve on your job. Learning should make you both humble and curious – humble about how much you do not know, and curious to gain more knowledge...

- Concept of behavioral leadership – you do not "tell" people what they must do as a result of your new-found knowledge; you provide a behavioral model for your subordinates and clients. You create your own future; you make things happen for the better as a result of your presence. As a leader, you should be an agent for planned, positive change in your organization.

Action research for organization development

Behavioral scientists began to have impact on organizations with their research, writings, and interventions six decades ago. Initially, this took the form of an intensive learning experience called the human relations laboratory. Under the sponsorship of the National Training Laboratories, professionals and managers from various organizations met in "T groups" for sensitivity training (now called the National Training Institute for Applied Behavioral Sciences (NTL)). Then, consultants began to conduct this "laboratory type education" inside organizations – with "family" groups – to increase the effectiveness of people who work together. The behavioral science technology thus spawned was called organization development (OD).

Organization development is a system for planned renewal of institutions. French and Bell (1984) have defined OD in this way:

> organization development is a top-management-supported, long-range effort to improve an organization's problem solving and renewal processes, particularly through a more effective and collaborative diagnosis and management of organization culture – with special emphasis on formal work team, temporary team, and intergroup culture; with the assistance of a consultant–facilitator and the use of the theory and technology of applied behavioral science, including action research.

This strategy then evolved into organization transformation (OT). Its practitioners believe that OD is focused on fixing here-and-now problems, while they favor a more visionary, futuristic approach. OT seeks to transform not only organizations, but also work and management in the process. They wish to unblock people, to recharge their energies, and to stimulate their intuition and innovation. They concentrate on personnel relationships and group processes, and on promoting a sense of purpose and more flexible responses.

Organizations are sometimes not in a position to benefit from the services of OD or OT consultants, either by contracting for external specialists or by hiring them as part of the HRD staff. However, most institutions do devote resources to training. This may be for professional development or personal growth, and may include learning about the people skills described in this book. Or such sessions may address issues such as wellness, networking, high performance, and team or transformational management. In-service education encompasses a wide range of concerns – from substance abuse and stress management to new technical or intercultural training. All of these training meetings and conferences are opportunities for utilizing action learning and its partner, action research, for data gathering and analysis. That is, HRD managers or trainers can conduct action research during these learning sessions, and follow up with reports to executives as a means of promoting feedback and change. The strategy is to use the training as an opportunity to accomplish some of the aims of OD or transformation. At least, it is a beginning of internal organization renewal until the external experts from consulting firms can be contracted.

For similar purposes today, the trend is to contract with specialists in "organizational effectiveness."

What is action research?

The term "action research" has different perspectives on its meaning. It has been defined as a process of collecting research data about an ongoing system relative to some objective goal or need of the system; then feeding these data back into the system based upon both the data and on hypothesis; and evaluating the results of actions by collecting more data. It is an approach to problem solving that can be incorporated into the organization's human resource management and development. It is a form of fact finding and experimentation that is ongoing and can be integrated into the action learning endeavors. It is a synergistic effort that requires the collaboration of managers and workers, and internal and external resource persons. It is pragmatic in that it seeks solutions that improve decisions, increase performance, and alter the status quo.

As a consultant, I have always been concerned with bringing about planned and significant change in the human systems that I serve. More often than not, I was employed by clients to design and conduct training programs to enhance personal and organizational effectiveness. Mostly, these clients understand and support management or executive development, although they are not familiar with such behavioral science buzzwords as "organization development" or "transformation." Therefore, I design my program interventions around this model: MD/OD. That is, I try to use management or executive development to achieve some organizational development or transformation. Thus, when departments of Los Angeles County asked me to design a management development institute, I used data gathering interviews and instruments to ascertain participant and organizational needs, as well as to design the training program. I used group process and survey instruments to collect data during the sessions. Then I summarized and analyzed the data and incorporated it into a written report and oral briefing of top management. With such action research, however, I only set the stage for organizational change; the wise consultant lets the information speak for itself, and merely offers recommendations based on the findings. This strategy has been successfully repeated by me with such diverse systems as the US Customs Service, and many other government agencies and the military, as well as with *Fortune 500* corporations.

I was suspicious when I read in the newspaper that a Congressional inquiry into riots in a military brig found they were caused only by poor staff morale and training. Therefore, I proposed to the Office of Naval Research an action research project in behavioral science leadership. When funded, I learned that the real cause of the conflict was cultural differences between the guards and the inmates in this military prison. In the process, I also developed the leadership program which is the basis of this book.

What is action learning?

The action learning/research strategy involves three entities: the learner or learning group – the immediate recipient of its benefits; the learning facilitator or trainer – the coordinator of the process; and the organizational sponsor or client – the investor and ultimate beneficiary of the learning when it is applied. As a result of the learning and research experience, all three parties should be positively changed.

The purpose of action research is to discover if that has happened. Was the learning both informative and fun? Will it achieve the results intended? Does it improve both individual and institutional performance? These and other questions for evaluation are answered in the process of action research (refer back to pages 204–219).

To determine the effectiveness of training efforts, some form of evaluation of the course design and its execution is important. An element of accountability is introduced when there is some attempt to measure the extent to which the educational objectives are set down before the learning experience has been realized. An experimental, inquiring approach to the planning and analysis of training programs can insure more relevant courses. The training process is cyclical – design, train, evaluate, redesign, retrain, re-evaluate, etc. A systems concept of learning would require that so much "input" by the trainer would require feedback control of the next "output" by that instructor. Thus, some form of applied research should be built into the HRD system.

Integrating action learning and research

A previous statement on action learning pointed out that learning can take place best when it meets the trainees', as well as the organization's, needs and goals. Action learning involves the learner in the process, while action research measures whether the training achieved its goals. The "climate" must also foster learning when the facilitator of training possesses competency and skill, especially in group dynamics. An assessment program for a training course, for example, is one application of action research. Furthermore, action learning emphasizes behavioral change in terms of knowledge, insight, understanding, attitudes, values, interests, and skills.

An evaluation of learning should focus on one or more of these elements with regard to the trainees.

Action research (AR) by human resource practitioners also centers investigation on people problems, to which it hopes to contribute solutions. It is a form of applied research that deals with social issues in an ongoing type of scientific analysis. Such research might center on a new technique for rehabilitating the alcoholic, drug addict, or criminal offender. Or, it might consider new ways for furthering organizational career development. AR relates to the daily activity of the worker, and that person's professional improvement. It seeks to measure the behavioral consequences of the innovative activity which is being tried out in the organization.

In its simplest form, AR might be a survey of opinion from the trainees as to their general reactions to the learning experience. In essence, the instructor invites the trainees to look at the learning experience together to see whether or not it was useful; the emphasis is on the "effect" of the training. The type and amount of feedback sought by the trainer can be expanded beyond this, depending on how he plans to analyze and use the data collected, or specific segments of the training program can be the subject of evaluation.

From such initial data gathering, the trainer can expand the research efforts in a variety of directions. Here are a few possibilities which could be undertaken depending on the research capabilities of the training director and the degree of assessment sought concerning the program:

- Design a pre/post instrument to ascertain attitudes or knowledge of the trainees before and after training (see samples in the Instrumentation section).
- Utilize a control group which is comparable to those in training, but which is not exposed to learning experience. The same pre/post instruments can be administered to this control group, and the results can be statistically compared between the trained and non-trained groups. In this way one can determine quantitatively the impact of the training upon the participants versus those who were not exposed to it.
- Seek an evaluation from the supervisors, peers, or subordinates of the trainees to discover if their behavior is any different as a result of the training (using subsequent instruments provided in this chapter and the next).
- Conduct a follow up study of the training group sometime after the learning experience to inquire about the long-term effects of the program. It is one thing to collect data from the group at the end of the last training session in the heat of enthusiasm, and another to obtain feedback three weeks, three months, or a year later when people have had an opportunity to test the application of the information and skills acquired in the training program.

Such action research efforts will help to gain greater credibility for the endeavors of a training division within an organization. By such an objective approach to educational efforts, management may be more inclined to support and expand programs for HRD if it receives some evidence that the investment in training is having some "pay-off." Furthermore, the data collected in such inquiries about training effects can be used to improve programs in their next administration.

Applied research is a valuable tool to refine a training design plan. For example, if the training coordinator makes a study of employee or member needs and organizational objectives, one may conclude that a particular type of training is in order. Before suggesting to the administration in the organization that the proposed educational program be undertaken with large numbers of trainees, however, try another strategy – design a pilot project in which part of the intended program would be tested on a limited sample of participants. Thus, the costs of the endeavor are scaled down to a reasonable proportion. If action research proves the training program to be effective, then a case has been made for further use of the "prototype training model."

Another reason to use action research is that organizational problems are not always what they seem to be. Executives may have ideas as to the problems, but, during training, the data gathered may indicate that such are not the real problems as identified by the workers. This chapter attempted to provide some rationale as to why a busy training coordinator should be concerned about a more objective assessment of his or her HRD efforts. Now it might be helpful to review what are some of the basic elements involved in the action learning and research process.

Steps in learning research

The issues or questions

Research is a systematic way of arriving at a new level of knowledge. Hopefully, it turns up something innovative and justifiable which can lead to improved thinking and action. It is more than mere fact finding, or experimentation, or statistical analysis of data, though it may include all of these functions. It begins with a question(s) on what the investigator proposes to study. The stating and selection of this question(s) is of prime importance, for it indicates the whole purpose or direction of the research, as well as its scope. Thus, a question on how a live training program compares to a self-learning instructional program on the same subject may lead to an experimental design for research.

Development of a new training model may indicate theoretical postulates and experiential data which can be united into a prototype. Logical development of it may lead to the establishment of criteria for the interpretation of the ideas. But if the original question was not clear, then nothing that follows it in the research process will be clear. When research is begun, the question(s) may be stated in the form of:

1 one or more inquiries;
2 a purpose(s);
3 a hypothesis or a series of hypotheses.

The hypothesis is a tentative proposition suggested as a solution to a problem or as an explanation of some phenomenon. It presents the researcher's expectations which one proposes to test in the research study. It is a part of a "theory" to investigate and evaluate.

Hypotheses in the field of learning research are often formulated around some innovation in methodology or content. Specifically, new ways for learning or training come into being in the following ways:

1 An individual conceives an idea for solving some training problem and develops it to the point where it can be introduced into a learning or training program. Such ideas often are adaptations of innovations which have appeared in other areas, in relation to other problems.
2 Innovations may arise not only as inventions, but as a result of systematic analysis and evaluation of existing procedures and materials. Improvement may come about as a result of systematic manipulation of training variables (e.g. a new or original use of a training device or technique).
3 A particular theory or broad concept may lead to hypotheses and deductions for improvements in adult education. It should be emphasized that only rarely are novel ideas subjected to careful tests or validation studies. Usually, they are either adopted or rejected without any real knowledge of their true value for learning or training. This can be seen in the testing of a new learning method or training technology.

The review

Lest we rediscover the wheel, one should, in the second stage of research, look into the roots from which the question has originated. What has been done in this area before? Who are the people, ideas, and procedures in checking the background of this inquiry? A professional approach would review published literature on the subject and all that is related to it. In such a review lies the real justification for doing the present research. It reveals what has been done on the question and equips the investigator with knowledge of the field so as to recognize the innovative and the significant. For example, in preparing to undertake the research on correctional training previously referred to, I reviewed literature on the following subjects: military criminal justice, correctional manpower and training, naval correctional reports, police training, behavior modification, and human relations training.

The library and other centers of information, especially the internet, become the focus of attention for the investigator who wishes to be thorough in his or her action research. The main sources of related literature are books, periodicals, research reports (such as graduate theses and dissertations), and information retrieval systems, including websites and electronic encyclopedias. The average busy manager or trainer in the process of designing a new training program has limited opportunity to survey the literature related to a proposed project. One may delegate this task to staff, but there are research tools available to help with the task. For locating up-to-date information in libraries, one might utilize various reference works which organize by topics that which has been written recently on the subject. A few examples of sources to be checked by trainers are: the Education Index, the *Reader's Guide to Periodical Literature*, and the Annual Review of Educational Research on Psychology. The Dissertations Abstracts, published by University Microfilms, Ann Arbor, Michigan, can provide microfilms on unpublished doctoral studies.

As an aid in educational research, the US Office of Education established ERIC (Educational Resource Information Center). By means of the computer, a clearing house of information is available to the investigator together with annotated bibliographies concerning a wide variety of topics dealing with education and training. Among the other such storehouses of knowledge, the Defense Documentation Center (a department within the Defense Supply Agency) has special meaning for those trainers who work with government agencies. Its National Technical Information Service provides bulletins, reports, announcements, bibliographies, and microfilm about government-sponsored research. Another useful data bank for managers and trainers is RISS (the Remote Interactive Search System). It is a combination of hardware, software, and "peopleware" that originated with NASA. Through its regional industrial applications centers (NIAC), technology transfer from R&D of NASA and other government laboratories is possible. Through a subscription service, NIAC associates gain instant access to information on almost any topic and from a variety of scholarly disciplines.

Too many organizations do not know their own history. A newly appointed HRD professional should seek to ascertain what the system has previously done with regard to an intended program. For example, the military has a high turnover in their training officers and administrators. I discovered in working with the US Marine Corps that current officers are often unaware of what has previously been tried, such as on the subject of leadership training. Beside checking organization histories and past contracts, it is wise to interview "old hands" who may have been involved in prior training schemes.

As the manager or trainer gathers data on what others have said or done relative to the subject under study, this information must be organized and stored for later reference. Again, a personal computer may be the means for setting up such document files; special software is available for this purpose. Then it becomes a matter of sorting out the most pertinent data, and setting priorities as to which material will actually be referenced in one's own proposal or report. This helps to substantiate the case that supports the research questions and strategies.

The research planning

The third stage in action research is to set down in some detail the systematic procedure you plan to follow in your investigation. You might start with a research design outline which can be expanded as warranted. Here you state the hypothesis or problem you wish to investigate, how you plan to test your hypothesis or seek solutions to the problem, a description of the procedures to be used, a description of the subjects or samples of population that will be involved, the logic or the criteria to be applied to the learning material or training model which you are proposing, the way you plan to analyze the data gathered (including statistical analysis), and the logistics of the research.

There are research style manuals which can assist you in organizing your thoughts in proper format. As much as possible, use a computer to record and analyze your data.

Sometimes a trainer has to seek moral or financial support from within or without the organization. In that case, one formulates a preliminary and/or final proposal. This can be simple or elaborate depending on the person for whom the proposal is intended and its purpose. The less complicated format might include the following: introduction, rationale, strategy, and tentative plan. The more formal approach would include sections such as: introduction, statement of the problem, scope of the work, research objectives, methodology, facilities, schedule and tasks, staffing, project costs, follow up research possibilities, and a statement of qualifications or biographical information on the researcher.

Back-up materials on the above can be included in the appendices. Essentially, then, what has been described in the previous paragraphs about a research plan has several applications:

1 it can be used as the researcher's own guidelines in pursuing the study;
2 it can enlighten those whose support one seeks for the investigation and be included in a proposal;
3 it can form the basis for parts one and two of a final report, namely, the description of the problem and the methodology.

The most frequent method used in action research by trainers is the survey technique. It is used to secure data in the behavioral sciences and in the field of education by means of questionnaires, the data from which is then analyzed and quantified. From this, a report may be drafted and conclusions and recommendations may be drawn about the experimental effort.

The report

The fourth stage of action research involves a report on one's findings after the data has been collected and analyzed. This information is presented and interpreted according to the plan set forth in the methodology. Findings must be related to the hypotheses the trainer set out to test. Were the findings statistically significant? Were there any strange, bizarre, or unexpected findings not anticipated in the hypotheses? A researcher must be detached and objective about what he discovers through the investigation.

Ideas about preferred styles for reporting findings and analysis of data can be obtained from the various reference works suggested in this chapter. These suggestions will range from how to illustrate the data through figures and tables to writing style. Computer software may be used for graphics that visually highlight important results. Generally, the last stage of the investigation and report is a summary in the form of a section or chapter. Sometimes, a report begins with an "abstract" or summary which pulls together briefly the statement of the problem, review of the literature, outline of procedure, and the principal findings. In addition, the investigator may offer his interpretation as to what the experiment or data reveal. This is listed as "conclusions."

With key executives who suffer from information overload, the following strategy may get their attention and ensure positive action on your recommendations. In addition to the full report, prepare an executive briefing of a few pages on well illustrated major findings and their implications. During oral briefings of top management, use this digest, but refer them to the full report for details. If those in leadership positions do not have the time to read the complete version, they may have their staff do it. Similarly, if the contents are not confidential, this digest may also be widely circulated within the organization in order to gain support for the necessary reforms.

To conclude, action research, especially of the human factor survey kind, should be regularly conducted for organizational diagnosis and improvement. However, the ongoing training programs offer an ideal situation to collect relevant data from the participants for their own benefit, as well as for the renewal of the system.

Values of action learning and research

Action learning is a dynamic process that is appropriate to mature trainees because it involves adults in a variety of intensive, educational experiences. Its advantages are:

- it stimulates learning at both the cognitive and affective levels, that is, by rational thinking and through the emotions or feelings;
- it is carefully prepared, timed, and paced to make optimum use of the training period;
- it promotes individual and group learning through a variety of input, interaction, and instrumentation;
- it focuses on results and requires planning for action that occurs because of the training.

The principal value of action learning is that it promotes positive and constructive change in people and their systems through increased awareness, knowledge, and skills. Action research compliments this approach by furthering organizational effectiveness through data gathering from its membership on individual and institutional performance. Meetings and training sessions are viewed as opportunities for this information collection. With a systematic analysis of findings, the merits of action research are:

- it aids organization diagnosis and development, helping to validate the need and the means for planned change;
- it evaluates the effectiveness of the HRD efforts;

- it provides measures of performance, productivity, and profitability;
- it improves the basis for decision making, planning, accountability, and career development.

Action learning becomes a synergistic means for action research. Combined, both are a powerful strategy for maintaining personal and organizational health. These are managerial tools suitable for an information age of knowledge and service workers. Many corporations have realized the value of marketing research and included such specialists on their staff. The new work culture requires expansion of such inquiry to go beyond surveys of public preferences and customer concerns, so that the broadening of human factor research encompasses all employees or members.

Every manager has a responsibility to develop his or her people, so action learning and research enable leaders to do so. When technicians and other specialists are assigned a training task, action learning and research strategies permit them to be more professional in their approach. Action learning and research are a means for capitalizing upon human assets.

Interaction

Throughout these chapters, I have provided guidance in this section on various ways to involve trainees in the learning process. In addition to a dozen possibilities for group dynamics already reviewed, an overview is now offered of twelve more adult education methods that will enhance action learning.

Adult education group methods
Audio visual aids

In an age of mass media, the imaginative group facilitator has numerous mechanical and technological aids in addition to traditional means of stimulating the senses and communicating more effectively by involvement of more senses within a person. The use of the new media not only conveys the message in a different, perhaps more startling way, but the medium chosen can itself be a message. Audiovisual (AV) aids may merely illustrate a point or serve as a catalyst for group discussion. With computers and presentation software, there are variety of ways to enliven the learning presentations.

Such devices may be purchased, loaned, or created. If mechanical equipment is being used with a group, then it is important that it be checked beforehand to ensure that it is in working condition. Any AV material to be shown should be previewed before a group assembles, so that the discussion leader is familiar with its contents and has devised questions or points for further analysis. The simplest visual aids are drawings or charts produced by the programmer or the group, preferably with the use of computer graphics. For this purpose, beside a projection screen, a new type of blackboard with both white and colored pens is helpful. A flannel board with felt symbols is also attractive, while a flip chart with plain newsprint or white cardboard may be employed with colored marking pencils. Sometimes groups find it useful to express themselves in this visual manner. Other materials, such as water and oil paints, paper cut-ups and wire and cloth, may be used by creative persons within a group to communicate a concept or design. Less used today is an opaque or overhead projector to project on a wall or screen; such use of printed or commercially produced illustrations or cartoons may stimulate group discussion. Also, this method allows materials from books or original slides to be projected for all to see.

The point is that instructors now have a variety of tools to help them in the visualization of learning materials. Slides and filmstrips in one, two, or three dimensions help the viewer to put himself into a scene. If desired, you can add audio by using a tape recorder or computer sound system. Homemade or commercial cassettes or disks can be played to accompany the visual presentation. Individual visual projection permits concentration on one scene for any length of discussion. DVDs and films in black and white, or color, offer a unique way to involve the group. However, long films are not the best for group discussion purposes; usually 12–30 minutes are adequate to stimulate communication. Slow motion can be used in any playback, but many projectors do not permit you to hold a still scene in the film for discussion. Guidelines for instructors sometimes accompany training films in order to foster discussion. Audio tapes, cassettes, or discs are excellent for groups to record their reports and discussions as a means of feedback for group analysis. The same approach can be used with videotape which has the added value of presenting visual, non-verbal communication. The recordings can be analyzed by the group itself or by external observers, or even key management. Of course, commercial audio or videotapes of outstanding guests or presenters may be then utilized by other training groups.

Television, live commercial, educational, or closed circuit, can be a unique learning tool. Since young people today are products of the Information Age, this media and other audiovisual devices are essential to keep people's interest. The group might employ videotapes and discs for the same purpose, or it might use them to record its own group interaction. The playback can have great impact on trainee growth. A group might observe another group through closed circuit television or it might engage in a cooperative project – such as the production of a television program or recording.

The local public library is a free source of videocassettes, CDs and DVDs, and even catalogs describing the offerings useful for management development. However, it is in the area of "interactive systems" that real breakthroughs are being accomplished in educational technology. These systems link computers with video and other AV capabilities. Current communication allows instructors to use a computer, tablet, or smart phone to download files on a wall or screen for a whole group view and discuss. These innovations are useful for both individual or group instruction and will dominate the future of training and education.[44]

Further, creative trainers may now use lightweight, comparatively inexpensive video equipment to record their own learning materials, customized to organizational needs. This video equipment can be used in training courses for skill development or to record high performers. To further customize media for trainees, trainers may also program computers with the appropriate learning on the internet.

Other forms of audiovisual communication with groups are the puppet show, pageant, pantomime, model congress, mock convention and trials. These are all unusual ways to present concepts and involve group members. A new dimension of group involvement through audiovisual aids is being experimented with today through various multimedia projects. These involve immersing group members in a kaleidoscope of sound and color, using colored spotlights, films, discs, and other "psychedelic" media.

Brainstorming

This technique can be used to stimulate creative thinking in a group and to permit members to participate in the decision making process. Brainstorming promotes a maximum number of ideas from a maximum number of people in a minimum amount of time. This form of problem solving can focus on one or more subjects for an hour, a day, or a weekend. By following a sequence of timed steps, a pressure is created which forces intense involvement. The person conducting the sessions encourages an open, non-judgmental atmosphere so that innovative ideas can be expressed without evaluation or recrimination on the part of any member. There are different ways to conduct brainstorming, and unblock the thought process. Such approaches include:

1 Have a short, warm-up session to "oil the brain"; practice on a light problem unrelated to the real issue. For example, "If you had a boatload of pipe cleaners in a foreign country where there was no market for that product, what new uses or markets could you develop for the item?" Then allow the group to free-wheel solutions for one minute and have a recorder note how many replies come forth. You may wish to have one more practice session, perhaps using paper clips as a theme this time and setting a minimum target of at least fifteen good uses within one minute.
2 Clarify the real problem and expand the time period for responses (five, ten, fifteen minutes). Arrange for some members of the group to record and number the answers on a blackboard, flip chart, or via a PowerPoint projector. To remove constrictions and mental blocks, inform the group that no comment or evaluation about their ideas will be made as they are offered by the group.
3 Allow the group to spend a few minutes screening the answers in order to note (by calling the number of the replies) whether there is any duplication or combining of similar ideas or a pattern of ideas to be observed in the responses.
4 Breaking into sub-groups to work out various plans for solving the problem based on the ideas already generated, the group may eliminate or expand upon these ideas recorded. Twenty to forty minutes should be sufficient. The small groups are instructed to present their plans to the total group by using the blackboard or large sheets of plain paper or cardboard (record their results with marking pencil).

5 Reassemble the whole group so that sub-group reporters can orally and visually present their consensus on the problem. A few minutes might be allowed again for a preliminary evaluation by the total group of the ideas that they prefer or find most emphasized in the various group reports. If desired, sub-groups may meet again to integrate or synthesize the above data into a final plan.

Small group dynamics

Buzz groups. When a film, lecture, or presentation is made to the total group, the audience can be divided into small groups of six to eight people who meet in a circle for approximately six to fifteen minutes to discuss the subject. A variation is to assign one question for the group to answer or prepare one issue in the presentation upon which they are to focus. The group discusses the subject freely after it has decided upon a recorder and spokesman. Groups should be given a two-minute warning that time is coming to a close and urged to conclude. The recorder or chairman then presents a summary or consensus of the group's reactions to the total audience.

Sometimes a variation of this method is referred to as the Phillips 66 Plan. The important elements are timing of the discussion period, small groups, and understanding of what is to be discussed and reported. If you wish, the groups can receive specific assignments before the presentation (e.g. take only one point of the lecture or form listening teams which listen from different viewpoints).

Discussion groups. These task oriented groups are assigned, or select, a topic or a series of related subjects for discussion. The whole group may investigate the same issue, or sub-groups may be formed out of common interest or to analyze different facets of the question. The discussion may be based on a committee report, a book or magazine article, a television or radio program, an audio or videotape, a lecture or sermon, a film or filmstrip. On the other hand, the subject may merely be announced and a free-swinging discussion permitted to ensue. The group may assemble for one meeting to discuss a single subject or meet for a series of sessions on the same, related, or different subjects. If all viewpoints are tolerated, sensitive communication is encouraged, and critical issues are analyzed, group discussion can be a very valuable approach. It is helpful for the group to lay down some basic ground rules for the discussion, to clarify its purpose, and to determine if any action or follow up is to flow from the discussion. The discussion is most meaningful when people are given time to prepare their thoughts about the subject rather than merely expounding on a subject about which they are uninformed. It can be a useful learning experience both from the perspective of content and human relations.

Case studies/critical incidents

To objectify a situation for group discussion, it helps if you set up the subject for discussion in the form of a case. The case may be printed for all members of the group to analyze, be read to the others by the group leader, or projected on a screen. The issue or problem brought out through the case should be one with which most members can identify, or be typical of the challenges they will have to solve themselves. By putting the matter in case style, you de-emotionalize the topic for a group solution. The study may center around a person who faces a problem common to the participants. It should include facts about the fictional or real individual, but include something of his background and the surrounding circumstances relative to the problem. Or it may concentrate on a critical incident in the life of a person or a group of people.

On the other hand, the case may simply describe a situation that involves a whole group, institution, or organization. Enough facts are provided to raise issues, but no solutions are presented. The introduction of the case may include a few questions about the case or critical incident to provoke discussion.

The language used should be informal and familiar to the audience reading or hearing the case. Personalize the story by including local names and references. Depending on the time available for analysis of the case, the length of the case may vary from one to several pages. When the incident is tailored to a real challenge which faces a particular group, then the members can get very involved in the discussion. Although it is possible to purchase books of case studies, it is usually more effective to compose your own case or incident, so that it is quite real to the participants. This technique can encourage non-directive learning by inserting specific issues and questions in the case that will expand the group's thinking.

Cases are written descriptions of actual events or situations that the trainees may confront in their own organizations. Encourage groups analyzing the case to:

- identify key issues and problems;
- diagnose and evaluate the problems and situations;
- identify alternative viewpoints and solutions;
- come to consensus on preferred strategy for meeting the challenges or resolving the problems.

Cases may be created by instructors and the participants, or purchased from publishers. Sometimes cases are supplements to a text book that is being used.

Debates

Any subject of concern to a group can be viewed from opposite positions. The group can be divided into two teams with a single chairman or moderator. The groups preferably should prepare their position for or against the issue by outside reading, investigation, and discussion. It is desirable to set ground rules for the debate as to time, procedure, and possible scoring of points. The teams should select a captain before returning to the next meeting at which they or their representatives will defend their position on the question at hand. The more contemporary and meaningful the subject is to the group, the better will be the debate. Each side should be permitted a summation of their position at the end of the specified time period.

Sociogram

The sociometric test permits members to express their feelings about others within the group with whom they would like to work or be in certain circumstances. It is designed to study the social structure of a group and its patterns of belonging. The basis for the choice must be real, not hypothetical, and members must know that action will follow the test results. The individuals are usually given three to five choices in order to show the relative position of a person in the group. Negative choices may also be added with the instruction that the purpose is not to pass judgment on anyone and that all the choices will be kept secret. The advantage is that members will reveal choices that they may not be willing to show in their group behavior. The results are plotted or pictured on a sociogram by drawing lines so that it is possible to analyze who is most frequently chosen, who is less frequently chosen, and what patterns of sub-groups exist. The group should then be given an opportunity to discuss the implications of this visual presentation of their preferred relationships.

Forum/assembly

A group can sponsor a forum to promote its ideas or can take part in one. This assembly procedure brings together large numbers of people for thought-provoking exchange on an announced subject. It may be conducted by a chairman, guest speaker, or discussion leader and may include questions from the audience. A panel of three to six persons can be appointed to discuss the speaker's points after his presentation. The procedure can be adapted to a symposium, in which several people present brief speeches on the subject to provide the audience with different perspectives on the topic. A question period usually follows the formal presentation.

Any large assembly can be broken down into smaller groups for more meaningful discussion by means of several techniques. One is listening teams, whereby the audience is divided into segments to listen to the presentation from a specific perspective or with a question in mind. For example, one group may be instructed to listen to the speaker from the viewpoint of "application" for his ideas, another from the viewpoint of "agreement," another for points of "disagreement," and still another for necessary points of "clarification." Each group meets after the speaker's address, compares its observations, and then appoints a spokesman to provide its reactions to the talk for the benefit of the whole assembly.

Another small group technique is circular response which may follow a formal speech or be used simply as a method of group discussion. Sitting in a circle of fifteen to twenty, the group takes up a point or question. After the first person speaks to the point, the next group member to the right expresses his or her views and so on until the discussion has gone around the circle. No member may speak out of turn until the whole group has provided input in sequence.

The buzz group (previously described) is another device to use before or after a speaker has made a presentation. When used to precede a talk, each sub-group may be given a quotation concerning the subject to discuss for six minutes in order to warm them up to the topic. When this method follows an address, the small groups of six to ten people are expected to discuss the subject matter for a limited time (ten to twenty minutes) and appoint a recorder to present the group's synthesis to the total meeting.

Dramatics

The dramatic approach may be utilized by a group to present a full-length play or a short skit of ten minutes or less. Essentially it involves role playing wherein the participant projects himself into another's position and acts as the other person would act in the situation created. In such a presentation, the script, the characters, or the materials used highlight material or issues for later group discussion. The participants may follow a regular script, read their lines, or converse extemporaneously. In the "sociodrama," the presentation stops at the climax, and the whole group is involved in the solution.

Sociodrama is a technique that employs the best of two methods – the case study and dramatics. It uses role playing, wherein participants project themselves into others' positions and act as other individuals would in the situation created. In such a presentation, script, characters, and issues provide material for later group discussion. This dramatic technique may be used to present a full-length play, a short skit of ten minutes or less, or merely a critical incident.

Such a social drama on real work situations offers the trainer an opportunity to guide the group to new insights and learning. The facilitator may assign the group a topic or situation or let the class choose the subject of its drama. It is important that the problem be defined or the general situation be sketched. It could be the issue of salespeople not filing proper contact reports, a conflict between salespeople and their manager, or a shortage of materials to sell. The point is that the subject matter should be familiar to the group, something they can identify with as real to their work environment. Human or organizational relations are always a fit topic for this purpose.

The presenters can be given a script which they read or act out extemporaneously, or they can be assigned the task beforehand with the freedom to develop their own script or situation. They should be urged to plan their presentation carefully, and to have a warm-up or practice run. Essentially, they are to create a situation just as it happens on the job, and then stop at the climax. They should discuss the characters, put themselves into their position, and use their language.

For example, suppose the issue is a salesman with much male ego who is assigned to a new female sales manager. His approach to women is typically chauvinistic; he uses them as playthings. Now how is he going to deal with this new situation? What are the manager's feelings likely to be? How will her judgments of his performance be influenced? What problems are likely to arise? How can he change his attitudes?

When the players have presented their drama, but provided no solutions, two alternatives are possible. The trainer may lead the problem solving discussion or permit the presenters to continue the discussion period. In the latter case, they would then have prepared some questions and would consider ways to stimulate the audience's thinking. One important consideration is to involve the whole class in the sociodrama – let them experience the emotions involved, the difficulties, the stresses, the possibilities. This is the time for analysis of the situation in depth, for behaviors to be illustrated, and for the issues at stake to be clarified.

Observers are challenged to seek the insights and understandings the actors try to convey. It is important to relate the discussion to the original problem under consideration. Players might be asked to comment on the characters they attempted to portray. The trainer should keep the group from evaluating acting talent and concentrate instead on solutions to the problem presented.

Finally, the audience should be asked to summarize what they learned through the experience. It is important that the group members have the opportunity to discover if they can explore a problem dramatically, break it down into its causal factors, and construct methods for meeting the issue effectively. If it is feasible, have the players act out some of the alternative solutions for further evaluation by the audience.

A creative trainer can work various options on the basic technique. For example, the trainer might encourage people to use masks to portray characters or to reverse their role by this means. Thus, a black is asked to portray a white; a male is asked to portray a female; a subordinate is asked to portray a supervisor; a salesman is asked to portray a customer.

A common tendency on the part of amateurs is to let a scene go too long, so the facilitator may have to cut it off when enough behavior has been exhibited for the group to analyze the problem; the group can imagine or project what would happen if the action continued; players have reached an impasse because of poor briefing or miscasting; a natural closing point has arrived.

Sociodrama allows groups to be objective about a situation which might be too painful for those concerned to deal with directly. Attitudes and feelings often unexpressed are brought out into the open. Dynamic factors in group process and human relations are brought out clearly. An artificial environment is provided within which a person may experiment with different behavior and attitudes, make mistakes, and try new skills without risking the hurt of the real life situation. And all this is accomplished in the presence and with the cooperation of co-learners, not judges. Dramatic skits and scripts may be original creations of instructors and trainees, or purchased from suppliers of learning materials.

Role playing

Role playing is an educational technique in which people spontaneously act out problems of human relations and analyze the enactment with the help of other role players and observers.

There are several values to this technique:

1 New skills can be developed for dealing with human relations problems, because a participant not only hears or tells about a problem but also lives through it by acting it out.

2 Understanding may be broadened since participants gain insight into their own and others' feelings.
3 Many new attitudes and feelings are brought before the group for review. Thus, role playing helps illustrate and objectify many frequently ignored causal and dynamic factors in group process and human relations.
4 Most important, role playing provides an artificial environment within which a person may experiment with behavior, make mistakes, and try new skills without risking hurts that experimentation in real life situations may involve; this in the presence of co-learners, not judges.

Necessary to the role playing process is a director, who is responsible for all procedures involved and who helps actors and other group members become emotionally involved with the situation to be acted out. The director is mainly concerned with helping actors' spontaneity in the presentation of characters and in helping audience–observers to analyze the situation and behaviors presented so that insights into problems and effective knowledge of how to deal with them are increased.

Role playing involves more than simple acting out of roles. It consists of a series of steps, which usually flow into one another quite naturally and have more or less importance in different role playing situations.

Steps in the role playing process:

1 *Defining the problem.* Role playing should be focused on a problem both meaningful and important to the entire group; chosen as a method only when particularly useful; concerned with clear, specific, valid problems in human relations.
2 *Establishing a situation.* The situation (design) of the role play is always dependent on learning outcomes desired or needed by the group. Planners must always work with the training purpose of the role play in mind. Some ways in which situations can be designed are:

   a. a sub-commitee can plan a situation and bring it to the group;
   b. the total group can make up a situation on the spot;
   c. a member or a leader can suggest an actual case which illustrates a particular problem (be careful that the scene does not become clogged with details about what happened).

3 *Casting the characters.* Responsibility for defining and casting characters may be taken by the whole group or delegated to certain members. In general, people should be chosen because it is thought that they can carry the role well. No one should be urged to take a role if he is unwilling to do so (if forced, a person is likely to give a constructed, unspontaneous version). When dealing with beginners, start with roles in which they feel at home and confident.
4 *Briefing and warming-up actors.* It is important to keep the problem to be studied before the group at all times and to remind members why they saw the problem as a significant one. No attempt should be made to use this process to structure

what actors are to say or to do in the action. The director sets the tone by point-ing out the job of observers: to look at actors in terms of their roles. It should be made clear that each actor is playing a specified role in a specific situation and is merely giving his spontaneous interpretation of a character's response in such a situation.

5 *Acting.* The mood of the play can be destroyed if the actors get out of character and talk about themselves.

6 *Cutting.* A common tendency is to allow scenes to last too long. Generally, a role play should be cut when:

a. enough behavior has been exhibited for the group to analyze the problem;
b. the group can project what would happen if the action were continued;
c. the players have reached an impasse because of miscasting or poor briefing;
d. there is a natural closing.

7 *Discussing and analyzing the situation and behavior.* It is important to relate dis-cussion to the original problem under study. Sometimes players are asked to comment first; sometimes discussion is begun by observers. The advantage to the players' beginning the discussion is that it allows them to set the tone for constructive criticism. If players show (by their own observations) lack of self-consciousness because they are analyzing characters portrayed, and not them-selves, observers are more likely to feel free to express their full reactions. Do not evaluate the acting ability of actors.

8 *Reviewing what is learned.* This involves making plans for further testing of insights gained or for practicing new behavior implied.

Some groups may be hesitant about role playing, either because of not seeing them-selves as actors or out of fear that such spontaneous expression and exploration of problems may come too close to personal anxieties. This type of group quickly learns to feel at ease when role playing is begun with some very simple situation which enables them to have a profitable discussion.

It is also important that group members have the experience of discovering that they can explore a problem, break it down into causal factors, and construct meth-ods of meeting the problem through changing their behavior in the role playing situation. A new group technique for role playing is to use masks and to reverse people's roles. For example, when dealing with an incident about racial prejudice, the white role player of a black person would use a black mask, while the black person uses a white mask.

Field trips

Group growth and cohesion can be enhanced by a visit to a public place, insti-tution, museum, exhibit, technology demonstration, or industrial plant or office. Ideally, the group is presented with an experience beyond its usual understand-ing and is given an opportunity to meet and talk with people at the location of the field trip. It may range from a visit to a newspaper plant or a museum to a state park or Amerindian reservation. The purpose can be for career information, social involvement, or enlightenment. It is one thing to have a group discussion on poverty; it is another for the group actually to visit the slums and talk with poor people. Some discussion precedes the event as to the field trip's purpose and what to look for. The group leader must make arrangements for an appointment and a guide, transportation and food, and plan for an evaluation period following the experience. The most valuable learning will come in the group discussion after the trip when participants share their perceptions and insights. Local service clubs such as Kiwanis or Rotary can be helpful in arranging field trips, while the Chamber of Commerce and the National Association of Manufacturers unit in your area may assist in such efforts.

Another variation is to break the group into smaller teams who then go out on a field investigation to a competitor, a high-tech industrial park, or a university to answer specific questions and then report back to the main group on their findings. Within a multinational corporation, for instance, the field trips could be to other plants, divisions, or subsidiaries. A trainee group can be subdivided, so each team goes to a different location or site, then reports back on their experience to the whole group (a cluster).

Exhibits

A group can find expression for itself in the joint task of developing an audio and/or visual display. This method not only provides training in working together, but it challenges the group to communicate its ideas to a larger audience. It permits the employment of creative talents within the group by the use of various media – art, sculpture, photography, film and slides, posters, cartoons, graphs, comic strips, and other graphic expressions. The exhibit may be portable or permanent, stationary or mobile. In conjunction with developing this presentation, the group meets to discuss what thoughts it wishes to convey through this means, how to best display information, and what assignments are necessary to get the project accomplished. Furthermore, a group can visit an exhibit of others, such as in an art or technology museum.

Projects

Like the exhibit or display, the project offers the group a task to accomplish which requires the exercise of skills of interpersonal relations as well as the special resources of members. The group or team determines the nature of these cooperative construction activities which may involve skills of painting, cooking, weaving, performing, or building. Investigation and research may have to precede the actual construction; the planning period allows for group participation and thinking. The atmosphere in the group should be such as to encourage, not stifle, creativity. Related to this approach is the report which may be conducted for the group by an individual or a committee. When the in-depth study is presented to the group, then discussion and decisions take place based on the information accumulated. The report may be written, oral, or a visual presentation such as a mock-up.

The computer lends itself to special projects that pull various members of a team together. For example, a group can devise a new software program that will be of benefit to the total group or organization, or construct a computer simulation that will enable the group to test out a new theory or strategy, make better choices, or anticipate future problems.

Now that the readers know a variety of learning methods to use with trainees, what type do professional trainers consider to be the most effective? In a recent survey of its membership, the American Society for Training & Development found the preferred techniques in the following six categories to be:

1 *Knowledge acquisition:* programmed instruction, lecture, conference method, and case study.
2 *Changing attitudes:* role playing, sensitivity training, conference and case study methods.
3 *Problem solving:* case study, business games, conference method, and role playing.
4 *Interpersonal skills:* role playing and sensitivity training.
5 *Participant acceptance:* conference and case study methods.
6 *Knowledge retention:* role playing, programmed instruction, conference, and case study methods.

Ninety-three percent of these respondents – all HRD specialists – ranked leadership training skills as the most important learning subject, while giving priority also to problem solving skills, decision making skills, performance appraisal, and time management. Note that some of these preferred methods can now be enhanced by the use of electronic technology, such as when the computer is used for programmed instruction or business games.

Instrumentation

While instruments can be purchased commercially, managers and trainers should not hesitate to construct their own data gathering forms, questionnaires, and inventories to suit their specific purposes. This book contains many illustrations of such devices, devised by me in the course of my action learning and research. Therefore, for those involved in survey and marketing research who seek to collect information from people, I recommend: S. Sudman and N. M. Bradburn *Asking Questions: A Practical Guide to Questionnaire Design* (San Francisco: Jossey-Bass 1983). Regardless of the format chosen, the manager or trainer wants to select a survey approach with these features:

- ease of administration and collection of data;
- appropriate and understandable wording or questioning;

- convenience for scoring and interpreting the results;
- viability for validity and comparative studies.

The computer now can be used to score responses, as well as to undertake statistical analysis of the results. For example, one behavioral scientist who assisted me with the original Office of Naval Research studies upon which this book is based, designed two interesting instruments. One was an "adjective rating scale," in which trainees were asked to respond (anonymously) to a dozen words. After each key term, such as "reward" or "punishment," the respondents checked the pair of adjectives that best described their personal reaction to the word cited. There were five pairs of adjectives from which to choose: good/bad, unimportant/important, strong/weak, inferior/superior, active/passive. The investigator was trying to gauge the group's attitudes toward certain topics before the training was undertaken. He also created a "modified polarity scale," consisting of sixteen statements to assess opinions on matters related to the learning program. For instance, since one of the learning modules was to be on change, two items dealt with the "changeableness of human feelings": one described change making life more interesting; the second described change as a sign of weakness in human beings. Respondents reacted to such statements in one of five ways: strongly agree, agree, don't know, disagree, and strongly disagree. The findings on both instruments were summarized and analyzed during the training program, then included in the project report for the benefit of management.

To improve your efforts at action learning and research, I will now include samples of forms that I have used in leadership or professional development institutes based upon the contents of this text. Such data gathering has several values:

- it creates awareness and sensitivity in the respondents relative to some of the key learning issues;
- it provides information on the trainees that can be used in program design and preparation, or in post-project reporting for purposes of OD and planning of future programs;
- it helps in the evaluation of the program's effectiveness, particularly regarding change in the learning group as a result of the training.

Instruments, whether they take the form of questionnaires, inventories, or checklists, are diagnostic tools that facilitate the identification of people and program needs. They are also a means for assessing performance and contribute to organizational effectiveness. Personally, over sixty years experience in education and training has convinced me that high performance can be achieved if organizations gather more data from their personnel, customers, and suppliers; then analyze that information to improve the system's performance. The next exhibits may be used to gather data about a class and training or research group before its first meeting.

Sample training forms

EXHIBIT 8.12   Personal information form

Directions. Please check the most appropriate answer or supply the information requested to the best of your ability. Begin with your full

Name_____

Address_____

Telephone_____

E-mail address_____

Website/blog_____

1 Organization_____

2 (a) Your division_____

   (b) Job title_____

3 Age_____

4 Length of job service_____ years_____ months

5 Total years of schooling you have had _____ years

6 Indicate your highest academic achievement:

   a High school diploma (or equivalent)_____

   b College degree_____ Major subject area_____

   c Master's degree_____ Major subject area_____

   d Doctor's degree_____ Major subject area_____

   e Post degree study (number of years completed)_____

   f Other educational credentials (certificates, etc.)_____

7 Are you currently enrolled in any of the following continuing educational programs (excluding this course)? Please check as appropriate:

   a In-service training   ( )

   b Online/correspondence courses   ( )

   c Non-degree course work   ( )

   d Video/audio courses   ( )

   e Degree course work   ( )

   f Other (specify)_____

8 Have you ever had any formal teacher training?   Yes ( ) No ( )

   If yes, specify:_____

9 Have you ever had any "Instructor" training?   Yes ( ) No ( )

   If yes, specify:_____

10 Are you presently engaged in teaching, training, or instructing?

   Yes ( ) No ( )

   If yes, indicate the category below which best describes your work:

   Trainer ( ) Instructor ( ) Counselor ( ) Other (specify)_____

Continued

---

11 If the answer to number 10 was "yes," please estimate the portion of your workday which is normally devoted to teaching (or instructing) and related activities:

Full time   ( )   Part time   ( )

Indicate the type of personnel for which you have a supervisory training responsibility:_____

12 In the field of HRD what is your major area of concern relative to the training of personnel?

Supervision   ( )   Technology training   ( )

Substance abuse   ( )   Human/diversity relations   ( )

Other (specify)_____

13 Please rate the assignment you now have in comparison to the other duties you have had:

Worst ( )   Fair ( )   Good ( )   Very good ( )   Best ( )

14 If you are engaged in any external activities related to this course, so indicate:_____

15 Upon completion of this course do you expect to be able to apply what you have learned in some type of HRD/educational work?

Yes ( )   No ( )

If the answer to the above was "yes," please specify the work you expect to do?

    a If the answer to the above was "yes," will the assignment specified be: A new job ( ) An additional duty ( ) Change in previous duty ( ) Same job as before ( ) As a mentor ( ) Other:_____

16 What are your expectations or hopes relative to participation in this career development program?

     (1) _____

     (2) _____

     (3) _____

     (4) _____

Date completed:_____

EXHIBIT 8.13   Pre-training self-evaluation inventory

As you begin this training experience, how would you rate your behavior in relating to other people? Please make a check mark on the left hand side if you perceive that you now possess the interpersonal skills listed. Leave blank those items in which you feel you do not possess average ability. Your honest personal reactions will help significantly towards an overall evaluation of the performance

Continued

of this group as it participates in these training sessions. Complete individual anonymity will be maintained. Your responses will be compared at the end of the course with a second administration of a similar questionnaire.

1 I am attentive in listening to others ( )
2 I take pains in putting my ideas across to others ( )
3 I am anxious to share information, both positive and negative, with others ( )
4 I usually understand what others communicate to me ( )
5 I am concerned to be understood by others, in both big and small matters ( )
6 I usually am able to take a firm stand on matters or issues ( )
7 I am able to express positive feeling toward others ( )
8 I often feel negatively toward others ( )
9 I express honest feelings and attitudes about myself ( )
10 I am willing to experiment with ideas coming from others ( )
11 I am normally helpful to other ( )
12 I recognize and commend others for work well done ( )
13 I am willing to experiment with ideas coming from others ( )
14 I am hasty with judgments on other people ( )
15 I am able to negotiate easily with people who do not know me well ( )
16 I am able to control my temper when others disagree with me ( )
17 I perceive myself as tolerant of others' differences and shortcomings ( )
18 I am patient with people who work and think more slowly than me ( )
19 I recognize prejudice and bias in myself and others ( )
20 I am usually able to accept others' negative criticism of me ( )
21 I can analyze my own shortcomings ( )
22 I am willing to seek help and consultation in overcoming my shortcomings ( )
23 I am willing to assume various group roles ( )
24 I am generally relaxed and at ease in group situations ( )
25 I am consciously considerate and attentive in my relations with those who may be in somewhat subordinate roles to mine ( )
26 I take responsibility for things for which I know I will never get recognition ( )
27 I take responsibility for things and actions expected of me ( )
28 I am usually sensitive to the needs of others ( )

In group situations:

29 I find I communicate normally ( )
30 I perceive myself as not dominating the discussions ( )

Continued

31 I allow others time to think and reply ( )
32 I get irritated when people do not understand, or question me ( )
33 I usually encourage participation by the more quiet and shy members ( )
34 I am conscious of how people are reacting to what I say ( )
35 I usually consult with my peers before making a decision ( )
36 I usually encourage a diversity of action by group members ( )
37 I consciously seek feedback to evaluate my performance ( )
38 I am willing to delegate functions to others ( )
39 I find myself able to stimulate others and to provoke discussion ( )
40 I am receptive to the contribution of others ( )
41 I am anxious to make contributions that are helpful ( )
42 I am anxious to resolve conflict as well accomplish a task ( )
43 I analyze sub-currents in groups and group processes ( )
44 I am concerned with the personal development of all members of the group, as well as accomplishing tasks ( )
45 Would you characterize yourself as a person who is open-minded or close-minded? ( )
46 Are you willing to change as a result of what you learn in this program? ( )

Conclusions. Over a period of time, people may change in the ways they work with and relate to other people. Personnel may also change in their attitudes and insights in operational ways as a result of meaningful learning experiences. Therefore, a HRD facilitator might wish to adapt the above questions into a Post-Training Inventory. Participants would then record on each item, any changes in perception or behavior relating to individual, group, or organizational relations in terms of before and after; a comparison then can be made on the effectiveness of a training program.

Next we provide a sample feedback form for evaluating a learning session after it has ended. For example, if you go back in this chapter to Exhibit 8.8, note that it provides a design for twelve learning modules within a HPLI. The next questionnaire could be utilized after the closing HPLI session to assess that training

EXHIBIT 8.14 High performance leadership institute

POST EVALUATION FORM

Date:_____ Your name or code #_____
Overall assessment – check as appropriate:

1 Were your expectations of this HPLI program fulfilled
  Very well ( ) Somewhat ( ) Very little ( )

Continued

2 Do you believe this learning experience will help to improve your performance as a leader
Very much ( ) Somewhat ( ) Very little ( )

3 Generally, how would you rate the speakers and discussion leaders?
Excellent ( ) Good ( ) Fair ( ) Poor ( )

4 In comparison to other learning or training experiences you attended, how would you rate the HPLI?
Excellent ( ) Good ( ) Fair ( ) Poor ( )

5 What changes would you propose for this program?

_____

Learning module assessment – check as appropriate:

Below are listed the titles of the lessons that have made up the program in which you have been participating. Please evaluate these lessons *individually* in terms of the potential (or current) usefulness to you in your work. Use the following scale:

5 = Excellent 4 = Good 3 = Average 2 = Fair 1 = Poor

Please feel free to list any other comments or suggestions for course improvements on the back of this page.

HPLI course
Learning module – first week   Usefulness rating

1 Dynamics of human and organizational behavior   ( )

_____

2 Understanding deviant behavior   ( )

_____

3 Improving communications skills   ( )

_____

4 Overcoming communication obstacles   ( )
5 Creative approaches to conference conflict resolution   ( )

_____

6 Insights from client feedback   ( )
7 Cultural influences on behavior   ( )

_____

Continued

8 Cultural influences on decision making ( )
9 Understanding group behavior in organizations ( )

10 Interpersonal skills for HRD ( )
11 Managing change and changing roles ( )
12 Behavioral strategies within organization and with clients ( )

9

ENERGIZING PERSONNEL THROUGH MEETINGS

Introduction

High performing leaders use their time effectively, especially with meetings, whether face-to-face or electronic. A meeting is a human encounter between two or more people. It is the means by which people exchange with one another, whether socially or for political and business purposes. A meeting is a junction; a place where we get together to get things done. Meetings can be used to clarify, negotiate, prepare, or solve problems.

Are you wasting too much time in meetings? A survey conducted by Burke Marketing Research in Cincinnati discovered that the average executive spends 16.5 hours a week, or twenty-one of the forty-hour work weeks, in a year at meetings. Another time management researcher has estimated that the average worker spends three years of his or her lifetime in meetings. The investigators concluded that top managers earn almost half their salaries by just sitting in such assemblages. That means organizations have a big financial investment in meetings, particularly if one estimate is true – that nearly one-third of those gatherings are considered unnecessary.

One of the ways that meetings waste time, talent, and money is the regularly scheduled sessions with no agenda. For example, an organization may have a tradition that certain key personnel meet once a week at 8:30 a.m., so everyone involved dutifully includes the time on his or her schedule whether there is any need for the meeting or not. Corporate headhunter, Robert Half, who commissioned one of the studies, laments that America does not lead the world in productivity, but in meetings.

Our concern in this book is for exercising high performance leadership. One way to do that is by finding innovative substitutes for the personal encounter, whether we confer with one person or a group. Fortunately, modern communication technologies offer a wide variety of media to utilize for the exchange of insights and information. Another way is to make better use of people's energies when they do gather for meetings. These two issues are the focus of this chapter, which flows naturally from our previous commentary on action learning.

The Input section discusses improving meeting effectiveness, using new meeting technologies, and making meetings more fun, as well as more productive. The Interaction section offers two methods for increasing learning at meetings through simulations and creative thinking exercises. Finally, the Instrumentation section provides a meeting and conference management checklist, as well as an inventory of a leader's capacities to energize people's performance at work.

As is customary, we begin with a profile of a HP global leader as a learning model – this time a chief executive officer who now serves on the board of two major corporations.

Social networking

EXHIBIT 9.1   Profile of a high performing CEO

David J. O'Reilly, a native of Ireland, was born in 1947. By 1968, he graduated from the University of Dublin with a chemical engineering degree. For almost forty years, he worked his way up in a global corporation called Chevron until he became its chairman and CEO. At the time of his retirement in 2009, *Fortune* magazine reported his last six-year average compensation to be $6.79 million. He also owns $11.2 million of Chevron stock. This is a remarkable record of high performance by an expatriate coming from outside the US system.

O'Reilly climbed the corporate ladder of this giant Californian energy company, serving in a wide variety of managerial positions, refinery plants, and countries. Chevron merged with Texaco in 2000 whilst he led this worldwide corporation. In eight years, O'Reilly would report record profits under his administration. No wonder that, in 2010, both Bechtel Corporation and Saudi Aramco invited him to join their board of directors. Throughout his career, O'Reilly was known for his helpful managerial style and team skills. During his time as a key executive, he reshaped Chevron through his Project Development Execution Plan. This strategy focused on stakeholders – the people who influence or are impacted by a major project. His cross-cultural competence was also evident in the many volunteer posts of leadership within his profession and community – ranging from the National Petroleum Council and the Business Roundtable, to the World Economic Forum and the San Francisco Symphony Board. For his service, O'Reilly received many awards and recognition – from an honorary doctorate of a science degree to a US State Department Award for Corporate Excellence.

Continued

O'Reilly proved his leadership in an international energy enterprise with interests in more than 180 nations. In many meetings, his emphasis was on the exploration and production of both oil and gas, including their refining, marketing, and transportation. In a period of economic recession, he offered a turn-around strategy based on operational excellence, lowering costs; maintaining a focused capital spending program on projects delivering long-turn value; and actively managing the corporate portfolio for robust returns. The son of a department-store buyer and homemaker, this honors student from Blackrock College also distinguished himself in sports as a long distance runner. From then on, he outdistanced colleagues in the world of business, especially as a new-style manager with a sense of humor and lack of status consciousness. A newspaper interview reported that his personal secret of success "isn't getting the most out of the ground, but getting the most out of people." He married an American lady, Joan Gariepy, and they are proud parents of two daughters.

Source: Dennis Harris, Chevron Petroleum Engineer, dennisharris@chevron.com.

Input

If we consider our organizations as energy exchange systems, then leaders have to be concerned that this energy flows properly and is channeled into the activities that will have the best pay-off. In that context, meetings are major loci of energy expenditure, because they consume so much personnel effort in preparing, conducting, and following-up. From the perspective of energy conservation, there are several questions: Is there a better way to confer and communicate than in the person-to-person format? Who are the required participants in a group encounter? How can we meet more productively? Many of the insights and methods of action learning and research (Chapter 8) can be applied here, because a learning or training session is a meeting. Similarly, what is offered in this chapter is equally applicable to all forms of instructional meetings, at all levels of education.

Increasing meeting effectiveness

To find out what can be done to improve meetings in an organization, ask the people who work there. This topic is perfect for action research, as long as the replies are anonymous and personnel are free to tell it like it is. A properly conducted survey can be done with questionnaires or interviews to ascertain what meetings are considered boring or unnecessary, what bothers people about the meetings, and what can be done to make the affairs more productive. The computer is a powerful tool for gathering feedback about the organization's meetings.

I was once a vice president in a corporation which held a weekly executive meeting. A common pattern prevailed – the president presided, made small talk and jokes, and dominated the proceedings. Rarely would the others present contribute to deliberations, and no real decisions were ever made. No agenda was ever set, no meaningful business was ever transacted, and everyone left frustrated, except the CEO's obsequious cronies. Knowing the company was losing money and going nowhere, I resigned to start my own enterprise. A few years later, after the first mentioned corporation had gone bankrupt, I discovered that, at the time of the meetings in question, the former president was going deaf, yet would not admit that he was unable to hear the contributions of others or wear a hearing aid. Thus, that strange meeting behavior contributed to the business failure. This was a company that did not welcome feedback from personnel, and, when it was given, tended not to act upon it. Trust, so critical in organizations, is something that can be developed through well conducted meetings. Three popular management themes – empowerment, engagement, and creativity – can also be developed through effective meetings.

Bradford D. Smart, president of Smart and Associates in Chicago, did a study as to what meeting characteristics bothered executives, particularly in team sessions. The respondents (fourteen board chairpersons, 358 presidents, 142 vice presidents, and 121 general managers) complained about:

1 poor preparation for the sessions by meeting planners or participants;
2 people drifting off the subject under discussion;
3 members not listening properly during the presentations and analysis;
4 participant wordiness during questioning or discussions;
5 lack of participation on the part of some;
6 emotional outbursts and conflicts;
7 ineffectiveness of methods or discussions;
8 excessive length.

The same executives reached some consensus as to ground rules during business meetings, including training sessions or team building:

• Each member must feel totally responsible for group effectiveness and team solutions, ensuring the maximum use of time and human resources available (e.g. invite silent ones to speak up and dominators to shut up).
• Telephone call interruptions and mobile phones should be banned except for serious emergencies of "life and death importance".
• Circular seating arrangements were requested, sometimes without tables.
• Participants should contribute to structuring the agenda and priorities, usually in the initial minutes and always in team meetings.
• Participative decision making achieved through group consensus is the desirable form of group action.
• Conflicts are to be confronted, used, and resolved, lest they hamper group effectiveness.
• Teams should learn how to diagnose and deal with problems of group process, including the appropriate use of instruments for this purpose.

Meeting guidelines

- Recognize that meetings have different purposes, requiring participants and methods suitable to the type of meeting proposed (e.g. meetings for regular staff business, for work programming, for unit feedback on progress, for problem solving, for information sharing, or for training) – therefore, plan accordingly.
- Realize there are meeting skills to be acquired relative to planning, chairing, controlling, facilitating, and coping with problems or obtaining solutions – develop these competencies.
- Consult resources that can assist in improving the technical presentations during meetings – seek training in multimedia methods, production of slides or videotapes, group dynamics, use of PowerPoint software.
- Use meetings to provide interaction opportunities for managers or supervisors of complex, interdependent operations – promote intragroup relations.
- Hold meetings, if possible, on one's own "territory," but ensure that the facilities are adequate for optimum performance, including all necessary supplies and equipment – site planning is essential.
- Seat participants for minimum conflict or collusion (e.g. divide antagonists and buddies) and maximum exchange (e.g. round tables, U-shaped table set up, or other logistic arrangements to promote eye contact and interaction) – devote attention to meeting preparations.
- Agendas are normally helpful to focus efforts and save time, while excluding undesirable and irrelevant subjects (except in unstructured meetings, in which the group develops the agenda). Issues are: who sets the agenda, how to get items on the docket, and when is this agenda to be distributed; does the leader establish the agenda or delegate this? Is there a procedure for members to contribute points for discussion? Is the agenda published in advance for preparation purposes, or held until the actual meeting?
- Control time in business meetings so that it is used productively – provide advance materials, set a time limit, use a timing device, limit individual input, establish meeting procedures.
- Facilitate the meeting process – provide for note taking and recording when desirable; invite and foster participation; encourage compromise and conflict management; replay people's ideas and synthesize input; use audiovisual aids; during sessions, articulate clearly and non-defensively; divide the group into subgroups or task forces to study critical issues; obtain support beforehand on critical decisions; offer positive reinforcement of sound strategies and positions; seek and obtain consensus (possibly by calling for a vote).
- Conclude meetings by clarifying action steps, establishing accountability, setting deadlines if necessary, confirming unusual contributions, encouraging feelings of accomplishment, and ending on time.

Andrew S. Grove, the founder and former president of Intel Corporation, observed that, in the course of a work day, he normally engaged in twenty-five separate activities, but that two-thirds of that time was spent in meetings. Obviously, then, this time must be used effectively – meetings provide the medium for most managerial activity, and, when conducted well, offer managerial leverage. In his book, *High Output Management* (Grove 1983), he described two basic types of business meetings:

1 *Process-oriented*. Knowledge is shared and information is exchanged; it should take place on a regularly scheduled basis and recorded on people's calendars for minimum interruption of production. Generally these are of three kinds:

> *One-on-one*, such as supervisor–subordinate, for mutual information exchange, learning, coaching, and problem solving; number and length may vary, but agenda is normally set by subordinate in outline form for note taking; usually is performance oriented; participants may "batch" key issues for discussion together or establish a "hold" file for those that are less urgent and can be put off until another encounter; supervisor welcomes authentic communication and sees these meetings as an opportunity to build organizational relationships; the face-to-face encounter may be supplemented by telephone and note exchanges.
>
> *Staff meeting*, in which supervisor and subordinates confer; opportunity for peer interaction and decision making; leader plays multiple roles of observer, expediter, questioner, decision-maker, and may share authority with the group in this context.
>
> *Operation review*, which brings together managers and peers from various parts of the organization to motivate, share progress and problems, and generally to inform of the larger operational activities; usually formal presentations, well-organized format; an opportunity for senior management to provide behavior models, to share the "big picture."

2 *Mission-oriented*. Ad hoc affairs aimed at producing a specific output, such as a decision, in a short time frame. The key is in the chairperson, who must understand why the meeting is necessary, what specific accomplishments are required, who must attend, and what logistical arrangements are critical. That person is also responsible for follow up action: minutes of the meeting, commitments pursued. No more than twenty-five percent of time devoted to meetings should be of this occasional, emergency type. Human exchanges now have moved far beyond formal meetings, as Exhibit 9.2 on social networking indicates.

EXHIBIT 9.2   A world of connections

People connect in a variety of ways, including through social networking. Sometimes this happens at meetings, such as the annual World Economic Forum in Davos – delegates of the great and good usually stay in touch with

Continued

one another long after the actual sessions end. To promote interaction among these global leaders, the Forum's organizers have introduced a secure online service so that participants could post mini biographies and other information, as well as create links to form collaborative working groups. Called WELCOM, this online network has some 5,000 members.

Facebook is now the second most popular site on the internet after Google. This social network has 845 million users worldwide. Other such networks serving specific purposes include My Space (music and entertainment); LinkedIn (targets career-minded professionals); Twitter (for short, 140 character messages); Muxlim (for the world's Muslims); Research Gate (connects scientists and researchers); Zyga (social gaming). Many other such networks now exist for individual countries, languages, religions, and interests such as gaming. Improved interfaces and security provisions for privacy now have engendered vast public spaces where millions may confer with one another. Humanity is thus upgrading mass communications. The human family is being brought closer together, while personal relationships are becoming more visible. In the business world, Enterprise 2.0 software connects new technologies and its practitioners. Social networking also spawns problems like executives who complain employees waste time "notworking" while "networking" for personal reasons.

In this new era of global interconnectedness, innovations spread faster than ever before. Further, the value of a network grows exponentially with the numbers of people connected to it. Most servers and databases can rapidly add services as they gather more users. The phenomenon creates a greater demand for software engineers, and programmers on open source memory systems which facilitate data retrieval. Also, digital cameras and video recorders reduce the costs of producing and publishing high-quality images. For operators, social networks produce a treasure trove of personal information that can be used in marketing, as well as for criminal purposes. There is no doubt that social networks are also "money spinners," so they attract venture capital. Businesses of all sizes see these networks are a bonanza for advertising products, and increasing income. Small businesses have discovered that Facebook and Twitter can increase sales. Even entrepreneurs are connecting to bring new products and services to the public. This technology is also employed by intelligence agencies to share information and counter terrorism. Global corporations find Enterprise 2.0 useful to connect with far-flung operations, and to exchange with other companies, while protected by a "firewall" from outsiders. Danone offers, by invitation only, private discussion groups among its 90,000 employees. Firms see these networks as a means of recruiting personnel, while job hunters also take advantage of them. They make it easier for individuals and institutions to exchange HRD data. Digital-savvy young people are entering the workforce and capitalizing on their abilities to search and integrate various social networks.

Continued

Social media makes it easier to manage a complex of relationships. Social computing and networks open up the labor market, and make both the public and private sectors more transparent and available. Millions worldwide already use their mobile telephones to tap into social networks. New ways of "geo-networking" applications are continuously discovered to boost productivity and generate fresh ideas. While there is always a minority who will misuse this marvelous tool, the majority of humanity is able to communicate and collaborate more freely via broadband internet connections. The world is better for it.

Source: Based on "A World of Connections – A Special Report on Social Networking," *The Economist*, 30 January 2010 (www.emerald-library.com).

Social media has become so important as a meeting method that Emerald Group Publishing is sponsoring a global research study on its impact.

Meeting innovations

When it comes to organizing professional meetings, the coordinators need to be high performers themselves. A competent meeting facilitator manages a whole range of activities: conference design and site selection; choosing media and learning materials; arranging for guest speakers and their needs; providing systems for registration, exhibits, presentations, evaluation and follow up. Exhibit 9.7 provides an instrument to assist in major meeting planning.

Meeting planners need to use imagination and innovate in the manner in which people are brought together. For more informal gatherings, there are a wide variety of possibilities. For example, when Dr Martin Apple was president of Adytum Inc., he used an unusual technique in this high-tech firm he founded. Apple held a daily stand-up meeting for all key researchers at 8:30 a.m.; normal work day for the plant began at 9:00 a.m. During the opening half hour, the group would brainstorm ideas for possible patents and the session was recorded. In the course of the day, the CEO would play back the ideas kicked around by the group in a very creative manner. Before leaving work that day, each member received a brief typed memorandum to the group from the chief executive on what concepts seemed feasible to pursue for patent filing. In this way, the knowledge workers were energized and enthused, knowing that they had a daily opportunity to meet with top management and contribute their creativity, which eventually might be rewarded. As a result of these unique encounters, this entrepreneurial activity prospered and a record number of patents were actually filed and recognitions given.

New meeting technology

Meeting performance can be enhanced by intelligent use of the many new electronic devices available to promote human interaction (as described in Exhibit 9.2). In fact, the "children of the television and information age" expect innovation when they attend meetings, conferences, and conventions. They not only have high expectations on the use of various media for presenting information and creating knowledge, but they want it done professionally in terms of content, format, and technical expertise. Thus, sound equipment has to be clear and understandable; live commentary has to be dynamic, appropriate and stimulating; the visuals have to be crisp and the pace fast. Whether attending a seminar or listening to a sales pitch, today's audience, products of mass media, demand that both medium and message be informative, sophisticated, and entertaining. This applies equally to live meetings, teleconferencing, or combinations of both.

Such expectations place an added burden on meeting planners, to see that films, video, slides, audio, computers, synthesizers, and other such technology is carefully chosen and combined for maximum impact. Therefore, planners ensure that:

- the proper hardware and/or software has been identified and selected;
- the pre-meeting testing of this proves satisfactory, especially in terms of sequence and integration of equipment and presentations;
- the provision has been made for alternative programming in case of technical breakdowns, power failures, or other emergencies;
- the plan makes for optimum use of the senses of those in the audience – the more individual powers involved, the better the chance that the message will be retained.

People enjoy variety at meetings, change of pace, and opportunities to directly participate in what is happening. Contemporary communication technologies make this all possible in dazzling ways. PowerPoint software offers one important presentation possibility. Live input can be alternated with mass media, group process, and even electronic involvement. Multiple projectors can now be synchronized for maximum impact. The planner might begin with a training film, supplement it by offering new dimensions of the same subject with two slide projectors, and then end the demonstration with live and active participation by actors or the audience; these methods can be used in sequence or simultaneously with multiple screens. Because annual corporate conferences may represent a considerable financial investment, a multidimensional transmission of a message may establish the right mood and learning environment. In addition to professional conference consultants, most conference facilities have personnel to assist planners with the use of meeting rooms, including colors, lighting, ventilation, seating, and sound or musical background. Then it becomes possible to immerse a group in a maelstrom of sight, sound, and feelings, providing a stimulating and, at times, almost psychedelic learning environment. To summarize, in this era of mass communication, imaginative meeting facilitators have numerous mechanical and technical aids, in addition to traditional means, to stimulate the senses and transmit the message more effectively. Indeed, there can be a message in the media chosen, as rock concert promoters have demonstrated.

Educational media publishers now offer a variety of instructional kits, learning packages, and other seminar aids to assist the manager or trainer conducting the meeting. For example, some distributors use a training systems approach, supporting management development films with instructor's guides and supplementary materials from CDs and DVDs to case studies and diagnostic instruments. Longman Crown of Reston, Virginia, offers computer-based training. These user-friendly, interactive systems can be used on personal computers and include learning strategies for drill and practice, tutorials and inquiries, simulations and computer-managed instructional methods. The subjects range from time and project management, to decision making and management performance. When these capabilities are combined with television receivers and CDs and DVDs, a learning system is created for individual or group training. Interactive video is the marriage of computer to video technology – a powerful new meeting, training and learning tool. Indications as to where some of this information is available is provided in the resource section at the end of this book.

Electronic meeting possibilities

The prospects for improving meetings through technology are staggering. These technologies include satellite communications, word processing systems, fiber optics, paging devices, and new digital uses of telecommuication long lines. High technology offers exciting opportunities at meetings or conferences to present graphics and simulations, to survey an audience for rapid response or texting purposes, to promote interactive, individual, or group learning, and to encourage networking. The power of the web has been examined in a new book on "wikinomics."[45] The following successful examples of meeting technology use may inspire further management leadership:

- Instantaneous, multisite, two way satellite meetings can be used for small groups or teleconferences of very large audiences; currently, there are three alternatives:
  - slow-scan video using standard video cameras and telephone lines for sound/video;
  - one way bandwidth video in which the audience may respond by two way audio telephone link;
  - two way full bandwidth for video and audio, so that participants both see and hear one another from remote locations and may exchange as if they were together at the same site.

  Major corporations, such as ARCO, TRW, Ford, Westinghouse, Sperry, and Merrill Lynch have their own telecommunication networks. Among the principal private enterprise communication network services are Satellite Business Systems of McLean, Virginia, and VideoNet of Woodland Hills, California.
- International hotel chains offer a combined service of meeting rooms and private satellite communications for conferencing purposes. For example, Holiday Inn, Intercontinental, and Hilton Hotels not only have electronic networks for

this purpose, but offer ancillary services such as story board development or exchange of hard copy across continents.

- Telephone conference calls for either audio or video meetings by combining the use of various visuals, computer video display terminals and electronic mail exchange. The range of network applications extends from telemarketing and teletraining to mass calling and electronic order exchange. Among the several telephone utilities offering such service, AT&T has the most comprehensive training and support system.
- Computer response systems for live meetings enables the presenter to profile the audience quickly, customize input, control audience attention, stimulate discussions, and create more intimate groups within large gatherings. Even testing by mobile phones can be used to answer surveys immediately.
- Electronic matchmaking between employers and potential employees eliminates the need for some job interviews or at least reduces the number of expensive meetings between the parties. The Corporate Interviewing Network of Fort Lauderdale, Florida, sends client companies video recorded interviews with candidates. Other firms now use satellite television to directly interview job applicants at remote sites, in preference to bringing them to corporate offices or sending out recruiters.
- Satellite Seminars is a new teleconferencing service which teams up the resources of the US Chamber of Commerce, American Management Associations, and BNA Communications. Subscribers receive a variety of seminars from marketing to management.

The venue one chooses for a major conference requires careful selection. For example, many meetings are being scheduled at theme parks or on cruise ships. The latter have proven popular for sea seminars. Meeting location is a critical factor for planners, and the choice often depends on convenience, cost, or location.

Another exciting development has been the explosion of online educational opportunities. Now working adults can enroll in university or college online courses that lead to Bachelors, Masters, and even PhDs. The University of Phoenix has become one of the world's largest with over 400,000 enrolled students. Many faculty members operate out of their homes as online professors. The Massachusetts Institute of Technology has put all its courses online. Communication technologies have brought distance education even to remote communities. There is a 3D mix digital design university to create art with people who think visually. Student teamwork produces international products, projects, and festivals.

In this post-industrial age, information and learning are the means to establish the authority of competence while furthering career development. Mass media is the means of obtaining solutions to problems and challenges. Leaders who are sensitive to their HRD responsibilities realize this, and make effective use of meetings to accomplish such purposes. Whether the situation requires a live or electronic meeting, innovators either master the professional methods or know where to obtain support services for achieving high performance through meetings. Such efforts contribute to creating a work environment that spawns productivity and happiness.

Interaction

Frequently at meetings, a manager or trainer is asked to lead a discussion group. Exhibit 9.3 provides fifteen guidelines for being more effective in this role that is provided by a professional meeting planner. Such specialists are available as consultants for major conferences.

EXHIBIT 9.3   Discussion group guidelines by Robert Letwin

1 State the objective of the session to the group and the area of discussion, explaining first that everyone participates, but there are to be no speeches.
2 To get started, you put a sharply defined question to the group. If no one responds, have an alternate question that is easy for anyone to answer. Resist answering your own question and entering into a monologue.
3 Test for the audience's objective. Is it the same as yours? If the audience would like to steer the discussion in another direction, make sure there is a consensus. If there is, discuss what the audience considers to be more important. Good discussion follows when everyone agrees on what to discuss.
4 Keep in mind what you hope will be the outcome. Ask questions that will focus on the agreed upon objective.
5 Have a member of the group serve as a reporter to keep a running record of problems, issues, facts, and decisions discussed. From time to time, have the reporter summarize. This is useful when the group starts to stray from the main topic.
6 Resort to easy-to-answer questions when discussion gets bogged down. For instance, ask a question about the time sequence, such as "What comes first, and next?" You can also ask "What is the biggest problem with...?" or, "What has been your experience with...?"
7 Ask for votes. Get a consensus on as many points as possible.
8 Do not rephrase what is offered by a group member. Repeat the statement exactly as it is given. Resist inserting your words or editing comments. This can be intimidating. No one wants his or her words corrected in public. This also tends to stifle discussion.
9 Do not feel you have to cover everything you know about the subject. That is not the purpose of discussion. Rather, the aim is to have everyone in the audience participate. It is better to have a lively, well-explored segment of a subject than breeze along quickly without deep reflections.

Continued

10 Summarize with the help of the reporter. Point out problems raised during the discussion. List bright ideas for all to read. Point out areas of agreement and disagreement.
11 If some members of the group do not have the courage to speak up, draw them in with non-threatening questions. Ask them to share their experiences.
12 It is best to toss questions to the entire group. But, if you want to ask a quiet person to speak, call the person by name before you ask the question. Say "John, what did you think when you first heard about...?" By starting with the person's name, you provide time for him or her to concentrate and think about an answer.
13 When someone tends to monopolize discussion, politely interrupt and ask someone else in the audience to comment on the monopolizer's statements. Allow the audience to straighten out its members instead of you doing it. Too tight a rein will cut off discussion.
14 At end of the discussion period, summarize the main points for the audience, possibly in writing.
15 Feel good about not covering all the points you had written in advance. This means you have led a wholesome discussion and were not prompted to inject your opinions in favor of those in the group.

Meetings can be fun and productive

The key to high performance is energized people who are interested and involved. One of the best ways to accomplish this at meetings is through play, games, and simulations. In addition to techniques already suggested in previous Interaction sections, further possibilities are now described. When people enjoy themselves at work, they tend to be more productive. The meeting, especially for training purposes, can be a useful mechanism for unleashing hidden creativity through play. It permits employees to reveal joyful, spontaneous, and even silly facets of themselves that are often restrained. Enlightened management takes advantage of this approach for creative problem solving and education, as well as for its mental health and recreational values.

Over many decades in leadership development, I have personally found that management games are very worthwhile because they:

- provide a change of pace in the training schedule or meeting schedule;
- foster experiential or affective learning;
- reveal behavior in a simulation that often occurs on the job;
- entertain while teaching important lessons of teamwork;
- build on the competitive spirit while demonstrating the disadvantages of; unrestrained competition and the synergistic value of cooperation or collaboration;

- offer opportunities for meaningful analysis and discussion after the play as to what happened and why;
- give incentive to extra team effort which can thus be rewarded, literally or figuratively.

In a meeting simulation, a real life experience is simulated or replayed through a "game-like" experience, but in a condensed time span. As in recreational games, a person acts out the situation according to established rules. A life experience that might require the passage of days or weeks can be telescoped into a short time frame of several hours. Practice in planning, decision making, and communication can be obtained through a simulated experience. As people get more deeply involved in the game, behavior which is often common in their real life is also exhibited in the game.

Simulation uses trial-and-error experimentation with a model for research, problem solving, or training purposes. A simulated group technique permits learning to take place through a group experience. It enables a trainer to demonstrate, by a simulated model within a short time period, a larger human relations truth that the participant may eventually experience in a different setting. Frequently, in business and industry, these techniques of group dynamics are employed for the purpose of management development. Principles are taught and insights gained which have application to the job situations. Behavioral games involve developing strategy, resolving conflict, and setting objectives. The most vital part of this action learning experience is when the game ends and the participants analyze what they learned.

Simulated exercises are used to teach a number of things not easily taught by any other method. These include:

1 the importance of planned, critically timed decisions;
2 the need for flexible, organized effort;
3 the need for decision-assisting tools, such as setting objectives and establishing criteria for measuring and evaluating performance;
4 the significance of reaching a dynamic balance between interacting managerial functions;
5 the power of the modeling concept for providing a scientific approach to problems.

An interesting use of the simulation is to train personnel through this "practice session" to prepare for the "real thing." War games have long been used for this purpose. Increasingly, the computer is being used for simulation purposes. Mathematical models of potential situations are programmed, and the trainees act out "live" work situations through the computer.

As previously indicated, a manager or trainer may purchase, borrow, or create a simulation game to meet a specific need. Two examples of helpful commercial games for management development are "StarPower" and "Relocation," both distributed by www.simulationtrainingsystems.com. "StarPower" teaches a group about the realities of power and its influence on behavior. "Relocation" examines the issues involved in moving a corporate headquarters, both from the viewpoint of the community and from the employees.

On the other hand, innovative trainers may use cardboard, sticks, glue, tinker toys, or other household items to create a structured learning experience that teaches managers the importance of cooperation or of "win–win." There are non-competitive games based on the approach that both teams either win together or lose. Two of my favorite homemade games of this type for managers are "Hollow Square" and "Blue Green."

At the beginning of the Hollow Square exercise (Exhibit 9.4), two teams are given various pieces of cardboard, which they are to assemble within a specific time frame. Each group is further divided into subgroups of planners and operators. The planners are to prepare a plan, like a plan for a jigsaw puzzle, for the operators to assemble the pieces into the correct pattern in this competitive game.

EXHIBIT 9.4   Hollow Square game

In this Hollow Square exercise, two designs are provided: (A) Overall Pattern, and (B) Detailed Assembled Pattern (Note: (A) is the incomplete design given to planners/operators. When properly assembled, the pieces make up this following pattern. (B) is the completed design that the winning team must produce with the pieces.)

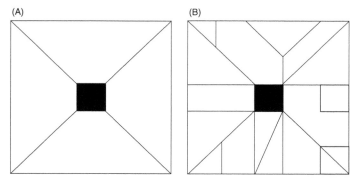

(A)   (B)

The team who uses the pieces to correctly assemble the pattern wins. There are also observers of the process going around the four groups of planners and implementers. Part B of Exhibit 9.4 illustrates the pattern of cardboard pieces properly assembled with its hollow square in the center. Following the simulation, the trainer hears reports from these observers on their own behavior and strategies. Exhibit 9.5 summarizes the instructions given to the planners, operators, and observers as well as knowledge gained. After the observers' reports, participants contribute their own insights from the learning experience. Part D provides a synthesis of the lessons real people have learned from this "game" – the principal one is that only when planners and operators collaborate, and when planners involve those who must implement their plans in the planning process, does the team succeed.

EXHIBIT 9.5 Hollow Square exercise: briefing sheet

Part A. Briefing sheet for planning team

(Note to Facilitator – There are two groups, each with two teams. For learning purposes, it is possible to influence the outcome by instructing one group to consider electing a team leader, while suggesting to the other group that they try participative management and share the leadership.)

Each participant will be given a packet containing four or more cardboard pieces which, when properly assembled with pieces from other participants, will make a hollow square design.

Your task. During a period of forty-five minutes you are to do the following:

1 Plan how these pieces, distributed among you, should be assembled to make the design.
2 Instruct your operating team on how to implement your plan so as to complete your task ahead of the other teams. (You may begin instructing your operating team at any time during the forty-five minute planning period, but no later than five minutes before they are to begin the assembling process).
3 You must keep all four pieces you have in front of you at all times.
4 You may not touch the pieces of other team members or trade pieces with other members of your team during the planning or instructing phase.
5 You may not show Sheet B (which contains the detailed design as shown in Exhibit 9.4) to the operating team at any time.
6 You may not actually assemble the entire square at any time (this is to be left to your operating team).
7 You may not number or otherwise mark the pieces.
8 Members of your operating team must also observe the above rules until the signal is given to begin the assembling.
9 When time is called for your operating team to begin assembling the pieces, you may give no further instructions, but are to step back from the table and observe the operation only.
10 All members of the planning team must be involved in the exercise; also, all members of the operating team.
11 If you have specific questions which may affect the way you propose to go about your task, it may be preferable to ask them of the Resource people privately rather than before the large group.

Part B. Briefing sheet for operating team

1 You will have responsibility for carrying out a task for four people according to instructions given by your planning team. Your planning team may call

Continued

you in for instructions at any time. If they do not summon you beforehand, you are to report to them anyway. Your task is scheduled to begin promptly at XX time, after which no further instructions from your planning team can be given. You are to finish the assigned task as rapidly as possible.

2 During the period when you are waiting for a call from your planning team, it is suggested that you discuss and make notes on the following:

    a. the feelings and concerns which you experience while waiting for instructions for the unknown task;

    b. your suggestions on how a person might prepare to receive instructions.

Your notes recorded on the above will be helpful during the work group discussions following the completion of your task.

Part C. Briefing for observing team

You will be observing a situation in which a planning team decides how to solve a problem and gives instructions to an operating team for implementation. The problem consists of assembling pieces of cardboard into the form of a hollow square. The planning team is supplied with the general layout of the pieces (Exhibit 9.4(B)). This team is not to assemble the parts but is to instruct the operating team on how to assemble the parts in a minimum amount of time. You will be *silent observers* throughout the process.

Suggestions for observation

1 Each member of the observing team should watch the general pattern of communication, but give special attention to one member of the planning team (during the planning phase) and one member of the operating team (during the assembling period).

2 During the planning period watch for such behavior as:

    a. For planners:

        i. the evenness or unevenness of participation among planning team members;

        ii. behavior that blocks or facilitates understanding;

        iii. how the planning team divides its time between planning and instructing (how early does it invite the operating team to come in?);

        iv. how well it plans its procedure for giving instructions to the operating team.

    b. For operators:

        i. what do members do with their time?

Continued

    ii. what evidence is there of anxiety, boredom, and feelings about planners?

    iii. what could the planners have done to alleviate the anxieties and/or negative behavior evidenced by the operating team?

3 During the instructing period (when the planning team is instructing the operating team) watch for such things as:

  a. Who in the planning team gives the instructions (and how was this decided)?

  b. What is significant about the management or leadership style followed in the group you are observing?

Part D. Knowledge gained from the Hollow Square game

Problems that may occur when one group makes plans which the other group is to carry out:

1 Planners sometimes impose restrictions on themselves which are unnecessary.
2 It is sometimes difficult for planners to see the task from the point of view of the operators.
3 Sometimes in planning, more attention is given to details while the larger clues and possibilities go unnoticed.
4 Planners sometimes fail to apportion their time wisely because they plunge into the act of planning before they think through their entire task and the amount of time available to them.
5 Planners sometimes have different understandings of their task and the boundaries in which they must operate.
6 When members of a planning team fail to listen to one another, time is lost in efforts to clarify.
7 Sometimes planners fail to prepare a proper physical setup for the working team.
8 Sometimes planners become so involved in the planning process that they do not plan their method of instructing the implementers.

Common problems when planners instruct operators:

1 Sometimes planners do not consider the operators' anxieties when they orient them to the environment and task.
2 Planners may not allow enough time for instruction, and to help the operators to "get set" and feel comfortable for the job.

Continued

3 Planners may not encourage questions from the operators and therefore assume greater understanding than the operators have.
4 The planners' own feelings of anxiety or security are likely to be transmitted to the operators.
5 Planners sometimes give detailed instructions before giving the operator an "overall" feel of the task.
6 Planners sometimes stress minute problems which concerned them while ignoring more important points.
7 The instructions may be given in a way that discourages members of an operating group from working as a team.

Common problems when operators carry out the plans of others:

1 If instructions are confusing, operators tend to display irritation toward each other as well as toward the planners.
2 If instructions are unclear, considerable time will be spent in clarification.
3 Members of an operating team will often have different perceptions of their instructions.
4 The factor of pressure will influence different operators in different ways – the efficiency of some will go up and the efficiency of others will decline.
5 If members of an operating group do not feel themselves to be a team, they will usually perform less efficiently (during some periods one person may be working on part of the problem all alone while the others wait inactively for him to complete the task).

Another, simpler, "Blue Green" game drives home the win–win philosophy. Two groups are told they are both separate divisions or subsidiaries of the same organization. They are instructed on procedures for amassing points, and told that within the specified time period, their group scores will be totaled to determine the winner. Although there is nothing in the ground rules preventing their mutual cooperation, each usually proceeds to gain points at the expense of the other group in a mad competitive battle. Only in the post-game learning analysis do the participants realize that the whole organization stands to lose because of their failure to cooperate as parts within the same system. This game teaches a powerful lesson about how the competitive race for profits may have destructive effects on the common good. Management games are useful tools for communicating about the new work culture norm of collaboration or team effort.

There are many training resources available that provide details on how to formulate and facilitate such games for the development of personnel. For example, Peter Garber has written *50 Communication Activities, Icebreakers, and Exercises* (www.hrdpress.com 2009). The same source has video-based simulations set around Grand Canyon adventures. Local computer software stores also can advise on what is available on the market in terms of computer simulations.

Creativity exercises

An effective strategy at the end of a training session or meeting is to propose creative problem solving on the question "How are we going to apply this learning, information, or technique back on the job?" Such an exercise can stimulate a group to produce action plans for performance improvement. In the Interaction section, one technique, "brainstorming" is outlined for this purpose, and four major steps in the creative thinking process are discussed in Exhibit 9.6 with examples. Such techniques can be used by a manager or facilitator at a meeting to "loosen up" the group's imaginative and intuitive capacities before turning them loose to creatively solve a real organizational problem. Dr Matt Weinstein developed a whole company to teach adults how to play at meetings and conferences – Playfair, Inc., based in Berkeley, California. His corporate clients use these services at meetings and conferences to help their employees decrease stress, increase productivity, and improve morale or camaraderie. As a replacement for the cocktail hour, he can engage a ballroom full of meeting attendees in free form play. There are no winners and losers; only celebration, bonding, and community results. When the meeting sessions are spread over days or weeks, it is essential to build into the conference design opportunities for physical and emotional release, so that participants are recharged for further intellectual effort. Thus "re-creation" can serve as a learning experience when so planned, such as a team golf game using the rules of "Scramble," in which individual scores are replaced by a group tally (combining the best performance of each member for each shot on every hole). Many resorts catering to conference groups have a variety of silly games to relax tired registrants – water-balloon tosses, egg-carrying relays, sandcastle building contests, or creative theme parties. The resulting laughter is good for morale, encourages conviviality and comradeship, and puts attendees on an equal footing. Meetings, a part of the whole work environment, can be made enjoyable in a variety of ways if creativity is exercised in the planning as described in the next exhibit.

EXHIBIT 9.6   Creative thinking techniques

1 Stating the problem

Creative problem solving requires that the problems be stated in such a way that the thinking of those who are attempting to solve the problem is not *unduly* restricted. For example, think of the old saw, "Build a better mousetrap and the world will beat a path to your door." The implied problem, "build a better mousetrap," is inadequate. A better problem statement is, "find a way to eliminate mice from *x* area." This latter statement permits us to think beyond an elimination that requires the presence of rodents. The former restricts us to thinking in terms of spring traps, gas, ultrasonic devices, and rodent-proof building construction.

Continued

The problem statement must not be unduly restricted nor must it be stated so broadly as to make it difficult to focus on constructive possibilities. For example, a problem solving team at one institute was to consider the problem of utilizing the knowledge gained about creativity at the conference. This is too vague, too broad, to handle effectively. A better statement was found when one of the group outlined his company's background and restated the problem as "How can we install an educational program on creative thinking in our company?"

Often, mechanical methods, such as the following, are big helps to coming up with a "best" problem stated. It is worth the time it takes to settle on the problem.

- Method 1. State the problem in ten words or less.
- Method 2. State the problem in a specified number of ways – at least five and, often, as many as ten.

The importance attached to problem stating cannot be overdrawn. The "old timers" and best technical men must be most wary that changing technology and conditions do not make yesterday's problems only apparent, but false, problems today. It is all too easy to work at solving problems which have become irrelevant in the course of time. Or just as bad, to deny ourselves the posing of certain problem statements *supposing* that solutions are beyond technical or human capability. In an age of increasing technical and organizational capability, virtually all problems may be stated without stating a pre-judged case.

2 Analytical operational techniques

These techniques employ a logical step-by-step approach to the problem. These approaches include attribute listing, the input–output method, and morphological analysis. These techniques have two basic rules: 1 all judgment or evaluation is eliminated from the idea-producing step; 2 all ideas, *even the most impractical*, are considered.

Attribute Listing was developed by Professor Robert Crawford at the University of Nebraska. Its procedures include:

a Isolate all the major characteristics or attributes of a product, object, or idea.
b Consider each in turn and change them in every conceivable way. No attempt is made to limit the suggested changes in any manner.
c After all the ideas have been listed, evaluate them in the light of the limitations posed by the problem and the situation.

Continued

Example: consider design improvements for the traditional telephone instrument.

The characteristics (attributes) are listed: usually black; has a handset and base, a dial for indicating the number desired, and is constructed principally of plastic.

Possible changes include: black color – could be any other color or transparent; could be two-tone; could utilize designs such as polka dot, abstract art designs, personalized designs (initials, names), or pictures. Handset and base construction – could design handset to fit hand (finger grooves); make it more square or more round in the base; oval base; higher or lower base; wall set; eliminate (use microphone and speaker). Dial – could use a push-button system; design the dial differently (numbers and letters outside the dial); lever system; abacus-type system; computer to interpret voice commands. Plastic construction – could be metal, glass, wood, hard rubber, stone, or lucite or other plastics.

Note: Unique attributes tend to produce the greatest opportunity for *original* variations. Attributes common to many products (i.e. color, shape, size, weight, etc.) tend to produce opportunities for fewer extraordinary original ideas. Consider how today's mobile phone comes in all colors and small sizes.

Input–output methods, developed by General Electric Company, are useful where the problem involves the use of one or more forms of energy.

a Establish the desired output, or end result. This "output" is the goal we are seeking to attain – the problem solution.
b The input is the starting point. The input includes the various forms of energy which are available to provide the initial stimulus which sets in motion the dynamic system involved.
c Analyze the input to determine how various forms of energy produced by it can be used to ultimately achieve the desired output.

Example (problem): to devise a fire warning system within a given building.

a Establish desired output – warning of the presence of fire.
b Determine input – fire.
c Analyze the input.

  i. Specifications. The warning must be received one mile away from the building site within a matter of seconds after the fire starts. Cost must be under $1000. System must be operative twenty-four hours a day, seven days a week. System must be relatively trouble-free and easy to maintain.
  ii. Problem attack.

Continued

- What outputs are produced directly by the input? Fire is characterized by the presence of a certain amount of heat and light and by the presence of the gaseous and solid products of combustion and smoke.
- Can any of these factors be used to produce the desired output directly? (Without referring to the specifications, we can say that once the fire became large enough, a combination of its light and smoke would supply its own warning signal, but by that time the fire would have devoured a good part of the building, thus making a solution of this kind unsatisfactory.)
- What reactions are caused by heat? light? smoke? Here a serious attempt should be made to list all the possible physical and chemical reactions. Those actions caused by heat include: expansion of various metals, liquids, and bases; melting of metals and glass; changes in the composition of certain chemicals. Light and smoke can cause various chemical and physical actions and reactions.
- Can any of these reactions be used to achieve the desired output? The melting of an alloy such as Wood's metal, which melts at a temperature below the boiling point of water, could be used to break a circuit or to open a valve. Actually, Wood's metal is used in sprinkler systems designed to extinguish undetected fires. The expansion of liquids is the principle used in the thermometer. The unequal expansion of bimetal strips when exposed to heat is the basis for the thermostat (a heat-actuated electric circuit breaker). Light can be detected by various chemicals.

Note: Only those problems that deserve extensive treatment would warrant use of the input–output method.

3 Forced relations techniques

In most instances, the forced relationship is established arbitrarily – often by mechanical means.

a *Catalog.* Open a catalog or other source of printed information and select any item or subject, or even a single word, at random without conscious effort. A second item, subject, or word is selected in the same arbitrary manner. These elements are then considered together, and the person using the technique attempts to create original ideas based upon this forced relationship.
b *Listing.* List a number of objects or ideas which are all associated with a general subject. After all items have been listed, give each one a number. Consider each item in turn with each other item. For example, a manufacturer of office equipment might consider the following objects: desk, chair, desk lamp, filing cabinet, bookcase. He would consider such combinations

Continued

as chair and desk, chair and lamp, chair and filing cabinet, and chair and bookcase – and others as possible marketable items. As with *all* other operational techniques, no attempt is made to judge any of the ideas produced until all possible ideas are collected.

c *Focused object*. The elements in the relationship are pre-selected with a definite purpose in mind.

 i Select the fixed element in the forced relationship. This may be a product, an idea, or a problem statement.

 ii Focus attention on some other element – usually something in the immediate vicinity. Once the fixed element and the element selected at random have been chosen, the forced or unnatural relationship has been established. This is then used as the basis for a free-flowing chain of free associations from which are to come new and original ideas. Usually the first ideas will come from a simple transfer of the attributes of the random to the fixed element. Example: a chair manufacturer might choose a chair as the fixed element and choose a light bulb as a random element. First level suggestions might be a glass chair, thinner chair, bulb-shaped chair, screw-plug construction, electrically operated chair, and chair with built-in reading light. Usually the most profitable ideas evolve from the second level ideas – ideas developed from free association of first level ideas.

d *Checklists*. An accumulation of points, areas, or possibilities that should be covered in a complete examination of a problem are put in checklist form. The following checklist, developed by Alex Osborn, the author of *Applied Imagination* (1953), can be used with the two basic rules of original thinking to develop many, many ideas.

Checklist possibilities: How can we put these finding to other uses? What new ways are there to use this as is? What possibilities are there to put this to other uses if modified? Such as:

- *Adapt*. What else is like this? What other idea does this suggest? Does the past offer a parallel? What could I copy? Whom could I emulate?
- *Modify*. New twist? Change meaning, color, motion, odor, form, shape? Other changes?
- *Magnify*. What to add? More time? Greater frequency? Stronger? Larger? Thicker? Extra value? Plus ingredients? Duplicate? Multiply? Exaggerate?
- *Minify*. What to substitute? Smaller? Condensed? Miniature? Lower? Shorter? Lighter? Omit? Streamline? Split up? Understate?

Continued

- *Substitute.* Who else instead? What else instead? Other ingredients? Other material? Other process? Other power? Other place? Other approach? Other tone of voice?
- *Rearrange.* Interchange components? Other pattern? Other layout? Other sequence? Transpose cause and effect? Change pace? Change schedule?
- *Reverse.* Transpose positive and negative? How about opposites? Turn it backward? Turn it upside down? Reverse roles? Change shoes? Turn tables? Turn other cheek?
- *Combine.* How about a blend, an alloy, an assortment, an ensemble? Combine units? Combine purposes? Combine appeals? Combine ideas?

Modification is an individual operational technique which consists essentially of attempting to modify or twist a given idea in as many ways as possible. In actual practice a goal consisting of a certain number of modifications is usually set. For some people it is helpful to specify twenty-five or more modifications of one basic idea.

"*The fresh eye*" is where an ordinary object is selected and examined with a great amount of concentration. An attempt is made to find beauty in this common object. This close scrutiny of a familiar object permits us to see it in a new "fresh" light and so may be the source of new ideas. This method is often used by people working in the fine arts.

4 Free association techniques

Free association techniques include brainstorming, the Gordon Method, buzz sessions, slip writing, and others which put a premium on quantities of ideas.

A. *Brainstorming.* A typical brainstorming session consists of a group of from six to twelve people seated about a table and spontaneously producing ideas designed to solve a specific problem. There are five basic rules as follows:

a Judicial judgment is not permitted.
b "Free-wheeling" is welcomed. The wilder the ideas, the better, because it is easier to "tame down" an idea than it is to build an idea into something more novel.
c Quantity of ideas is wanted.
d Combination and improvement are sought.
e Rule out the negative and traditional.

Note: By ruling out judicial judgment and making all ideas acceptable, an unusually psychologically safe climate is created. The pressures that one finds in an ordinary conference are removed by the conditions established. Because no time is devoted to discussion or criticism, a great many more ideas per conference hour are expressed than in the usual conference.

Continued

Choose people for a brainstorming session with as much diversity in background as possible. It is often helpful to include some people in the group who have little direct experience with the problem area – they are not aware of the dos and don'ts that experts may have developed. The expert can also be a valuable member of the group because he is a source of useful information. However, the expert must not be permitted to indicate any negative reaction or positive reaction or, as a result, the implied disapproval or sanction will likely destroy the effectiveness of the session.

It is often useful to have mixed groups – men and women, highly active and relatively quiet people.

Do *not* mix widely differing ranks within the organization in the same group. The junior men are likely to hold back any ideas that are unusual because they feel that their superiors are judging them, and that their future success depends upon their reputation for sound judgment. The boss is also restrained because he has a certain dignity and aloofness to maintain.

Equipment for the best brainstorming sessions will include:

- An audio recorder. A note-taker may take down the ideas, but he/she will often miss a few. A tape recorder can capture all of them for later review.
- A smart blackboard or flip chart. The participants can use the blackboard to help others in the group to visualize the problem and certain kinds of ideas.
- A conference table, preferably round, permits easy communication between members of the group.

Brainstorming sessions may last from forty minutes to an hour. This time range seems to be best for the better sessions. The evaluation of the ideas may be conducted by the brainstorming group, by another group, or by an individual. If the same group that brainstorms the ideas is called upon to evaluate them, usually it is done several days after the session.

B. *Gordon Technique.* Professor William J. Gordon of Harvard University, and of the Arthur D. Little Company, developed this highly valuable method:

A group conference is held in which unevaluated free-flowing discussion is encouraged. No one except the group leader knows the exact nature of the problem under consideration. Example: the leader has in mind a particular type of fastener or, rather, he has a problem such as "how to close and open a space suit easily and quickly." The leader asks the group questions and receives answers similar to the following hypothetical circumstance:

Leader: "If we can't use our hands, how can we close things?"
      "Suppose we have *heavy* gloves on."

Continued

Ans: Wish it closed.

Ans: Have an insect close "it" on command.

Ans: Have a beetle with large pincers do the job.

Ans: Use steel loops that easily slip together and as easily can be taken apart even with heavy gloves on the hands.

Other methods of brainstorming are in the previous chapter, while *imagineering* will be discussed in the next chapter.

Reverse Brainstorming, developed by the Hotpoint Company, works some-what opposite to brainstorming. Still the same is the procedure, but the product, idea, or problem statement are subjected to a barrage of ideas as to why and how they are inadequate. The object of the group session is to think of all the possible limitations, shortcomings, and failings of a product or idea. After the session, the ideas are evaluated to find true problem areas. The new problems are then made the focus of standard creative problem solving methods.

Slip Writing is a method best described as brainstorming limited to a single person. The person formulates his problem statement and writes or tapes all the ideas on the problem that come to his mind. As with other methods, the goal is for a great quantity of ideas. The quality of each idea is to be judged in a separate session.

Another form of slip writing, developed by Dr C. C. Crawford, requires each member of a group or audience to perform as described in the preceding paragraph. The slips are then collected and the ideas are evaluated. Remember, being creative and innovative is the norm of the new work culture.

Conclusions

The principal conclusions to be drawn from both our Input and Interaction sections are that HPLs invest more care and professionalism into meeting arrangements and implementation. Whether it is a weekly staff meeting, an annual stockholders' gathering, a regional sales conference, an employee retreat, an appraisal interview, or a regular meeting between supervisor and subordinate, performance can be enhanced on such occasions. This can be accomplished:

- by utilizing established guidelines and group dynamics in the planning, conducting, and evaluating of such events;
- by employing multimedia technology to interest and involve participants;
- by remembering the human element – making provision for people's comfort and relaxation.

The manager or trainer has many resources to call upon for assistance in improving meetings – the organization's HRD specialists, the staff at the meeting site, the external speakers or consultants employed as presenters, and the suppliers of meeting or game materials and services.

Instrumentation

As indicated throughout this text, meetings can be used for data gathering, especially by means of instruments. This same device can provide information during a meeting for group discussion and analysis of the findings. Apart from their feedback and other values, questionnaires, inventories, and checklists can be devised to improve the performance of the manager or trainer. Our last two examples, the Meetings Management Planning Inventory (Exhibit 9.7) and the Managing People Skills Inventory (Exhibit 9.8), will help leaders to assure that meetings are planned and conducted effectively, as well as to provide a means for further evaluating how people are managed in the workplace.

EXHIBIT 9.7 Meetings management planning inventory

To assure an effective meeting, conference, or seminar, this instrument provides thirty critical check-points for planners. Included are intercultural factors in case the meeting is cross-cultural or international in scope. Developed in the form of a rating scale, the meeting planner, or his/her supervisor, may evaluate the individual from one (lowest) to ten (excellence). A wide range of planning activities are covered from meeting content input, objectives, site, and budget to site visitation, international protocol, and detail preparations and arrangements. The scoring allows for skipping of some items which may not be appropriate in specific circumstances. With regard to the cultural diversity of the participants, I have supplied a useful tool to accompany this inventory in my text, *Managing Cultural Differences* (8th edn, 2011; www.elsevier.com).

Meeting Management Planning Inventory (MMPI)
Directions. Please supply the following information:
Name of the organizational sponsor_____
Date of the meeting_____
Site of the meeting_____
Purposes of the meeting_____
_____

Number and function of attendees expected for the meeting:

Type of meeting being planned:
Conference ( ); Seminar ( ); Operational review ( ); Regular staff meeting ( );
One-on-one encounter ( ); Other_____
   In planning this meeting, please rate yourself on a scale of ten as to how you have carried out the following functions. Use the box on the right column to

Continued

place your score: one would be lowest, five would be average, and ten would be the highest rating for excellence. If the item is not applicable, just skip it and move on to the next number.

1 Input was sought from both management and potential participants on this meeting's purposes and agenda. [ ]
2 Objectives were clearly stated and circulated with a schedule to the intended audience or attendees. [ ]
3 Adequate and comfortable site/facilities were selected, and successful negotiations concluded with operators of facility. [ ]
4 Proper budgeting or provisions were made for the meeting expenses (and income if any). [ ]
5 Adequate arrangements were made for the selection and/or pre-registration of attendees, as well as on-site registration and/or welcome of meeting participants. [ ]
6 Adequate negotiations and arrangements were completed for all guests, presenters, exhibiters, and other human resources required for this meeting. [ ]
7 If meeting off site, adequate provisions were made for transportation and registrants were so informed. [ ]
8 If residential meeting, adequate arrangements were made for housing and alternatives; registrants, guests, exhibitors, and staff so informed. [ ]
9 Adequate design planning as to program activities, variety, sequence, time, and pacing. [ ]
10 Appropriate, adequate provision included for relaxation and play. [ ]
11 Adequate arrangements ensured for ordering all program equipment, learning materials, and exhibits. [ ]
12 Adequate provisions ensured for on-site monitoring and management of external support service, meeting staff, and procedures (e.g. registration and hospitality desk, refreshment and food services, exhibits, handout materials distribution, etc.). [ ]
13 Adequate pre-meeting briefing of registrants and resource staff, plus coordination with site management. [ ]
14 Arrangements made for special needs of participants (e.g. handicapped, non-smokers, session recordings, etc.). [ ]
15 If necessary, shipping or mailing arrangements completed for all material and equipment on-site (or for their purchase/lease/rental on-site). [ ]
16 Final checking executed satisfactorily on functional logistics (e.g. the details and set up of meeting rooms, media equipment, exhibits, food and beverage services, etc.). [ ]
17 Final confirmation of arrangements and site opportunities to all concerned (e.g. mailing of schedule or agenda with travel directions to participants,

Continued

staff, presenters, and possibly entertainers, exhibitors, suppliers, and site managers). [ ]

18 Provisions made for staff person or contractor to select, communicate, and coordinate with resource people (e.g. speakers, facilitators, panelists, entertainers, exhibitors, travel guides). [ ]

19 Provisions completed for entertainment and informative program alternatives if spouse or family accompany attendee. [ ]

20 If appropriate, arrangements completed for public relations program in conjunction with meeting (e.g. press release, media coverage, follow up stories). [ ]

21 Arrangement completed for recording the meeting or conference (in writing, stenotype, or audio/video); if appropriate, for editing and publishing the proceedings, and distribution and/or sale of recordings/proceedings. [ ]

22 Arrangements completed for evaluating the meeting as to its effectiveness and implementation of action plans set at the meeting. [ ]

23 Provision for payment of all gratuities and invoices for services contracted, including any reimbursements due the participants. [ ]

24 Provision for letters of appreciation or commendation to be sent to appropriate persons connected with meeting. [ ]

Note: If this is an international meeting, then continue with the inventory.

25 Prior to the meeting, a personal visit ensured that the overseas' facility and services were adequate. Such as:

a. equipment and power incompatibilities were resolved;
b. negotiations with contractors had achieved mutual cultural understanding and agreement as to what is being provided;
c. problems of overseas shipping and entry of materials/equipment had been resolved with customs in home/host countries (whenever possible, equipment leased or rented abroad, while contracting for local supplies). [ ]

26 Observance of all the foreign formalities regarding international meeting amenities, such as:

a. invitations and confirmations to government or corporate officials invited to receptions, luncheons, and banquets;
b. selection of local representatives to welcome participants, give addresses or lectures, and bestow honors/rewards. [ ]

27 Preparations made to facilitate intercultural communication with the locals or among participants from other countries (e.g. business cards in both languages, proper use of titles and seating arrangements, multilingual

Continued

presentation of learning materials, and slides, interpreters and simultaneous translation equipment, etc.). [ ]

28 Arrangements made for participants to enjoy the international resources, such as:

a. extra group services and discounts of airlines and travel agencies;
b. use of local stately mansions, grand estates, or convention centers;
c. optional offerings for local or supplemental sightseeing tours and appropriate field trips. [ ]

29 Incorporation into schedule of host culture's food/dress, as well as music/festivals. [ ]

30 Cultural briefings on the foreign customs, protocol, opportunities and dangers. [ ]

31 Pre-departure briefings provided to all participants by mail or in person on customs regulations, currency issues, tipping, security issues, and other relevant matters (e.g. host country cuisine "pros and cons," public safety and terrorism, cultural differences regarding meeting activities and participation, role of men/women in country). [ ]

32 Arrangements made for translations of meeting/conference proceedings in the major participant languages, as well as editing, printing or recordings' reproduction, and distribution of volumes or cassettes. [ ]

Total ratings:_____

Note: To obtain a total score, among the thirty-two possible selections add up the number of items for which it was appropriate for you to respond; then tally up the number of rating scores. To attain an evaluation average, divide the total number of items into the total of ratings.

EXHIBIT 9.8 Managing people skills inventory (MPSI)

For those concerned about the human side of enterprise and its impact on productivity, this rating instrument can be quickly used on one's self or by another colleague or subordinate. Twenty-four key questions are raised concerning people skills – the behavioral science management concerns which complement technical proficiency of managers. A five-point rating scale is utilized for assessment ratings which range from poor to excellent. The content covers behavior and innovative management practices to human relations and communication. The totaling of ratings permits assessment in three categories: need for improvement, average, and high performance. The inventory is supplementary to the HPMI in Chapter 2 (Instrumentation), but apply inquiries to performance at meetings.

Continued

Instructions. For yourself or a colleague, use a five-point scale to evaluate one's effectiveness as a leader in the human relations competencies at work. In the column at the right, rate the manager by inserting the number which best describes his or her present performance or behavior at work:
5 = Excellent; 4 = Good; 3 = Average; 2 = Inadequate; 1 = Poor

The manager being assessed is (check one):

( ) Myself_____

( ) My subordinate named_____

( ) My colleague named_____

Since we are to be learning managers concerned about high performance on the job, I rate this person as follows:

1 Possesses and practices a positive management philosophy regarding people. [ ]
2 Is a behavior model to workers of the desired attitudes and performance on the job. [ ]
3 Is innovative in dealing with people, being quite open-minded and flexible. [ ]
4 Is sensitive to people and opportunities around him/her. [ ]
5 Is positive and encouraging with personnel, not given to falling back on negative statements. (e.g. "It can't be done"; "it's never been done before"; "it's not the way we do things around here"). [ ]
6 Is aware of the differences in people, capitalizing upon their uniqueness. [ ]
7 Understands the influence of culture upon individuals and institutions, but is able to change it or move beyond. [ ]
8 Is results, not task, oriented; places emphasis on accomplishments and rewarding performance. [ ]
9 Is goal oriented with self and subordinates – sets realistic objectives, targets, and deadlines. [ ]
10 Maintains high performance standards – values competence, professionalism, and measurable growth. [ ]
11 Operates on the principle of expect/inspect – each employee reporting to him/her comprehends the job expectations, is encouraged to ask questions, but is held accountable to achieve measurable standards. [ ]
12 Provides performance leadership by dynamic achievements, inspiring personnel to stretch and achieve their potential. [ ]
13 Trusts people by delegating, giving them freedom to perform in their own unique way, thus building self-reliance. [ ]
14 Fosters reasonable risk-taking and creativity in others. [ ]
15 Re-enforces cooperation and collaboration, rather than interpersonal or intergroup competition. [ ]

Continued

16 Seeks continually to learn, even from failure; promotes personal and career development for self and others. [ ]
17 Endeavors to capitalize on human assets, helping people to experience success and results. [ ]
18 Searches to understand his/her own, as well as others' needs and attempts to satisfy them through work. [ ]
19 Believes in positive re-enforcement, so confirms people's self-concept when it is healthy or assists them to gain in a strong sense of personal identity and confidence. [ ]
20 Enables people to gain control over their work space, thus sharing in the exercise of power. [ ]
21 Communicates authentically with co-workers, customers, and suppliers, giving and receiving appropriate feedback. [ ]
22 Provides recognitions and rewards customized to the individual worker's needs and values. [ ]
23 Arranges for training opportunities for employees so that performance may be improved or new skills acquired. [ ]
24 Manages conflict constructively and acts as a facilitator. [ ]

Total ratings:_____

Note: Tally up the rating scores and insert the total in the space provided. A high performing manager would gain a score of 100 or more; an average manager would obtain ratings of 75+, indicating a need for gradual improvement. Scores below that level should raise questions about this person's suitability for management. In developing goals for performance improvement, go back over the items in which a score of three or less was recorded. If this was a self-evaluation, one might ask a supervisor or colleague to rate you, and then compare the assessment on each of the twenty-four items.

10

FUTURE OF LEADERSHIP IN THE TWENTY-FIRST CENTURY

Introduction

If humanity is to achieve its potential on Earth and beyond, then more people will have to exercise leadership to move us ahead. This is particularly true at this critical juncture of our species' evolution as we go aloft to explore and discover new worlds. Some claim that leaders are born, while others maintain they can be developed.[46] As biologists research the field of management, it is evident our genes do account for differences in individuals, and variances in their performance, so that some lead others. But behavioral scientists like myself still believe that some leadership is largely situational, and that people can also learn to be leaders. Thus, it is interesting that in 2008 the US Congress passed the Genetic Information Nondiscrimination Act banning the use of DNA information in job recruitment.

Next generation of HPLs

In this Information Age and its knowledge culture, there is a special need for online leaders who can manage the stream of news and data that comes into daily business life. As Carol Bartz, former CEO of Yahoo, observes, top management is needed who can cut through the information clutter so as to make clear decisions without apology. Further, leaders are needed who can interpret both valued news and disinformation. As Bartz said, "There are wonderful opportunities for leadership – employees, investors, customers, and business partners are heartened by executives who can sift through the avalanche of opinion and clearly communicate what matters or doesn't to the enterprise." She recommends that listening to all is a key aspect of leadership, along with identifying and mentoring high potential employees. Thus, business leaders can learn to leverage, clarify, and use information to advance strategy and satisfy stakeholders.

But, effective leaders also are able to transform information into useful knowledge. They follow the research of neuroscientists on brain matters, especially with reference to robotics and artificial intelligence. Brain-based devices will increasingly take over the work environment through simulated nervous systems. These new tools are already capable of pattern recognitions; neural connections and categorizations; simulating organisms and learning by conditioning; self-generated movement, perception and vision; signaling synchronization and tactile sensing; predictive thinking, episodic and maze memory; navigation and moving.

HPLs themselves function on intrinsic motivators and rewards. Therefore, author Daniel Pink advises giving knowledge workers more control over their own lives, allowing them to pursue their own projects, providing customized incentives to productivity, allowing flextime and time off, and encouraging self-determination and creativity.[47] Such management practices also have implications with senior, aging, and even blue collar workers. Mentoring systems are especially helpful in developing people potential, and retirees can be most useful in this role.

As a professional futurist, my hope for the twenty-first century is that visionary leaders will emerge especially to advance knowledge intensive and space industries, as well as social entrepreneurship. HP leaders are willing to learn new and better ways of performing from varied sources. For example, corporate executives might gain insights from studying non-profit organizations.[48] These "charities" can teach business how to get more for less, especially through volunteers and by motivators that inspire both workers and donors. Another arena for HP leaders to explore is "wellness" strategies. Better to keep personnel healthy and happy, than to lose their services through illness and accidents. Some management psychologists call this applying "emotional intelligence in the workplace," especially during times of high stress and depression. Authentic leaders discover ways to optimize positive performance even under pressure. Organizations can do much to further both employee and community mental health. To cope with an imperfect world and all its banalities requires a new type of "neuroleadership." Advances in scientific research and information technologies (IT) erode the middle-skilled and middle-income occupations. To avoid developing a permanent underclass, mass educational reform challenges shared leadership to create new learning environments and instruments appropriate for a knowledge culture.

Jim Clifton, CEO of Gallup, is rightly concerned about the next generation of leadership. He contends they are the ones who will manage tomorrow's ideas and talent by knowing the state of mind of their constituencies. Jim wants leaders who explore business frontiers, such as through science and behavioral economics. Clifton expects these future leaders to use knowledge to create economic growth, especially by formulating better quality products and services at lower cost. This will require more innovation, talent, and entrepreneurship. Jim thinks such leaders will exercise skills in quantification, so they make decisions based on data and not assumptions. Thus, to build a sustainable culture, Gallup is now creating the biggest data base on behavioral economics.

Perhaps the Society for Human Resource Management summarized best the essence of this book with this advertisement:

> In today's global marketplace, people are your competitive advantage. As organizations expand abroad, human resource leaders are using new business strategies to deliver greater productivity, agility, and success. From tapping into the global talent pool to managing a diverse workforce as a team, HR is helping plan for what's next.

(www.weknownext.com)

Tomorrow's leaders envision the future as opportunity. But such HPLs are at work now making it happen. Take, for example, just one emerging field – smart technology.[49] Smart systems are causing the convergence of the real and digital worlds; a proliferation of connected sensors, cameras, wireless networks, communications standards, and human ingenuity are making it possible. Innovators are formulating "societal information technology systems." Leaders in world corporations are putting together networks of data centers for thousands of servers bound together in "computer clouds." IBM, for instance, is working on a project called "Smarter Planet" using digital technology to make energy, transportation, and other areas of human endeavor "more intelligent." Our Input section has further insights on these possibilities for future HP leadership.

HPLs are found everywhere, and in all forms of human endeavor. Two widely different examples are Russell Simons and Hamad bin Khalifa. Russell, a hip hop singing star, was chosen by *USA Today* as "one of the twenty-five most influential people of the last 25 years!" In a Volpe Lecture at St Francis College in Brooklyn Heights, NY, Simons, an African American, emphasized "People who are happy with what they have are rich. Focus on work – that is a gift." This UN goodwill ambassador is CEO of Rush Communications; he uses their Community Affairs division to "give back" by focusing on empowering at-risk youth through education, arts, and social engagement. Over in the Middle East, the Emir of Qatar has led his tiny Gulf state to a gross domestic product of $84,000 per person (2009). The world's largest producer of liquefied natural gas, its emir, Hamad bin Khalifa, is known as the most dynamic of Arab global leaders. This peacemaker's wife, Sheikha Mozah, is helping him to bring world-class education and culture to their people by attracting top foreign universities and museums there.

Our last profile will demonstrate visionary leadership in a person who "thinks big and thinks ahead."

EXHIBIT 10.1 Profile of a HP futurist[50]

> Valentin Peretroukhin lives in Toronto, Ontario, and is active in the National Space Society. He won a prize in a writing contest sponsored by The Moon Society. His futuristic thinking is reflected in these excerpts from his essay:
>
> **Continued**

- The twentieth century saw great leaps of innovation that allowed humans to not only travel in space, but also to set foot upon a completely different celestial body and return home safely.
- Mankind is an incredibly social species. Our evolutionary supremacy on this planet stems from our competitive nature, our ability to work in groups, and our ability to share information so as to pass on relevant knowledge... One of the main arguments against human-based planetary travel, and perhaps why so few countries have attempted it since the Apollo missions, is the high costs of developing technologies safe and practical for sending humans to another world.
- Astronauts bring an entirely different approach to exploring different planets and moons. Humans are also incredibly dynamic and can perform many things that a robot simply cannot do. An astronaut can provide a holistic overview of a new unknown environment.
- Thus, in just over 150 years since its conception, space exploration is now a crucial element for human development. In a changing, multidimensional world, it is imperative that we continue to challenge ourselves to explore distant frontiers ... The future generations of humanity will rely on our courage and ingenuity as we move out of our cradle. In the words of H. G. Wells, "life, forever dying to be born afresh, forever young and eager, will presently stand upon this Earth as a footstool, and stretch out its realm among the stars!"

In the above slightly edited words of Val Peretroukhin, we express our hopes for future HPLs off-world.

So, to conclude this volume, we invited a guest expert to contribute our last Input section on "the future of leadership." My esteemed colleague, Bill Howe, has a bachelor's degree from Northwestern University, Master's degrees from both Harvard University and the University of Massachusetts, plus another Master's and Doctorate from Stanford University. Indeed, his credentials and experience offer readers observations worth heeding.

Input

The future of leadership

By William S. Howe PhD.

Introduction

As we hear so often today, leadership is about change – transformation, continuous improvement, restructuring, re-strategizing. We are, as Peter Vaill has reminded us, paddling in permanent whitewater, facing the challenges of constant change and the need to constantly renew our organizations and ourselves to adapt and to remain competitive.

But rarely, I must confess, do I encounter discussions of leadership that move beyond the need to address the changes of *today*. Simply addressing the generic need for present-day change in a changing world seems shortsighted to me. What about addressing where the world is going and what it may become in the coming decades? What will leadership look like in a world that is significantly different from the world of 2012? I suggest that it – and in fact all organizations and all social life – could look radically different from what it seems today.

Back in the mid-1990s, I spoke at a conference and outlined some ideas that I thought might help us take the field of leadership studies in new directions. At that time I felt as though leadership studies was rather static and not moving ahead with the generation of new theoretical proposals, innovative research, or significantly different practices. I suggested, for example, that researchers push the envelope on the unit of analysis in leadership studies – that is, from teams and organizations, to organizational fields, and even to macro-level entities such as global organizations (e.g. United Nations), nation states, and geographical regions (e.g. European Union). I suggested, too, that we investigate how non-human species exercise or exhibit leadership. Given the relatively common genetic makeup of animal life in general, perhaps we might discover clues that could potentially inform human leadership. In addition, I suggested that we give increased emphasis to how the arts and the humanities can inform the study and practice of leadership. To be honest, my suggestions were met with puzzled and even incredulous stares – quite similar, I would say, to what young Marty McFly met with when, in the movie *Back to the Future*, he started playing a fast-paced Chuck Berry rock and roll song on an electric guitar a decade or so before rock and roll music emerged. My audience just did not seem to understand my desire to push leadership studies into the coming decades.

But what of our future beyond 2012? What lies ahead, and how may impending or potential changes influence leadership and leadership studies in the coming decades? Rather than suggesting some of my own ideas for future directions, let me try here to outline some ideas put forth by scholars from various disciplines – molecular biology, physics, neuroscience, cognitive science, computer science, astrophysics, geophysics, cosmology, nanotechnology, information science, quantum-mechanical engineering, and genetics. Then, given the benefit of these insights, I will offer some thoughts concerning how their implications may assist improvements in leadership studies, development, education, and practice. Related ideas, I might note, were offered within Margaret Wheatley's *Leadership and the New Science*, though she was talking primarily about leadership as a phenomenon that can be situated within the new science, while I am seeking to offer areas of potentially imminent change that may well affect and even transform the way we conceive and practice leadership.

One caveat to remember – the future is uncertain and highly unpredictable. Nevertheless, I propose the following fifteen areas of change that could, according to scholars across a variety of disciplines, *potentially* change our lives dramatically and, in consequence, our conceptions of – and practices of – leadership. These areas of change are broad enough, I believe, to offer credible scenarios for the coming decades. More than mere science fiction, they represent changes that we, as leaders or leadership scholars or educators, would do well to envision and to consider. Leadership, of course, is often defined in terms of vision. I suggest that we envision the world that is quickly emerging in terms of leadership itself.

Areas of change and their potential impact on leadership

1 *Life extension.* Researchers within neurobiology, molecular biology, gerontology, and other fields affirm that humans will live increasingly longer lives and, in fact, could potentially live indefinitely once we "defeat" aging as a "disease." Scholarly investigators are confronting aging on numerous fronts – genetics, cellular biology, tissue and whole organ regeneration through stem cells and other means, the enzyme telomerase, significant life extension experiments with the worm *C. elegans*, and calorie restriction. Many believe that we will actually be able to "defeat" aging within a few decades. How, then, will we lead populations that are increasingly "older," that may not retire, that may make numerous career shifts and develop numerous new interests over scores or hundreds of years, that may see work in a radically different way, and that may approach truth, beauty, goodness, and other values in ways we do not yet understand? Clearly, the implications for leadership of longer lives or of infinite life spans are enormous.

2 *Robots and artificial intelligence.* Varied researchers now argue that robots, super-computers, entities that are part biological and part robotic, or entities whose identity as either biological or robotic is entirely unclear or indeterminable, yet will be among us soon. Some even suggest that we may be able to download our entire memories and neuronal systems into computers that would, with our input plus their own capacity to learn, far surpass our current levels of human intelligence. How will we lead robotic entities or supercomputers that may be far more capable of understanding and practicing leadership than we are? How will we "empower" biological/robotic entities or entirely robotic entities to exercise leadership? And to extend this line of thought, how might we lead downloaded selves – that is, "people" whose complete memories have been downloaded in silica and who are thereby immortal? Here too, the implications are extraordinary, almost surely putting into question the way we currently conceive leadership.

3 *Exposure of many long-held assumptions.* Physicists, biologists, neuroscientists, cognitive scientists, cosmologists, and others tend to agree that in the coming decades we may have to shed, or at least confront as potentially problematic, many long-held assumptions that, given evidence, will seem increasingly illusory. Such assumptions may include time (particularly as a continuous "flow"), mind, soul, spirit, objectivity, external empirical world, individuality, consciousness, and an afterlife. Such assumptions have often undergirded some

leadership practices and, at a deeper level, the cultural behaviors of some countries. How will we lead if these or similar assumptions are called into question, and how might such questioning affect the ontological, theological, metaphysical, and epistemological attitudes many people, Western and Eastern, have held for millennia?

4 *Species intermixing or transformation.* If we can transform one species – i.e. *Homo sapiens* – into another simply by changing the DNA in our cells, or if we are capable, as many scientists believe we are, of intermixing human and other species, then what will that mean for leadership? My suggestion above that we might learn something about leadership by looking at other species pales in comparison to this notion, entertained by many, of combining or altering species through genetic engineering or other means. What will leadership look like for or among these new species? And how adaptable will leadership have to be if we produce many new human-related species, each one quite different from the other?

5 *Virtual reality.* In the future, many argue, the distinction between physical reality and virtual reality will be blurred or even obliterated. At present, of course, we conceive of leadership as something that is exercised within what we take for granted as our physical reality. Certainly, however, there will be virtual realms that stand alone on their own or are indistinguishable from physical reality. How will we conceive and practice leadership within virtual worlds or within worlds that may or may not be virtual or physical? Will we have virtual leaders and virtual followers perhaps?

6 *Entanglement.* Quantum physics indicates, of course, that particles at great distances from each other (even light years apart) may be "entangled," meaning that they seem to "communicate" with each other across the distances or at least to act in accord across the distances. Can larger entities be similarly entangled, or interactive, or mutually charged? If so, what might such entanglement mean for leadership practices? How, for example, might we lead in a world wherein everything may somehow be entangled with everything else? Surely this would take current notions of collaboration, mutual influence, cooperation, and shared decision making to a completely new and far more elaborate level. Csikszentmihalyi (2003) suggests that it is now crucially important "to understand events, objects, and processes in their relationship with one another [rather] than in their singular structure... It is now time to take synthesis seriously." While that notion is extremely important, it almost seems to pale when seen next to the counter-intuitive idea of universal entanglement put forth by quantum physics.

7 *Living outside planet Earth.* Many scientists and futurists believe that we will colonize another planet during the current century, thus initiating the potential to spread life well beyond Earth. Living and working off-world will not only change our image of the species, but will alter us both physically and psychologically. What will leadership look like in these new environments? Will we simply replicate the kinds of leadership we have known on Earth, or will we create entirely new forms of interaction and leadership?

8 *Synchronized brains.* Some scientists now argue that we need to understand how different brains become synchronized and then put this synchronization to good use. It is possible that brains, for example, may be able to synchronize across huge distances and over time, particularly if, as recent research demonstrates, we can understand and utilize the function of "mirror neurons" – "brain cells that respond to the actions of other individuals as if one were performing them oneself" (Brockman 2010). While we know much about group dynamics, crowd behavior, empathy, social intelligence, and other related behaviors and attitudes, new knowledge deriving from these notions of mirror neurons and synchronized brains could help us see leadership in some remarkably different ways. As with entanglement, such knowledge could help us rethink collaboration, mutual interaction, teamwork, and cooperation.

9 *Telepathy.* At present we communicate with one another through language or through non-verbal cues, both of which have been identified for many decades as integrally important to leadership. Many leadership scholars, in fact, have argued that communication – i.e. speaking, writing, listening, reading – may well be *the* key leadership skill and may provide the foundation for all leadership processes. How, then, would we exercise leadership if communication were telepathic – that is, if we could transmit and read each other's thoughts? Powell (as cited in Schein 2010) suggests that transmitting thoughts is "not terribly farfetched" and "would break down one of the most profound isolations associated with the human condition … Transmitting specific, conscious thoughts would require elaborate physical implants to make sure the signals go to exactly the right place – but such implants could soon become common anyway as people merge their brains with computer data networks." Powell says he gives "synthetic telepathy" a seventy percent chance of coming about within his lifetime. Obviously, this may raise serious ethical considerations, but the ramifications for leadership practice would be truly astounding, particularly if thought transmission could occur across global dimensions. At the very least, it now seems, we are moving rapidly away from a text-based world into an increasingly audio-based and video-based world, a transition that will send significant ripples through leadership practices.

10 *Advanced education/training strategies.* Many researchers and thinkers argue that our current education/training systems, embedded in centuries of institutionalized notions of how people learn, are antiquated and anachronistic. Despite new and emerging technologies, we all too often remain wedded to old learning models – lecturing to passive learners, persisting with rows of desks or seats and grades that emphasize individual learning and achievement, departmentalized learning, and the separation of disciplines into bounded – even protected – concerns. How will we lead people who *graduate* from these old systems and move on to new systems that are highly interactive, engaging, and relevant because they utilize advanced technological, scientific, and entertainment discoveries? Cosmides and Tooby (2005) envision the use of "Hollywood post-production techniques, the compulsively attention-capturing properties

of game design, nutritional cognitive enhancement, a growing map of our evolved programs ... an evolutionary psychological approach to entertainment, neuroscience-midwived brain-computer interfaces, rich virtual environments, and 3D imaging technologies." How will leadership learning – not to mention on-the-job learning – become transformed in such an extraordinary educational/training environment?

11 *Multiple dimensions.* Many quantum physicists argue that the universe is composed of multiple dimensions – perhaps ten or eleven it seems, rather than the four we now take for granted. Indeed, many of those physicists, along with many cosmologists, suggest that there may be multiple universes. What if we were to break through to other dimensions or universes? Though this potential area of change may seem even further afield than others I am offering, it certainly is a major focus of much contemporary physics and cosmology, and for many substantive reasons. How would we lead across multiple dimensions or bring multiple dimensions to bear upon the practice of leadership? What would leadership look like within an as yet unidentified dimension?

12 *Split identity.* It is quite possible, some researchers claim, that we may in coming decades be able to split ourselves so that we exist in our bodies in one location but are able to experience – partially or fully – through robotic interface or other means at another location or at several other locations (e.g. Yuki 2011). Geary and Sanother (2011) suggests that we could see brain-machine interfaces where one "could be lying on a beach on the east coast of Brazil, controlling a robotic device roving on the surface of Mars, and be subjected to both experiences simultaneously, as if ... in both places at once." Assuming that leaders and those who "follow" them could participate in such possibilities, who then are the leaders and the led? This might seem to give new meaning to the old idea of the leader-as-individual, particularly if the individual is in himself multiple.

13 *Social aggregation.* We have only scratched the surface of the possibilities of the internet. One possibility is that we will increasingly look to systems of ranking or rating information, not just to gathering it. Hence the popularity of Google and other search engines. Orrigi (as cited in Northhouse 2009) envisions a new "Age of Reputation" wherein, "thanks to the tremendous potential of the social Web in aggregating individual preferences and choices to produce intelligent outcomes," we will be guided by collective cyber judgments. Clearly, such guidance could form a new "substitute for leadership" in which we are led by our collective decisions about information. Clearly too, such guidance could create a problematic situation in which we are dictated to by collectivism and thus lose track of the creative and innovative outliers, almost as though we will have taken marketers' strategies of optimizing via numbers and overlaid that on all information processing. There are, then, some serious ethical considerations with this and other potential areas of change.

14 *Empowerment of people around the globe.* Here too, the Internet may be the key. At present there are, by some estimates, about four billion of our nearly seven

billion people on Earth who are illiterate, have no access to the Web, not to mention clean water and adequate food, and are not participating in the knowledge revolution (Harari 2003). Once these four billion obtain access to that revolution – and they will in rapidly increasing numbers – how will we lead them? Perhaps a more appropriate question will be how will they participate in leading themselves and the world? No doubt they will assume awesome power and will demand the kinds of resources enjoyed by the three billion who have utilized the Earth's resources, often in abundance. Once most people on our planet become part of the social network, our very conception of leadership will almost surely shift dramatically.

15 *Extended brain power.* Though some of the areas noted above already hint at this potential advance, it is worth describing briefly at this point. In the future, some believe, our brains will be able to control machines, tools, and, thus, various production processes. "Neural control" is already here in the form of prosthetic devices. But it could become far more powerful in the years ahead, especially if we could manipulate machines and tools at a distance through thought processes. To be sure, the implications for leadership with such a change would be staggering, particularly in terms of leadership as defined by task completion and productivity. Leaders might even become extraneous if everyone could exercise mind control over machines and tools.

Conclusions

Some of the areas of change outlined above may be far closer to us in time than we realize; others may be more remote and may not occur within our lifetime, or may not occur at all at any point in the future. Still, they are ideas that have been offered by some of the most astute, intelligent researchers/thinkers on the planet today who honestly believe that many of the ideas will become a "reality" within the next several decades.

Looking across those ideas, here are eight conclusions to challenge readers of this book on leadership:

1 In the future, leadership will be conceived and practiced without many of the spatial and temporal boundaries that constrain it today – that is, it will potentially become a phenomenon that moves well beyond the bounds of specific locations, including planet Earth, and temporal restraints.

2 In the future, leadership may function according to completely new and strangely different metaphysical, ontological, epistemological, and theological assumptions about life, learning, time, space, mind, and other key concepts, with the new assumptions even serving to transform current ideas about who and what man is. Briefly perhaps, the new assumptions may include a purely subjective notion of reality and change, and a far more diffuse notion of what man is as a biological and/or robotic entity, a "real" and/or virtual person, a single and/or multiple being.

3 In the future, leadership may be exercised also by robotic entities, by biological-robotic entities that blur any distinction between biology and robotics, by mixed

species entities, or by split human entities that can operate in different places simultaneously, as well as – or perhaps instead of – humans as we currently know them.

4 In the future, leadership will be increasingly shared, democratic, collaborative, interactive, and characterized by synthesis, with far more of the planet's population participating in leadership processes and activities. Obviously it will move light years away from the old theories of the "great man" or even individual leaders' traits, styles, or behaviors, though elements of those perspectives may continue to have a residual impact.

5 In the future, leadership will focus on the needs of far different populations than today – e.g. on people who are living well past one hundred and perhaps indefinitely or as long as they wish, on entities that combine biology and robotics, on robots themselves, and perhaps even on entities that inhabit virtual worlds or places that combine the virtual and the "real." Leadership will be associated with both "real" and virtual contexts, or with contexts that blur distinctions between "real" and virtual. This will certainly give new meaning to theories of contingency or situational leadership.

6 In the future, leadership will be exercised through new forms of communication that move far beyond our centuries-old reliance on text. These will increasingly include audio and visual forms and could potentially include telepathy, the use of brains to manipulate distant machines and tools, or as yet unimagined forms.

7 In the future, leadership will be learned through intensive strategies that will make current learning approaches seem ancient. The new strategies will be highly engaging, entertaining, and, through seemingly "real" virtual interaction, relevant to actual practices.

8 In the future (and this may obviate the above), leadership and leaders may be unnecessary and extraneous. In short, the future, with the potential for genuine sharing and interaction that can be performed with abundant technological assistance, may spell the end of leadership as we know it. For much of human history, we seem to have needed leaders and leadership processes to guide our actions and to create change. Soon, however, we may cast aside the very ideas of leaders and leadership and see them as elitist notions that were congruent only with an elitist past in which many people were marginalized and disempowered, in which mankind existed within highly constrained spaces and for limited life spans, in which man was a singular being who could not interact instantaneously with the "real" and various virtual worlds, and in which man lived amidst hierarchies rather than in a vast interconnected web.

For years some scholars or writers have suggested that "leadership is dead," almost in echo of Nietzsche's infamous phrase "God is dead." They have argued that great man leadership is dead, that executive leadership is dead, and even that any conception of leadership as featuring a singular leader is dead. Surely the future will put many nails in the coffin of leadership, particularly since the very present in which we live seems to sense that traditional "leadership" – the word but also the concept and practice – may be outworn, a kind of dinosaur whose hide cannot be stretched to fit a world that is rapidly becoming increasingly democratic, connected, and empowered. "Leadership," it seems, cannot live on as a watershed word, concept, or practice that continues to *mean* through attempts to resurrect it as "shared leadership," "leader-full teams," "substitutes for leadership," and so on. We may be approaching its funeral, which in itself would perhaps signal the birth of a truly empowered and enlightened humankind.

All citations are to selections within a single provocative and compelling text.[51]

About the contributor

William S. Howe PhD was Associate Editor of the *International Leadership Journal*. He is Dean of Academic Affairs at the University of the West in Rosemead, California. Formerly, he served as Dean of Graduate Studies at California International Business University, San Diego, California, as well as Dean of the School of Graduate and Professional Studies at Bethune-Cookman University in Daytona Beach, Florida. In addition, Dr Howe teaches online courses within the School of Business and Management at Thomas Edison State College in New Jersey, teaches writing courses at the University of California at San Diego, and serves on dissertation committees at the University of Maryland. He earned his doctorate at Stanford University. He encourages thoughts on or reactions to this input article: williamh@uwest.edu.

Interaction

In this section we offer three forms of group process that a manager can use with staff or teams to improve their attitudes and skills in the management of change. As an exercise, "Imagineering" is a creative means to involve the group in planning and preparing for change. To stimulate capacities in this regard, I recommend regular reading of these publications for leaders: *The Futurist* (World Future Society); proceedings of Foundation for the Future; and *Mind Play*, newsletter of Innovative Thinking Network.

Imagineering

In the new work culture, people will be expected to make more use of their imagination and intuition, as well as to be more future oriented. Imagineering has been successfully used with managers all over the world and from all types of systems. It is useful to preface this process with the showing of a short educational film on change or future shock. Having stirred up the participants' imaginations, invite them to project themselves into the future of their organization, industry, or profession. Since the New Millennium is underway, leaders may like to use the years 2025 or 2050 as points of reference. For example, with a large audience considering the future of a specific multinational corporation at midway in the twenty-first century, the facilitator can divide up participants into smaller groups representing various operations, such as a particular subsidiary, division, or product line. Another way is to assign each group to consider the future of the company in terms of only one dimension, such as HRD, personnel policies and practices, technology, marketing, manufacturing, and customer services. Before the exercise begins, each group is instructed what their frame of reference is to be in the designated future time target. They are asked to base their projections on what they know of present trends. Of course, the same technique can be used with individuals who project their lives and career decades into the future.

With an audience of representatives from an occupation or career, the imagineering procedure is simpler. Instructions for management information specialists might begin: "Given what you know about changes in your field, about developments in a distributed information environment, growth in the use of personal computers and online activities, and other emerging trends, what will happen to your vocational or professional role by the year 2025 or later? Another forecast: what will be the impact of advances in artificial intelligence, or the future of leadership (refer to Input section)? Take off your perceptual binders and use your imagination."

The steps for conducting an "imagineering" session are outlined below. Final reports should be recorded with PowerPoint software, or audio/video disks, or a flip chart. These reports should be edited, for feedback to key executives and planners. The process fosters participative management and shared leadership.

Procedures for imagineering

HRD leaders explain that this technique aims to expand their horizons and to assist them in developing new psychological *constructs*. Everyone views reality through the perspective of his/her own private world or life *space*, as Kurt Lewin called it. Personal and professional development requires the participants to revise their perceptions, or the way in which they read meaning into their "worlds." Staff input and discussion should encourage a change in opinions, attitudes, and thinking.

To help participants become more future oriented, rather than past oriented, imagineering is especially helpful in sessions dealing with management of change, forecasting, and planning. This technique can be used for predictions relative to a career field, such as selling, to a department or division, such as marketing, or to the whole organization or career field. The approach helps to get the group out of the rut of status quo or "the way we always did it," by using imagination to anticipate tomorrow's realities based on today's trends.

Consider how much better prepared salespeople might have been for their changing role in an economy of scarcity if, five years ago, they had done some "imagineering." This technique encourages trainees to think "unthinkable" thoughts and to take risks in stating their prognosis.

Specific steps in this group forecasting process are:

- The audience is invited to take a fantasy trip into the future and to let imagination flow freely. The manager might dim room lights to provide a setting for this forecasting exercise.

- Next, the trainees are asked to close their eyes and to project ahead one, five, ten, thirty, or even fifty years. For example, the manager might comment "Imagine it is now 20XX. Place yourself in that time frame and consider what kind of world will be likely by that year in the future." Specifically, ask the group to fantasize in terms of their occupation (or some specific subject, industry, or company). Then identify four or five changes that are probable in the time frame of the assignment. For instance, if considering changes within the field of communication technology over the next decade, participants would be encouraged to think creatively about likely changes ahead in the near future. To loosen their perceptual and psychological "binds," up to five minutes might be devoted to this task. One minute before the end of the exercise, the manager reminds the group again: "Now it is 20XX, and you should have identified some specific changes that may likely occur in your field."

- If the lights were turned off or dimmed, they may be readjusted to normal functioning. Trainees are asked to jot down three, four, or five of the changes that they have predicted for the time period ahead. Then break into small groups of six or eight people who sit in a circle with no table between the members. A PowerPoint screen can be used to record their prognosis on changes (or an easel or flip chart pad provided along with a large felt-tip marking pen).

- Each member is asked to take turns and to share with the group his/her insights without elaboration; the group is requested to hold back comments until every participant in that group has provided his/her input. Based on these projections, the whole group is asked to arrive at some consensus concerning five to eight major trends in their field.

- Instruct each group to summarize findings on likely changes. The group should name a reporter for this purpose. Allow twenty to thirty minutes for this portion of the assignment. Meanwhile, the facilitator makes provisions for displaying group consensus before all. A five-minute warning reminds the group recorder to prepare. Each group then gives a five-minute oral report on the written outline to explain the reasoning behind the selections. The facilitator notes any pattern which emerges from the group reports, for example, a similar idea mentioned by more than one group; such concepts might be underlined or starred. The use of laptop computers in this recording and reporting will facilitate the process.

In conclusion, the HRD leader might inquire what the participants should be doing *now* to plan ahead for such changes which they identified as likely to occur. A general discussion on the implications of the combined data might be undertaken.

Instrumentation

After reading this book, those who would become HPLs may wish to complete the following inquiries:

EXHIBIT 10.2 Preparing for the future questionnaire

1 If you have altered your concept of leadership, explain below:

2 Why is high performance necessary in a knowledge culture?

3 What changes in the work environment do you expect during the next decade?

4 What new communication skill or language will you acquire in the next year?

5 Why should you gain more cross-cultural insights and skills?

6 How should you view accelerating change today?

7 Why is team management and development important?

8 Why is your organization a dynamic energy exchange system?

9 Why should you promote a HPLI and a strategy to identify peak performers in your organization?

10 What action plans should you make to ensure your future leadership?

EPILOGUE

The learning leader

To be a leader in this information society, dominated by knowledge and service workers, an executive or manager promotes a learning environment within the organization. As a thinking leader, he or she facilitates continuous self-development, both personal and professional. Beginning with oneself as the model, this responsibility is extended outward to all who report to that person, as well as to their own family members.

The rationale for this has been discussed throughout this volume, particularly in Chapters 1 and 10. A radically different job market exists in this twenty-first century.

Both jobs and job categories are disappearing, while smart systems are creating new vocational activities. Today's knowledge culture is more demanding, so workers have to learn more, including new techniques and skills, to maintain their marketability. Since lifelong learning is becoming a necessity, Dr Selwyn Enzer, of the University of Southern California, offers these guidelines for those who wish to prepare for the changing work environment:

- master the basic principles underlying your discipline so as to be able to innovate, or face machine replacement;
- cultivate creativity, learning how to analyze alternatives and open-ended problems;
- recognize the limitations of current methods and products, stay open to improved approaches;
- keep abreast of changes in your own field, and be ready to make career changes.

As a futurist, I naturally agree with these observations, but it may help to explain why our emphasis in this text is upon continuous lifelong learning.

As a strategy, what organization development (OD) does for the renewal of institutions, professionals in human resource development (HRD) do for enhancement of individual potential. Because a learning manager exercises leadership in both processes, I have highlighted in this text some of the enabling skills required. Although there are also many technical competencies to be acquired by contemporary leaders and their colleagues, we have focused here on human skills that can be learned in order to:

- increase performance through motivated personnel;
- use communication and culture for systems development;
- collect, analyze, and apply human data for the improvement of organizational relations and effectiveness;
- foster productivity through team building, monitoring, and management;
- plan for organizational changes that redesign and enrich the work environment, especially by personnel participation;
- channel human energy in the organization toward more innovative work accomplishment and goal achievement.

Globalization, especially of the market and economy, contributes to changing social expectations and foreign competition. Thus, leaders re-examine the way in which they deal with their diverse and better educated associates. The trends are toward a system of mutuality in the workplace; the emphasis on learning and collaboration among workers; and the giving of more voice to personnel relative to job performance and goal setting. This results in a new commitment along with change in managerial control. The concept of sharing leadership, especially in the business world, is gaining acceptance. Joint stewardship is evident especially in information technology companies. Another emerging paradigm calls for more synergistic participation in large-scale, complex projects that require collaboration among professions, institutions, and nations. Macro-management challenges have to be met in renewing terrestrial infrastructure, as well as to build space infrastructure on the high frontier. Such large-scale enterprises demand cooperation instead of wasteful competition or conflict. The International Space Station, now completed in orbit, is an example of such global synergy.

In a study and report on *The Learning Enterprise*, Carnevale (1986) underscored the scope of educational efforts by US business and industry. This economist reported twenty-five years ago that financial investment then in workplace training and development was approximately equivalent to that of the entire elementary, secondary, and higher education systems. Corporate learning has itself become a $50 billion industry – many world-class corporations have their own universities, and the number of private, for-profit universities have risen dramatically in both numbers and students worldwide. The major arenas for further company-sponsored training are science, technology, mathematics, managerial ethics, and leadership. Continuous, online learning often determines what a person earns throughout a lifetime. Today the amount of investment in education and training is escalating. The correlation between learning and salaries is confirmed in the USA's 2010 census report. In essence, institutions have to be transformed into learning organizations.

Peak performance

Research also confirms the arguments in this book for high performance leadership. The landmark investigations by clinical psychologist and mathematician, Charles Garfield (1986), of the University of California's Medical School in San Francisco, provides further insight. In his reporting, some twenty-five years ago (*Peak Performers: The New Heroes of American Business*), he shared results of his studies with 1,500 prominent top performers. Garfield concluded that these high performers, whether in management, marketing, or the professions, excelled because they learned a basic set of skills which substantially improved their potential. The peak performers profile that emerged in his studies indicated the presence of these six attributes:

1 a strong sense of mission;
2 well-defined goals;
3 a capacity for self-observation and self-analysis;
4 the ability to bring out the best in others;
5 the mental agility to steer a critical path through complex situations;
6 the foresight to anticipate and adapt to major changes without losing momentum.

Obviously, management and other professional development programs would be well advised to include training for higher performance, and to use high performing employees as "trainers" and problem-solvers. Some of the suggested input, interactions, and instrumentation offered in our own volume help the learning leader to cultivate these qualities in one's self and others (see HPLI Exhibits 8.8 and 8.14). The next report summarizes one global corporation's strategy with this challenge.

EXHIBIT E.1   ExxonMobil's policy with peak performers

This world corporation's Global Management Training system (GMT) aims to develop competency in individual employees so that work groups achieve peak performance. GMT improves the organization's scale in the global marketplace by providing a more efficient, effective, and sustainable approach to developing the potential of personnel. The objective is to help employees to excel in varied components from safety and environmental protection to flawless operations. GMT emphasizes gaining knowledge by understanding a subject, developing skills leading to expertise, and application of such in diverse circumstances. It utilizes the concept of adult learning science that offers varied methods –

Continued

self-contained modules for classroom or self-learning featuring customized training and hands-on mentoring. The outcome is mastery of job roles and team participation. Work teams have already developed 5,000 such learning modules that include intranet training tools. Before any of their 25,000 employees are credited with completing such modules, verification is sought by tests, task demonstrations, simulation with problem scenarios, and interviews. GMT represents an investment in people to foster individual and team success, so that the organization is more effective and competitive.

Source: Based on "Training for Peak Performance," *The Lamp*, 2010: Number 2: 30–32.

Peak or high performance can be found anywhere and at any time. Wolfgang Amadeus Mozart proved that in the eighteenth century when he composed 800 pieces of extraordinary music during a lifetime of only thirty-five years. High performers are diverse, and not limited by gender, race, or nationality. In *Developing High Performance Leaders*, we have provided many profiles of such people to inspire the reader to greater efforts in developing his or her potential. To confirm our premise, Exhibit E.2 offers two more contemporary examples for your last consideration.

EXHIBIT E.2 Diverse high performers

Mary Anne Fox, sixty-three, a wife, mother, and chemist, received in 2010 the National Medal of Science. A native of Canton, Ohio, she received the United States highest scientific honor for her many accomplishments. A prolific researcher, she holds three patents and authored several books, but is noted for her studies of molecules behavior, renewable sources of energy, and creation of university–industry partnerships leading to many spin-off companies and job creation. In 1998, she became Chancellor of the University of North Carolina where her leadership boosted research funding by an outreach program to industry. In 2004, Dr Fox was chosen as Chancellor of the University of California – San Diego. There she has already raised $1 billion in research contracts. Among her other recognitions are membership of the National Academy of Science, Fellow of the American Academy of Arts and Science, and the 2005 Parsons Award for outstanding public service. Now that is a high performing lady.

Fazle Hassan Abed, son of a distinguished Bangladeshi family, was educated in Britain, admires Shakespeare and Joyce, and retired as an accountant with Shell Oil. In 2010, he was knighted by Queen Elizabeth the Second for his unusual work of combating poverty in his homeland. Specifically, he was

Continued

honored for founding a non-governmental organization called BRAC, the largest non-governmental organization in the world, and one of the most businesslike. BRAC is known for its successful micro-financing operations, disbursing over a $1 billion a year. BRAC is also an internet-service provider; has a university and primary school system; and runs feed mills, chicken farms, tea plantations, and packaging factories. In his book, *Freedom from Want*, author Ian Smillie describes BRAC's impact on community development as, "Undoubtedly the largest and most variegated social experiment in the world." Sir Fazle began his humanitarian efforts in 1973 when he founded the Bangladesh Rehabilitation Assistance Committee to provide assistance to cyclone victims in Chittagong. Their motto is "building resources across communities." BRAC channels Western aid so that it is honestly spent on the needy poor. Sir Fazle's approach is not only businesslike, but combats social stratification in his country which helps the rich at the expense of the poor. BRAC's micro-financing is focused on women at the bottom of society who need help for themselves and their children. Its tiny loans also help small companies and village enterprises that are productive. Sir Fazle and BRAC are proven high performers.

Source: "Honoring a Life Devoted to Science," *The San Diego Union-Tribune*, 16 October 2010: A1 and A3. "BRAC in Business," *The Economist*, 20 February 2010: 60–61.

Critical human resources issues

Among the driving forces changing the leader's role in human resource management and development, the following six issues are significant for those aspiring to high performance leadership:

1 The alteration in our perception of the corporate human resources' function. Leaders who deal effectively with the people issues (hiring, firing, promotion, pay, benefits, discipline, training, and union relations) are rising in power and influence within organizations. Human resources (HR), whether considered a staff or line function, is taking on the business–driven attributes of sales, marketing, and finance. The change in corporate philosophy is another reflection of the competitive business environment – especially when coping with acquisitions, mergers, spin-offs of divisions, entering new businesses, or getting out of old ones. Strategic decisions are involved in these continuous institutional changes, and HR considerations are primary (e.g. matching skills with jobs, retaining key personnel and re-training them, coping with the human and cultural problems associated with introduction of a new technology, or the closing of a plant). Those in management with HR insights and competencies are increasingly used by enlightened CEOs as advisors to keep the corporation on the competitive edge, especially in terms of productivity. As unions decline in power, those with

personnel and training skills are valued to deal with broad labor and social issues involved in redeployment, offshore activities, "intrapreneurialism," and many other systems innovations.

In the microcomputer and related communication technologies, line managers have new tools for taking on human resource management activities. In every level of supervision, managers can be enabled to understand and take action on employee difficulties on the job, so as to turn around the performance situation. Furthermore, decentralization is occurring relative to the HRD responsibilities. The trend puts training into line management hands, and the HRD professional's role changes to that of consultant and facilitator. Increasingly HR corporate philosophy is client-centered – the line manager has the charter to improve subordinates' competencies; training is to solve performance deficiencies, to help people acquire the skill necessary to perform their jobs optimally. If a training or HRD department exists, then its function now is to provide managers with the tools and resources for adult learning, and to show the link between competence and results, the connection between lack of knowledge and lack of productivity. HR professionals provide managers with counsel, feedback systems, and training program aid. HR expert power is diversified, managers learn to become trainers and call upon a HR support function or resources for assistance, such as with team building.

2 The whole culture is in transition toward more effective information processing, technology, and computers that expand learning and knowledge. Therefore, learning, whether in formal institutions of education or within organizational training settings, must focus on these subjects. Anthropologist Edward Hall (1987) reminded us that any culture is primarily a system for creating, sending, and storing information. Communication underlies everything we do, and the new communication technology is the means to rapidly and widely disseminate both information and learning. As Strassman (1985) maintained, "Information technology, wisely employed, provides leverage to greater productivity and performance pay-off." Corporate strategies should give priority to learning its mastery for valued-added results. Since this technology is constantly advancing, continuing education is a necessity. The impact of automation and robotics on work is profound, causing a transformation in relationships and the operations of offices and plants. Thus leadership is needed both in IT and the optimization of a knowledge culture.

3 There is a mismatch in the work environment between employee skills and the expertise required within the emerging job market.

One of the biggest challenges in this area is renewal of educational curricula to provide the new skills required in this century's work environment. Until that happens, the existing workforce will have to be retrained to meet today's performance needs. Massive re-training and new educational programs are necessary to meet the needs of business and the professions in an Information Age. To convince top management that proposed learning programs can bring a return on such investments, the cost of learning will have to be quantified and perceived as a capitalization of human assets, not merely as expenses to be written off. Further, to benefit more fully from technical and other training, some personnel need to learn how to acquire and apply the information being presented more efficiently. This may be especially important for managers whose backgrounds in science and technology are deficient.

To curb the emergence of an underclass, the whole public and private education program requires drastic reformation. The poor, especially, need not only better schooling, but improved technological literacy and mathematical education, so as to take advantage of new educational opportunities, and qualify for the new work culture.

4 Leadership development programs, whether internal or external, can affect not only the outcome of the learning, but the survival and growth of social institutions. Human systems are revitalized by the injection of new knowledge and learning. Learning applications in the work environment are enhanced when:

a. overall organizational and strategic goals for promoting learning are evident when leaders model behavioral change as a result of the learning experience;
b. learning programs are linked to promotions, new assignments, and incentives;
c. post-program support is evident through management debriefings, establishing informal "alumni" groups, and follow up training to advance and ensure career development;
d. HRD leadership focus is on creation of high performance teams.

5 The new work culture and environment emphasizes positive re-enforcement – people's work performance improves with enjoyment and satisfaction, rather than from fear or punishment.

Building upon the research of psychologist, B. F. Skinner (1986), behavior management provides on-the-job positive reinforcement of desirable behavior such as high performance. Management can do this in a systematic fashion, such as by the redesign of assembly line jobs so the worker is more involved in the finished product, or offering sustained psychological or other rewards for productive behavior. Again new learnings are implied in this applied behavior methodology or modification.

Giving employees "ownership" in learning or an organization tends to improve their performance. This can be accomplished figuratively or literally. For example, some companies use top performing workers as instructors, tutors, or mentors with new trainees, while other corporations offer stock options to their high performing personnel. However, the strategy is often supplemented by performance-related rewards.

6 HRD increasingly directs its attention to developing cross-cultural leaders who are effective in a global marketplace. The globalization of business and markets requires managers and technical representatives who are cross-culturally skilled (Moran, Harris, and Moran 2011). Going international means training not only in foreign area studies and economics, but how to cope with cultural differences to produce synergy. It also implies developing leaders with foreign language skills.

High performance leadership is also manifest in the promotion of synergy between and among various disciplines, industries, systems, and nations. Those strategies need wider applications through learning managers and professionals who foster synergistic relations within their organizations and communities.

Readers who act upon the above six trends, and other messages in this book will discover for themselves the "pay-off" in higher performing personnel.

Conclusions

The speed of changes in the work environment creates new norms for twenty-first century institutions and systems. The role of human resource professionals, within organizations and industries, is being enhanced. The individual who holds that position must not only be competent, but also a high performance leader. Such people are challenged to assume responsibility for transforming executives, managers, supervisors, technicians, and workers so they function more effectively within the changing workplace. The HR leader, then, becomes the principal agent of change within older organizations, as well as a catalyst within start-up enterprises (Harris 2009). The HR leader enables the system or institution to cope with such cultural changes as:

- diversity in the workplace and globalization of the marketplace;
- extending worker and family benefits, ranging from child care provisions to employee fitness/wellness centers;
- counseling or group education on organization/future shock, whether caused by mergers, acquisitions, restructuring, or introduction of new technologies;
- developing leaders who can resolve conflict in peaceful ways;[52]
- preparing personnel for tomorrow's new realities, including climate change, by utilizing forecasting strategic planning, and futures research.

A caution to high performers: expect opposition and jealousy from low performers who may be threatened psychologically by a HPL's achievements. This undermining may take the form of malicious gossip, degrading jokes, and even lies to top management. It is often hard to be a cultural hero. Also, not all HPLs start out well. For example, Louis Zamparini, whose biography was published when he was ninety-three (see L. Hillerbrand, *Unbroken* published by Random House in 2010). Zamparini was a juvenile delinquent who transformed himself into a track star at the 1936 Olympics in Berlin, then became a Second World War combat bomber pilot who survived forty-seven days drifting in shark-infested seas, eventual capture by the enemy, and subsequent torture as a prisoner of war. However, he overcame his nightmares thanks to the evangelist, Billy Graham, who turned Louis's life around again. Resilience comes in many forms, and high performers are often found among survivors.

High performers should also be promoters and creators of innovation. In large enterprises, they may even fill the role of chief innovation officer. In his writings on the subject, renowned innovation architect, Josh Abend, maintains that businesses cannot survive on the hope that innovation will miraculously emerge – hope is not a strategy, but choosing the right innovation model is (www.innovationcity.com).

HPLs are also distinguished for their capable stewardship of resources – human, physical, natural, and financial. They are not given to the exploitation of either the environment or others. Possibly our greatest need today in our human relationships, especially in business and the professions, is for HPLs who are ethical, sensitive to others, and foresighted.[53] Some of the new industries in information and finances are noted for technical whizzes who are very loose with the truth or standards of behavior, while demonstrating little concern for others. They neither respect shareholders or stakeholders in their drive to profit. These types are in stark contrast to real leaders who change the world for the better because of their presence.

Finally, the main message of this book is that HPLs utilize the insights from behavioral science management research. Furthermore, they promote the career development of HRD professionals within their organization. Thus, we can all contribute to the realization of human potential. Perhaps the next illustration of humanity's evolution defines the HPL challenge best.

AFTERWORD

When you have the chance to work with "the best of the best" how do you teach them? What do you say that can improve on the raw talent factor of their leadership? These are the questions that Dr Phil Harris has dealt with in this remarkable book, based upon his stellar career of leadership education. Do "high performance behaviors" need to be brought out? Is this a gene in every soul, or are there but a few men and women who are gifted and need to be nurtured? Dr Harris unfolds this mystery and how everyone can seek, recognize, and potentially realize moments of peak performance. We seek it in our leaders; we attempt to bring it forth in ourselves. The mystery is unlocked in Harris' concepts, cases, and lifetime examples.

Developing High Performance Leaders offers a synopsis of insights from behavioral science management as applied to leadership development. In each chapter, the Input sections contain profound thoughts for consideration by future leaders. The unique Instruments enable readers to engage in astute self-assessment. The Interaction sections provide an array of group dynamic techniques for instructional purposes, or for use in a High Performance Leadership Institute (HPLI). The material on action learning and research alone is worth investment in this volume, which would also make an excellent textbook in schools of business or education.

Michael McManus, PhD
President, California International
Business University, San Diego, CA

GLOSSARY OF ABBREVIATIONS

AR	Action research
CBC	Canadian Broadcasting Company
CRI	Cultural Relations Inventory
CSC	Corporate Service Corps
DOD	Department of Defense
EP	Emerging Participative
ERIC	Educational Resource Information Center
FIRST	For Inspiration and Recognition of Science and Technology
GMT	Global Management Training
HPL	High Performing Leader
HPLI	High Performance Leadership Institute
HPMI	High Performance Management Inventory
HPMW	High Performance Management Workshop
HR	Human Resources
HRD	Human Resource Development
HRI	Human Resources Inventory
IB	Input Bombardment
IPO	Initial Public Offerings
ISS	International Space Station
KAUST	King Abdullah University of Science and Technology
KC	Knowledge Culture
KM	Knowledge Management
KMC	Knowledge Management Consortium
LMI	Leadership Motivation Inventory
LPO	Legal Process Outsourcing
MbO	Management by Objectives
MCI	Management Communications Inventory

MPSI	Managing People Skills Inventory
NTL	National Training Laboratory
OCS	Organizational Culture Survey
OD	Organizational Development
OT	Organizational Transformation
OTV	Orbital Transfer Vehicle
PERT	Program Evaluation and Review Technique
R&D	Research and Development
RISS	Remote Interactive Search System
RR&R	Read, React, and Report
SI	Simulated Identity
TA	Traditional Authoritarian
TOPS	The Outstanding People Seminar

FURTHER READING

In addition to references provided in chapter endnotes, the following is a selection of classic and contemporary books, especially leadership and behavioral science management works of value to HPLs.

Andriessen, A. *Making Sense of Intellectual Capital*. Oxford, UK: Elsevier/Butterworth-Heinemann, 2004.

Argyris, C. *Reasoning, Learning, and Action – Individual and Organizational*. San Francisco: Jossey-Bass/Wiley, 1982.

Avolio, B. J. *Full Range Leadership Development*. Newbury Park, CA: Sage, 2010.

Bass, B. *The Bass Handbook of Leadership: Theory, Research, and Managerial Implications*. New York: Free Press, 2008: 4th edn.

—— with R. E. Riggio, *Transformational Leadership*. Mahwah, NJ: Erlbaum Associates Inc., 2006.

Beckhard, R. and Harris, R. T. *Organizational Transitions: Managing Complex Change*. Reading, MA: Addison-Wesley, 1987.

Bellingham, R. *Ethical Leadership*. Amherst, MA: HRD Press, 2010: 2nd edn.

Bennis, W. *Still Surprised – A Memoir of a Life in Leadership*. San Francisco, CA: Jossey-Bass/Wiley, 2010.

Blake, R., Moulton, J., and Allen, R. *Spectacular Teamwork*. Somerset, NJ: John Wiley & Sons, 1987.

Bradford, D. L. and Cohen, A. R. *Managing for Excellence: The Guide to Developing High Performance in Contemporary Organizations*. New York: John Wiley & Sons, 1984.

Burns, J. M. *Transforming Leadership*. New York: Grove Press, 2004.

Carkhuff, R. R. *The Art of Helping*. Amherst, MA: HRD Press, 2010: 9th edn.

Carleton, R. *Implementation and Management of Performance Improvement Plans*. Amherst, MA: HRD Press, 2009.

Carnevale, A. P. "The Learning Enterprise," *Training and Development Journal*, January 1986, 40, 1: 18–29.

Center for Creative Leadership, *Leading the Organization. Leading Others. Leading Yourself. Leadership Systems*. Greensboro, NC: Center for Creative Leadership, 2010.

Cohen, N. H. *The Manager's Pocket Guide to Effective Mentoring*. Amherst, MA: HRD Press, 2008.

Cosmides, L. and Toohy, I. *What is Evolutionary Psychology*. New York, NY: Amazon Books, 2005.

Csikszentmihalyi, M. *Good Business Leadership*. New York, NY: Penguin Books, 2003.

Davenport, T. H. *Thinking for a Living: How to Get Better Performance Results from Knowledge Workers*. Boston, MA: Harvard Business School Press, 2005.

Deming, W. E. *Out of the Crisis*. Cambridge, MA: Massachusetts Institute of Technology Press, 1986.

Drucker, P. E. *Innovation and Entrepreneurship*. New York: Harper & Row, 1985.

Dyer, W. G. *Team Building: Issues and Alternatives*. Reading, MA: Addison-Wesley, 1987.

Elashmawi, F. and Harris, P. R. *Multicultural Management*. Burlington, MA: Elsevier/Gulf Publishing, 1993.

Flamholtz, E. G. *Human Resource Accounting*. San Francisco, CA: Jossey-Bass/Wiley, 1986.

Forester, T. (ed.) *The Microelectronics Revolution – The Complete Guide to the New Technology and Its Impact on Society*. Cambridge, MA: MIT Press, 1985.

French, W. C. and Bell, C. H. *Organizational Development*. Saddle River, NJ: Prentice Hall, 1984.

Garber, P. R. *Giving and Receiving Performance Feedback*. Amherst, MA: HRD Press, 2009.

Garfield, C. *Peak Performers: The New Heroes of American Business*. New York: William Morrow, 1986.

Geary, J. and Sanother, I. *The Secret Life Metaphor and How It Shapes How We See the World*. New York, NY: HarperCollins, 2011.

Gill, R. *The Theory and Practice of Leadership*. Newbury Park, CA: Sage, 2006.

Gladis, S. *The Executive Coach in the Corporate Forest. The Trusted Leader*. Amherst, MA: HRD Press, 2010; 2011.

Greiner, L. E. and Schein, V. *Power and Organization Development*. Reading, MA: Addison-Wesley, 1988.

Groff, T. R. and Jones, T. P. *Introduction to Knowledge Management*. Burlington, MA: Elsevier/Butterworth-Heinemann, 2003.

Grove, A. *High Output Management*. New York: Random House, 1983.

Gudykunst, W. B., Stewart, L. P., and Ting-Toomey, S. (eds) *Communication, Culture and Organizational Processes*. Newbury Park, CA: Sage Publishing, 1985.

Hall, E. T. and Hall, M. R. *Hidden Differences: Doing Business with the Japanese*. Garden City, NJ: Doubleday, 1987.

Harari, O. *The Leadership Principles of Colin Powell*. New York, NY: McGraw-Hill, 2003.

Harris, P. R. *New Worlds, New Ways, New Managements*. New York: AMACOM, 1983.

—— *Management in Transition – Transforming Managerial Practices and Organizational Strategies for a New Work Culture*. San Francisco, CA: Jossey-Bass/Wiley, 1985.

—— *High Performance Leadership*. Glenview, IL: Scott, Foresman and Company, 1989.

—— *The New Work Culture*. Amherst, MA: HRD Press, 1998.

—— *Managing the Knowledge Culture*. Amherst, MA: HRD Press, 2005.

—— *Space Enterprise – Living and Working Offworld in the 21st Century*. New York: Springer-Praxis, 2009.

—— *Toward Human Emergence*. Amherst, MA: HRD Press, 2009.

Harrison, A. A. *Spacefaring – The Human Dimension*. Berkeley, CA: University of California Press, 2001.

Heifetz, R. A. and Linsky, M. *Leadership on the Line*. Boston, MA: Harvard Business Press, 2002.

Heil, G., Bennis, W., and Stephens, D. C. *Douglas McGregor, Revisited: Managing the Human Side of Enterprise*. New York: John Wiley, 2000.

Hersey, P. and Blanchard, K. *Management of Organizational Behavior: Utilizing Human Resources*. Upper Saddle River. NJ: Prentice Hall, 1988: 5th edn.

Herzberg, F. *One More Time: How Do You Motivate Employees. The Motivation to Work*. Boston, MA: Harvard Business Review Classics, 2008.

Hubbard, E. E. *The Manager's Pocketguide to Diversity Management*. Amherst. MA: HRD Press, 2008.

Hughes, R. L., Ginnett, R., and Curphy, G. *Leadership: Enhancing the Lessons of Experience*. Boston, MA: McGraw-Hill/Irwin, 2006: 6th edn.

Kirby, A. *The Encyclopedia of Games for Trainers*. Amherst, MA: HRD Press, 2009.

Kilmann, R. H., Saxton, M. J., and Serpa, R. *Gaining Control of the Corporate Culture*. San Francisco: Jossey-Bass/Wiley, 1985.

Knowles, M. *Andragogy in Action – Modern Principles of Adult Learning*. San Francisco, CA: Jossey-Bass, 1984.

Kouzes, J. M. and Posner, B, Z. *The Leadership Challenge*. San Francisco, CA: Jossey-Bass, 2003, 4th ed.

Kouzes, J. and Posner, B. *The Leadership Challenge*. San Francisco, CA: Jossey-Bass/Wiley, 2008: 4th edn.

Kozmetksky, G. *Transformational Management*. Cambridge, MA: Ballinger/Harper & Row, 1985.

Kuhn, R. L. (ed.) *Handbook for Creative and Innovative Managers*. New York: McGraw-Hill, 1987.

Lawler, E. F. *High Involvement Management*. San Francisco: Jossey-Bass/Wiley, 1986.

Likert, R. *New Patterns of Management*. New York: McGraw-Hill, 1961.

Lippitt, G. L., Langseth, P., and Mossop, J. *Implementing Organizational Change*. San Francisco: Jossey-Bass, 1985.

Loden, M. *Feminine Leadership*. New York: New York Times Books, 1985.

London, M. *Change Agents: New Roles, Strategies for Human Resource Professionals*. San Francisco: Jossey-Bass/Wiley, 1988.

McClelland, D. C. *The Achieving Society*. New York: The Free Press, 1967.

—— *Human Motivation*. Glenview, IL: Scott, Foresman, 1984.

MacCrimmon, K. R. and Wehrung, D. A. *Taking Risks: The Management of Uncertainty*. New York: The Free Press, 1986.

McGregor, D. (ed.) *Human Side of Enterprise 25th Anniversary Printing*. New York: McGraw-Hill, 2006.

McManus, M. L. and Hergert, M. L. *Surviving Merger and Acquisition*. Glenview, IL: Scott, Foresman, 1988.

Maslow, A. "A Theory of Human Motivation," *Psychological Review*, 1943, 50, 4: 370–396.

Maslow, A. *Toward a Psychology of Being*. New York: John Wiley, 1998: 3rd edn.

Maslow, A. *Maslow on Management*. New York: John Wiley, 1998: revised edn.

Maxwell, J. S. *Ethics 101 – What Every Leader Needs to Know*. New York: Time Warner, 2005.

—— *Leadership 101 – What Every Leader Needs to Know. The 21 Irrefutable Laws of Leadership*. Nashville, TN: Thomas Neeson Inc., 2007.

Meyers, B. *Take the Lead*. New York, NY: Simon & Shuster, 2011.

Miller, D. B. *Managing Professionals in Research and Development*. San Francisco, CA: Jossey-Bass/Wiley, 1986.

Miller, J. G. *Living Systems*. New York: McGraw-Hill, 1978.

Moran, R, T. and Harris, P. R. *Managing Cultural Synergy*. Houston, TX: Gulf Publishing, 1982.

Moran, R. T. and Youngdahl, W. E. *Leading Global Projects for the Professional and Accidental Project Leader*. Burlington, MA: Elsevier, 2008.

Moran, R. T., Harris, P. R., and Moran, S. V. *Managing Cultural Differences*. Burlington, MA: Elsevier/Butterworth-Heinemann, 2011: 8th edn.

Morrison, A. M., White, R. P., and Van Velsor, E. *Breaking the Glass Ceiling – Can Women Reach the Top of America's Largest Corporations?* Reading, MA: Addison-Wesley, 1987.

Morton, J. *The Science of Managing Organizational Technology*. Philadelphia, PA: Gordon & Breach, 2010.

Nadler, L. (ed.) *The Handbook of Human Resource Development.* New York: John Wiley & Sons, 1984.

Nadler, L. and Nadler, Z. *The Comprehensive Guide to Successful Conferences and Meetings.* San Francisco, CA: Jossey-Bass/Wiley, 1997.

Nohria, N. *Handbook of Leadership Theory and Practice.* Boston, MA: Harvard Business School Publishing Corp., 2010.

Northouse, P. G. *Leadership: Theory and Practice.* Newbury Park, CA: Sage, 2006: 4th edn.

Northhouse, P. G. *Leadership Theory and Practice.* Thousand Oaks, CA: Sage Publications, 2009.

Osborn, A. *Applied Imagination.* New York, NY: Charles Scribner & Sons, 1963.

O'Toole, J. *Vanguard Management.* New York: Doubleday, 1985; paperback edn, New York: Berkeley Publishing Group, 1987.

Ouchi, W. *Theory Z: How American Business Can Meet the Japanese Challenge.* Reading, MA: Addison-Wesley, 1981.

Parker, G. *Parker Team Series: Teamwork, Vol. 1; Effective Meetings, Vol. 2; Team Leadership, Vol. 3; Creating a Positive Team Atmosphere, Vol. 4; Team Communications, Vol. 5.* Amherst, MA: HRD Press, 2010.

Passmore, W. A. *Using Sociotechnical Systems to Design Effective Organizations.* New York: John Wiley & Sons, 1985.

Peters, T. *Leadership Alliance.* New York: Alfred Knopf, 1989.

Pike, C. W. *Creative Training Techniques Handbook.* Amherst, MA: HRD Press, 2009.

Prahalad, C. K. *The Fortune at the Bottom of the Pyramid.* New York, NY: McGraw-Hill, 2009.

Revens, R. W. *The Origins and Growth of Action Learning.* London, UK: Chartwell Bratt Publishers, 1982.

Robson, M. (ed.) *Quality Circles in Action.* Brookfield, Vt.: Gower Publishing, 1984.

Schein, E. *Organizational Culture and Leadership.* San Francisco: Jossey-Bass/Wiley, 1985.

Schein, E. H. *Organizational Culture and Leadership.* San Francisco, CA: Jossey-Bass, 2010.

Sears, W. H. *The New Manager's Primer: Winning with People at Work; Front Line Guide to Communicating with Employees; to Mastering the Manager's Job; to Creating a Winning Management Style; to Thinking Clearly; to Building High Performance Teams.* Amherst, MA: HRD Press, 2010; 2008.

Simons, G. F., Vazquez, C., and Harris, P. R. *Transcultural Leadership – Empowering the Diverse Workforce.* Burlington, MA: Elsevier/Gulf, 1993.

Skinner, B. F. *Upon Further Reflection.* New York: New York University Press, 1986.

Stark, P. and Flaherty, J. *The Competent Leader.* Amherst, MA: HRD Press, 2009.

Stein, G. *Managing People and Organizations: Peter Drucker's Legacy.* Bingley UK: Emerald Group Publishing, 2010.

Strassman, P. A. *Information Pay-off: The Transformation of Work in the Electronic Age.* New York: Free Press/Colliers-Macmillan, 1985.

Tannenbaum, R., Margulies, N., and Massarik, F. *Human Systems Development – New Perspectives on People and Organizations.* San Francisco, CA: Jossey-Bass/Wiley, 1985.

Thomas, K. "Conflict and Conflict Management," in M. Dunneete (ed.) *Handbook of Industrial and Organizational Psychology.* New York: Rand McNally, 1976: 889–937.

Thurow, L. *The Management Challenge: Japanese View.* Cambridge, MA: MIT Press, 1985.

Tichy, N. M. *Managing Strategic Change – Technical, Political, and Cultural Dynamics.* New York: John Wiley & Sons, 1983.

Tichy, N. M. and DeVanna, M. A. *The Transformational Leader.* New York: John Wiley & Sons, 1986.

Tubesing, N. L. and Tubesing, D. A. (eds) *Structured Exercise in Stress Management,* Vols. I & II; *Structured Exercises in Wellness Promotion,* Vol. 1. Duluth, MN: Whole Person Press, 1983.

Tung, R. L. *The New Expatriates: Managing Human Resources Abroad.* Cambridge, MA: Ballenger/Harper & Row, 1987.

Wheatly, M. J. *Leadership and the New Science*. San Francisco, CA: Berret-Koelher, 1999.

Wheelwright, S. C. and Makridakis, S. *Forecasting Methods for Management*. New York: John Wiley & Sons, 1985.

Wibbeke, E. S. *Global Business Leadership*. Oxford, UK: Routledge/Taylor & Francis, 2012.

Wiig, E. *People-Focused Knowledge Management*. Oxford, UK: Elsevier, Butterworth-Heinemann, 1994.

Wilson, J. Q. and Herrnstein, R. J. *Crime and Human Nature*. New York: The Free Press, 1985.

Yuki, G. A. *Leadership in Organizations*. Saddle River, NJ: Pearson/Prentice Hall, 2011.

NOTES

1 This and subsequent passages are from Dr Cribbin's book, *Leadership – Strategies for Orga-nizational Effectiveness*. New York: Amacom, 1981. An esteemed behavioral scientist, Jim died in 2008 at the age of ninety-four, much beloved by his family, students, and clients.

2 Michael Maccoby, *The Leader, a New Face for American Management*. New York: Simon and Shuster, 1982.

3 V. Allee, *The Future of Knowledge: Increasing Prosperity Through Value Networks*. Oxford, UK; Burlington, MA: Butterworth Heinemann/Elsevier, 2003. Curley, K. F. and B. Kivowitz, *The Manager's Pocket Guide to Knowledge Management*. Amherst, MA: HRD Press, 2003.

4 Refer to these knowledge management resources: www.kmci.org; www.find-whitepapers.com; www.brint.com/km (accessed 18 April 2012).

5 E. S. Wibbeke, *Global Business Leadership*. Oxford, UK: Routledge/Taylor and Francis 2012. The Rose Leadership Institute has an online forum and certification program for would-be GEO leaders: www.roseleadershipinstitute.com (accessed 18 April 2012).

6 Based on books by P. R. Harris, *Management in Transition*. San Francisco, CA; Jossey-Bass Wiley, 1985: 88–98; *New Worlds, New Ways, New Management*. New York: AMACOM, 1983.

7 From P. R. Harris, *The New Work Culture*. Amherst, MA: Human Resource Development Press, 1998.

8 P. Hersey, and K. Blanchard, *Management of Organizational Behavior*. Upper Saddle River, NJ: Prentice Hall, 2000, ninth edn; and K. Blanchard, *Self-Leadership and the One Minute Manager*. New York, NY: Harper-Collins, 2005.

9 B. Bass and R. E. Riggio, *Transformational Leadership*. Mahwah, NJ: Lawrence Erlbaum Associates Inc, 2005.

10 James O'Toole, *Vanguard Management*. New York: Doubleday/Berkeley Publishing Group, 1987.

11 Thomas H. Davenport, *Thinking for a Living: How to Get Better Performance Results from Knowledge Workers*. Cambridge, MA: Harvard University Business School Press, 2005.

12 Daniel Andriessen, *Making Sense of Intellectual Capital*. Burlington, MA: Elsevier/Butter-worth-Heinemann, 2004.

13 Ronald J. Burke (ed.) *The Human Resources Revolution: Why Putting People First Matters.* Burlington, MA: Elsevier/Butterworth-Heinemann, 2006.

14 I am indebted to my colleagues, Jack Hayes and Bruce Qualset, for my knowledge and experience with HPMW, gained while associated with their Innovation Management Consultants in La Jolla, California.

15 Reproduction of single copies of the instruments in this book may be made for personal use by readers. For multiple copies to be reproduced for training sessions, order P. R. Harris' *Twenty Reproducible Assessment Instruments.* Amherst, MA: Human Resource Development Press, 1995. Available from Human Resource Development Press (25 Amherst Road, Amherst, MA 01002, USA; www.hrdpress.com). Also inquire about J. Robert Carleton, *Implementation and Management of Performance Improvement Plans.* Amherst, MA: Human Resource Development Press, 2010.

16 See "The Maslow Window" in Bruce Cordell, *21st Century New Waves* blog; http://21st CenturyWaves.com/2009/07/05/buzz-aldrin-a-man-for-all-maslow-windows (accessed 18 April 2012).

17 M. Pinkus, "On Friends," *The Economist's The World in 2011,* Nov 2010; www.economist.com/node/17509376.

18 V. Nayar, *Employees First, Customers Second.* Boston, MA: Harvard Business Press, 2010.

19 Permission granted to reproduce only one personal copy of this LMI inventory. For group use, order P. R. Harris' *Twenty Reproducible Assessment Instruments.* Amherst, MA: Human Resource Development Press, 1995: www.hrdpress.com (accessed 18 April 2012).

20 David Kirkpatrick, *The Facebook Effect: The Inside Story of the Company that is Connecting the World.* New York, NY: Simon & Shuster, 2010.

21 Kenneth Cluker, "Data, Data Everywhere," *The Economist,* 27 February 2010: 18.

22 P. R. Harris, *Toward Human Emergence.* Amherst, MA: Human Resource Development Press, 2009.

23 D. Tapscott and A. Williams, *Macrowikinomics: Rebooting Business and the World.* New York, NY: Portfolio Penguin, 2010.

24 For further information on the subject of this chapter, refer to R. T. Moran, P. R. Harris, and S. V. Moran, *Managing Cultural Differences.* Burlington, MA: Elsevier Butterworth-Heinemann, 2011: 8th edn.

25 Additional inventories to assess a group or team's behavior are available in Philip R. Harris, *Twenty Reproducible Assessment Instruments*, Part 2. Amherst, MA: Human Resource Development Press, 1995.

26 See P. R. Harris, *Space Enterprise – Living and Working Offworld in the 21st Century.* New York: Springer-Praxis, 2009; Marsha Freeman, *Krafft Ehricke's Extraterrestrial Imperative.* Burlington, ON, Canada: Apogee Books, 2008.

27 See A. A. Harrison, *Spacefaring – The Human Dimension.* Berkeley, CA: University of California Press, 2001; M. Freeman, *The Challenges of Human Space Exploration.* New York, NY: Springer-Praxis, 2000.

28 R. H. Hall, *Dimensions of Work.* Newbury Park, CA: Sage Publications, 1985.

29 John Sherwood, "Creating Work Cultures with Competitive Advantages," *Organization Dynamics.* American Management Association (Winter 1988: 5–26).

30 Schumpter, "Overstretched," *The Economist,* 22 May 2010: 72.

31 F. Guerreram, H. Sender, and P. Jenkins, "Damning Insight into Corporate Culture Sheds Light on Fall of a Wall Street Giant," *Financial Times,* 14 March 2010: 2–18.

32 J. Fouts, "Al-Andalus 2.0," *Saudi Aramco World,* July/August 2010: 10–15.

33 Permission to reproduce single copies of these instruments for reader use. For quantity copy reproduction, obtain P. R. Harris, *Twenty Reproducible Assessment Instruments.*

Amherst, MA: Human Resource Development Press, 1995: www.hrdpress.com (accessed 18 April 2012).

34 Mary M. Connors, Albert A. Harrison, and Faren R. Akins, *Living Aloft: Human Requirements for Extended Spaceflight*. Washington, DC: National Aeronautics and Space Administration, 1985.

35 For an update, refer to A. A. Harrison, *Spacefaring – The Human Dimension*. Berkeley, CA: University of California, 2001: Chapter 8.

36 R. T. Moran and W. E. Youngdahl, *Leading in Global Projects for the Professional and Accidental Project Leaders*. Burlington, MA: Elsevier, 2008.

37 Permission is granted to reproduce single copies for personal use of all inventories in this book. However, to replicate multiple copies, obtain P. R. Harris *Twenty Reproducible Assessment Instruments* from www.hrdpress.com. In that volume there are related items: Organizational Roles and Relationship Inventory; Group Maturity Analysis; Team Synergy Analysis.

38 G. Hamel, *The Future of Management*. Boston, MA: Harvard Business School Press, 2007.

39 Peter Drucker, *The Essential Drucker – The Best of Sixty Years of Peter Drucker's Essential Writings on Management*. New York: Harper Collins, 2008. See his "Next Society Survey," in www.economist.com (accessed 1 November 2001).

40 Alan Murray, *The Wall Street Journal's Essential Guide to Management*. New York: Wall Street Journal, 2010.

41 B. Krone (ed.) *Beyond Earth – the Future of Humans in Space*. Burlington, Ontario, Canada: Apogee Press, 2006. J. Spencer, *Space Tourism*. Burlington, Ontario, Canada: Apogee Press, 2006, 2004, 2001. L. Morris and K. J. Cox (eds), *Space Commerce – The Inside Story*. New York: Aerospace Technology Working Group Book, 2010.

42 The next two instruments may be reproduced for reader personal use. For multiple copies, go to P. R. Harris, *Twenty Reproducible Assessment Instruments*. Amherst, MA: Human Resource Development Press, 1995.

43 Refer to R. T. Moran, P. R. Harris, and S. V. Moran. *Managing Cultural Differences*. Burlington, MA: Elsevier Butterworth-Heinemann, 2011: 8th edn.

44 New digital applications are continually being developed to enhance instructional methods, for example the Flash Drive which enables teachers or trainers to utilize courses from the Kahn Academy or Google Maps.

45 D. Tapscott and A. Williams, *Macrowikinomics: Rebooting Business and the World*. New York: Penguin/Portfolio, 2010.

46 Refer to S. Shane, *Born Entrepreneurs, Born Leaders – How Genes Affect your Work Life*. Oxford, UK: Oxford University Press, 2010.

47 Daniel Pink, *Drive: The Surprising Truth of What Motivates Us*. New York: Barnes & Noble, 2009; Daniel Pink, *A Whole New Mind: Why Right Brainers will Rule the Future*. New York: Penguin/Berkeley Group, 2006.

48 Schrumpeter, "Profiting from Non-Profits," *The Economist,* 17 July 2010: 72.

49 L. Siegele, "It's a Smart World," *The Economist,* 6 November 2010.

50 V. Peretroukhin, "The Case for Manned Space Exploration," *Moon Miners Manifesto,* June 2010, #236: 4–5: www.moonsociety.org (accessed 18 April 2012). For additional insights, read P. R. Harris, *Lunar Pioneers – A Science-based Novel About Living, Working, and Settling on the Moon in 2050*. New York: Infinity Publishers, 2010.

51 J. Brockman, *This Will Change Everything: Ideas That Will Shape the Future*. New York: Harper Perennial, 2010; A. De Grey, *Ending Aging: The Rejuvenation Breakthroughs That Could Reverse Human Aging in our Lifetime*. New York: St. Martin's Griffin, 2007; B. Greene, *The Fabric of the Cosmos: Space, Time, and the Texture of Reality*. New York:

Vintage Books, 2004; S. Hawking, *A Brief History of Time* (10th edn). New York: Bantam, 1996; S. Hawking, with L. Mlodinow, *A Briefer History of Time*. New York: Bantam, 2008; Immortality Institute, *The Scientific Conquest of Death: Essays on Infinite Lifespans*. Immortality Institute in Alabama: Libros En Red, 2004; M. Kaku, *Hyperspace: A Scientific Odyssey through Parallel Universes, Time Warps, and the 10th Dimension*. New York: Anchor Books, 1994; M. Kaku, *Physics of the Impossible: A Scientific Exploration into the World of Phasers, Force Fields, Teleportation, and Time Travel*. New York: Anchor Books, 2008; R. Le Poidevin, *Travels in Four Dimensions: The Enigmas of Space and Time*. Oxford, UK: Oxford University Press, 2003.

52 M. Saskin, *Conflict Style Inventory*. Amherst, MA: HRD Press, 2010.

53 R. Bellingham, *Ethical Leadership*. Amherst, MA: HRD Press, 2010: 2nd edn.

INDEX

abdicratic leadership 23
Abend, Josh 309
abstract 233
abstraction 75
achievement learning 64
action learning 204–10, 227–8, 233–4
action learning programs 210–19
action plans 205
action research (AR) 225–7
adaptability 170–2
ad-hocracy 179, 182
adjective rating scale 246
adult education 221; methods 234–45
agenda 257
Aldrin, Buzz 44
alternative learning activities 214–15
analytical operational techniques 273–4
andragogy 204
appearance 106–7
applied research 229
AR *see* action research
Arapakis, Maria 51–2
Argyris, Chris 206
artificial intelligence 291
artisan 16
assessment program 227
associative person 184
assumptions 83
attitude change 173, 245
attitudes 109, 110
attribute listing 273–4
audio visual (AV) aids 234–6
automation 21, 25
autonomy 20, 25
AV *see* audio visual

Bartz, Carol 287
Bass, Bernard 25, 42
behavior 3, 45–6, 137, 307; cultural influences 102–3

behavioral change 227
behavioral deviancy 48
behavioral games 266
behavioral science management theory 42–3, 113
beliefs 109
bias 82
Bloom, Benjamin 49
Blue Green 271
body language 83
book reading 88
brain-based devices 287
brainstorming 174, 236–7, 277–9
Brennan, Thomas 50
bureaucracy 179, 181
buzz groups 91, 237

capability 14
case studies 114, 237–8
change 163; management 164–5, 173–4; organizational communications 173–4; resistance 177–8
change agent 173
change inventory 191–4
change strategy 174
charisma 24
checklists 276
child care 45
chronomics 107
circular interaction 76, 77
Clifton, Jim 287
cohesion 139
collaboration 111, 148
collusion 257
communication 3, 306; barriers 82–3; circular interaction 76, 77; culture 20, 106; group 139; high-tech 84–8; leadership 31, 33–4, 73–6, 84; self-image 78; systems 79–82
communication capacities 76–7

communication technologies 7, 79, 87, 165, 263
compensation 27
competency 26, 52, 64, 109
computer-based training 262
computer response systems 263
computer viruses 85
concept 1, 4–5
conferencing by video 87
conflict 3, 47, 147–8, 257
conflict management 146–8
congruence 76
connectivity 85
control group 228
cooperative 16
coordination 32, 34–5
corporate culture 26, 53
corporate image 80
corporate learning 302
corporate social responsibility 80
cosmopolitan leaders 5
cosmopolitans 5
creative deviants 48
creative risk taking 189–90
creativity 256, 272, 287
CRI see cross-cultural relations inventory
Cribbin, James J. 8–9
criminality 48
critical incidents 114, 237–8
critical pay-off functions 58–60
critical thinking 88
cross-cultural collaboration 111–12
cross-cultural leaders 14, 307
cross-cultural relations inventory (CRI) 121–33
cultural awareness 31, 33, 104, 113
cultural conditioning 101, 103, 105
cultural understanding, simulations 114–17
cultural universals 103
culture 100–11, 137, 306; see also knowledge culture; organizational culture; work
culture
culture lag 11, 103
customer relationships 108
cyberculture 167–8, 170
cybernation 169
cybernetic model 1
cyber security 85

data bases 86
debates 238
decentralization 306
developer 16

digital information 86
discussion groups 237, 264–5
division of labour 110
dramatics 114, 240–1
dress 107
Drucker, Peter 14, 163, 164
dyad 136

education 293–4
educational media 261–2
Educational Resource Information Center (ERIC) 231
electronic matchmaking 263
electronic meetings 262–4
electronic networking 112
emotional intelligence 287
empathy 84
employee support 26
empowerment 256, 294–5
energy exchange systems 1, 2
energy forces 195
engagement 256
entanglement 292
entitlements 21
entrepreneur 15, 20, 26
Enzer, Selwyn 301
ERIC see Educational Resource Information Center
exhibits 244
expectations exercise 213

Facebook 85, 259
family 108
feedback 26, 151, 250–2
feeding customs 107
field trips 243–4
financial management 32, 35–6
flexibility 26, 114, 287
food 107
forced relationships 275–7
force field analysis 174, 195–200
formal communication systems 79
forums 239–40
free association 277
fresh eye 277
From, Eric 144
frustration 47
future 286–9

gamesman 16
Garber, Peter 271
Garfield, Charles 303
Gates, Bill 44
GEO leadership 14–15

Gibb, Jack 81
globalization 11, 302
goal setting 26, 51
good will 80
Google 87
Gordon Technique 278
group 136; affiliation 138; alignments
    140–1; atmosphere 139; background
    138–9; cohesion 139; communication
    patterns 139; goals 140; leadership 140;
    participation patterns 139; performance
    141–2; procedures 140; standards 140
group direction 14
group dynamics 137
Grove, Andrew S. 26, 257

Hall, Edward 306
Hare, Robert 48
healthy personalities 49
helping relationship 149–51
Herzberg, Frederick 42
high performance behavior 49–50
high performance cultures 111–13
high performance learning institute (HPLI)
    207, 217–18, 250–2
high performance management inventory
    (HPMI) 18, 31–9
high performance management workshop
    (HPMW) 29–30
high performance organizations 52–5
high performance work environment 25–8
high potential workers 113
high-tech communications 84–8
Hollow Square 267–71
houses of wisdom 10–13
housewives 40
Howe, William S. 289
HPLI see high performance learning
    institute
HPMI see high performance management
    inventory
HPMW see high performance management
    workshop
HRI see human resource inventory
human development 169–70
human-machine relations 108
human relations 64, 134, 200
human resource development 55
human resource inventory (HRI) 64–72
human resource management 32, 36–7,
    162, 305–8
human resource revolution 28
hypothesis 229

IB see input bombardment
IBA see individual behavior analysis
identity 106
imagineering 297–9
implementation 32, 35
incentive awards 27
incentives 21, 27
individual behavior analysis (IBA) 152–9
informal communication systems 79
information age leadership 74
information management 86
information search engines 87
information technology (IT) 22, 85, 287,
    306
innovation 26, 230, 260
input bombardment (IB) 56–8
input-output methods 274
instrumentation: change inventory 191–4;
    cross-cultural relations inventory
    121–33; feedback form 250–2; force
    field analysis inventory 195–200; high
    performance management inventory
    31–9; human resource inventory
    64–72; individual behavior analysis
    152–9; leadership motivation inventory
    60–4; learning 216, 245–6;
    management communications
    inventory 92–5; managing people skills
    inventory 283–5; meetings
    management planning inventory
    280–3; organization communications
    analysis 95–9; self-evaluation inventory
    248–50; team performance survey
    159–61; training forms 247–8
integrator 16
integrity 25
intellectual capital 28
interaction skills 73
intergroup relations 134
internet 84–5, 88, 230
interpersonal communication 75
interpersonal skills 134, 245
interview questions 211
intragroup relations 134
intrapreneurialism 18, 306
IT see information technology

jargon 106
jet lag 107
job analysis 210
job motivational factors 62–4

Kelly, Kevin 88
KM see knowledge management

KMC *see* knowledge management consortium
know-how 6
knowledge 6–7
knowledge acquisition 235
knowledge culture 4–10, 106
knowledge factories 11
knowledge management (KM) 13–14, 28
knowledge management consortium (KMC) 14
knowledge retention 245
knowledge work culture 45
knowledge workers 4–6, 11, 28–9, 221, 287
Knowles, Malcolm 205–6

leadership 4; change inventory 191–4; change management 165–6; communication 73–6, 84; development 175; future 289–97; high performance teams 142–4; image 137; knowledge-based 8–9; knowledge management 13–14; management games 265–6; organizational relations 137–8; organization energy exchange 2; roles 81–2; self-assessment inventory 15–17; situation 24; styles 15–17, 23; training 231, 307; transactional 24; transformational 24, 25; *see also* high performance leader
leadership motivation inventory (LMI) 60–4
learning 109–10, 113, 202–3; *see also* action learning; education; training
legal process outsourcing (LPO) 112
Lewin, Kurt 2, 174
life extension 291
lifelong learning 11, 168, 203–4, 221, 301
life space 45–6, 76, 137, 174–5, 298
life values 64
line managers 306
Lipp, Dorothy 7–8
Lippitt, Gordon 144
listening skills 81, 89–91
literature review 230
LMI *see* leadership motivation inventory
low performers 308
loyalty 21
LPO *see* legal process outsourcing

McClelland, David C. 51, 64
Maccoby, Michael 9, 131
McGregor, Douglas 42, 111
macro-culture 104, 109
maintenance behavior 89

management: change 164–5, 173–4; communication 73; teams 134; *see also* high performance management
management communications inventory (MCI) 92–5
management development 56–8, 226
management games 265–6
managing people skills inventory (MPSI) 283–5
Maslow's hierarchy of needs 43–5
mass media 263
materials resource management 32, 36
matrix management 110
MCI *see* management communications inventory
media 76, 79
meetings 3, 253–6, 279; behavior 89; coordinator 219–20; guidelines 257–8; innovations 260; technology 260–2
meetings management planning inventory 280–3
mental habits 109–10
mentoring 287
meta-performance 49
Miller, James Grier 136
Millians-Roche, Anne 41
minority cultures 104
mirror neurons 293
mission-oriented meetings 258
modifications 277
modified polarity scale 246
morale 3, 21, 24
motivation 42–6, 60–4
MPSI *see* managing people skills inventory
multiple dimensions 294
Murray, Alan 164
mutuality 302
MySpace 85

national culture 104, 106
networking 21, 112
neural control 295
neuroleadership 287
new management 20, 45, 57
non-profit organizations 287
norms 51, 108–9

observers 150–1
OCA *see* organization communications analysis
occupational gradations 110
OD *see* organizational development
OEE *see* organization energy exchange
online learning 263, 302

operation review 258
organization 136, 166
organizational change 163–4, 167–70,
    177–8, 180–4, 195
organizational communications 78–84,
    173–4
organizational cultures 18, 106, 113–14,
    137
organizational development (OD) 163,
    225–9, 302
organizational growth 184
organizational knowledge 7
organizational relations 3, 22, 137–8, 142–3
organizational transformation (OT) 163,
    178–9, 225
organization communications analysis
    (OCA) 95–9
organization energy exchange (OEE) 1, 2
organization shock 179–80
OT *see* organizational transformation
O'Toole, James 27
outcomes 24
outsourcing 112
overload 82, 113, 233
ownership 307

participant acceptance 245
participation 20, 22, 139
peak performance 303–5
peer management 21
perceptual field 45, 76
Peretroukhin, Valentin 288–9
performance culture 26
performance evaluation 32, 37–8
performance improvement 40, 51–2
performance standards 27
performance surveys 159–61
personal assessment 38–9
personal growth 144
personal motivators 61–2
personal networking 112
planned change 163, 172–3
planning 3, 32, 35
positive reinforcement 48
PowerPoint 57, 86, 261, 298, 299
prejudice 78, 103
prework package 213
problem solving 29, 145, 245, 272–9
process conflict model 146–7
process-oriented meetings 258
productivity 3, 10, 21, 22, 58
professionalism 21
project management 110
projects 244–5

psychological contract 136
psychopaths 48
public relations 31, 34
punishment 48

quality 22
quality circles 119–20
questionnaires 245

rating scales 246
real time information 87
reception 77
reference works 230–1
rejection 82
relationships 108, 135–6
religion 107
Relocation (game) 266
Repole, Mike 19–20
research 229; planning 231–2; reports
    232–3
resource allocation 165
responsibility 58–60
restructuring 167
reverse brainstorming 279
rewards 27, 46
robotics 21, 291
role models 25, 26, 82
role playing 114, 241–3

sabbatical leaves 21, 45
screen reading 88
Sears, Woodrow 58
Second Life 118
self-actualization 44, 50–2
self-assessment inventory 15–17
self-concept 76
self-evaluation 64, 248–50
self-image 78, 137
self-learning 27, 202
self-management 21
sexuality 108
sexual prejudice 141
Sherwood, John 113
Simons, Russell 288
simulations: cultural understanding 114–17;
    meetings 266
situation leadership 24
slip writing 279
small group dynamics 237
Smart, Bradford D. 256
smart grids 85
smart technology 288
social aggregation 294
social media 85, 260

social networking 6, 85, 168, 170, 254–5
societal information technology systems 288
sociodrama 240–1
sociogram 239
spaceflight 170, 292
split identity 294
staff meetings 258
StarPower (game) 266
stereotyping 116
structural conflict model 146
super industrial person 183
supervision skills 32, 37
support services 26
surveys 232
suspicion 83
symbols 75
synergistic leadership 9
synergy 27, 111–13, 165
system analysis 186
systems approach 136–8

task behavior 89
team building 58, 148–9
team conflict resolution 146–8
team culture 106
team decisions 144–5
team management 134
team performance survey (TPS) 159–61
teamwork 3
technology transfer 231
teleconferences 262
telepathy 293
thinking cosmopolitans 5
time consciousness 107
top performers 50–1
TPS *see* team performance survey
traditions 103

trainer 212
training 27
training forms 247–50
training needs analysis 211
training programs 221–5
transactional leadership 24
transformational leadership 24, 25
transmission 77
transparency 54
Treybig, James 21
triad 136
trust 54
Twitter 79, 85

underclass 11, 221, 307
unit monitoring 32, 37

values 108
video conferencing 87
virtual reality 88, 292
virtual reality simulations 118

WELCOM network 259
wellness strategies 21, 287
Wibbeke, Eileen Sheridan 14
wikinomics 262
wisdom 10–13
work culture 20–1, 101–2, 105–6, 110–11, 119–20, 142, 307
work environment 2, 18–20, 25–8, 55–6, 168
work life 21
work relationships 79, 81, 136
worth ethic 110

Zamparini, Louis 308

For Product Safety Concerns and Information please contact our EU
representative GPSR@taylorandfrancis.com
Taylor & Francis Verlag GmbH, Kaufingerstraße 24, 80331 München, Germany

www.ingramcontent.com/pod-product-compliance
Ingram Content Group UK Ltd.
Pitfield, Milton Keynes, MK11 3LW, UK
UKHW021851240425
457818UK00020B/804